CISTERCIAN STUDIES SERIES ONE HUNDRED SIXTY–EIGHT

Franz Posset

Pater Bernhardus: Martin Luther and Bernard of Clairvaux

Plate 1: *The Crucified Embraces Bernard and Luther*. Bronze sculpture by Werner Franzen, 1986/87. Photo: Alexander Glaser. Altenberger Dom-Verein, Germany.

CISTERCIAN STUDIES SERIES ONE HUNDRED SIXTY–EIGHT

Pater Bernhardus: Martin Luther and Bernard of Clairvaux

by

Franz Posset

Foreword by Michael Casey

Preface by †Bernhard Lohse

Cistercian Publications
Kalamazoo, Michigan—Spencer, Massachusetts

© Copyright Cistercian Publications Inc. 1999

Cistercian Publications Inc. Editorial Offices
Institute of Cistercian Studies
Western Michigan University
Kalamazoo, MI 49008

The work of Cistercian publications is made possible in part
through the support from Western Michigan University
to the Institute of Cistercian Studies

Library of Congress Cataloguing-Publication information available on request

Dedicated to
Kenneth Hagen

Table of Contents

Foreword

ⓘT HAS NOT BEEN EASY, until recently, to find a balanced presentation of the life and philosophy of Martin
Luther. During the cold war of the Counter-Reformation,
lives of Luther fell victim to the prejudices of both advocates
and opponents and, as a consequence, the interpretations offered
depended more on how the Reformation was evaluated than on any
honest attempt to confront the complex reality of Martin Luther
and his role in the events that led to the division of the western
church.

One of the happy exceptions to this general polarisation was
the early Redemptorist, St Clement Mary Hofbauer (1751–1821).
Five years before his death he wrote to the publisher Friedrich
Perthes an assessment of the German Reformation that is as worth
pondering today as it was unusual among his contemporaries.

> Ever since I have been in a position to compare, as papal
> legate, the religious situation of Catholics in Poland with that of
> Protestants in Germany, I have become certain that secession
> from the church has come about because the Germans both
> did and do feel the need of being religious. The Reformation
> has spread and taken root, not purely on account of men who
> were heretics and philosophers, but on account of men who
> genuinely sought after a religion of the heart. I have said this
> to the Pope and cardinals in Rome, but they did not believe

me, maintaining rigidly that the cause of the Reformation was hostility to religion.[1]

Despite this fair-minded assessment it was only in the twentieth century that Catholic scholars began to acknowledge the reality of abuses in the Church that cried out for reform and thereby opened the way to accepting Martin Luther as a *homo religiosus* whose actions were dictated by genuine religious sentiment and did not spring from perversity, contentiousness or psychological troubles, as their more polemical forebears had claimed.[2] In the climate of post-Vatican II ecumenism, a greater understanding of the *theologia crucis*[3] and an appreciation of Luther's solid biblical expositions brought to the attention of Catholics some of the riches of Luther's non-controversial writings. Although the foundations had been laid by F. X. Kiefl in 1917 and by Joseph Lortz in his 1939 landmark, *Die Reformation in Deutschland*, it was only in a later irenic climate that a broad consideration of Luther's spiritual teaching and personal piety became feasible. In 1968, Jesuit Jared Wicks published a study of Luther's early spirituality which was

1 Translated in Karl Blockx, 'Si Quae Culpa . . . ,' *Eastern Churches Quarterly*, 16 (1964) p. 276.

2 This evolution is charted by Richard Stauffer in *Luther as Seen by Catholics*, Ecumenical Studies in History (London: Lutterworth Press, 1967). This is a shortened version of the 1966 french original. The Catholic historian Erwin Iserloh concludes his 1966 book, *The Theses Were Not Posted, Luther; Between Reform and Reformation* (ET London: Geoffrey Chapman, 1968) by citing 'the theological and pastoral failures of Luther's interventions—and not any intrinsic wrongness of the actions themselves. The work inspired by Heiko Oberman clarifies the religious context of the late medieval period. It is important both in demonstrating how far scholastic theology had wandered from its Golden Age and in identifying some of the forces operating in Luther's own formation. The whole area is evoked in Charles Trinkaus and Heiko A. Oberman (ed.), *The Pursuit of Holiness in Late Medieval and Renaissance Religion: Papers from the University of Michigan Conference*, Studies in Medieval and Reformation Thought 10 (Leiden: E. J. Brill, 1974).

3 This is credited especially to Walter von Loewenich's 1929 *Luther's Theology of the Cross* (ET of the fifth German edition, Christian Journals Limited, Belfast, 1976). This classic presentation is, perhaps, limited by having been strongly influenced by the agenda of dialectical theology but, at the very least, it served the purpose of introducing the topic into theological awareness. An example of how seriously Catholics are beginning to take the theme can be seen in Brunero Gheradini, *Theologia crucis: L'eredità di Lutero nell'evoluzione teologica della Riforma*, Teologia 25 (Rome: Edizioni Paoline, 1978).

well but not uncritically received by lutheran scholars.[4] Likewise appeared interest in the Reformer's monastic career and his contact with the mystical tradition such as Bernard, Bonaventure, Tauler, and the *Theologia Germanica*.[5]

The traditional character of Luther's thought has begun to appear more evident. This awareness has been helped by the de-absolutising of the role of Thomism in Roman Catholic theology. So long as the method and agenda of Scholasticism were regarded as normative for theology, Luther's unsystematic and emotive discourses would be judged defective. In such a perspective, the only way to rehabilitate his theological reputation among Catholics would be a tortuous process of harmonisation.[6]

Wherever there is an appreciation of the content, method, and style of patristic theology (and this term includes medieval monastic works), a greater affinity is felt with Luther than with Scholasticism. In the context of the evolution of theology, Luther appears to hark back to an older model of theology that had been in decline in the latin Church since the late twelfth century. It was Scholasticism that was innovative.

Part of the novelty of scholastic thought was its reliance on Aristotle. For centuries platonising philosophy had been the principal vehicle for theological speculation and discourse. Despite obvious drawbacks in the platonic systems, Plato had been gradually baptised. Generations of christian usage had filtered out the errors and inconsistencies and had gradually reintegrated many themes into a coherent synthesis of theology and spirituality.[7] Aristotle was

4 Jared Wicks, *Man Yearning for Grace: Luther's Early Spiritual Teaching* (Washington: Corpus Books, 1968). See Bengt R. Hoffman, *Luther and the Mystics: A Re-examination of Luther's Spiritual Experience and his Relationship to the Mystics* (Minneapolis: Augsburg, 1976) pp. 126–127.

5 ET by Susanna Winkworth (London: Stuart and Watkins, 1966), a reprint of the Macmillan re-edition of 1893. The influence of both Tauler and the *Theologia Germanica* is especially discernible in the pietist stream of lutheran tradition.

6 See, for example, Stephanus Pfürtner, OP, *Luther and Aquinas: A Conversation* (London: Darton, Longman and Todd, 1964).

7 The major thematics of monastic spirituality have their origin in what may be loosely termed 'platonic tradition'—recognising that there is also substantial input from Stoicism and other schools of thought and a certain selectivity in the ideas embraced. These include anthropological themes such as image and

largely ignored, dismissed as an 'atheist'. When Aristotelianism did find entry into schools of theology, it often came by way of jewish and arab mediators, unintegrated with christian faith. Aquinas, who regarded Aristotle as the Philosopher *par excellence*, also accepted Averröes (Ibn Rashid of Toledo) as the Commentator *par excellence*. Despite the resistance of traditionalists, the deductive analytic approach associated with the new wave of philosophy began to fashion a new style of theology. By the time of Luther much of what passed for theological writing had become, in the words of *Zen and the Art of Motorcycle Maintenance* 'emotionally hollow, esthetically meaningless and spiritually empty'.[8] Even devotional works tended to be dry, apodictic, and sometimes out of touch both with the central realities of christian revelation and the practical struggles of daily life. Theology had rationalised itself to the point of absurdity.

Luther was formed as an Augustinian. It is not surprising that, as early as 1517, he was already affronted by the dominant Aristotelianism of scholastic theology.[9] Luther wrote optimistically in the spring of that year:

---

likeness, the tripartite structure of the soul, the emphasis on interiority and on memory, the importance attached to self-knowledge. These, in turn, led to certain moral perspectives; for example the understanding of the passions and hence the emphasis on abstinence, *apatheia*, ascesis, and purification. Positive spirituality emerges in such themes as desire for God, contemplation, ecstasy, illumination, and spiritual marriage. In all of these matters monastic spirituality, drawing on the great teachers of Alexandria and Cappadocia as well as Augustine, sought to explain christian experience by using the language and categories of platonic thought, progressively adapting the themes to approach the reality ever more nearly.

8 Robert M. Pirsig, *Zen and the Art of Motorcycle Maintenance: An Inquiry into Values* (London: Corgi Books, 1976) 110. See also, M. Casey, " 'Emotionally Hollow, Esthetically Meaningless and Spiritually Empty": An Inquiry into Theological Discourse', *Colloquium* 14.1 (1981) 54–61.

9 See several numbers of Luther's 'Disputation against Scholastic theology':

41. Virtually the entire *Ethics* of Aristotle is the worst enemy of grace. This in opposition to the scholastics.
43. It is an error to say that no man can become a theologian without Aristotle. This in opposition to common opinion.
44. Indeed, no one can become a theologian unless he becomes one without Aristotle.
45. To state that a theologian who is not a logician is a monstrous heretic—this is a monstrous and heretical statement. This in opposition to common opinion.

Our theology and St Augustine are making good progress and are dominant in our university, thanks to what God has done. Aristotle is gradually declining and is approaching his final demise.'[10]

Luther's Augustinianism was as much outraged by contemporary theology as was his piety by thinly-veiled simony. His was a cry of the heart both for reform in the Church and for a theology more apt to nurture devotion. These dispositions inevitably brought Luther into Bernard's ambit. Bernard was also a reformer, a master of language, and adept at robust polemic. Although he was spared the worst ravages of rampant Scholasticism, Bernard was aware from its beginnings of its likely disruptive effect on devotion. He was a spiritual master of similar outlook to Luther in that the twelfth century was also an age in which the practice of religion was infected with guilt, scrupulosity, and even superstition. Much of the pastoral concern in the sermons of the twelfth-century Cistercian Fathers was expressed to neutralise fears and to build confidence in grace. No wonder Luther was to find comfort in what Bernard had written!

As long as scholastic theology exercised a monopoly in western theology, the work of Bernard of Clairvaux, in common with monastic/patristic theology in general, was marginalised and largely ignored. Bernard was honoured as a saint and as having been an influential figure in his own times. His intellectual status, however, was reduced to the level of his being thought a 'pious author'. In fact, this situation continued unchallenged until our own century. It was finally remedied by opposite consensus generated first by the 1934 book of Étienne Gilson,[11] and accelerated by

50. Briefly, the whole Aristotle is to theology as darkness to light. This is in opposition to the scholastics.

Translation by Timothy F. Lull, *Martin Luther's Basic Theological Writings* (Minneapolis: Fortress Press, 1989) p. 16.

10 Quoted and contextualised in Gerhard Ebeling, *Luther: An Introduction to his Thought* (London: Collins/Fontana, 1972) p. 19.

11 *La Théologie mystique de saint Bernard* (1934) ET by A. H. C. Downes, *The Mystical Theology of Saint Bernard* (London: Sheed and Ward, 1940; rpt Kalamazoo, 1990).

the Dijon Congress on 'Bernard the theologian' and the practical disenfranchisement of Scholasticism that followed Vatican II.[12] With Bernard rehabilitated and Luther viewed somewhat more objectively, it was inevitable that the extent of Luther's well-known attachment to Bernard would need to be assayed professionally. The work of Dr Franz Posset, already initiated in many published articles, reaches its culmination in this present volume. He has undertaken a comprehensive survey of all the texts in which Luther makes reference to the abbot of Clairvaux, analyses them, and melds them into a nuanced synthesis. What makes this present work particularly valuable is that Dr Posset has not only journeyed through the well-traversed highways of Luther's major theological utterances but has also scrutinised the byways of his less formal discourses to ensure that his portrayal of the relationship is well-rounded.

Dr Posset finds a congeniality between the two outspoken christian apologists and, on Luther's side, an enduring respect for *Pater Bernhardus*. This is not to say that Luther uncritically agreed to everything Bernard propounded. As his own thought developed and the polarising effect of controversy solidified, Luther experienced deep reservations regarding many traditions which Bernard accepted without question. Luther's characteristic theological stance evolved according to its own inner logic and on many points Bernard was inevitably left behind. The result was that, on the surface, there are substantial differences between the two theologies. The fact remains that even when the disjunction was strongest Luther retained a love and respect for Bernard as one who truly understood the grace of God and lived in obedience to it.

The four centuries that separate Bernard from Luther witnessed many changes in society and in the church. These necessarily shape the products of theological reflection in such a way that it becomes difficult to compare work done in difference orbits. In particular, the massive change in human awareness that occurred

12 See Michael Casey, 'Bernard of Clairvaux: Forty Years of Scholarship,' in John S. Martin, ed., *St Bernard of Clairvaux: The Man* (Parkville: University of Melbourne, 1992) pp. 31–45.

around the sixteenth century, whereby the object of philosophic reflection shifted from being to consciousness,[13] left its mark both on the style and the content of theological discourse. In some senses, any 'dialogue' between Bernard and Luther has to span this significant chasm. Such bridging can come about only as the result of an accurate, sensitive, and detailed examination of positions. Dr Posset's work is a much-appreciated step in this direction.

Comparison of two minds requires the researcher to master the specific qualities of both thinkers. It also demands a quality of heart; one has to be broad enough to encompass within oneself two distinctive viewpoints and philosophies so as to be able to map both concordances and disjunctions. In this present feat of scholarship Dr Posset has, in an eminent degree, demonstrated Bernard's impact on Luther—and, by implication, his potential influence on all Christians. For this we thank him.

Michael Casey

Tarrawarra Abbey

---

13 Colin Morris argues for the beginning of this process in the twelfth century. See, *The Discovery of the Individual: 1050–1200* (Toronto: University of Toronto Press, 1987). Some important qualifications are added by Caroline Walker Bynum, 'Did the Twelfth Century Discover the Individual?' in *Jesus as Mother: Studies in the Spirituality of the High Middle Ages* (Berkeley: University of California Press, 1982) pp. 82–109.

𝔓𝔯𝔢𝔣𝔞𝔠𝔢

SINCE 1987 Franz Posset has published several scholarly articles on the significance Bernard of Clairvaux had for Martin Luther. He has now finished his extensive investigation under the title *Pater Bernhardus*, for which I have been invited to contribute this preface. In his dissertation on *Luther's Catholic Christology* (directed by Kenneth Hagen) Dr Posset, a Roman Catholic lay theologian, used primarily a systematic theological approach, not a church historical one. Recent Roman Catholic Luther research has attempted to bring out what remains in common between Protestants and Catholics despite the split that occurred in the sixteenth century. This common ground, as is often emphasized, is based not least on the fact that Luther retained essential elements of the heritage of undivided Christianity and that he highly esteemed those elements. In this vein, Posset's dissertation presented the catholicity of Luther's image of Christ.

In a similar way, in his several other studies Posset has elaborated on what Bernard and Luther have in common. He has especially tried to show Bernard's comprehensive significance for Luther. Luther learned from Bernard's sermons a theology which was not scholastic, but one which concentrated on questions of spirituality—such as temptations, salvation, faith, and hope. He claims that there was something congenial between Bernard and Luther, and that Bernard may, in Luther's eyes, have taken on the

15

role of pastor or of a brother in the spirit, even a companion in the midst of temptations.

In his Bernard studies Posset echoes tendencies which can be observed in a series of investigations on Bernard in recent years. The most comprehensive study to have appeared so far is the theological dissertation of the Dutch Catholic, Theo Bell (*Bernhardus Dixit. Bernardus van Clairvaux in Martin Luthers Werken* (Dissertation Amsterdam, 1989, printed at Delft, 1989); revised German edition: *Divus Bernhardus: Bernhard von Clairvaux in Martin Luthers Schriften* (Mainz, 1993). That it is primarily Roman Catholic scholars who publish such studies gives food for thought. So far, Protestant Luther scholars have only very sporadically made similar comparisons. My own research efforts on the relationship between Bernard and Luther were presented in my book *Mönchtum und Reformation. Luthers Auseinandersetzung mit dem Mönchsideal des Mittelalters* (Göttingen, 1963). There I concentrated on Luther's criticisms of monasticism in the years after 1513; these eventually led to his breach with monasticism and to his marriage with Katharina von Bora. There I described the concepts of monasticism which were represented by important medieval theologians and which were then criticized by Luther in the sixteenth century. Needless to say, this line of questioning dealt not so much with the shared catholicity as with the deep dissent between Luther and Bernard. Indeed, Luther did not spare Bernard when criticizing medieval monasticism. Yet in Luther's early phase, and partly also later on, we find an essential dependence on some of Bernard's thoughts. At the same time, however, Luther in his early years did not accept Bernard's vehement stress upon the monastic ideal and later he sharply criticized his praise of the *vita monastica*. Yet Luther did not distance himself from Bernard's spirituality and Christocentrism. This is quite remarkable in that Luther in other cases was led from his criticism of medieval concepts and rites to a sharp rejection of various traditions and figures. This was not so in the case of Bernard.

In Posset's latest, broad investigation, *Pater Bernhardus*, we observe the continuation of Luther's earlier method within a larger framework. In a comprehensive way Posset presents Bernard's influence on Luther's theology on numerous important points.

He describes Luther's high esteem for 'Father Bernard' and his
indebtedness to the monastic tradition in his emphasis on grace
alone, faith alone, Christ alone, and evangelization alone. Here,
too, Posset pursues a systematic theological line. What he is able
to demonstrate in this context is remarkable and deserves the
full attention of both scholars and ordinary Christians, Catholic
and Lutheran alike. If there were any further need of proof, this
intensive investigation into the doubtlessly existing relation and
congeniality between Bernard and Luther once more demonstrates
how deeply connected the Catholic and Protestant traditions are.
They have in common not only the doctrine of God, the centrality
of Christ, and belief in the presence of the Holy Spirit within the
life of the Church, but also the conviction that faith lies at the heart
of human response and the certainty that ultimately as Christians
we will stand before God with empty hands and can only hope
that God will accept us. Thus, Posset demonstrates the deep bond
between Catholics and Protestants at the core of their spiritualities.

Posset declares on the basis of his investigation that while
Luther referred many times to Saint Bernard, he never mentioned,
for instance, Master Eckhart (d. 1329) or Henry Suso (d. 1365), two
representatives of German mysticism. Equally remarkably, Luther
never referred to or quoted from any works of Saint Bernard's foe,
the famous Peter Abelard. And with equal right, Posset emphasizes that one cannot distinguish Bernard's evangelicity from his
catholicity, for both are reciprocally related; they condition each
other. So general a statement can easily be made today without fear
of ignoring the specifics of either the Catholic or the Evangelical
tradition.

The question of how Luther came to know Bernard and how
widely he really read the abbot's work is important, if one wants
to establish a connection between Bernard and Luther. If indeed
Luther actually read and studied several of Bernard's works, he
must have gained a broad and thorough knowledge and he then
also saw and evaluated certain bernardine sentences which became
important to him personally. By his investigation Posset offers
a remarkable and noteworthy study, even though one or another
idea may not prevail in the scholarly discussion that will grow
out of it.

18   Bernhard Lohse

One issue may yet be raised which did not arise in the immediate context of Posset's investigation, but which is important for a comprehensive Luther interpretation. That is the issue of Luther and the medieval theological tradition in general. Otherwise stated: What is Bernard's significance for Luther when compared to other traditions. The complex field of 'Luther and the tradition' or 'which traditions shape Luther's career?' cannot be presented conclusively and definitely. During the past twenty years, new ways of looking at it have surfaced. Some of them are still under discussion. Posset takes a position which is shared by a group of scholars specializing in Bernard and Luther. There are others, however, who come to different conclusions and underscore the differences between Bernard and Luther. Doubtlessly these existed. It is good when divergent research positions are presented sharply. Scholarly discussion will lead to the most convincing position based on the best arguments.[1]

Of other theological traditions which had an impact on Luther, we may say this: there is no doubt that Luther came to know Occamism during his studies of philosophy and theology at Erfurt. But it was an Ockhamism of the milder sort, as represented by Gabriel Biel (d. 1494). Also beyond doubt is the fact that Luther dealt with Augustine, probably as early as his student years. Still debated in this regard is whether he came to the study of Augustine by way of his superior in his Order, or whether he began these studies on his own. Furthermore, it is certain that the noble Johann von Staupitz (d. 1524) influenced Luther at least in the midst of his temptations and perhaps in his theological work as well. It remains to be seen at what point Staupitz and Luther came into closer encounter; whether already in Luther's early days at Erfurt, or in 1510 in connection with the conflict in the Order of the Austin Friars over the issue of the strict observance of the Rule. Also undeniable is the influence certain writings of the german mystics, especially Johannes Tauler (d. 1361), but also the anonymous author of *Theologia Germanica*, had on Luther.

1 My own contribution may be found in 'Luther und Bernhard von Clairvaux' in *Bernhard von Clairvaux. Rezeption und Wirkung im Mittelalter und in der Neuzeit*, ed. Kaspar Elm (Wiesbaden: Harrassowitz Verlag, 1994).

Yet no definite date when Luther came to know Tauler's sermons can be determined. Besides these figures and movements, whose influence has been recognized for some time, the thesis is now being promoted that already to some degree during his studies at Erfurt, and even more during his Wittenberg years, Luther came into contact with humanism and accepted its premises. The precise degree and intensity of humanistic influence on Luther is still the subject of discussion.

That Luther learned a great deal from Bernard during his monastic years at Erfurt, whether from his own reading or from listening to sermons read to the friars, is beyond doubt. If one wants to determine more precisely the impact Bernard had on Luther, then one must correlate this impact with the influences indicated here in terms of date and substance. This means that investigations have still to be conducted on whether Augustine's and Bernard's influence on Luther complemented each other or whether perhaps the bishop's impact is to be sought in such theological issues as the righteousness of God and the abbot's impact perhaps more in practical spirituality and in living faith. Furthermore, it needs to be asked whether Bernard and the german mystics helped Luther in similar ways, or whether, here too, differences exist, and why. Franz Posset has made an important contribution in illuminating the relationship between Luther and Bernard, and all those who wish to go into greater detail, need to give his work careful consideration. For this he has earned our gratitude and recognition.

Bernhard Lohse

Hamburg

Author's Preface

ONE OF THE GREATEST protestant theologians of the twentieth century, Karl Barth, always felt that the critical edition of Martin Luther's *opus* of more than one hundred volumes was like Pandora's box; he had to cover it with a rug for 'protection'. Barth made this witty comparison because he evidently felt that as a protestant theologian, he was entrusted with Luther's works just as Pandora had been given her box of unknown contents, and like Pandora he could not contain his curiosity but opened it. From Pandora's box every human ill and plague escaped into the world, leaving only 'hope'.

To many people, learned or not, Luther's work represents something valuable and tempting, but once opened, it has often turned out to be a 'curse' in some sense, or so it appeared to me. Through the ecumenical environment of the University of Tübingen, Germany, where I studied in the 1960s, attending lectures in both catholic and protestant theology faculties, I was prepared for opening this 'box'. Yet the first time Luther's 'box' was really opened to me happened at the University of Münster in the summer semester 1967. I was probably the only Roman Catholic participant in Kurt Aland's *Luther Sozietät* in which the Reformer's concept of the pastoral office in the Church was being investigated. Since then I have not been able to resist the temptation of opening the Luther 'box' time and again. After a prolonged pause, I felt compelled early in the 1980s to take a second, closer look at the 'hope' left in the 'box'. This second look resulted in my PhD dissertation under the direction of Kenneth Hagen, published in 1988 under the title *Luther's Catholic Christology According to his Johannine Lectures of 1527*. This enterprise filled me with hope for the future of ecumenism; this dissertation, completed at a Jesuit university, was published by a Lutheran church press. By then addicted to the Luther 'box', I had to take a third look into it, and I found many precious sparks of hope which turned into essays or articles about Luther and the greater catholic tradition. Still unable to curtail my curiosity, I dug deeper into the 'box' and discovered Bernard of Clairvaux, whom Luther affectionately called 'father' and whose writings he recommended for diligent study. It was Luther who led me to Bernard! I began faithfully to follow Luther's advice in anticipation of the great international 'birthday party' for Saint Bernard's nine-hundredth birthday in Kalamazoo, Michigan in 1990. On that occasion I presented some of my research in the company of Theo Bell from Holland.[1] To my pleasant surprise, I found out that we both were catholic Luther researchers and born in the same year.

I had hoped that my major work on Bernard and Luther (a forerunner of the present book) would be published by the year 1990, as a contribution to the nonacentenary celebrations of Bernard's birthday. However, the contract with Cistercian Publications was not signed until 1991, and when its publication was delayed even further, I asked the editorial director to give me the chance to integrate the most recent research results which had become available only after I had finished my original manuscript in 1989. The result is the present volume.

1 Theo Bell, 'Testimonium Spiritus Sancti. An Example of Bernard-Reception in Luther's Theology', *Bijdragen: Tijdschrift voor filosofie en theologie* 53 (1992) 62- 72. This is a summary of his dissertation, *Bernhardus Dixit: Bernardus van Clairvaux in Martin Luthers Werken* (Delft: Eburon, 1989); the revised German edition was published under the title *Divus Bernhardus: Bernhard von Clairvaux in Martin Luthers Schriften* (Mainz: Verlag Philipp von Zabern, 1993). The paper I presented at that congress was published as 'Divus Bernhardus: Saint Bernard as Spiritual and Theological Mentor of the Reformer Martin Luther'. *Bernardus Magister. Papers Presented at the Nonacentenary Celebration of the Birth of Saint Bernard of Clairvaux, Kalamazoo, Michigan, Sponsored by the Institute of Cistercian Studies, Western Michigan University 10–13 May 1990*, John R. Sommerfeldt, ed. (Kalamazoo, 1992) 517–532.

I want to thank Kenneth Hagen, who put me on the track of reading Luther in a medieval catholic context, and for his encouragement to carry on with my research. I also thank Roger van Haren and Russ Stommel for their critical reading of the various drafts of the manuscript, or parts of it, since 1988, and for their helpful hints. I also wish to acknowledge Robert J. Goeser, who was one of the first readers of my manuscript. Furthermore, I am grateful to Fr Vincent Hermans from Saint Benedict Abbey in Achel, Belgium, for his help in locating quotations through his *Bernard Kartoteek Konkordanz*. Last but not least I thank Cistercian Publications and the anonymous referees for accepting the manuscript into its publication program, and Michael Casey (Australia) and Bernhard Lohse (Germany) for contributing their much appreciated forewords.

F P

Beaver Dam, Wisconsin
On the Feast of Saint Bernard

Abbreviations

THE WORKS OF BERNARD OF CLAIRVAUX:

SBOp	Sancti Bernardi Opera. 8 volumes. Rome, 1957–1977
Abb	Sermo ad abbates
Abael	Epistola in erroribus Abaelardi
Adv	Sermo in adventu domini
Ann	Sermo in annuntiatione domini
Asspt	Sermo in assumptione BVM
Circ	Sermo in circumcisione domini
Conv	Sermo de conversione ad clericos
Csi	De consideratione libri v
Dil	Liber de diligendo Deo
Div	Sermones de diversis
Epi	Sermo in epiphania domini
Gra	Liber de gratia et libero arbitrio
Miss	Homelium super *Missus est* in laudibus virginis matris
Nat	Sermo in nativitate domini
Nat BVM	Sermo in nativitate BVM
O Asspt	Sermo dominica infra octavam assumptionis
OS	Sermo in festivitate Omnium Sanctorum
Pasc	Sermo in die paschae
Pre	Liber de praecepto et dispensatione
PP	Sermo in festo Ss. apostolorum Petri et Pauli
Pur	Sermo in purificatione BMV
QH	Sermo super psalmum *Qui Habitat*

25

Quad	Sermo in quadragesima
Res	De resurrectione
SC	Sermo super *Cantica canticorum*
Sent	Sententiae
V Nat	Sermo in vigilia nativitatis domini

The Works of Martin Luther:

AWA	Archiv Weimarer Ausgabe
WA	Weimarer Ausgabe
WA Br	Weimarer Ausgabe, *Briefe* (Letters)
WA TR	Weimarer Ausgabe, *Tischreden* (Table Talks)

PERIODICALS AND SERIES:

ABR	*The American Benedictine Review*
AC	*Analecta Sacri Ordinis Cisterciensis; Analecta Cisterciensia* 1945-
ARG	*Archiv für Reformationsgeschichte*
CC	Corpus Christianorum Series, Turnhout, Belgium: Brepols, 1953-
CCCM	Corpus Christianorum, Continuatio Mediaevalis
CF	Cistercian Fathers Series. Spencer, Washington, D. C., Kalamazoo, 1970-
CP	Cistercian Publications
Cîteaux	*Cîteaux: Commentarii cistercienses; Cîteaux in de Nederlanden*, Westmalle, Belgium
Coll	*Collectanea Cisterciensia; Collectanea o. c. r.*
CS	Cistercian Studies Series. Spencer, Washington, D. C., Kalamazoo, 1970-
CSQ	*Cistercian Studies Quarterly*
CTQ	*Concordia Theological Quarterly*
DSp	*Dictionnaire de Spiritualité*. Paris, 1932-
LThK	*Lexikon für Theologie und Kirche*. Freiburg im Breisgau, 1957–1967
MnS	*Monastic Studies*. Montreal, 1963-
NCE	*New Catholic Encyclopedia*, New York, 1967-
PL	J.-P. Migne, *Patrologia cursus completus, series latina*
San	Studia Anselmiana Series. Rome, 1933-
ZKG	*Zeitschrift für Kirchengeschichte*

List of Plates

Plate 1   (Frontispiece): *The Crucified Embraces Bernard and Luther.* Bronze sculpture by Werner Franzen, 1986/87. Photo: Alexander Glaser. Altenberger Dom-Verein, Germany.

Plate 2:   *Holy Communion in Bernard's Vicarious Faith.* Glass window, originally from the cistercian monastery of Altenberg, Germany. Sixteenth-century. Photo: Ludwig Stiftung für Kunst und Internationale Verständigung GMBH, Aachen, Germany.

Plate 3:   *Mary, the Christ Child, and Saint Bernard.* Woodcut, Title Page of *Sermones Bernardi In Duytssche.* Zwolle: Peter van Os, 1495. Photo: Institute of Cistercian Studies Library, Western Michigan University.

Plate 4:   *The Devil Reveals the 'Eight Verses' to Bernard* (*Octo versus Bernardi / Septem Versiculi Sancti Bernardi*). Book of Hours, fol. 132; no. C03273; Lyon: 1480/90. Private ownership. Photo: Swiss National Museum, Zurich, Switzerland.

Plate 5:   The Crucified Embraces Saint Bernard (*Amplexus Bernardi*). Minature attributed to a dutch iconographer of the School of Bruges and Ghent, from a vernacular *Seelengärtlein, Hortulus animae,* from the 1520s. Vienna, Österreichische Nationalbibliothek, Codex 2706, fol. 273v. Photo. Leutner Fachlabor, Vienna.

Plate 6:   *Bernard and a Rustic Bet on Attentive Prayer.* Glass window, originally from the cistercian monastery of Altenberg, Germany. Sixteenth-century. Today in north window of Saint Mary's Church, Shrewsbury, England. Photo: Sonia Halliday Photographs, Buckinghamshire, England.

Plate 7:   *Bernard Under Trees in the Company of Biblical Authorities and Students of the Scriptures.* Glass window, originally from the cistercian monastery of Altenberg, Germany. Sixteenth-century. Today at the Castle Stolzenfels, Koblenz, Germany. Verwaltung der staatlichen Schlösser Rheinland-Pfalz, Mainz. Photo: Landesamt für Denkmalpflege Rheinland-Pfalz, Mainz, Germany.

Plate 8:   *Bernard Preaches to his Monks on God's Mercy.* Glass window, originally from the cistercian monastery of Altenberg, Germany. Sixteenth-century. Today at Schnütgen Museum, Cologne. Photo: Rheinisches Bildarchiv (no. 130515), Cologne, Germany.

Plate 9:   *Maulbronn Crucifix with Royal Crown.* Bronze. Originally from the cistercian monastery of Maulbronn, Germany. Approx. 1125–1150. Photo: Württembergisches Landesmuseum (no. 11233), Stuttgart, Germany.

Plate 10:   *Maulbronn Crucifix without Crown.* Bronze. Originally from the cistercian monastery of Maulbronn, Germany. Approx. 1200. Photo: Württembergisches Landesmuseum (no. 1967–47), Stuttgart, Germany.

Plate 11:   *Meran Crucifix with Headband* (crown filed off). Originally at St. Clare's nunnery in Meran, Italy. First half of the twelfth century. Today in private possession. Photo: Württembergisches Landesmuseum, (no. L 1984–92), Stuttgart, Germany.

Plate 12:   Detail of *Meran Crucifix* (previous plate). Photo: Württembergisches Landesmuseum (no. L 1984–92), Stuttgart, Germany.

Plate 13:   *The Crucified Embraces Bernard (Amplexus Bernardi).* Painting by Michael Wolgemut for the altar of the augustinian friary at Nuremberg, 1487. Photo: Bayerische

Staatsgemäldesammlungen (no. 5791), Munich, Germany.

Plate 14: *Bernard's Meditation of the Man of Sorrows.* Woodcut by Lucas Cranach the Elder. Approx. 1515, in *Hortulus animae: Lustgertlein der Seelen.* Wittenberg: Georg Rhau, 1547/48. National Gallery of Art, Washington, D.C. Rosenwald Collection (1949.3.2859.B-5940).

Plate 15: *Bernard's Meditation of the Man of Sorrows.* Woodcut, anonymous, middle of the sixteenth century. From Johannes Ficker, 'Hortulus animae', *Buch und Bucheinband* (Leipzig: K.W. Hiersemann, 1923), p. 68. Photo: author.

Plate 16: *Luther's Seal* (so-called 'Luther Rose'), 1530. Photo: Internet.

Plate 17: *Mary, the Christ Child, and Saint Bernard.* Enlarged detail of illuminated page 88 of an *Antiphonale Cisterciense*, originally from the cistercian monastery of Altenberg, Germany. 1544 (D 34). Photo: Universitätsbibliothek Düsseldorf, Germany.

Plate 18: Enlargement of the detail of bottom of page 88 (previous plate).

Plate 19: *Mary, the Christ Child, and Saint Bernard.* Book illustration of *Manuale pietatis*, Saint Bernard-op-'t-Schelt. Approx. 1524. Photo: Bibliotheek van de Faculteit der Godgeleerdheid, Catholic University of Louvain, Belgium. Photo: author.

Plate 20: *Christ Enthroned on a Rainbow.* Green colored seal of the former augustinian friary in Grimma, Saxony, used after 1426. From: *Urkundenbuch der Stadt Grimma und des Klosters Nimbschen*, Ludwig Schmidt, ed. (Leipzig: Giesecke & Devrient, 1895) no. 5.

Plate 21: *Bernard's Vision of Mary and the Christ Child*, combined with *Bernard's Fight with a Demon.* Enlarged detail of an illustration in an *Antiphonale Cisterciense*, originally from the cistercian monastery of Altenberg, 1547 (D 36, fol. 207v). Photo: Universitätsbibliothek Düsseldorf, Germany.

Plate 22: Enlargement of the letter 'P' (previous plate).

Introduction

MANY BOOKS have been published about Saint Bernard of Clairvaux, and even more about Martin Luther. Books on the german reformer and his relationship to the french cistercian abbot remain, however, very rare. The significance of both men is more than hinted at by the fact that in 1996, the four-hundred and fiftieth anniversary of Luther's death, and in 1990, the nine-hundredth birthday of Bernard, were celebrated around the world.

In the following pages I want to let Bernard and Luther speak for themselves, in particular on those issues which Luther found worth quoting from Bernard's *opus*, and which demonstrate their congeniality. This means that some of the dust, collected over the centuries, is to be wiped off the old 'boxes' of narrow interpretations by which generations of interpreters have made Luther an 'arch-heretic' to some and a 'saint' to others, and which have made Bernard a distant figure of the 'dark Middle Ages' to some, but a spiritual master to others, especially to monks and nuns. Along with the dust of centuries, some glitter also may come off these two figures. I want to reach the real, historical Luther and the real, historical Bernard who as prophets to the Church Catholic were called to help the Gospel shine in it and in the world.

By this concentration on the relationship of Bernard and Luther, a new phase in Luther research is rung in, one which has yet to come to terms with the entire monastic heritage in Luther's

works. The development of such a new phase is hindered when
one does not differentiate between monastic theology and monastic
life style. This methodical distinction is needed as the attempt is
made here to uncover Luther's bernardine monastic theological
insights from beneath the suffocating blanket of the reformational
rejection of monasticism, which Luther and lutheran interpreters
misunderstood as the quintessence of work righteousness.[1]

In interpreting Luther and Bernard, one has to leap across
the centuries. This may pose problems. First, we take the leap
into the distant twelfth century and its elitist monastic milieu,[2]
from there to the sixteenth century, and then into the present time.
Bernard and Luther moved in different worlds, of course, several
hundred years apart.[3] The leap from Bernard to Luther may appear
less daring once one realizes that the whole of the later medieval
and early modern religious thought is permeated by Bernard's
thinking[4] (and Augustine's, of course). Bernard had an impact,
for instance, on Francis of Assisi, the Franciscans Bonaventure
and David of Augsburg,[5] and on the nuns at Helfta in the thirteenth

1 See Franz Posset, 'Monastic Influence on Martin Luther'. *Monastic Studies*
18 (Montreal, 1988) 136.

2 See Michaela Diers, *Bernhard von Clairvaux: Elitäre Frömmigkeit* (Münster: Aschendorff, 1991) 11–27.

3 See Bernhard Lohse, 'Luther und Bernhard von Clairvaux'. *Bernhard von
Clairvaux. Rezeption und Wirkung im Mittelalter und in der Neuzeit.* Kaspar Elm,
ed. (Wiesbaden: Harrassowitz Verlag, 1994) 271–301, here 282–85.

4 See Giles Constable, 'The Popularity of Twelfth-Century Spiritual Writers
in the Late Middle Ages'. *Renaissance Studies in Honor of Hans Baron.* Anthony
Molho and John A. Tedeschi, eds., (Dekalb, IL: Northern Illinois University
Press, 1971) 5–28. Jean Leclercq, 'The Image of Bernard in the Late Medieval
Example Literature', *Thought* 54 (1979) 291- 302. Theo Bell, *Divus Bernhardus*,
17–25. David N. Bell, " 'In Their Mother Tongue": A Brief History of the
English Translation of Works by and Attributed to Saint Bernard of Clairvaux:
1496–1970'. *The Joy of Learning and the Love of God: Studies in Honor of
Jean Leclercq.* CS 160. E. Rozanne Elder, ed. (Kalamazoo and Spencer: CP,
1995) 291–308. With Peter Dinzelbacher one must point out that the history of
Bernard's impact on later centuries is not written yet, see his *Christliche Mystik
im Abendland: Ihre Geschichte von den Anfängen bis zum Ende des Mittelalters*
(Paderborn: Ferdinand Schöningh, 1994) 120. Pierre Riché, 'Postérité de saint
Bernard'. *Saint Bernard & le monde Cistercien*, eds. Léon Pressouyre and Terryl
N. Kinder (Paris: CNMHS/Sand, 1990) 137–139.

5 On Bonaventure, see Jacques Guy Bougerol, 'Saint Bonaventure et Saint
Bernard', *Antonianum* 46 (1971) 3–79; Bougerol, 'L'influence de Saint Bernard

century.[6] Bernard also had great influence on the carthusian Guigo de Ponte at the end of the thirteenth century, who quoted Bernard by name about thirty times (Augustine is quoted only ten times) in *On Contemplation*.[7] Bernard also had an impact on such diverse spiritual and theological authors as Joachim of Fiore,[8] Thomas Aquinas,[9] Duns Scotus,[10] the german dominican friars Meister Eckhart, Henry Suso, and John Tauler;[11] Gottfried of Strasbourg,[12]

sur la pensée franciscaine', Coll 52 (1990) 284–298. On David of Augsburg, see Georg Steer, 'Virtus und Sapientia. Der Einfluß Bernhards von Clairvaux auf Davids von Augsburg deutsche Traktate "Die sieben Vorregeln der Tugend" und "Der Spiegel der Tugend" ', *Zisterziensische Spiritualität: Theologische Grundlagen, funktionale Voraussetzungen und bildhafte Ausprägungen im Mittelalter*, Clemens Kasper OCist. and Klaus Schreiner, eds. (St. Ottilien: EOS Verlag Erzabtei St. Ottilien, 1994) 171–187.

6 See Johanna Lanczkowski, 'Der Einfluss der Hohe-Lied-Predigten Bernhards auf die drei Helftaer Mystikerinnen', *Erbe und Auftrag* 66 (1990) 17–28. Ulrich Köpf, 'Bernhard von Clairvaux in der Frauenmystik'. *Frauenmystik im Mittelalter*. Peter Dinzelbacher and Dieter R. Bauer, eds. (Ostfildern: Schwabenverlag, 1985) 48–77.

7 See *Carthusian Spirituality. The Writings of Hugh of Balma and Guigo de Ponte*, Dennis D. Martin, trans. and ed. (New York and Mahwah: Paulist Press, 1997) 173–253.

8 See Bernard McGinn, '*Alter Moyses:* The Role of Bernard of Clairvaux in the Thought of Joachim of Fiore'. *Bernardus Magister,* 429–448.

9 See Jean Chatillon, 'L'influence de s. Bernard sur la pensée scholastique au XII et au XIIIe siècle'. *Saint Bernard Théologien. Actes du Congrès de Dijon 15–19 Sept 1953.* ASOC 9 (Rome, 1953). M. Basil Pennington, 'The Influence of Bernard de Clairvaux on Thomas Aquinas', *Studia Monastica* 16 (1974) 281–291; Pennington, *The Last of the Fathers: The Cistercian Fathers of the Twelfth Century: A Collection of Essays* (Still River: St. Bede's Publications, 1983) 97–107; Mark D. Jordan, 'Thomas Aquinas on Bernard and the Life of Contemplation'. *Bernardus Magister,* 449–460; Jacques Verger, 'Saint Bernard et les scholastiques'. *Vies et légendes de saint Bernard de Clairvaux. Création, diffusion, réception (XIIe–XXe Siècles). Actes des Rencontres de Dijon, 7–8 juin 1991*, ed. Patrick Arabeyre, Jacques Berlioz, and Philippe Poirrier (Cîteaux: Commentarii Cistercienses, 1993) 201–210; hereafter quoted as *Vies et légendes*.

10 See William A. Frank, '*Sine Proprio:* On Liberty and Christ, A Juxtaposition of Bernard of Clairvaux and John Duns Scotus'. *Bernardus Magister,* 461–478.

11 See Andre Rayez, 'The Golden Age of Medieval Devotion: The Fourteenth and Fifteenth Centuries,' *Jesus in Christian Devotion and Contemplation* Edward Malatesta, ed. (St. Meinrad: Abbey Press, 1974) 48–85 (translation of the entry 'Humanité du Christ [Devotion et contemplation]', DSp 8:1033–1108 (Paris: Gabriel Beauchesne et ses Fils, 1969). See Bernard McGinn, 'Bernard and Meister Eckhart', *Cîteaux* 31 (1980) 373–386. Concerning Bernard's influence

Dante Alighieri,[13] the author of the *Cloud of Unknowing*,[14] Bridget of Sweden,[15] John Ruusbroec[16] in the fourteenth century, and leaders of the *Devotio Moderna* Geert Grote, Gerard Zerbolt of Zutphen, and Thomas a Kempis.[17]

As for Erasmus of Rotterdam, the prince of the humanists, Bernard was of interest primarily as the elegant preacher, including the preacher of the second crusade, and as the author of the *Book in Praise of the New Knighthood*.[18] While Luther could not have cared less about this aspect of Bernard's work and life, he shared Erasmus' concerns for good preaching and found a superb model in

---

on the german mystics such as Tauler, see Louise Gnädiger, 'Der minnende Bernhardus: Seine Reflexe in den Predigten des Johannes Tauler', *Cîteaux* 31 (1980) 387–409; Georg Steer, 'Bernhard von Clairvaux als theologische Autorität für Meister Eckhart, Johannes Tauler und Heinrich Seuse', *Bernhard von Clairvaux*, ed. Elm, 233–60; Dennis E. Tamburello, 'Bernard of Clairvaux in the Thought of Meister Eckhart', CSQ 28 (1993) 73–91.

12 See Karl Allgaier, *Der Einfluss Bernhards von Clairvaux auf Gottfried von Strassburg* (Frankfurt etc.: Peter Lang, 1983).

13 See R. W. Englert, 'Bernard and Dante: Rituals of Grief', ABR 38 (1987) 1–13; Raymond D. DiLorenzo, 'Dante's Saint Bernard and the Theology of Liberty in the *Commedia*', *Bernardus Magister*, 497–515; M. Aversano, *San Bernardo e Dante. Teologia e poesia della conversione* (Salerno: Edisud, 1990); S. Botterill, 'Life after Beatrice: Bernard of Clairvaux in "Paradiso XXXI" ', *Texas Studies in Literature and Language* 32 (1990) 120–136.

14 See *The Pursuit of Wisdom and Other Works by the Author of The Cloud of Unknowing,* James A. Walsh, ed., preface by George A. Maloney (New York, Mahwah: Paulist Press, 1988) 101–102.

15 See James France, 'From Bernard to Bridget: Cistercian Contribution to a Unique Scandinavian Monastic Body'. *Bernardus Magister,* 479–495.

16 See Albert Ampe, 'Bernardus en Ruusbroec', *Ons Geestelijk Erf* 27 (1953) 143–179.

17 On Groote, see Heinrich Gleumes, 'Gerhard Groot und die Windesheimer als Verehrer des hl. Bernhard', *Geist und Leben: Zeitschrift für Aszese und Mystik* 10 (1935) 90–112. Edmond Mikkers, 'Sint Bernardus en de Moderne Devotie', *Cîteaux* 4 (1953) 149–186. On Zerbolt, see his 'Spiritual Ascents', which is filled with Bernard references; see John van Engen, *Devotio Moderna. Basic Writings* (New York and Mahwah: Paulist Press, 1988) 243–315. On Thomas a Kempis, see Heinrich Gleumes, 'Der geistige Einfluss des hl. Bernhard von Clairvaux auf Thomas von Kempen', *Geist und Leben: Zeitschrift für Aszese und Mystik* 13 (1938) 109–120; K. Lauterer, 'Bernhard und die Devotio moderna', *Bernhard von Clairvaux und der Beginn der Moderne*, Dieter R. Bauer and Gotthard Fuchs, eds. (Innsbruck and Vienna: Tyrolia, 1996).

18 See Gerhard B. Winkler, 'Die Bernhardrezeption bei Erasmus von Rotterdam'. *Bernhard von Clairvaux*, Elm, ed., 261–270.

Bernard. Furthermore, Bernard had an impact on such german Augustinian friars as Johann von Paltz and Johann von Staupitz, who was Luther's superior,[19] and on such other sixteenth century figures as Thomas More,[20] John Calvin,[21] John of the Cross,[22] Ignatius of Loyola,[23] Luis de León,[24] and on still later spiritual authors like

19 See Robert H. Fischer, 'Paltz und Luther', *Lutherjahrbuch* 37 (1970) 9–36, here 33, who counted about sixty Bernard quotations in Paltz's works. See Franz Posset, 'St Bernard's Influence on Two Reformers: John von Staupitz and Martin Luther', CSQ 25 (1990)175–187; on Staupitz: 177–182. William O. Paulsell, 'The Use of Bernard of Clairvaux in Reformation Preaching', *Erudition at God's Service: Studies in Medieval Cistercian History* XI, John R. Sommerfeldt, ed., CS 98 (Kalamazoo: CP, 1987), 327–338; Pietro de Leo, 'La postérité spirituelle'. *Colloque de Lyon-Cîteaux-Dijon, Bernard de Clairvaux: Histoire, Mentalités, Spiritualité* (Paris: Cerf, 1992) 659–698; 674 (on sixteenth century developments). Franz Posset, 'Saint Bernard in the Devotion, Theology, and Art of the First Half of the Sixteenth Century', *Lutheran Quarterly* 11 (1997).

20 See Germain Marc'hadour, 'Saint Bernard et saint Thomas More', Coll 44 (1982) 26–59.

21 See Anthony N. S. Lane, 'Calvin's Sources of St Bernard', ARG 67 (1976) 275f; Lane, 'Bernard of Clairvaux: A Forerunner of John Calvin?' *Bernardus Magister*, 533–545; Lane, 'Calvin's Use of Bernard of Clairvaux'. *Bernhard von Clairvaux*, Elm, ed., 303–332; Lane, *Calvin and Bernard of Clairvaux* (Princeton: Theological Seminary, 1996); Jill Raitt, 'Calvin's Use of Bernard of Clairvaux', ARG 72 (1981) 112–113; W. Stanford Reid, 'Bernard of Clairvaux in the Thought of John Calvin', *Westminster Theological Journal* 41 (1978) 127–145; Reid, 'The Reformer Saint and the Saintly Reformer. Calvin & the Legacy of Bernard of Clairvaux,' *Christian History* 8 (1989) 28f; C. Izard, 'Jean Calvin à l'écoute de Saint Bernard', *Etudes théologiques et religieuses* 67 (1992) 19–41; Luke Anderson, 'The Imago Dei Theme in John Calvin and Bernard of Clairvaux'. *Calvinus Sacrae Scripturae Professor*. W. H. Neuser, ed. (Grand Rapids: Eerdmans, 1994) 178–198. Dennis E. Tamburello, *Union with Christ: John Calvin and the Mysticism of St. Bernard* (Louisville: Westminster John Knox Press, 1994).

22 See M. Huot de Longchamp, 'Saint Bernard au secours de saint Jean de la Croix', Coll 52 (1990) 307–317; R. M. Garritty, *Bernard of Clairvaux and John of the Cross: Divergent views of human affectivity in Christian spirituality* (Washington: Dissertation, Catholic University of America, 1990).

23 See Joseph de Guibert, *The Jesuits: Their Spiritual Doctrine and Practice*, George Ganss, ed., William J. Young, trans. (Chicago: Loyola University Press, 1964) 216f; B. de Vregille, 'De saint Bernard à saint Ignace', Coll 52 (1990) 238–244. In the year 1570 the Jesuit College at Loreto possessed fifteen meditations books of Saint Bernard, see Klára Erdei, *Auf dem Wege zu sich selbst: Die Meditation im 16. Jahrhundert: Eine funktionsanalytische Gattungsbeschreibung* (Wiesbaden: Otto Harrassowitz, 1990) 167.

24 See R. Cao Martinez, 'Sobre la presencia de San Bernardo en Fray Luis de León', *Actas. Congreso internacional sobre san Bernardo e o Cister en Galicia e Portugal*. 17–20 outubro 1991. Ourense/Oseira. IX Centenario de San Bernardo (Ourense, 1992) 137–171.

Francis de Sales and the German Lutheran Johann Arndt,[25] Blaise
Pascal, and others in modern times.[26] Bernard's influence can be
demonstrated as well in medieval and late medieval prayerbooks,
and in such collections of 'legends' as *The Golden Legend*.[27] All
in all, it is not an exaggeration to call Bernard a 'Teacher of All
Christians', a *doctor communis*.

Bernard was considered 'the last of the fathers' because he
taught in continuity with the patristic tradition and in contrast to
the scholastic style of doing theology which was on the rise in
his day. Luther also tried to move within the tradition of biblical,
patristic, and monastic theology, and thus in discontinuity with
much of the scholastic tradition, as he perceived it and as it had been
established in a position of dominance. A simplistic view which
would equate 'catholic tradition' with 'scholasticism' was to see
Luther as the breaker with tradition in general. But he really wanted
to break away only from the scholastic philosophical tradition and
its impact on theology. Since Bernard's *epitheton ornans* 'last of the

25 On Francis de Sales, see René-Jean Hesbert, 'Deux âmes fraternelles: S.
Bernard et S. François de Sales,' Coll 44 (1982) 210–37; Viviane Mellinghoff-
Bourgerie, 'Bernhard von Clairvaux in der französischen Frömmigkeitsliteratur
des 17. Jahrhunderts: François de Sales'. *Bernhard von Clairvaux*, Elm, ed., 389–
420. On Arndt, see Johann Arndt, *True Christianity*. Translation and Introduction
by Peter Erb, preface by Heiko A. Oberman (New York, Ramsey, Toronto:
Paulist Press 1979) 165, 223, 279; Ernst Koch, 'Die Bernhard-Rezeption im
Luthertum des 16. und 17. Jahrhunderts'. *Bernhard von Clairvaux*, Elm, ed, 333–
352; Johannes Wallmann, 'Bernhard von Clairvaux und der deutsche Pietismus'.
Bernhard von Clairvaux, Elm, ed., 353–74. According to Paul Althaus, the
augustinian-bernardine mysticism entered the lutheran prayerbooks of the sixteenth century, see his *Forschungen zur evangelischen Gebetsliteratur* (Gütersloh
1927, reprint Hildesheim: Olms, 1966) 61; see Erdei, *Auf dem Wege zu sich selbst*,
228.
26 See Jean Mesnard, 'Pascal et Bernard de Clairvaux'. *Bernhard von
Clairvaux*, Elm, ed., 375–388. For a general survey of Bernard's impact, see
John Eudes Bamberger, 'The Influence of St Bernard', CSQ 25 (1990) 101–114.
On the nineteenth and twentieth centuries, see G. Penco, 'S. Bernardo tra due
centenari: 1890–1990', *Benedictina* 38 (1991) 19–33; Philippe Poirrier, 'Saint
Bernard; enjeu idéologique et politique? Deux siècles de commémoration à Dijon
(XIXe-XXe siècles)'. *Vies et légendes*, 346–370; Michel Albaric, 'Saint Bernard
dans l'imagerie de piété, XIXe-XXe siècles'. *Vies et légendes*, 371–384.
27 See Brian Patrick McGuire, 'A Saint's Afterlife. Bernard in the Golden
Legend and in Other Medieval Collections'. *Bernhard von Clairvaux*, Elm, ed.,
179–212; Alain Boureau, 'Saint Bernard dans les légendiers dominicains au XIIIe
siècle'. *Vies et légendes*, 84–90; Peter Ochsenbein, 'Bernhard von Clairvaux in
spätmittelalterlichen Gebetbüchern'. *Bernhard von Clairvaux*, Elm, ed., 213–232.

fathers'[28] was always understood in an anti-scholastic sense, it is
not surprising that Luther wanted to return to him, for he understood
the pre-scholastic authorities as the preferable interpreters of the
Word of God. He wanted to 'employ' the church fathers as helpers
in his profession as a preacher and professor. The issue for Luther
was not so much 'either' Scripture 'or' Tradition, but biblical
theology versus philosophical (scholastic) theology, and he must
have sensed the same or similar preferences in Bernard for the
Scriptures. The cistercian abbot mistrusted any philosophical role
(especially in contemplation) because it jeopardized the primacy
of Scripture as the Word of God, and he himself was mistrusted
by philosophers for his aversion to 'reason' alone and 'lack of
modernity'.[29]

Apparently, Luther had no problem going back to Bernard and
grasping his theological insights, drawn from scriptural meditations. In contrast, Luther did not select Peter Abelard (or Thomas
Aquinas) as his theological mentor(s). From all the patristic and
medieval 'channels' at his disposal, he chose primarily Bernard
(along with Augustine, Tauler, and some others). His selections
probably had something to do with the theological preferences of
his augustinian Order. In any case, the result of his intense selecting
and viewing of the traditional 'channels' was the formation of his
own 'transmitter station' which later beamed out his reformation
theology.

28 *Ultimus inter Patres* (Mabillon's preface to the edition of Bernard's
works), PL 182:26. *Vir bonus dicendi peritus* (Wibald of Stablo, 1149), PL
189:1255. See O. Rousseau, 'Le dernier des Pères', *Saint Bernard Théologien*.
ASOC 9 (1953) 306–308, as referred to by M. B. Pranger, 'Bernard van Clairvaux, de laatste der Vaders?' *Millennium: Tijdschrift voor middeleeuwse studies*
2 (1988) 41–46; Pranger, *Bernard of Clairvaux and the Shape of Monastic
Thought—Broken Dreams* (Leiden: Brill, 1994) 163.

29 On the primacy of the Bible, see Jean Leclercq, 'Saint Bernard et l'Ecri-
ture Sainte'. *Saint Bernard mystique* (Bruges and Paris: Desclée de Brouwer,
1948) 483–489; Leclercq, 'Essais sur l'ésthetique de saint Bernard', *Studi me-
dievali* 9 (1968) 688–728, here 691. Jean Figuet, 'La Bible de Bernard'' données et
ouvertures', *Colloque de Lyon-Cîteaux-Dijon, Bernard de Clairvaux: Histoire,
Mentalités, Spiritualité*, 237–269. With Emero Stiegman, one must state that
'Bernard is biblical, in a sense that, perhaps, has not been sufficiently clarified':
'The Light Imagery of Saint Bernard's Spirituality and Its Evidence in Cistercian
Architecture'. *The Joy of Learning*, 365. On Bernard's 'lack of modernity', see
Pranger, *Bernard of Clairvaux and the Shape of Monastic Thought*, 8.

The leap across centuries may be facilitated and simultaneously complicated by viewing Luther in the context of what is
called 'renaissance humanism', which looked back to the sources
(*ad fontes*).[30] The reader needs to know that the augustinian friars
themselves, whom Luther joined at Erfurt, had been affected by the
humanistic movement coming from Italy. Luther studied at Erfurt
University, which was the first in central and northern Germany to
introduce humanist studies into its curriculum and which played a
pivotal role in the development of northern 'renaissance humanism'. This movement sought to gain access to the best sources of
the past, which included Saint Bernard as the last of the Fathers.
The humanistically-inclined augustinian friars at Erfurt made sure
that Bernard's books were accessible in their library where they
were available to Luther.[31] Without doubt Luther moved in and
was moved by not only the traditional monastic milieu, but also
in and by the contemporary humanistic air which fostered a return
to non-scholastic authorities and ultimately to the Bible.[32] Luther

30 See Lewis W. Spitz, 'The Renaissance: Humanism and Humanistic Research', *Luther and German Humanism* (Brookfield, VT: Variorum, 1996), I:1–
40, especially 2–5 ('Defining Renaissance Humanism').

31 Jun Matsuura, 'Restbestände aus der Bibliothek des Erfurter Augustin-
erklosters zu Luthers Zeit und bisher unbekannte eigenhändige Notizen Luthers'.
*Lutheriana: Zum 500. Geburtstag Martin Luthers von den Mitarbeitern der
Weimarer Ausgabe* (Cologne: Böhlau, 1984) 318–326.

32 For the relationship between humanism and the augustinian order, see
especially Rudolph Arbesmann, *Der Augustinereremitenorden und der Beginn
der humanistischen Bewegung* (Würzburg: Augustinus Verlag, 1965). Little is
known, for instance, about Caspar Amman, a humanist trained in Italy, who
was the provincial of the Augustinians in southern Germany, and who corre-
sponded with Luther on philological issues and on translating Mt 16:18; see
their correspondence in 1522: WA Br 1:607–10 (no. 543). Like Spitz one is
surprised that 'modern secular scholars' all too often have not taken the fact
into account that the monasteries were important centers for the new learning,
see Spitz, *Luther and German Humanism*, V:205; on the augustinian friar Luigi
Marsigli at Florence in the fourteenth century, see I:8; on other italian and
german augustinian humanists, see VII:97–99. Maria Grossmann, *Humanism in
Wittenberg 1485–1517* (Nieuwkoop: B. de Graaf, 1975). Helmar Junghans, *Der
junge Luther und die Humanisten* (Weimar: Hermann Böhlaus Nachfolger, 1984;
Göttingen: Vandenhoeck & Ruprecht, 1985). Ulrich Asendorf, 'Das kulturelle
Paradies: Reformation und Humanismus gingen ursprünglich Hand in Hand',
Lutherische Monatshefte (1994) 35–38; Charles Nauert, *Humanism and the Cul-
ture of Renaissance Europe* (Cambridge and New York: Cambridge University
Press, 1995); Erika Rummel, *The Humanist-Scholastic Debate in the Renaissance
and Reformation* (Cambridge: Harvard University Press, 1995). *Humanismus*

ully shared the aversion many contemporary humanists had to the scholastics. The cultural climate of the early sixteenth century in what is today the Netherlands, Germany, Austria, and Switzerland was permeated by *Klosterhumanismus* ('monastic humanism')[33] with its sometimes strong feelings against scholasticism, but also with its inclination toward the renewal of meditation of which the leading humanist, Erasmus, wrote in his *Enchiridion (Dagger)* in 1503.[34] In this humanistic climate, new editions of the Church Fathers' works were published and Luther made eager use of them.

The renaissance humanists' interest in the rhetorical tradition must have contributed to Bernard's attractiveness at the beginning of the sixteenth century; Bernard was famous as a medieval rhetor and preacher, heir to the classical tradition.[35] *Flores Bernardi* circulated that included chapters rhetorically structured according to bernardine texts combining either two concepts (such as ascent and descent), or three concepts (such as triple grace) or four concepts (such as four affections of the soul).[36]

Luther's chief assignment besides teaching was preaching. In

---

und Wittenberger Reformation. Aspekte eines Transformationsprozesses, Michael Beyer, Günther Wartenberg, and Hans-Peter Hasse, eds. (Leipzig: Evangelische Verlagsanstalt, 1996). As to 'monastic' and 'biblical humanism' of that time, see Klaus Ganzer who pointed out that benedictine and cistercian monasticism had established a long tradition of biblical monastic theology, and that the humanist and benedictine abbot Trithemius (d. 1516) considered the study of the Scriptures the crowning of any monastic studies, 'Zur monastischen Theologie des Johannes Trithemius'. *Historisches Jahrbuch* 101 (1981) 385–421, here 399; see also Noel L. Brann, *The Abbot Trithemius (1462–1516): The Renaissance of Monastic Humanism* (Leiden: Brill, 1981).

33 Richard Newald, *Beiträge zur Geschichte des Humanismus in Ober-Österreich* (1926) appears to have coined the expression *Klosterhumanismus*; see Franz Machilek, 'Klosterhumanismus in Nürnberg um 1500', *Mitteilungen des Vereins für Geschichte der Stadt Nürnberg* 64 (1977) 10–45. Spitz, *Luther and German Humanism*, V:205, with right stresses the monasteries as transmitters of humanistic culture, and he refers, as examples, to the cistercian monastery of Adwert (which Rudolph Agricola, the 'father of german humanism' frequented) and to the benedictine monastery of Sponheim where Trithemius was abbot.

34 See Erdei, *Auf dem Wege zu sich selbst*, 67 (on the renaissance humanism and its efforts of renewing Scripture meditation).

35 See Luke Anderson, 'The Rhetorical Epistemology in Saint Bernard's *Super Cantica*'. *Bernardus Magister*, 95–128.

36 As part of the medieval encyclopedia by Vincent Beauvais (Venice, 1494), or separately (Nuremberg, 1472 and later editions). See Ulrich Köpf, 'Die Rezeptions- und Wirkungsgeschichte Bernhards von Clairvaux. Forschungsstand und Forschungsaufgaben'. *Bernhard von Clairvaux*, Elm, ed., 5–65, here 15–17.

the light of the high expectations people had of preachers at the
time, it is probably correct to say that Luther was assigned to
earn his doctorate in theology in order to become a good preacher,
and not primarily to become a professor. Key preaching positions
(*Prädikantenstellen*) in the imperial cities of German-speaking
lands were usually given only to priests with doctorates.[37] Luther,
the preacher, picked only the best from the rhetorical tradition:
Bernard's monastic theological 'sermons' with their rhetorically
skilled structures. These bernardine sermons served as models.
They emerged easily from memory if not from direct copies, as they
are well structured, often along the rhetorical concept of triplicity:
triple grace ('convictions') in the *First Sermon on the Annunciation*; three kisses in the initial *Sermons on the Canticle;* the triple
advent of Christ in the *Advent Sermons*; the triple miracle at the
incarnation in the *Christmas Sermons*; triple (pastoral) feeding in
an *Easter Sermon* and in *Sermon 76 on the Canticle*. But we also
find in Luther the double concept: Christ's double right to heaven
is one of the most favorite concepts Luther learned, not, however,
from a bernardine sermon, but from medieval Bernard legends. A
comparison of Bernard's and Luther's 'rhetoric' and 'metaphoric'
would be enticing, but cannot be the goal of this study. Here we
can say only that both were gifted orators: Bernard was 'one of
the greatest masters of christian rhetoric',[38] 'the greatest master of
language in the Middle Ages'.[39] And in a recent biography Luther
has been called the 'German Cicero'.[40]

According to custom Bernard's eighty-six sermons on the Song
of Songs, his four 'homilies' on Luke 1 (*Missus est*), and the
'sermon' to the Knights Templar were traditionally listed under
the classification 'writings', and not under 'preaching'. Actually,

37 See the section 'The Preacher-Positions in the Late Middle Ages' in my
article 'Preaching the Passion of Christ on the Eve of the Reformation', CTQ 59
(1995) 280–282.

38 Erich Auerbach, *Literary Language and Its Public in Late Latin Antiquity
and in the Middle Ages*, Ralph Manheim, trans. (London: Routledge & Kegan
Paul, 1965) 274.

39 David Knowles, *The Evolution of Medieval Thought* (New York: Vintage
Books, 1962) 147.

40 Horst Herrmann, *Luther: Ketzer wider Willen* (Munich: Bertelsmann,
1983) 272, 392.

the texts on Luke 1 were called by Bernard himself a *disputatio*,[41] a category Luther detested. These bernardine works are not exegetical commentaries in the modern sense; they are medieval spiritual literature. Nevertheless, Luther took Bernard's famous sermons on the Song as products of his Scripture meditations, which to him mirrored Bernard's intense love for the Word of God. This great love for Scripture drove Bernard 'to perfect the beauty of his own words, to make the human word less volatile and to fix in his audience's memory the word of God conveyed by the words of Bernard'.[42] Luther must have been very impressed by this love for the Scriptures and thus for Christ. The medieval classification of the bernardine works as 'sermons' and as 'writings' has another significance generally overlooked by Luther scholars: if Bernard's early works on Mary, the so-called four 'homilies' on Luke 1 (*Missus est*), were understood by Bernard himself and by later medieval readers (even up to Luther) not so much as 'sermons', but as 'writings' or as a *disputatio*, then they may indeed fall under the rubric 'disputation' in the general sense in which Luther apparently used the term when he dismissed the category as 'impious disputations'.

Justifiably or not, Luther perceived in Bernard a double image: (1) Bernard the preacher of Christ, and (2) Bernard the disputer of monastic stuff. Late in his career (in 1540) he declared himself to this effect:

> If you shake him [Bernard] out, you will find him two[faced]. For when he is by himself in faith, then he teaches Christ most beautifully; he preaches his benefits, sets the spirits on fire for the embrace of Christ; here then he is [all] roses and honey. On

41 *Interim autem ex devota scintillantis sideris contemplatione, ferventior reparabitur in his, quae sequuntur, disputatio*, SBOp 4:35,18–20; see Jean Leclercq, 'Le Bible dans les homélies de S. Bernard sur "Missus est" ', *Recueil d'Études sur Saint Bernard et ses Écrits* (Rome: Editioni di Storia e Letteratura, 1969) 3:248; see Leclercq, *Introduction* to the American edition of the *Song of Songs* II, Kilian Walsh, trans. (Kalamazoo: CP, 1976) xiii.

42 See Beverly Mayne Kienzle, '*Verbum Dei et verba Bernardi*: The Function of Language in Bernard's Second Sermon for Peter and Paul'. *Bernhardus Magister*, 158.

the other side, when he disputes about matters of law, then he disputes just like a Turk or a Jew who does not know Christ or who negates [Christ]. Anyone who reads any of his disputations on the monastic life, about obedience toward abbots and so forth, will see that I speak the truth.[43]

If Luther meant to include Bernard's early four pieces on Mary, the *Homelium super Missus est in laudibus virginis matris*, which were traditionally incorporated among the 'writings' of Bernard, then his rejection of them as 'impious' becomes more plausible in that in them Bernard glorified Mary more than Christ in Luther's view, expressed in the table talk of 1531.[44] This is understandable once one realizes that Luther's hermeneutical axiom was to promote whatever promotes Christ (*was Christum treibet*) and thus, by implication to neglect whatever does not promote Christ. Any bernardine 'sermon' or 'disputation' like the *Missus est* was to be left aside, in Luther's opinion in another of his table talks (no. 494).[45] If Luther's definition of 'disputation' as 'writings which do not teach Christ' is understood to include Bernard's four marian homilies, then Luther's use of the singular ('sermon')[46] when talking about this text makes sense, and is explained in the very fact that the Reformer apparently took them as one piece of 'writing'

43 WA 40-III:354,17–24 (on Ps 130, printed in 1540); see Bell, *Divus Bernhardus,* 341- 352; Lohse, 'Luther und Bernhard von Clairvaux', *Bernhard von Clairvaux,* ed. Elm, 271- 301.

44 *Sic Bernhardus multa scripsit impiissime sicut in sermone: Missus est Angelus et aliis locis de Maria,* WA TR 1:45,24f (no. 118).

45 *Sed ein christ lest disputationes stehn* ('But a Christian leaves disputations aside'), WA TR 1:219,8 (no. 494).

46 *Sicut in sermone* [sic]: *Missus est Angelus,* WA TR 1:45,25 (no. 118); *Bernardus consumit totum sermonem* [sic] *in laude virginis Mariae,* WA TR 1:219,6 (no. 494, 1533). Theo Bell, 'Luther's Reception of Bernard of Clairvaux', CTQ 59 (1995), note 14 (where it should read 'no.', not 'note' 494) noticed Luther's use of the singular for the so-called four bernardine 'sermons' on Mary. Bell, however, drew the unnecessary conclusion that 'possibly he [Luther] had never read them'. If Luther took all four 'homilies' as one 'sermon' (losely speaking) or as one despicable 'disputation' on Mary, then Bell's concusion is not cogent at all. Luther may very well have read this one *homelium* on Mary, but did not like his concentration on Mary, as it smacked too much of a tract or a 'disputation'. Luther much preferred his Christ-centered sermons for the feast of the Annunciation, as he mentioned this in his Table Talk no. 494.

and not as four individual 'sermons', as we are inclined to view them today.

This negative evaluation of bernardine 'disputations', in contrast to his Christ-centered preaching, is found elsewhere in Luther's table talks: 'Bernard is the best of all the teachers in the Church as long as he preaches, but in his disputations he becomes a different person'.[47] The distinction between two Bernards comes through in the statement: 'The Fathers and teachers such as Augustine, Jerome, Hilary, Bonaventure, etc. are to be held in high esteem for their faith testimony. . . . Bernard preaches most beautifully, but not so when he disputes'.[48]

The leap across the centuries into Bernard's time may not be as easy for modern readers (without a monastic mentality) as it was for Luther (with his monastic mentality). Usually the modern reader fails to feel the immediate impact of Bernard's texts because his mental training differs from the 'monastic memory'. As B. Pranger pointed out:

> Just as the twentieth-century entertainer expects his audience to have a basic knowledge of modern life, so the medieval monastic preacher was able to draw on a presence of biblical language in the minds of his audience which he could appeal to, not only in his routine commentary but also in more sophisticated moves of hints and allusions.[49]

The scope of this book is neither rhetorical, nor literary, nor linguistic (nor purely historical either); it is primarily ecumenical-theological. Therefore, a reader with mostly historical interests will perhaps miss the desirable contextualization of passages quoted here, especially those of Bernard. I must live with the criticism if it should arise in this regard. My theological focus is on the overall interpretation of Bernard and of Luther. Therefore, I emphasize two major fields of scholarly research: monastic theological studies and Reformation theological studies. Among the works I tend

47 WA TR 1:272,7f (no. 584).
48 WA TR 3:294,34–295,2 (no. 3770a).
49 Pranger, *Bernard of Clairvaux and the Shape of Monastic Thought*, 12.

to rely on are, first the research of Jean Leclercq and his very helpful separation of scholastic and monastic theology,[50] and other scholars' recent monographs on Bernard.[51] With Ulrich Köpf, and following Étienne Gilson and Jean Leclercq, I view Bernard as the originator of the theological treatment of devotions in general and mysticism in particular, something not known in the same way in the western world up to his time. Bernard is more than an author of edifying spiritual literature, as he was viewed for a long time. Bernard was a biblical, monastic, and mystical theologian.[52] The most significant elements of his theology are the interrelatedness of knowledge of self and of God (or 'religious experience'), the centrality of the belief in salvation through Christ alone, and the triple coming of Christ: the miracle of his incarnation, his coming in glory on the Day of Judgment, and his spiritual advent in the believer's heart, where the encounter of God and man is experienced.[53] Herein may lie Bernard's greatest contribution to western civilization, for 'nothing is so significant and seminal in his spirituality as his respect for experience'.[54] 'Experience' is a notion to be investigated not only in Bernard's work, but

50 See Jean Leclercq, *The Love of Learning and the Desire for God: A Study of Monastic Culture,* Catharine Misrahi, trans. (New York: Fordham University Press, 1960).

51 See Etienne Gilson, *The Mystical Theology of Saint Bernard,* A. H. C. Downes, trans. (New York: Sheed and Ward, 1940; reprint: Kalamazoo: CP, 1990); Ulrich Köpf's study on religious experience according to Bernard: *Religiöse Erfahrung in der Theologie Bernhards von Clairvaux* (Tübingen: Mohr, 1980); Michael Casey, *A thirst for God: Spiritual Desire in Bernard of Clairvaux's Sermons on the Song of Songs.* CS 77 (Kalamazoo: CP, 1988). Michael Casey, 'Bernard of Clairvaux: Forty Years of Scholarship'. *St Bernard of Clairvaux: The Man,* John S. Martin, ed. (Parksville: University of Melbourne Press, 1992) 31–45. Dagmar Heller, *Schriftauslegung und geistliche Erfahrung bei Bernhard von Clairvaux* (Würzburg: Echter Verlag, 1990). John R. Sommerfeldt, *The Spiritual Teachings of Bernard of Clairvaux: An Intellectual History of the Early Cistercian Order.* CS 125 (Kalamazoo: CP, 1991). Adriaan H. Bredero, *Bernard of Clairvaux Between Cult and History* (Grand Rapids: William B. Eerdmans, 1996).

52 See Köpf, 'Die Rezeptions- und Wirkungsgeschichte Bernhards', *Bernhard von Clairvaux,* ed. Elm, 50. Köpf, 'Bernhard von Clairvaux – ein Mystiker?', *Zisterziensische Spiritualität,* 15–32.

53 See Köpf, *Religiöse Erfahrung in der Theologie Bernhards von Clairvaux,* 227f; Claudio Stercal, *Il 'Medius Adventus': Saggio di Lettura degli Scritti di Bernardo di Clairvaux* (Rome: Editiones Cistercienses, 1992) 10.

54 Stiegman, 'The Light Imagery', 372; see Norman F. Cantor, *The Civilization of the Middle Ages,* revised edition (New York: Harper Collins, 1993) 339–343.

also in Luther's, each in terms of his theological starting point. A
remarkable congeniality is uncovered across the span of more than
three and a half centuries: the quest for God and God-experience
in faith.[55]

Second, we presuppose the research results of reformation
historians/theologians like Bernhard Lohse, Lewis W. Spitz, Bernd
Moeller, Heiko A. Oberman, Reinhard Schwarz, Kenneth Hagen
and many other Protestants, who have helped to redirect Luther
research by contextualizing Luther within the medieval world. I am
indebted to Roman Catholic scholars such as Joseph Lortz, Erwin
Iserloh, Jos Vercruysse, Jared Wicks, and especially Peter Manns,
Otto Hermann Pesch, and Theo Bell.[56] As to Luther himself, I dare
to think that he was impressed most of all by Bernard the biblical

55 See Johannes Jürgen Siegmund, 'Bernhard von Clairvaux und Martin
Luther – Ein erfahrungstheologischer Vergleich', *Cistercienser Chronik* 98 (1991)
92–114.

56 To mention a few: Bernd Moeller, *Die Reformation und das Mittelalter:
Kirchenhistorische Aufsätze,* Johannes Schilling, ed. (Göttingen: Vandenhoeck
& Ruprecht, 1991). Heiko A. Oberman, *Luther: Man Between God and the Devil*
(New Haven, 1989). Darrell R. Reinke disclosed Luther's monastic style in one of
his Reformation tracts: 'The Monastic Style in Luther's *De libertate christiana,'
Studies in Medieval Culture* X, John R. Sommerfeldt and Thomas H. Seiler, eds.
(Kalamazoo: The Medieval Institute, Western Michigan University, 1977) 147–
154. Reinhard Schwarz, 'Luther's Inalienable Inheritance of Monastic Theology',
trans. Franz Posset, ABR 39 (1988) 430–50. Kenneth Hagen pleaded to view
Luther as monastic interpreter of the 'sacred page': *Luther's Approach to Scripture
as seen in his 'Commentaries' on Galatians 1519–1538* (Tübingen: J. C. B. Mohr
[Paul Siebeck], 1993) 35–48. Specifically on Bernard and Luther: Carl Volz,
'Martin Luther's Attitude Toward Bernard of Clairvaux'. *Studies in Medieval
Cistercian History: presented to Jeremiah F. O'Sullivan* (Spencer: CP, 1971) 186–
204. Erich Kleineidam, 'Ursprung und Gegenstand der Theologie bei Bernhard
von Clairvaux und Martin Luther,' *Dienst der Vermittlung. Festschrift zum 25-
jährigen Bestehen des philosophisch-theologischen Studiums im Priesterseminar
Erfurt,* Wilhelm Ernst, Konrad Feiereis, Fritz Hofmann, eds. (Leipzig: St. Benno
Verlag 1977) 221–47. Wilhelm Maurer, 'Cisterciensische Reform und reformatorischer Glaube', *Cistercienser Chronik* 84 (1977) 1- 13. Peter Manns, 'Zum
Gespräch zwischen M. Luther und der katholischen Theologie: Begegnung zwischen patristisch-monastischer und reformatorischer Theologie an der Scholastik
vorbei,' *Thesaurus Lutheri: Auf der Suche nach neuen Paradigmen der Luther-
Forschung.* Referate des Luther-Symposiums in Finnland 11.-12. November
1986, Tuomo Mannermaa, Anja Ghiselli, and Simo Peura, eds. (Helsinki 1987)
105–106; reprinted in Peter Manns, *Vater im Glauben: Studien zur Theologie
Martin Luthers.* Festgabe zum 65. Geburtstag am 10. März 1988, ed. Rolf
Decot (Stuttgart: Steiner Verlag Wiesbaden, 1988) 441–532. Lohse, 'Luther und
Bernhard von Clairvaux,' *Bernhard von Clairvaux*, ed. Elm, 271–301, and most
of all Theo Bell's publications whose investigations are greatly appreciated and
used here for controling my own research results. For summaries of recent studies,

theologian and the theologian of the religious experience of the encounter between God and man. Bernard's theological concerns emerge in Luther's theology, which may surprise some people, especially Bernard scholars. Luther, after all, was a 'protestant reformer'; how can the two have anything in common? Indeed, Luther appears to be much less interested in Bernard as a representative of what has been called 'romanesque mysticism'[57] than he was eager to learn from Bernard the preacher and interpreter of Scripture. As R. W. Scribner wrote, 'the Reformation itself was predominantly a preaching revival'.[58] One may add that Bernard's model sermons played a major role in it, as we shall see.

Luther scholars may be surprised that Bernard had so great influence if they are accustomed to thinking of Luther's witness to the christian truth in terms of originality and unique giftedness or if they limit medieval influence on Luther to the rhenish mystics, the Modern Devotion, and a hard-to-define late medieval 'nominalism'. A reinterpretation of Luther's theology in the light of the bernardine tradition appears therefore, appropriate. Luther scholarship may have to abandon the idea that Luther's 'theology of the cross' was unique and independent of any previous cross-centered spirituality. Never before the twelfth century had there been a 'theology of the cross' such as we observe in Bernard. It was he who achieved a breakthrough.[59]

---

see Kenneth Hagen, ed., *Luther Digest: An Annual Abridgment of Luther Studies* 4 (1996) 199–225.

57 The observation concerning Luther's preference for Bernard as the Scripture theologian surfaced earlier in this century in a different context, as follows: Luther had less interest in the so-called *romanische Mystik* as compared to the *deutsche Mystik*, see Erich Vogelsang, 'Luther und die Mystik'. *Lutherjahrbuch* 19 (1937) 32–54, here 40f.

58 Robert W. Scribner, *For the Sake of Simple Folk. Popular Propaganda for the German Reformation* (Cambridge and New York: Cambridge University Press, 1981) 2. Bernd Moeller: Luther is to be understood primarily as pastor (*Seelsorger*) and reformer of spirituality, and not so much as ecclesiastical rebel (*Kirchenrebell*), see Moeller's *Reformationstheorien: Ein kirchenhistorischer Disput über Einheit und Vielfalt der Reformation*. Berndt Hamm, Bernd Moeller, Dorothea Wendebourg, eds. (Göttingen: Vandenhock & Ruprecht, 1995) 17.

59 *Nie zuvor wurde in der Theologiegeschichte bis zum 12. Jahrhundert das Leiden und Sterben Jesu Christi zu Ansätzen einer 'theologia crucis – Theologie des Kreuzes' entwickelt, wie bei Bernhard.* Siegmund, 'Bernhard von Clairvaux und Martin Luther', 99; see Köpf, 'Schriftauslegung als Ort der Kreuzestheologie

Is Luther still to be regarded as the reformer, or more as a 'returner' to Bernard and Augustine? He is both. In particular he is a reformer of spirituality, a concept which has become acceptable in recent years beyond Catholic circles and is used to describe Luther's piety.[60] A 'spirituality of the heart' is distinctive to both Luther and Bernard. While Bernard has been known for it for some time,[61] only very recently have we read of Luther's 'spirituality of the heart';[62] but unfortunately Bernard's impact on it has not been taken into consideration. The fundamental congeniality between the two will be unfolded in the course of this study. Their spiritualities of the heart are closely connected to their respective theologies of humility. Young Luther copied several sentences from a bernardine sermon on humility; he did not, however, consult Bernard's treatise on humility. This demonstrates once more Luther's interest in Bernard as a preacher rather than as the author of treatises or 'disputations'.

Bernhards von Clairvaux', *Bernhard von Clairvaux und der Beginn der Moderne*, 194–213.

60 See George S. Yule, 'The Spirituality of Luther and Calvin', *Christian Spiritual Theology,* Noel J. Ryan, ed. (Melbourne: Dove, 1976) 205–210. Hans Bungert, ed., *Martin Luther: Eine Spiritualität und ihre Folgen.* Vortragsreihe der Universität Regensburg zum Lutherjahr 1983 (Regensburg: Mittelbayerische Verlagsanstalt, 1983). Bengt Hoffman, 'Lutheran Spirituality' *Spiritual Traditions for the Contemporary Church,* Robin Maas and Gabriel O'Donnell, eds. (Nashville: Abingdon Press, 1990) 145–161. A. Skevington Wood, 'Spirit and Spirituality in Luther', *The Evangelical Quarterly* 61 (1989) 311, as quoted by Egil Grislis, 'The Spirituality of Martin Luther', *Word & World* 14 (1994) 453–459. Grislis, 'Piety, Faith, and Spirituality in the Quest of the Historical Luther', *Consensus: A Canadian Lutheran Journal of Theology* 19 (1993) 29–51; Bryan V. Hillis, 'Spirituality and Practice: Luther and Canadian Lutheran Spirituality', *Consensus: A Canadian Lutheran Journal of Theology* 19 (1993) 53–76.

61 *'Theologia cordis'*, see Pacificus Delfgaauw, 'An Approach to Saint Bernard's Sermons on the Song of Songs', Coll 23 (1961) 148–161; Bernard Bonowitz, 'Custody of the Heart in the "Sermons on Diverse Subjects"', *Word and Spirit: A Monastic Review* 12 (1990) 134–147; Jean Leclercq, 'From the Tender Heart of Christ to his Glorified Body According to Bernard of Clairvaux'. *Word and Spirit: A Monastic Review* 12 (1990) 80–91; Michael Casey, *The Undivided Heart: The Western Monastic Approach to Contemplation* (Petersham: St. Bede's Publications, 1994), especially 36–40 ('Cardiomimesis'), here 36.

62 See Jared Wicks, 'Martin Luther: The Heart Clinging to the Word'. *Spiritualities of the Heart: Approaches to Personal Wholeness in Christian Tradition,* Annice Callahan, ed. (New York, Mahwah: Paulist Press, 1990) 79–96. Bertrand de Margerie, 'The Heart of Christ: Revelation of the Heart of the Father According to Martin Luther', *Faith and Reason* 17 (1991) 109–114.

In addition to this major sermon passage on humility other lengthy quotations from bernardine sermons are to be found in Luther's works. The longest is taken from the *First Sermon on the Annunciation*, as we shall see in dealing with the priority of grace. This sermon was referenced explicitly by Luther as *B. Bernardus ser. 1 de annunciatione Dominica*. Another, less elaborate quotation, taken from his Sermon 27 on the Song of Songs, concerns the people of faith, and Luther quoted it verbatim in his *Dictata* on Psalm 8:4. These are the three longest, most impressive quotations from Bernard's sermons. They probably carry the greatest theological weight in Luther's repertoire of Bernardine sermons. Of equal importance theologically was the concept of Christ's double right to heaven, which Luther found in a medieval Bernard legend and which he qualified as 'golden'. Other bernardine phrases Luther often used have the character of adages and were easily memorized because of their conciseness and impressiveness.

An examination of Luther's Bernard quotations and references, of which there are more than five hundred, has recently been made by Theo Bell, who (in his own words) 'concentrated above all on quotations of Bernard and probable allusions to him'. Bell wisely added: 'By no means, however, has the subject been thereby exhaustively treated'.[63] In the present work, I include these quotations along with concepts which I find to be similar in Bernard and in Luther, even though Luther did not make explicit reference to Bernard on every occasion.

Before ending these introductory notes, one needs to mention the terminology 'monks' and 'friars'. Often in secondary literature one reads of 'the monk Luther'. This is an inappropriate designation because he never was a 'monk' in the strict sense. He was a member of the reformed Order of Saint Augustine; 'reformed'

63 *Le nom de Bernard apparait plus de cinq cents fois dans les oeuvres de Luther*, Theo Bell, 'Pater Bernardus: Bernard de Clairvaux vu par Martin Luther', *Cîteaux* 41 (1990) 233- 255, here 251; see Bell's annotation in his 'Luther's Reception of Bernard of Clairvaux', 264, on his own previous studies in Dutch, French, and German. Posset, 'Divus Bernhardus', 517: 'Saint Bernard is quoted or mentioned more than five hundred times in the critical edition of Luther's works'.

in the sense of strictly observant of the Rule,[64] and Augustinians technically are friars, not 'monks'.

The recently perceived closeness of Bernard's and Luther's spiritualities was expressed in 1986/87 in a sculpture called *The Crucified Embraces the Two Theologians of the Cross, Bernard and Luther* (Latin: *Amplexus*) by the German artist Werner Franzen. It serves as our frontispiece and requires a brief comment. Franzen's *Amplexus* is part of a series of sculptures which depict the life of Saint Bernard: The Writer, The Preacher, The Mystic, and The Embraced (*Amplexus*).[65] Franzen's Christ has his feet still nailed to the cross, one foot over the other, but he has lifted both hands from the beam and placed them on the two men who kneel by his cross: Bernard and Luther. Bernard is depicted with a crozier, his hands crossed over his chest and his coat of arms by his knees, facing Luther whose coat of arms is also at his knees. So as to leave no doubt about the identity of the two men, the artist has inscribed their names next to their coats of arms. Luther, with only one knee on the ground, holds a Bible scroll in his hands—the artist's way of conveying Luther's career as Scripture professor and his theological axiom 'Scripture alone'. Luther is presented as a young friar, Bernard as an old monk. Christ's right hand is firmly placed on Bernard's shoulder, while his left hand lightly touches Luther's. Bernard contemplates the Crucified; Luther respectfully observes Bernard's eye contact with Christ. The Lord's face is not turned to either of them.

What inspired this modern artistic depiction of the *Embrace of Bernard and Luther* was the medieval motif of the *Amplexus Bernardi*, which may or may not have been known to Luther.[66] This

64 See Bede K. Lackner, 'Martin Luther and Monasticism', *Studiosorum Speculum: Studies in Honor of Louis J. Lekai, O.Cist,* Francis R. Swietek and John R. Sommerfeldt, eds. (Kalamazoo: CP, 1993) CS 141, 173–200, here 173. The Augustinians officially became a 'mendicant order' in 1567.

65 See Arno Paffrath, *Bernhard von Clairvaux. Band 2. Die Darstellung des Heiligen in der bildenden Kunst* (Bergisch Gladbach: Heider,1990) 125.

66 Theo Bell, 'Luther's Reception of Bernard', 261, claims that the motif was known to Luther. However, Bell did not provide any clues for his assumption. The only locus in Luther's works, that one could think of, which perhaps hints at the *amplexus* idea in a general way is on Ps 130, in 1540: Bernard 'sets the

unusual adaptation is grounded in the contemporary ecumenical movement in Germany, with its insights into the close affinity between Bernard's and Luther's theologies of the cross. This iconographic innovation appeared in the homeland of Luther's Reformation and the land of modern ecumenical raprochement between the two traditions dominant in Germany, i. e. 'Roman Catholics' and 'Lutheran Catholics' (Lutherans claim to be Catholic, too!). The artist was evidently aware of recent insights into Luther's dependence on Bernard, for he has Luther look at Bernard who is looking at Christ. The artist took the medieval image of Christ embracing Bernard and added Luther. By this daring innovation in christian art the artist simply expressed with the means specific to his craft what historians of theology have emphasized in recent years, that Bernard and Luther are united in their central concern with proclaiming salvation through Christ crucified, although they represent two different christian traditions.[67]

Finally, I have tried to incorporate a number of scenes from Bernard's life which came into being in the early sixteenth century (sometimes earlier) in order to give a flavor of what Luther and his contemporaries may have known. Most of the illustrations represent a bernardine story, scene, or concept to which Luther himself referred at some time. It is my hope that these illustrations will make reading this book more enjoyable. Dealing with either Bernard or Luther by himself is difficult enough; dealing with both of them at the same time can be compared to entering an

spirits on fire for the embrace of Christ', WA 40-III:354,17–24. But this is not the specific iconographic motif of the *Amplexus Bernardi*. See below, Chapter Four.

67 Among the more recent german publications on Bernard and Luther prior to 1986 which may have inspired the artist to create the *Amplexus* sculpture of Bernard and Luther, are the following: Carl Stange, *Bernhard von Clairvaux: Studien der Luther-Akademie* (Berlin: Verlag Alfred Toepelmann, 1954); Hedwig Bach, 'Bernhard von Clairvaux und Martin Luther,' *Erbe und Auftrag* 46 (1970) 347–351; 453–459; and 47 (1971) 36–43; 121–125; 193- 196. Theo Bell, 'Sermon von der Geburt Christi: Bernard van Clairvaux en Johann Tauler in Luther's Kerstpreek van 1520', *Bijdragen: Tijdschrift voor filosofie en theologie* 39 (1978) 289–309. Ernst Werner, 'Reformation und Tradition—Bernhard von Clairvaux in den Schriften Martin Luthers'. *Martin Luther Kolloquium: Sitzungsberichte der Akademie der Wissenschaften der DDR* (Berlin: Akademie-Verlag, 1983) 28–33. See also the other studies mentioned already, especially Kleineidam's.

'ocean'.[68] Bernard has been called not only a 'difficult saint', but also a 'difficult writer'.[69] As contemporary hagiographer William of Saint Thierry reported, Bernard's sermons on spiritual matters were difficult to understand, and his hearers failed 'to catch what he was saying. . . . His preaching would be more of a stumbling block to them than a source of edification'. But out of respect for Bernard the monks 'treated with reverence even the parts they did not comprehend'.[70] I hope we may do the same.

68 *Luthers Theologie ist ein Ozean*, Paul Althaus, *Die Theologie Martin Luthers* (Gütersloh: Gütersloher Verlagshaus, 1963) 8. *Man gerät auf ein Meer, wenn man sich in das Studium seines [Luthers] Schrifttums begibt*, Gerhard Ebeling, *Luther: Einführung in sein Denken* (Tübingen: J. C. B. Mohr [Paul Siebeck], 1964) 41.

69 Brian Patrick McGuire, *The Difficult Saint: Bernard of Clairvaux and his Tradition*, CS 126 (Kalamazoo: CP, 1991); Bernardo Olivera, 'Help in Reading St. Bernard'. *Word and Spirit: A Monastic Review* 12 (1990) 3–20, here 7: 'difficult writer'. M. Basil Pennington and Yael Katzir, *Bernard of Clairvaux: A Saint's Life in Word and Image* (Huntington: Our Sunday Visitor, 1994) 10: 'in some ways difficult to read'.

70 Vita Bern, Book 1.6,28; PL 185:243; Martinus Cawley, trans., *Bernard of Clairvaux. Early Biographies. Volume I by William of St Thierry* (Lafayette, OR: Guadalupe Translations, 1989) 37f.

Plate 2: *Holy Communion in Bernard's Vicarious Faith.* Glass window, early sixteenth century, originally from the cistercian monastery of Altenberg, Germany;
today in the possession of the Ludwig Stiftung für Kunst und Internationale
Verständigung GMBH, Aachen. The inscription in the top left-hand corner represents the words of the doubting monk who is dragged before Bernard by two
fellow monks, saying that he knows that he will go to hell because of his disbelief:
*Ego nullis assertionibus ad hoc potero induci, ut panem et vinum, quae in altari
proponuntur, credam esse verum corpus et sanguinem Christi, et propterea scio
me ad infernum descendurum.* Bernard tells the doubting monk to receive holy
communion in his (Bernard's) vicarious faith because nobody from Clairvaux
will be going to hell: *Pietas e [Clara]valle in infernum descendit? Absit. Si tu
fidem non habes, per virtutem oboedientiae praecipio t[ibi:] vade communica
fide mea.*

1

Luther's High Esteem for 'Father Bernard' and His Indebtedness to the Monastic Tradition

N THIS CHAPTER we shall attempt to unfold what Luther liked so much about Saint Bernard and what his Bernard sources may have been, including his medieval sources on Bernard. Placing Luther within the tradition of monastic theology by demonstrating his indebtedness to it, we will reflect on what may be called Luther's *sacra pagina* approach to the Bible, i. e. his prayerful study of the Sacred Scriptures as the Word of God in 'prayer, meditation, and temptation', and his view of Bernard's experience of tasting the 'sweetness of the Lord'. We conclude the chapter with Luther's evaluation of Bernard's strained use (*catachresis*) of the Scriptures.

I. LUTHER'S 'FATHER BERNARD'

1. '*I venerate Saint Bernard*'

A number of Luther's early phrases express his knowledge and veneration of Saint Bernard, but also his critical distancing of himself from a contemporary use of pseudo-bernardine material.

These phrases show Luther's interest in Bernard as a spiritual writer and in issues of folk piety and morality.

When Luther quoted Bernard for the first time in his first lectures on the Psalms (*Dictata*,1513), in expounding Ps 14, he used in a positive way a spurious bernardine saying on detraction. He returned to this saying, when he had the honor of delivering the sermon at his Order's chapter meeting at Gotha in 1515, by referring twice to Bernard and his detestation of the evil of slander. Apparently he did not hesitate to demonstrate to an audience of augustinian friars his knowledge of what he considered Bernard's saying. This quotation, however, is not genuinely bernardine. A precise source cannot be located in the critical edition of Bernard's works (SBOp), and possible loci (*On Consideration* 2.13 and SC 24) on 'detraction and righteousness' are not specific enough to qualify as sources. It is likely that Luther consulted contemporary theological manuals and trustingly copied the (Pseudo) Bernard references on 'detraction' which they provided. Luther's wording of the allegedly bernardine phrase best matches entries in two major manuals on *detractio* or *detrahere*: (1) Rainer von Pisa, *Pantheologia* (Augsburg: 1475, two vols.; Nuremberg: 1477, three vols.; Venice: 1486, two vols.); and (2) Petrus Berchorius, *Repertorium* (Nuremberg: 1489, three vols.).[1]

While this example shows Luther using reference works uncritically, another instance reveals Luther critically distancing himself from a contemporary misuse of Bernard. At about the same time (1515/1516) he came across a booklet by Marcus von Weida op (1450–1516) on the confraternity of the rosary. It was printed in 1515 under the title *Zum Spiegel hochlöblicher Bruderschaft des Rosenkranzes Mariae*, Luther angrily objected to the author's use

---

1 *Quia secundum Bernardum vterque habet diabolum, detractor et auditor, ille in lingua, iste in aure,* WA 55-I:110f (WA 3:101,30f). *Bernhardus in Quadragesimali serm. 23 et sermo 36 de restitutione honoris, Art. 3* (Sermon of 1515, *Contra vitium detractionis*), WA 4:681,4–11; see WA 4:481,5; WA 1:49,38f; *triplex homicida,* WA 1:473,6f (1516–18); WA 1:120,7f (1 January 1517); WA 25:428,5–6 (1527). Rainer von Pisa's manual has the following reference which is quoted in WA 55-I:111,39–41: *Bern[ardus] in quodam sermone sic ait: Detractor et libens auditor uterque diabolum portat, detractor in lingua vel in ore, auditor in aure.* See Bell, *Divus Bernhardus,* 76f, 244, 333. Bell 244, note 21 has a reference to WA 6:681,4ff which must be a mistake because vol. 6 only has 632 pages.

of a saying attributed to Bernard about praying the Lord's prayer repeatedly over a year's period of time: 'What the devil; where do so many lies and similar stuff come from'?[2] Apparently Luther did not want Bernard associated with this kind of piety, and he may already at this time have developed an aversion to the Dominicans which would come to a climax in the controversy over indulgences in 1517.

In 1518, when Luther wrote on the preparation of one's heart for reception of the Eucharist, he referred to a story about Bernard and a fellow monk who did not want to receive holy communion because of his lack of faith in the real presence of Christ in the Eucharist. Bernard allegedly told him: 'receive in my faith'. The monk obeyed and was healed of his disbelief. This story was so famous that it also found visual expression in one of the glass windows of the cistercian monastery at Altenberg, Germany, near the beginning of the sixteenth century. Bernard's banderole as shown on the window has its wording lifted from the medieval Bernard hagiography (Plate 2) and was used by Jean Gerson, Gabriel Biel, and Caspar Schatzgayer. Biel included it in his manual on the Mass, which Luther studied in preparation for his ordination to the priesthood. The story showed up as well in Luther's own tract on the Mass in 1521.[3] Apparently, these spiritual writers, including Luther, were all deeply impressed by the story.

2 *Teuffel, Wo her so viel lugen vnd so mancherley*, WA 60:188,25–28 (approx. 1516). Luther's opposition to the rosary at such an early date may be a bit surprising. A facsimile edition of the book by Marcus von Weida op was edited by Anthony van der Lee (Amsterdam: Rodopi, 1978).

3 The wording in the Bernard hagiography is slightly different from Luther's, and therefore it is not certain that he lifted it directly from Vita *Bern*, Book 7.8–9; PL 185:419. For controling purposes I use Martinus Cawley, *Bernard of Clairvaux. Early Biographies*. Vol. I by William of St Thierry. Vol. II by Geoffrey of Auxerre and others (Lafayette, OR: Guadalupe Translations, 1990); quoted from here on as Cawley 1 (for Vol. I) and Cawley 2 (for Vol. II); here: Cawley 2:85. See Conrad of Eberbach, *Exordium Magnum Cisterciense*, 2.6. See Arno Paffrath, *Bernhard von Clairvaux: Leben und Wirken - dargestellt in den Bilderzyklen von Altenberg bis Zwettl* (Cologne: Du Mont, 1984), illustration 15; see Michael Eissenhauer, ed., *LudwigsLust - Die Sammlung Irene und Peter Ludwig* (Nuremberg: Germanisches Nationalmuseum, 1993), illustration 90b (as part of a series of six glass windows depicting Bernard's life). Luther: *Sic B. Bernhardus . . .*, WA 1:333,26–29; see also WA 8:451,5–9. The reference to Bernard's utterance is found again in the work *Libellus auro praestantior de animae praeparatione in extremo laborantis, deque praedestinatione et tentatione*

Luther, however, did not borrow blindly from unidentifiable late medieval spirituality which may have preserved or misrepresented Saint Bernard's ideas over the centuries. It can and will be shown that the Wittenberg professor used original bernardine source material as it was available to him in the library, along with second-hand sources. It can be proven that at times he made very precise source references; for instance to Bernard's twenty-seventh *Sermon on the Song of Songs*, to his *First Sermon on the Feast of the Annunciation*, to the fourth book of *On Consideration*, or to the sermon about Naaman the leper (the third *Sermon on the Resurrection*). When Luther made general references—'according to Saint Bernard', 'as Saint Bernard says', 'as Saint Bernard distinguishes', *Sic Bernardus in Canticis*—he usually had specific quotations in mind or cited them directly or at least in part or paraphrased the content. Using the typical humanistic expression *divus* for 'Saint', Luther cited this respected authority in his 1519 commentary on Gal 6:1 on fraternal correction: 'Just as Saint (*divus*) Bernard taught his followers that if one was unable in any way to excuse a brother's sin, at least one should say that it was a great and insuperable temptation by which he was overtaken, and that he was seized by what was more than he could bear'.[4]

---

fidei, which is attributed to Luther by Martin Brecht, 'Der 'Libellus auro praestantior de animae praeparatione in extremo laborantis, deque praedestinatione et tentatione fidei: eine unbekannte frühe Predigt Luthers?' *Lutheriana*, AWA 5 (1984) 333–350, here 349; Brecht's thesis is questioned by Markus Wriedt, 'Ist der 'Libellus . . .' eine Lutherschrift?', *Lutherjahrbuch* 54 (1987) 48–83. Brecht retorted in: 'Zum Problem der Identifizierung namentlich nicht gekennzeichneter Lutherschriften'. *Lutherjahrbuch* 56 (1989) 51–58. Luther may have encountered this story when he read Gabriel Biel, *Canon Missae expositio*; see the edition by Heiko A. Oberman and W. J. Courteney (Wiesbaden: Steiner Verlag, 1963) 1:65, or perhaps when he read Jean Gerson who also used this story, as has been pointed out by Walther Köhler, *Luther und die Kirchengeschichte nach seinen Schriften, zunächst bis 1521* (Erlangen, 1900; reprint: Hildesheim, Zurich, New York: Georg Olms Verlag, 1984) 310, note 1. Gerson, *De praeparatione ad missam* chapter 3: *Dixit ei . . . Bernardus . . . 'Vade frater et in fide mea celebres',* (*Oeuvres* 9.39); Caspar Schatzgeyer also used the story; see Bell, *Divus Bernhardus*, 197–199.

4 . . . *sicut divus Bernhardus suos docuit* . . . , WA 2:602,8–11 (on Gal 6:1); see WA 2:15,18 (*Acta Augustana*, 1518); Luther used humanistic vocabulary here, as he spoke of *divus Bernhardus*. The humanists used *divus* synonymously with 'saint' (*sanctus*), see Erasmus: *Diuus Bernardus in libris quibus titulum fecit De consideratione* (letter to Jodocus Jonas of May 10, 1521), Allen edition 4:487 (no. 1202). *Divus Paulus* was the patron saint of the theological faculty of Wittenberg, see Junghans, *Der junge Luther und die Humanisten*, 58.

If his erudition was challenged in this regard, Luther felt compelled to set matters straight. In the famous Leipzig Disputation with Dr Eck in 1519 the challenging professor from Ingolstadt told Luther to inform himself better on Bernard's book *On Consideration*. Apparently the disputation had reached a point where the correct interpretation of Bernard, the church fathers, and the scriptural sources were under dispute. Luther countered that he did not hold Saint Bernard's views in contempt at all; in fact, he venerated *Divum Bernardum*. This confession apparently is still so impressive today that it was mentioned in the recently published papers of the Catholic-Lutheran dialogue (Dialogue VIII).[5]

On another occasion, in his response to the conservative Latomus at Louvain in 1521, Luther angrily objected to Latomus' implications that he, Latomus, had the church fathers on his side against Luther: 'As for Augustine, Jerome, Ambrose, Gregory, and Bernard,' he retorted, 'I know them, and so it is in vain that you raise such clouds [of witnesses] against me'.[6] From this perspective one gets the impression at times that the Reformation conflict was primarily a fight over the right interpretation of the theological tradition, i. e., of the church fathers' thinking. Luther claimed to be well versed in the theology of these ecclesiastical authorities and later in his career boasted: 'I have read more than they think'![7]

The older Luther continued to use Bernard, especially in his exposition of the Book of Genesis, where Luther referred to him several times, including a passage in SC 65 for which he could not remember the exact source:

In his sermons on the Song of Songs Bernard inveighs against certain religious who dwelt together with girls (*mulierculis*) and declared in spite of this that they were chaste. Thus before these times priests associated with women. . . . Therefore Bernard says: 'It cannot be believed that you live chastely; for to dwell

5 *Respondeo: Divum Bernhardum veneror et eius sententiam non contemno*, WA 59:441–445 (Leipzig Disputation); see *The One Mediator, the Saints, and Mary: Lutherans and Catholics in Dialogue VIII*, George Anderson, J. Francis Stafford, and Joseph A. Burgess, eds. (Minneapolis: Augsburg, 1992) 26.

6 WA 8:102,15–16 (Against Latomus).

7 WA 50:519, 27–28 (1539).

with a woman, and not to learn to know her—is this not more
[difficult] than waking the dead'?[8]

In the same commentary Luther summed up his observations about
Bernard by saying that his writings show him to be the most
knowledgeable man of *religio*.[9]

From his early years as a friar until his last exegetical work as
an aging Bible interpreter, Luther appears to have had a bountiful
supply of Bernard references at hand, often quoting from memory,
which may explain an occasional inaccuracy. Luther's knowledge
of the last of the church fathers showed his great respect for
Bernard, and prompted him to praise the Cistercian as his spiritual
father in true religion.

Some time in the 1530s, when the conversation at table came to
the subject of the great cistercian abbot, Luther praised him again,
calling him the 'most sincere man' and 'the most perfect monk':

> Saint Bernard was the most sincere man whom I venerate more
> than all the other monks, even though he dared to say that it is
> a certain sign of damnation, if someone would not stay in the
> cloister. He had three hundred monks, and none of them was
> supposed to be damned? After his <Bernard's> death somebody
> wrote rather impious things saying that before Bernard's death
> no soul would have been saved, although the monastic life is
> against nature and church. Saint Bernard lived in dangerous
> times under the Emperors Henry IV and Henry V, Conrad and

8 WA 44:362,21–30; LW 7:77. *Cum femina semper esse, et non cognoscere
feminam, nonne plus est quam mortuum suscitare?* SC 65.4; SBOp 2:175,3–11;
CF 31:184. Already in the immediate preceeding and succeeding context Luther
referred to Bernard, see WA 44:361,20 and 363,16. Luther seemed to quote from
memory. This observation may explain the fact that Luther quoted Bernard out
of context. Bernard spoke out against the abnormal behavior of some religious
fanatics, while Luther thought Bernard was talking about priests who cohabit
with women. A more elaborate treatment of the elder Luther's use of Bernard
is presented in my essay 'The Elder Luther on Bernard: Part I', ABR 42 (1991)
22–52; Part II, ABR (1991) 179–201.

9 *Ac antefero omnibus Bernhardum: Habuit enim religionis optimam cognitionem: sicut ostendunt eius scripta,* WA 42:453,42–454,1; LW 4:269. On the
notion *religio*, see Ernst Feil, *Religio: Die Geschichte eines neuzeitlichen Grund-
begriffs vom Frühchristentum bis zur Reformation* (Göttingen: Vandenhoeck &
Ruprecht, 1986) 235–246 (on Luther, who uses *religio* also in the meaning of
'religious Order'); Feil skipped the treatment of Bernard.

Lothar. Therefore he was the most perfect monk. . . . Oh, that
only the monastic life would not have been forced but free, then
it could be tolerated.[10]

The source reference here is obscure. It is difficult to determine
which text Luther had in mind. While Luther severely criticized
the monasticism of his time, he can be seen advocating it if it is not
'forced' upon people (as apparently was the case at times). This
is, however, not the place to elaborate on Luther's attitude toward
the religious life of his day.

In quoting Bernard on a regular basis throughout his career,
Luther surely meant to demonstrate his respect for him. One of the
finest compliments ever paid by Luther the interpreter of Scripture
was to Saint Bernard as biblical interpreter and to his 'art' of
meditating on Scripture. Luther observed in his second course on
the Psalms that Saint Bernard was an admirable and exceptional
expert in the profession they shared: 'I see that *divus Bernhardus*
stands out with this art and that he learned the entire wealth of
his erudition from it'.[11] These expressions of great admiration for
Bernard did not cease in later years, as this sympathetic statement
from 1538 shows: 'Whenever monks were saved, however, they
were constrained to crawl to the cross of Christ again. This is what
Saint Bernard did. I regard him as the most righteous (*fromsten*) of
all the monks. . . . He is the only one worthy of the name 'Father
Bernard' (*Pater Bernhardus*) and of being studied diligently'.[12] In
his colorful vernacular expression, Luther described Bernard as
'creeping to the cross of Christ,' and regarded him therefore as
'the most righteous monk' (*den aller fromsten Munch*). The term,

10 See WA TR 4:480,16–24 (no. 4772, Latin); 481,18–26 (German); see
Posset, 'The Elder Luther on Bernard: Part I', 46.

11 *Video Divum Bernhardum hac arte praestitisse* . . . , AWA 2:63,26f.

12 . . . *und er ist auch allein werd, das man ihnen Pater Bernhardus nenne
und den man mit vleiss ansehe* . . . , WA 47:109,18–29; LW 22:388 (on Jn 3:19,
1538). On the german notion *fromm*, see Hugo Moser, "Fromm' bei Luther und
Melanchthon: Ein Beitrag zur Wortgeschichte in der Reformationszeit'. *Studien
zu Raum- und Sozialformen der deutschen Sprache in Geschichte und Gegenwart*
(Berlin: Schmidt Verlag, 1979) 54–74; see Jun Matsuura, 'Zu 'fromm' bei Luther'.
Doitsu Bungaku/Die Deutsche Literatur, Japanese Society of German Studies,
ed. (Fall 1984) 124–137, as quoted by Ebeling, *Lutherstudien* (Tübingen: J. C. B.
Mohr [Paul Siebeck], 1985) 3:100, note 88.

fromm in Luther's German also designated the 'justified' sinner. Accordingly, Saint Bernard would be the 'most justified monk'. Luther added that he preferred him to Saint Dominic. Bernard alone he considered worthy of being called a father in the faith, the one to whom one needs to turn 'with assiduity' (*mit vleiss*). Even though he was 'stuck in the cowl', Bernard did not hold it up against God's judgment (in self-justification); instead he 'grasped Christ' (*ergreifft Christum*) as his only salvation.

Luther's comment on 'Father Bernard' occurs in a passage in which he admonished that if monks and nuns want to be saved, they, too, must crawl to the cross as Saint Bernard had done and must not pride themselves on their monastic life style on the Day of Judgment. To Luther the cowl became an anti-symbol; it represented monkish work-righteousness, while true righteousness is found in faith alone, faith in the cross of Christ. Luther praised the christocentric piety of the monk Bernard, i. e., his concentration on the passion of the Lord, in the middle of an anti-monastic text. Lutheranism seems to have been overwhelmed by Luther's criticism of monasticism while Luther's high esteem for Bernard the monk fell into oblivion. Today Bernard's influence usually escapes the student of Luther's life and work.

The eulogy of *Pater Bernhardus* is found in Luther's sermon on Jn 3:19 ('The judgment of condemnation is this: the light came into the world, but men loved darkness rather than light because their deeds were wicked'). Luther saw johannine 'darkness' expressed in the monks' undeserved reliance on 'the Fathers, Councils, religious Orders, rules etc.', while Bernard alone—who 'grasped Christ'—is worthy to be called *Father*. According to Luther, the monks/friars who persecuted him would not let 'their thing' (*ihr ding*), their monastic way of life, be condemned, but began to rage; thus they remained in darkness from which they called upon the 'Fathers, Councils'. The only thing which counted in Luther's opinion was the faith of these saints, not their works; this Luther stressed in his sermon, hinting at Hebrews 13:7, by which he interpreted John 3:19. And in this same context Luther (fortifying his position) returned again to the example of Bernard, who regarded as salvific not his chastity, but only his 'faith in the Son of God'. Therefore 'Do this with Saint Bernard',[13] Luther recommended.

The Reformer did not hesitate to write to the councilmen of Germany in 1524 that 'Saint Bernard was a man of [such] great mind that I almost venture to set him above all other celebrated teachers both ancient and modern'.[14] On another occasion he compared Saint Augustine and Saint Bernard, declaring (perhaps to the surprise of some) that 'Bernard with his sermons excels over all other teachers, and even over Augustine himself'.[15] Perhaps none of Luther's other table talks expresses more colorfully Luther's appreciation of Saint Bernard's preaching than the one in which he proclaimed: 'Saint Bernard is golden when he teaches and preaches'.[16] Behind this can be seen his conviction that the monks of old were the best teachers of the Word of God: 'No one could better teach the Word of God than the monks, as Saint Bernard and others did'.[17]

2. *Luther's Bernard Repertoire*

As we have indicated, Luther made extensive use of Bernard's spiritual insights, primarily those in his 'sermons'. Yet occasionally insights found in Bernard's treatises and letters may also be identified in Luther's works. In the following pages, an overview of Luther's Bernard repertoire is attempted. Subsequent chapters will provide precise source references to Luther's works; at this point I restrict myself to listing those works of Bernard of which Luther somehow had knowledge and which he evidently used, whether he knew them directly, by reading Bernard in the original, or indirectly, by lifting bernardine sentences from the vast medieval

13 WA 47:109,26–29; LW 22:388.

14 *Sanct Bernhart ist eyn man von grossem geyst gewesen, das ich yhn schier thuerst uber alle lerer setzen, die beruembt sind, beyde allte und newe,* WA 15:40,30–41, 3; LW 45:363.

15 *Bernhardus in suis praedicationibus excellit omnes alios doctores vel ipsum etiam Augustinum* (no. 3370a); . . . *quia pulcherrime praedicavit Christum,* (no. 3370b) WA TR 3:295,3–10; see WA TR 3:435,32–436,3 (no. 872).

16 WA TR 1:272,4–10 (no. 584).

17 WA 8:648,25–27 (1521).

literature he consumed. I omit bernardine references which Luther hardly ever utilized:[18]

I. *Homelium super 'Missus est' in laudibus virginis matris*

Luther sometimes called this *homelium* 'a sermon' on the *Glories of the Virgin Mother.* In later table talks he referred to it in general as a despicable 'disputation'.[19]

II. *Sermones per annum*

From among the sermons on the liturgical seasons of the year Luther used the following, usually in a positive way:

1. The Advent sermons, *In adventu Domini*, especially sermons one, three, and possibly sermons five and seven.[20]
2. The Christmas Eve sermons, *In vigilia nativitatis Domini*, especially sermons two and three.
3. The Christmas sermons, *In nativitate Domini*, especially sermons three and four.[21]
4. Probably all three sermons on the Circumcision of the Lord, *In circumcisione Domini.*
5. The sermons for Epiphany, *In epiphania Domini,* especially sermons one and three.
6. The sermons on the Purification of Mary, *In purificatione BVM*, especially sermons two and three.
7. The Lenten Sermons, *In quadragesima*, especially sermon five.[22]

---

18 For controling purposes, see Bell, *Divus Bernhardus*, 384–87; Bell, 'Luther's Reception of Bernard of Clairvaux', CTQ (1995) 248–254.

19 Bell, *Divus Bernhardus,* 136 and 384, assumed that Luther may have used ('possibly') also Miss 4, while Bell did not list Miss 1. Bell, *Divus Bernhardus,* 322, rightly pointed out that a passage from Miss 2 may have been used by Luther in 1537, WA 45:319,22. Luther may have referred to Bernard's Adv 1 instead of Miss 3. As to 'disputation', see my INTRODUCTION.

20 Bell, *Divus Bernhardus,* 385, for some reason did not take sermons five and seven into consideration; see on this Posset, 'Bernard of Clairvaux as Luther's Source', CTQ 54 (1990) 294f.

21 Bell, *Divus Bernhardus,* 274 included also Nat 2,4.

22 Bell, *Divus Bernhardus,* 386 listed Bernard's QH 6. However, one can argue that this is not necessarily so, see Franz Posset, 'Bernhard von Clairvauxs Sermone zur Weihnachts-, Fasten- und Osterzeit als Quellen Martin Luthers'.

8. The sermons on the Annunciation, *In annuntiatione dominica*, especially sermon one.

9. The Easter sermons, *In resurrectione Domini*, especially sermons two and three.[23]

10. The sermon on the Feast of the Birth of Mary, the famous 'Aqueduct' sermon, *In nativitate beatae Mariae*.

III. *Sermones super cantica canticorum*

Of the eighty-six sermons *On the Song of Songs*, about thirty provided materials 'exploited' by Luther; they are: 1–9, 16, 17, 20, 22, 23, 27, 31, 33, 34, 37, 40, 42, 43, 44, 46, 47, 51, 56, 61, 62, 65, 66, 69, 76.[24]

Lutherjahrbuch 61 (1994) 93–116, here 100–107. Bell, *Divus Bernhardus,* 53, indicated that Luther only indirectly mentioned Bernard's exposition of Ps 90. However, in *Divus Bernhardus,* 112f, and in his later article, 'Bernhard von Clairvaux als Quelle Martin Luthers', *Bijdragen: Tijdschrift voor filosofie en theologie* 56 (1995) 7–10, Bell expressed the conviction that Luther, when saying *et ut Bernhardus psal. xc vocat* (AWA 2:240,15–17 on Ps 5) wanted to refer to Bernard's QH series, which traditionally is called *Qui Habitat.* If, however, Luther would have wanted to identify this specific source here, he probably would have quoted this series of sermons in the traditional way by referring to the first few words of the text which is the subject of the respective sermon, namely *Qui Habitat* (= the beginning of Psalm 90 in the Vulgate version), which Luther, however, in this case did not do. In other cases Luther quoted sermon series in the traditional fashion such as when he referred to the *'sermo' Missus est.* Or, Luther simply followed the conventional designation of a famous sermon when he quoted, for example, Bernard's *De lepra Naaman* as *de Naaman leproso* (i. e. the third sermon on Easter), or when he referred to an Advent sermon of Bernard as to *b. Bernardus sermone de adventu,* or when he referred to the first sermon on the Annunciation as *B. Bernardus ser. 1 de annunciatione Dominica.* It seems to me that Luther simply wanted to point out what Bernard said about Ps 90. It is of secondary importance to know from where he ultimately may have lifted it. Since elsewhere he mentioned having read SC, one may safely assume that he referred to SC 33, while he otherwise did not refer as explicitly to Bernard's QH.

23 Bell, *Divus Bernhardus,* 386 listed only Bernard's Res 3.1 (Bell mistakenly wrote of *In die Paschae* 3.1). In *Lutherjahrbuch* (1994) 109–112, I argued that not only Bernard's third (Res 3.1), but also his second Easter sermon (Res 2.3) needs to be taken into consideration. Bell in his 'Bernhard von Clairvaux als Quelle Martin Luthers', 12, preferred, however, to take Bernard's Sent III,41 as Luther's source; this thesis may be questioned because Luther nowhere else mentioned Bernard's *Sententiae.* And so it is unlikely that he here used the *Sententiae.*

24 See Bell, *Divus Bernhardus,* 386, whose list differs from the one I work with here. In contrast to Bell, I tend to include also SC 31, 44, 46, 47, and 76 (the latter on pasturing the sheep on the Scriptures). Also in contrast to Bell, *Divus Bernhardus,* 71 and 330f, I doubt that Luther quoted from SC 58 and SC 73.

IV. *Liber de praecepto et dispensatione*

Some insights appear to be taken from Chapters Four and Twenty. One may doubt whether Luther actually read this text in its entirety.[25]

V. *De consideratione libri v*

All five books of this advice to a pope.

VI. *Epistolae*

Brief, adage-like references appear to be excerpted from the following *Letters*: no. 77 on baptism (=treatise); no. 91 (perhaps also nos. 96, 254, and 385) on spiritual progress; no. 106 on the spring and rivulets; no. 201 on the triple feeding of the flock.[26]

This list of Bernard texts represents the likely Bernard repertoire from which Luther borrowed at every stage of his life. Unfortunately, we do not possess any copy of Bernard's works with Luther's annotations, which would greatly simplify the task of tracking down Luther's sources. He could have used any one of the almost three hundred editions printed between 1464 and 1500 alone, or any of the three hundred editions which appeared later,

---

25 Luther's use of certain parts of this book may have been mediated via Gerson's *De vita spirituali animae* which is based on Bernard's Pre. This is all the more likely, as Luther did not appear to have related the idea of monastic vows as 'second baptism', as found in Bernard's Pre 54, to any bernardine text. If Luther had read this entire tract, he certainly would have come across and criticized Bernard's theory of the 'second baptism'. Luther never connected Bernard to this idea, which he rejected vehemently. Thus, one is led to conclude that he probably did not read Bernard's book at all. However, Bell, 'Luther's Reception of Bernard of Clairvaux', CTQ (1995) 252, insists that 'Luther, indeed, knew the book, but rarely mentioned it'. I beg to differ.

26 However, one must realize that Luther never referred to any 'letters' of Bernard. One may find in his works some hints at bernardine sentences which are, indeed, traceable to his letters. When Luther made reference 'to Eugenius' (*ad Eugenium*), he did not have the letters to this pope in mind, but Bernard's Csi which was written for Pope Eugenius. Bell in his *Divus Bernhardus*, 386, accepted only Epp 91, 96, 254, and 385, while in his later article, 'Luther's Reception of Bernard of Clairvaux', CTQ (1995) 252, he stated that 'it is not very likely that Luther was aquainted with Bernard's letters as such'. I used to agree with Bell's 1995 insight, but now I take the possiblity more seriously that Luther also read Bernard's letters, especially since I know that they were available in a printed edition from Strasbourg since 1470.

during Luther's lifetime (1483 to 1546).[27] Luther could have had access, for example, to the following editions; I list the most famous first; the numbers in parenthesis refer to Leopold Janauschek's *Bibliographia Bernardina* of 1891:

> *Melliflui deuotique doctoris sancti Bernardi abbatis Clareuallensis Cisterciensis ordinis opus preclarum*: Paris: Jehan Petit [=Johannes Clein, or Cleyn, or Parvus], 1508 (no. 350); this edition was prepared by Andreas Bocardus; later editions are of 1513 (no. 379), 1515 (no. 388, appeared also in Lyon), 1517 (no.402), 1520 (no. 423). The editions of 1527, 1538, 1540, 1544, and 1546 were printed by Claudius Cheuallonius. The most likely edition used by Luther may have been the one which the Wittenberg library catalogue of 1536 shows as Bernard's *Opera*, (Lyon: Johannes Clein [=Jehan Petit], 1515).

Individual bernardine works or collection of letters and sermons were available after 1470; among them were:

> *Epistulae cum aliquot tractatibus*: Strasbourg: Heinrich Eggesteyn, 1470 (no. 3).

27 See Lohse, 'Luther und Bernhard von Clairvaux', 271–301. Concerning the Bernard editions, see Leopold Janauschek, *Bibliographia Bernardina* (Vienna: 1891; reprint: Hildesheim: Georg Olms, 1959) 3–74 (prints from 1464–1500); 74–130 (prints from 1500 to 1546). The title page of the Zwolle edition of 1495 is shown in M. Sabbe, M. Lamberigts and F. Gistelinck, eds., *Bernardus en de cisterciënzerfamilie in België* (Louvain: Bibliotheek van de Faculteit der Godgeleerdheid, 1990) 14; see Edmond Mikkers, 'Hoe kwam Bernardus tot ons?' *Bernardus en de cisterciënserfamilie*, 132–134. A selective list of sources is provided in Reinhard Schwarz's introduction for the new edition of Luther's *Dictata* (1993), WA 55-I: page XL. As to the Paris edition of 1508 by the humanist and theologian Judocus Clichtoveus, see WA Br 1:602, note 3. The title pages of the 1515 edition and of the 1520 edition of *Melliflui deuotique sancti Bernardi abbatis Clareuallensis Cisterciensis ordinis opus preclarum . . .* are shown in Riccardo Cataldi, ed., *Melliflui Doctoris Opera: Edizioni delle opere di san Bernardo di Clairvaux* (Casamari: Ministerio per i bene culturali e ambientali biblioteca statale del monumento nazionale di Casamari, 1992) 28 (1515) and 32 (1520); the latter depicts Bernard venerating the Virgin, who exposes her breast, with the Christ Child sitting on her lap; Bernard's banderole says: *Monstra te esse matrem*. Interestingly, Pseudo-Bernard's *Meditationes* (Paris: Georg Mittelhus, 1493) were translated into english as *Medytatcions of saynt Bernarde* (Westminster: W. de Worde, 1496); an italian version was published as *Devote Meditationi Di San Bernardo* (Venice: Francesco Bindoni, 1559) and a french version by Jean Guyot became available as *Les Méditations, les sermons de la mort et Passion de Jésus-Christ* (Paris 1582); see list of sources in Klára Erdei, *Auf dem Wege zu sich selbst*, 255.

Plate 3: *Mary, the Christ Child, and Saint Bernard.* Title Page of *Sermones Bernardi In Duytsche.* Zwolle: Peter van Os, 1495, woodcut. The words between Bernard's and Mary's heads read: *Mo[n]stra te e[ss]e matre[m]* ('Show yourself a mother') which is a direct quotation from the fourth stanza of the ninth-century hymn *Ave maris stella.*

Homiliae super Missus est: Cologne: Arnoldus ther Hoernen, 1472; Antwerp: Gherardus Leeu, 1487 (no. 93).

Sermones varii: Mainz: Petrus Schoyffer, 1475 (no. 30); later editions in 1481,1494, 1495, 1497.

De consideratione: Augsburg: Anton Sorg, 1476/77 (no. 37), which was available to Luther at Erfurt.

Opuscula, no location given, ca. 1470 (no. 7); Paris 1495 (no. 174). This edition includes *De diligendo deo*; *Ad fratres de monte Dei* (Pseudo Bernard); *Apologeticum*; *De preceptis et dispensatione*; *De libero arbitrio et gratia*; *Ad eugenium papam de consideratione*; *Meditatione* (Pseudo Bernard).

Sermones in cantica: Rostock (Germany): *Fratres Communis vite,* 1481 (no. 60); Pavia (Italy) 1482, Paris 1494; the editions by Martin Flach, Strasbourg 1496 (no. 195) and 1497 (no. 207), included the forty-seven sermons by Gilbert of Hoyland as the continuation of Bernard's Canticle interpretation.

Sermones [Bernardi In Duytsche]: Two volumes of Bernard's Sermons in German/Dutch: Sermons for the liturgical seasons from Advent to Easter: Zwolle: Peter van Os, 1484 (no. 75); for the remaining liturgical year: Zwolle: Peter van Os, 1484 (no. 83).; reprinted in 1495 (no. 176); see Plate 3.

Sermones de tempore et de sanctis et de diversis: Basel: Nicolaus Kesler, 1495 (no. 179).

Speculation over the Zwolle editions is not far-fetched since (a) the german augustinian friars under Johann von Staupitz's leadership had good connections with the Low Countries, where the book was issued, and (b) Luther was very interested in spiritual literature in the vernacular.

It remains doubtful whether Luther read the following works of Bernard: The one-hundred twenty-five *Sermones de diversis*; the seventeen *Sermones super psalmum 'Qui habitat'* (*On the Psalm [90] 'He Who Dwells'*). The two treatises *Liber de gradibus humilitatis et superbiae* (*On the Steps of Humility and Pride*) and *Liber de gratia et libero arbitrio* (*On Grace and Free Choice*) may have been known to Luther, but only indirectly through other, unidentifiable channels.[28] In addition, there are instances where

28 See Manns, 'Zum Gespräch zwischen M. Luther und der katholischen Theologie', 105; Posset, 'Bernard of Clairvaux as Luther's Source', CTQ 54

Plate 4: *The Devil Reveals the 'Eight Verses' to Bernard.* Book of Hours, Lyon, around 1480/90. Fol. 132. Swiss National Museum, Zurich. The little devil is not very visible.

Luther mentioned Bernard's faith and good example, probably without having a specific text in mind.

Whether or not Luther's Bernard citations could have been taken from any of the medieval or contemporary Bernard anthologies[29] must be left unresolved. So too must the question whether or not Luther got information about Bernard from specific contemporary or late medieval sources of unknown origin, as may have been the case with his references to *ein gedichte* ('a story') or to an *historia Bernhardi*.[30]

3. *Luther's Use of Medieval Sources on Bernard or Attributed to Bernard*

Luther's knowledge of pseudo-bernardine and medieval secondary sources about Saint Bernard shall be briefly considered, as there are references to allegedly bernardine texts which cannot be located

---

(1990) 286; Bell, *Divus Bernhardus,* 276–278, 347; Bell, 'Luther's Reception of Bernard of Clairvaux', 250f. Bell, 'Bernhard von Clairvaux als Quelle Martin Luthers', *Bijdragen* 56 (1995) 7–10, argues that Luther *wahrscheinlich* knew the series of sermons on Psalm 90. I am not convinced of that.

29 One has to reckon with the possibility that Luther lifted some of the adage-like sayings from medieval anthologies, since numerous such collections existed as, for instance, the *Flores seu sententiae ex S. B. operibus depromptae*, which stems from Bernard's time, or the *Flores Bernardi*, also called *Florilegium Bernardinum, Bernardinus,* or *Liber Florum Bernardinum* by William, monk of Saint Martin de Tournai, from the thirteenth century, printed, for instance, at Nuremberg in 1472 and more often later on, see Ferdinand Cavallera, entry 'Bernard (Apocryphes attribué à saint)', DSp I:1499–1500 (Paris: Gabriel Beauchesne et ses Fils, 1937); see M. Bernards, 'Zur Verbreitung der Bernhardflorilegien'. *Studien und Mitteilungen zur Geschichte des Benediktinerordens und seiner Zweige* 64 (1952) 234–241. In 1494, the encyclopedia *Speculum historiale* was published in Venice, originally compiled by Vincent of Beauvais in the thirteenth century; it contains 128 chapters in its volume 28 with sayings of Bernard; see Köpf, 'Die Rezeptions- und Wirkungsgeschichte Bernhards', 14–17, especially note 37. Most recently Bell observed that Luther's quotations from Bernard most likely came from anthologies, or indirectly through other authors like Gerson, Biel, Bonaventure, and Ludolph of Saxony: 'Luther's Reception of Bernard of Clairvaux', 248.

30 *ex historia Bernhardi,* WA TR 5 (no. 6476); see WA 47:598, 23–34; concerning the 'poem' (*gedichte*) which Luther mentioned, one may think of the *Carmen uita sancti Bernardi* by Theophilus Brixanus in *Opuscula Diui Bernardi Abbatis Clareuallensis* (Brixen: Angelus et Jacobus de Britannicis, 1495), as described by Cataldi, ed., *Melliflui Doctoris Opera,* 24f. I did not have the opportunity to examine this text as to its content and possible source for Luther.

in Bernard's authentic *opus*. Occasionally, such material found expression in Bernardine iconography (Plate 4).

'The Eight Verses of Saint Bernard'

The text known by the title *Octo versus sancti Bernardi* was a prayer, widely known both in Latin and in German, for a happy death. Sometimes it was referred to also as 'the six' or 'the seven' verses of Bernard. They probably originated in France. The mistress of King Charles VII, Lady Agnes Sorel (1422–1450), wrote these verses in her book of hours and apparently prayed them before she died. The prayer was used by the mother of the german artist Albrecht Dürer, as she spoke it for his father on his deathbed.[31] It was more widespread in vernacular versions (including dutch and german dialects) than in Latin.[32]

Legend attributed it to a revelation the devil made to Saint Bernard during a debate they had about death. Bernard somehow forced the devil to reveal the eight psalm verses which protect against a sudden death.[33] The prayer goes as follows (I have added the Vulgate psalm references):

31 On Agnes Sorel, see Bredero, *Bernard of Clairvaux Between Cult and History*, 5. Dürer's words, *sant Pernhartyz fersch for gesprochen* ('[mother] has spoken Saint Bernard's verses'), see *Albrecht Dürer: Schriftlicher Nachlaß*, H. Rupprich, ed. (Berlin 1956) 1:36, as quoted by Ochsenbein, 'Bernhard von Clairvaux in spätmittelalterlichen Gebetsbüchern'. *Bernhard von Clairvaux*, Elm, ed., 216.

32 See Ochsenbein 214.

33 This prayer (with an illustration) was found under the title *Septem versiculi sancti bernardi* in a prayerbook of 1480/90 from Lyon, France, see Peter Jezler, ed., *Himmel Hölle Fegefeuer: Das Jenseits im Mittelalter* (Zurich: Verlag Neue Zürcher Zeitung, 1994) 208 (exhibition catalague); see Plate 4. See also Roger S. Wieck, *Time Sanctified. The Book of Hours in Medieval Art and Life* (New York: George Braziller, 1988) 108 (with the "Seven Verses" and an image of Bernard in his study). An enlarged, color plate with the motif 'Bernard and the devil's revelation of the psalm verses' by Jean Fouquet from the *Heures d'Etienne Chevalier* (1461; Musée Condé, Ms. 71, fol. 36) is reproduced in *Saint Bernard & le monde Cistercien*, 71, and there is another depiction mentioned: *Heures de Frédéric d'Aragon* (beginning of the sixteenth century; National Library, Paris, lat. 10 532, p. 330); *Saint Bernard & le monde Cistercien*, 158. A german version of the legend can be found in a late fifteenth century prayerbook, see Ochsenbein 213. This same prayer (with an illustration) surfaced also in 1490, printed either at Augsburg or at Salzburg, and it was known in manuscript form in nunneries, see Köpf, 'Die Rezeptions- und Wirkungsgeschichte Bernhards von Clairvaux', 24, 62 with illustration 4. The german title indicates that the purpose of the prayer was to prepare for a happy end of one's life: *Die acht Verss S. Bernharts, umb ein seligs end zubitten*, as it is found in the edition of Johann Koberger, *Hortulus animae*, printed in 1516. The literary category of *Hortulus* meant a prayerbook for

The Eight Verses of Saint Bernard:

Give light to my eyes
that I do not fall asleep when dying:
so my enemy may never say:
'I prevailed against him' (12:4b–5).
Into your hands I commend my spirit:
You have redeemed me, O Lord, God of truth (30:6).
I was told in my own language:
Make known to me my end, O Lord.
And what is the number of my days,
that I may learn how frail I am (38:5).
Grant me a proof of your favor,
that my enemies may see, to their confusion,
that you, O Lord, have helped and comforted me (85:17).
You have loosed my bonds:
To you will I offer sacrifice of thanksgiving:
and I will call upon the name of the Lord (115:16b-17).
I have lost all means of escape;
there is no one who cares for my life.
I cry out to you, O Lord; I say,
'You are my refuge,
my portion in the land of the living' (141:5f).[34]

Erasmus, in his *The Praise of Folly* (1509), ridiculed people's confidence in this prayer. He called the verses *magicos versiculos,* and acknowledged that they were attributed to *Divus Bernardus.*[35] Luther's superior, Johann von Staupitz, made uncritical use of this

---

lay people. Ochsenbein, 213–218, located numerous prayerbooks which contain these eight Bible verses.

34 The english text presented here is the reconstruction of the latin version provided in WA 55-I:877–79 (and in note 1 of WA 4:442).

35 *Quid autem stultius iis, imo quid felicius, qui septem illis sacrorum Psalmorum versiculis quotidie recitatis, plus quam summam felicitatem sibi promittunt? Atque hos magicos versiculos Daemon quispiam, facetus quidem ille, sed futilis magis quam callidus, Divo Bernardo creditur indicasse, sed arte circumventus miser. Et haec tam stulta, ut me ipsam propemodum pudeat, tamen approbantur, idque non a vulgo modo, verum etiam a religionis professoribus. Morias Enkomion id est stultitiae laus, Opera Omnia Desiderii Erasmi Roterodami* (Amsterdam: North-Holland Publishing Company, 1969) IV-3: cap 40. See Lewis W. Spitz, *The Protestant Reformation* (Englewood Cliffs: Prentice-Hall, Inc., 1966) 16; see Ochsenbein 216f; Bell, *Divus Bernhardus,* 278f, did not take into consideration Erasmus' text as the potential source for Luther's shared criticism of this prayer.

pseudo-bernardine prayer in his booklet on the art of dying, *Von der Nachfolgung des willigen Sterbens Christi* (1515), Chapters 14–15.[36] When Luther lectured on these *Eight Verses of Bernard* in his first course on the Psalms (at about the time Staupitz published his booklet), his critical attitude was perhaps inspired by Erasmus' criticism.

Luther spoke on this issue at least at two occasions: on Ps 115 and again on Ps 141. Both psalms were used in the 'Eight Verses'. When Luther interpreted Vulgate Ps 115:16f, 'You have loosed my bonds: To you will I offer the sacrifice of thanksgiving: and I will call upon the name of the Lord', he mentioned the alleged effect of this particular verse and traced it back to Cassiodorus. At this point Luther quoted in full Cassiodorus' *Explanation of the Psalms* (on Ps 115:16) that 'We must observe that this verse was believed to have such power that some claimed that sins could be forgiven by it if a person repeated it at the end of his life by a third confession'. Luther warned against using it in a superstitious way (*superstitio cavenda*).[37]

When he came to lecture on Ps 141:5f, he remembered that this text, too, was part of the popular 'Eight Verses of Saint Bernard'. He called such use of the verses an *error*.[38] He spoke of them again in his exposition of the Lord's Prayer (1518); and again, he did not like the idea of considering these verses the equivalent of the 'entire Psalter'.[39] In 1522 Luther tried to replace such prayers and

36 See Helmut Appel, *Anfechtung und Trost im Spätmittelalter und bei Luther* (Leipzig: M. Heinsius Nachfolger, 1938. Schriften des Vereins für Reformationsgeschichte no. 165) 99. See Albrecht Endriss, 'Nachfolgung des willigen Sterbens Christi: Interpretation des Staupitztraktates von 1515 und Versuch einer Einordnung in den frömmigkeitsgeschichtlichen Kontext'. *Kontinuität und Umbruch: Theologie und Frömmigkeit in Flugschriften und Kleinliteratur an der Wende vom 15. zum 16. Jahrhundert,* Josef Nolte, Hella Tompert, and Christof Windhorst, eds. (Stuttgart: Klett-Cotta, 1978) 130–135.

37 WA 4: 267f; Cassiodorus on Ps 115:16: *Cassiodorus: Explanation of the Psalms,* P. G. Walsh, trans. Ancient Christian Writers 53 (New York/Mahwah: Paulist Press, 1991) 3:158.

38 Luther's gloss: *Hic error notetur de 8 versibus totius psalterii, quorum iste unus ponitur, velut b. Bernardo a Diabolo revelatis,* WA 4:442,17–19. See Ursula Stock, *Die Bedeutung der Sakramente in Luthers Sermonen von 1519* (Leiden: Brill, 1982) 98f. However, in her note 24 on p. 98, Stock wrote of Bernard's seven psalm prayers (nine with Staupitz).

39 WA 9:134,11–14; see Bell, *Divus Bernhardus,* 278, where the story is said to stem from 'a french legend'.

prayerbooks by publishing his own german *Betbüchlein* ('prayer booklet'), which reached seventeen editions within two years.[40] As late as 1530, Luther objected to the abuse of these *Eight Verses*, supposedly as good 'as eight entire Psalters'.[41] Luther went with the humanistic flow which tried to reform people's piety and make it less superstitious. He was very much concerned with a healthy folk spirituality. He did not fault Bernard for any deformations in people's spiritual lives, but he nevertheless criticized the wrong use of prayers attributed to Bernard.

'Heavenly consolation'

Another phrase which Luther attributed to Bernard but which is difficult to locate in Bernard's works is 'heavenly consolation'. During his first lectures on the Psalms, on Ps 119:46, Luther spoke on this bernardine phrase, saying that since divine consolation is precious, it is not given indiscriminately. The most likely source for this phrase is the pseudo-bernardine text *Declamationes ex S. Bernardi sermonibus*, i. e. exercises 'from Simon's conversation with Jesus, as collected from Saint Bernard's sermons' (LV,66), fabricated by Bernard's secretary Geoffrey. The bernardine sermon which best lent itself to Geoffrey's summary is likely the third Advent sermon, in which Bernard exhorted his brethren to celebrate the Advent of the Lord, to be delighted by so much divine consolation, to be excited by so much worthiness, and inflamed by so much love. The quotation also bears some similiarity to a sentence in a bernardine lenten sermon. Perhaps these two passages in authentic Bernard sermons prompted Geoffrey to contract them into one saying, which he then handed down in his *Declamationes*.[42] Luther referred to this bernardine phrase in both Latin and German. His

40 See WA 10-II:331–495; see Schwarz, *Luther*, 126f.

41 See WA 30-II:253,10 (1530).

42 *Ita ut recte B. Bernardus dixerit, quod delicata est consolatio divina et non datur admittendibus alienam*, WA 4:331,14–15. Luther has *admittendibus* which in the original pseudo-bernardine text reads *admittentibus*. Geoffrey: *Pretiosa siquidem divina consolatio est, nec omnino tribuitur admittentibus alienam. Declamationes de colloquio Simonis cum Iesu ex S. Bernardi sermonibus collectae*, 55.66; PL 184:472; *Geoffrey d'Auxerre: Entretien de Simon-Pierre avec Jésus. Introduction, Texte, Traduction et Annotation*, Henri Rochais, ed. (Paris: CERF, 1990, *Sources Chretiennes* 364) 276. See Adv; SBOp 4:182,3- 5; see QH 9; SBOp 4:440,14–18. See Posset, 'Bernard of Clairvaux as Luther's Source', 293 with note 48; see Bell, *Divus Bernardus*, 57.

latin version may best be understood with the help of his german, which he gave elsewhere as: 'But God's Word is so tender that it does not tolerate any addition; it wants to be all by itself or not at all'.[43] Luther's reference in German is close to that of John Tauler who also quoted the phrase as a bernardine saying and also in German: Divine consolation is so tender that it does not admit in any way any other consolation from anywhere else.[44] Luther may have received Bernard's dictum through Tauler. It appears that Luther blended Bernard's with Tauler's teaching; and not only here, but also, for instance, in his Christmas sermon of 1520.[45]

Hagiographies, and medieval and contemporary secondary literature on Bernard

Among medieval secondary literature on Saint Bernard Luther had knowledge and made use of Jacobus de Voragine's *Golden Legend* (*Legenda aurea,* also known as *Historia Lombardina*). Most of his biographical information about Bernard may have been drawn from this collection of readings on the saints whose editor likely lifted most of what he knew about Bernard from the *Sancti Bernardi vita prima* (*Vita Bern*) compiled and composed by William of Saint Thierry and others. Luther commented in a general and negative way to *The Golden Legend* and to the *Catalogue of the Saints* by Peter Natalibus (Lyons, 1508) by saying: 'I am quite annoyed with the nonsense and the lies to be found in the *Catalogue* and *The Golden Legend*'.[46] Apparently he exempted the Bernard story, which he often used. *The Golden Legend* enjoyed

---

43 Luther's german version: *Aber gottis wort ist sso tzart, das es keynen tzusatz mag leyden, es wil alleyn seyn, oder gar nichts seyn,* WA 8:143,34–36 (on confession, 1521).

44 Tauler presented it in his own german translation within one of his sermons in which he contrasted worldly and divine consolation, see Gnädiger, 'Der minnende Bernhardus', 406. Tauler: *gottlicher trost sol sin also zart, das er in keine wise gestot do man andern trost enphohet.* See Martin Treu, 'Die Bedeutung der consolatio für Luthers Seelsorge bis 1525'. *Lutherjahrbuch* 53 (1986) 12. The phrase played a role also in the literature of the Modern Devotion: *Per manna, quod habebat omnem suavitatem saporis, spiritualis consolatio designatur, quae iuxta verbum Bernardi delicata est nec datur admittendibus alienam,* as quoted by a spiritual master of the Windesheim Congregation, see Gleumes, 'Gerhard Groot und die Windesheimer als Verehrer des hl. Bernhard von Clairvaux',108, note 62.

45 See Bell, 'Sermon von der Geburt Christi', 289–309.

46 Luther's letter to Spalatin of August 24, 1516, WA Br 1:50.

wide circulation at the time, a sort of illustrated layman's lectionary available after 1471 from a printer at Augsburg. It was readily available in many editions in the vernacular. Originally called *Legenda Sanctorum*, the 'Readings in the Lives of the Saints',[47] it was so enthusiastically received that it soon came to be known as golden; 'for in lyke wyse as gold is moste noble above al other metalles, in lyke wyse is thyse legende holden moost noble above al other werkys', as William Caxton explained in his foreword to his translation from Latin into English published in 1483,[48] the year Martin Luther was born.

From *The Golden Legend* (or directly from the *Vita Bern*) Luther probably learned about Bernard's way of dealing with concupiscence of the flesh. The story reported how young Bernard once caught himself girl-watching and tried to deal with this temptation by jumping into 'ice-cold water', staying in it until he almost fainted. Luther embellished this cure by telling how Bernard sought remedy from desire by making snow women and lying down with them.[49]

47 On the famous print of *The Golden Legend* with illustrations, see the article "book illustration" in Thomas G. Bergin and Jennifer Speake, *The Encyclopedia of the Renaissance* (New York, Oxford: Facts On File Publications, 1987) 58. On the wide diffusion of the *Legenda aura*, see *Legenda Aurea: Sept Siècles de Diffusion. Actes du colloque international sur la Legenda aurea: texte latin et branches vernaculaires à l'Université du Québec à Montréal 11–12 mai 1983*, Brenda Dunn-Lardeau, ed. (Montréal: Editions Bellarmin, and Paris: Librairie J. Vrin, 1986).

48 The quotation from Caxton is found in the foreword to *The Golden Legend,* page v. From here on, when I refer to the latin title, *Legenda aurea*, I mean the edition by Th. Graesse in its reprint of 1969: Jacobi a Voragine, *Legenda aurea vulgo historia lombardica dicta* (Osnabrück: Otto Zeller Verlag, 1969); when I quote it in English, I indicate first the page in the 1948 reprint edition, *The Golden Legend of Jacobus de Voragine*, trans. and adapted from the latin by Granger Ryan and Helmut Ripperger (New York, London, Toronto: Longmans, Green and Co., 1948) and then the new translation as Ryan: Jacobus de Voragine, *The Golden Legend: Readings on the Saints*, William Granger Ryan, trans. (Princeton: Princeton University Press, 1993) 2 vols.

49 *Vita Bern*, Book 1.3,5; PL 185:230; Cawley 1:11. *Legenda aurea,* 529; *The Golden Legend* 466; Ryan 2:99. *Et Bernhardus, dum quandam foeminam fixe fuisset intutus, gravi ultione seipsum coercuit*, WA 1:495,40–496,1 (1518). Bell, *Divus Bernhardus,* 261, did not consider *The Golden Legend* as Luther's source for this story on Bernard. The Bernard hagiography knows of the young man (not yet a monk) leaping into ice cold water; Luther lumped Bernard and Francis together on this, saying that they made snow men and snow women and lay down with them, WA 47:326,20–23 (1537–1540). *The Golden Legend* talked

In Bernard's letter 106 of around 1125 to the Englishman Henry Murdac we read that the saint prayed and contemplated while working outdoors. In *Vita Bern* we find the amplification that Bernard learned the meaning of the Scriptures while in the woods and the fields, thinking about what he had read: 'And among his friends he jokes merrily of having had no other masters for such lessons but the oaks and beeches.'[50] *The Golden Legend* picked up this story and simply reported that Bernard confessed that whatever he knew about the Scriptures he had learned while 'meditating and praying in the woods and the fields'; that he told his friends that 'he had no teachers except the oaks and the beeches', and that 'finally, he admitted that at times, as he meditated and prayed, the whole of Scripture appeared to him as though spread open and explained'.[51] *The Golden Legend* is not as explicit as *Vita Bern* 1.4,23f that Saint Bernard loved to read the Sacred Scriptures very often and in simplicity, and that he preferred drinking from this original spring to the rivulets of later interpreters.[52] Luther knew this element of the Bernard story either from reading it in *Vita Bern* (which formed part of the *Opera Bernardi* editions after 1515) or through a vernacular version,[53] or by lifting it from some unidentified secondary literature. Luther used the spring and rivulets comparison on several occasions after 1519, at times without mentioning Bernard. This leads us to guess that he like the contemporary humanists drew it

---

about Francis throwing himself naked into the deep snow: *Legenda aurea*, 666; Ryan 2:223.

50 Ep. 106.2; SBOp 7:266f. *Vita Bern*, Book 1.4,23; PL 185:240f. See Bredero, *Bernard of Clairvaux Between Cult and History*, 125f and 141f.

51 *Legenda aurea*, 531; *The Golden Legend* 469; Ryan 2:101; see McGuire, 'A Saint's Afterlife. Bernard in the Golden Legend and in Other Medieval Collections'. *Bernhard von Clairvaux*, Elm, ed., 189.

52 *Vita Bern*, Book 1.4,24; PL 185:241; Cawley 1:32. This hint at Bernard was used also by Luther's contemporary, Caspar Schatzgeyer (Luther's later adversary) in 1501, see Köhler, *Luther und die Kirchengeschichte*, 327, note 4; Bell, *Divus Bernhardus*, 166f, where references to possibly ancient classical sources are provided.

53 *Leben sant Bernharts*: Augsburg: Ginther Zeiner, 1472; Nuremberg: Hannsen Sensenschmidtz, 1475; Augsburg: Johannes Baemler, 1475, 1480; Augsburg: Anton Sorg, 1478, 1482, 1486, 1488; Augsburg: Hans Schoensperger, 1499; see Janauschek, *Bibliographia Bernardina*, 3–74, where in the nos. 428, 429, and 636 prints of sixteenth-century translations are described, and in nos. 222, 332, and 391 the abbreviated translations of the *Vita Bern*; see Bredero, *Bernard of Clairvaux Between Cult and History*, 162.

probably from classical sources such as Ovid and Cicero. Humanistic and bernardine concerns meshed here. What Luther wrote in his commentary on Deuteronomy of 1525 sounds very much like a humanist's concern for simplicity and return to the sources:

> But since in this age everything begins to be restored, as if that day of restoration of all things (Acts 3:21) were near, I got the idea to try whether perhaps Moses could be restored and I might return the brooklets to the spring (*rivulos ad fontem*). . . . I have taken pains, however, first to treat everything in the simplest manner. I have not allowed myself to be snatched away into so-called 'mystic' interpretations if at times laws came up that appear absurd or foolish to some.[54]

There is yet another story which only the *Vita Bern* mentioned: Bernard's stomach problems. The hagiographer reported that because of his ruined digestion Bernard frequently vomited, but chose not to leave the communal prayer services in the church because of it. Instead he 'arranged to have a spitoon dug in the ground' next to his stall in the church. Only after this solution became 'intolerable' to the monks did he retire from the community and live separated from them.[55] Luther talked about Bernard's problem in terms of his 'bad breath' in his lectures on Genesis and on several other occasions.[56] He criticized Bernard for ruining his health by his exaggerated mortification of the body, done for the purpose of domesticating his libido. He should not have done so. God created body and soul, and God wanted the recreation of both, but with moderation. Luther commented that Bernard admitted that he had overdone his ascetism.[57] According to the *Vita*

54 WA 14:499,16–22; LW 9:6 (On Deuteronony, 1525); WA Br 1:602,42–46 (no. 235; December 1519); WA 7:100,25–27 (1520). WA 10-III:176,12 (sermon of 1522, no mention of Bernard); WA 50:519,32;520,3; 525,24–30; 657–58; see Bell, *Divus Bernhardus*, 166 and 289. Bell assumes that Luther did not lift it from the *Vita Bern* directly. This saying may have its origins in the classical tradition, and was used also by Erasmus.

55 See *Vita Bern*, Book 1.8,38–40; PL 185:250; Cawley 1:52.

56 WA 43:331,24–28; WA 47:62,30–34.

57 *Also list man von sant Bernhardo* . . . , WA 10-III:376,25f. See also WA 40-II:113,6; WA 11:43,21; WA 12:282,28–32; WA 24:448,4; WA 43:63,3; 85,12; 326,23; WA 49:213,14; WA 12:282,32; WA TR 3:607,1f (no. 3777). Bell, *Divus*

Bern Bernard in hindsight accused himself of wrongdoing in this regard: 'He unashamedly accuses and charges himself . . . with indiscreet fervor, for having enfeebled that body until it became all but useless'.[58]

Only in the *Vita Bern*, in Book Seven, do we find the story Luther told about Bernard telling a monk to receive holy communion on his (Bernard's) faith.[59] On various occasions, Luther retold this story without mentioning any source. One may take the fact that Luther's wording differs from that of the *Vita Bern*, as a hint that he took it from another source, possibly from a vernacular Bernard hagiography, or perhaps from Jean Gerson and/or Gabriel Biel.[60]

Both the *Vita Bern* and *Legenda aurea* report yet another story: Bernard's loss of the sense of taste as a result of his strict ascetic life. Thinking it was butter, Bernard had eaten 'raw animal fat' which had been placed in front of him, and he had drunk oil instead of wine.[61] Luther spoke only of the incident with oil. In his late commentary on Gen 27:23, he mentioned this confusion not so much with regard to Bernard's loss of the sense of taste as in regard to his deep meditation. Bernard drank oil instead of wine, Luther stated, while engaged in earnest meditation.[62]

Bernhardus, 295, suggested the Augustinians' breviary as an additional source for Luther's knowledge about Bernard's fasting. This recourse is unnecessary if one assumes that Luther knew the passage in the *Vita Bern* referred to in the following note.

58 *Vita Bern*, Book 1.,41; PL 185:251; Cawley 1:54.

59 See *Vita Bern*, Book 7.8–9; PL 185:419; Cawley 2:85.

60 WA 1:333,26–29. On Gerson and Biel, see above, note 3.

61 Both sources speak of *sanguinem crudam*, 'raw blood', but this wording must be a mistake of copyists who mistook it for the more likely *saginam crudam*, 'raw animal fat'. *Vita Bern*, Book 1.7,33; PL 185:247; Cawley 1:45. *The Golden Legend,* 468; Ryan 2:101; see McGuire, 'A Saint's Afterlife. Bernard in the Golden Legend and in Other Medieval Collections'. *Bernhard von Clairvaux,* Elm, ed., 188. See the modern german edition by Paul Sinz, ed. and trans., *Das Leben des heiligen Bernhard von Clairvaux (Vita Bern)* (Düsseldorf: Patmos Verlag, 1962) 272, with note 20.

62 *De Bernardo . . . oleo pro vino*, WA 43:520,24; WA 13:662,4f. However, *Vita Bern*, Book 1.7,33; PL 185:250, speaks of drinking oil instead water (not wine, as Luther has it). The incident with the oil was mentioned a second time in the *Vita Bern*; PL 185:304. Based on the *Golden Legend*, it is also found in the thirteenth century vernacular collection of legends, *Das Passional. Eine Legenden-Sammlung des dreizehnten Jahrhunderts*, Karl Köpke, ed. (Quedlinburg and Leipzig: Gottfr. Basse, 1852) 401.

Yet other sayings of Bernard were handed down concerning salvation for members of the Cistercian Order, and these appear to have been familiar to Luther. According to these, Bernard declared that even Judas would have been saved if only he had become a Cistercian, and that remaining faithful in the Order would be sufficient to obtain eternal salvation.[63] In one of his table talks, Luther claimed that Bernard had allegedly said that those who chose not to remain in the cloister would surely be damned. In contrast, Luther pointed out that being clothed like Bernard would not lead a person into heaven, because Christ who is the Way alone will do this.[64]

Luther knew statistics drawn from Geoffrey of Auxerre's *Vita Bern* Book 5.5f, and mentioned in *The Golden Legend*, on the hundred sixty monasteries founded by Bernard.[65] He spoke of it several times. He also knew about the emperors of the time and introduced Bernard as the most sincere monk and someone he 'venerates'.[66] He repeated also the central story about Saint

63 See *Vita Bern*, Book 7.7; Cawley 2:84. See Herbert of Clairvaux's *Liber Miraculorum*, Caesarius of Heisterbach's *Dialogus Miraculorum,* Conrad of Eberbach's *Exordium Magnum Cistercience* 2.5, and John the Hermit's *Vita Quarta* of Bernard (PL 185:545), as mentioned by McGuire, *The Difficult Saint,* 165 and 177.

64 *Bernhardi vestis non me ducit in coelum, non enim potest, solus Christus potest qui est via in coelum* (sermon of March 25, 1538), WA 46:227,24f. *Signum damnationis, si non manserint in monasteriis,* WA TR 4 (no. 4772); Bell, *Divus Bernhardus,* 346, did not mention the source material which is given in the previous note; he, therefore, still listed Luther's saying in this Table Talk (no. 4772) under the unidentified bernardine phrases (*Divus Bernhardus,* 387).

65 *Vita Bern,* Book 5.5f; Cawley 2:67; *Legenda aurea,* 538; *The Golden Legend,* 477; Ryan 2:107; see McGuire, 'A Saint's Afterlife. Bernard in the Golden Legend and in Other Medieval Collections'. *Bernhard von Clairvaux,* Elm, ed., 203.

66 Luther in Table Talk no. 6353: *36 annos fuit abbas . . . 160 klöster gebauet,* WA TR 5:616,39f; German verison: 617,4–8; *multa coenobia,* WA 20:745,8; WA 47:597,34; WA 53:156; WA 50:610,13. It is unclear what Luther meant by *Historien.* The WA-editor refers us to the *Chronik* of Nauclerus. However, Luther may very well have lifted this number (of 160 monasteries) from *Vita Bern,* Book 5 or from the Bernard story in the *Legenda aurea.* In his study on monastic vows Luther indicated also some historical knowledge about Pope Anastasius IV being a 'disciple of Bernard': *ut Anastasius, Bernhardi discipulus,* WA 8:643,23 (on vows, 1521). Luther's exact source in this regard is not known. Most likely he took this historical information from the story about Pope Pelagius in *The Golden Legend,* where the following names are mentioned: Pope Eugene as former abbot of Saint Anastasius, and the Emperors Henry

Bernard being sick in bed and having a vision of Satan accusing him at judgment before the eyes of God. Bernard's words in this connection made a great impression on Luther. He may have taken it from *The Golden Legend*, or directly from either the first or second Bernard hagiography.[67]

It is very possible that Luther learned of Bernard's advice on fraternal correction, echoed in his testament, from *The Golden Legend*. There Bernard is quoted as saying: 'I have wished to give scandal to no one, and if scandal occurred, I have kept it secret as best as I could: I have always trusted the opinion of others more than my own: I have never sought to avenge an injury. Charity, humility, patience, these are the three things I leave you'.[68] Luther recalled this saying of *divus Bernhardus* as he lectured on Gal 6:1, on fraternal correction, but without mentioning any source.[69] The clue (until now not identified[70]) is the Bible verse which Luther was expounding at the moment and which is cited in Bernard's Sermon on the Canticle 44, where he speaks of gentle fraternal correction in the context of interpreting Sg 1:3, the balsam shrubs which grow in En-gedi:

IV, Henry V, Conrad III, and Lothar III, all contemporaries of Bernard. The same imperial names appear in Luther's Table Talk no. 4772: *S. Bernhardus est sincerissimus, quem omnibus aliis monachis veneror. . . . S. Bernhardus vixit periculosis temporibus sub imperatoribus Henrico 4. et Henrico 5., Conrado et Lothario*, WA TR 4:480,16–24.

67 See WA 8:601,22–31 (1521). On the 'double right to heaven', see Posset, 'St Bernard's Influence on Two Reformers', 175–187. Bell, *Divus Bernhardus*, 208, correctly pointed out that Luther used this story already in his treatise on the monastic vows, and that it can be found originally in *Vita Bern*, Book 1.12,57f; PL 185:258; Cawley 1:70. I stand corrected. However, there might still be a connection between Luther's becoming aware of the Bernard legend and Luther's doubts about the value of the monastic life. As to Luther's first use of the bernardine phrase about the right to heaven, Bell is mistaken when he assumed that it is found in Luther's tract on the monastic vows. The first use appears to be in the *Dictata* of 1513, see WA 55-II,1:120,5ff.

68 *The Golden Legend*, 477; Ryan 2:107.

69 WA 2:602,8–11.

70 No source reference was listed in the WA 63 index, where the quotation was considered as unidentified. Bell, *Divus Bernhardus*, 387, also listed it as unidentified, and he (Bell 109) correctly rejected Volz's suggestion that Bernard's SC 35.5–7 was the proper source, see Volz, 'Martin Luther's Attitude Toward Bernard of Clairvaux', 191.

By the vines of En-gedi therefore we may understand the peoples of the Church, which possess a liquid balsam, the spirit of gentleness, to soothe and cherish the tenderness of those who are still 'babes in Christ' (1 Cor 3:1), and to ease the sorrows of repentant sinners. So if a brother sins (Gal 6:1), let a man of the Church, who has already received this spirit, come to his assistance with all gentleness, not forgetting that he himself may be tempted. . . . If a man, conscious of his own sins, refuses to be angry when he sees a fellowman committing an offense, but instead approaches him with a love and sympathy that comfort him like the sweetest balsam, here is something whose source we know, about which you have already heard, but perhaps without grasping its significance. What I said is, when a man reflects on his own conduct he ought to feel impelled to be gentle with all (2 Tim 2:24). Following the wise counsel of Saint Paul, he must learn to love those who are caught in habits of sin (Gal 6:1), not forgetting that he himself is open to temptation.[71]

The Golden Legend incorporated bernardine material from outside the immediate cistercian tradition: Bernard curing a gambler; Bernard betting with a boor over inattentive prayer. The latter Luther most likely lifted from *The Golden Legend*.[72] The former he did not mention.

In general, we may assume that the *Legenda aurea*, this famous collection of 'golden readings', which Luther mentioned at one point, may have provided his main source of information on Bernard's life. Yet there are two hagiographical stories he uses which are not found in it: Bernard sending a confrère to receive holy communion on his faith (1); and Bernard's spitoon (2). Nor do we find the spring/rivulets metaphor in it (3). We are led to conclude that the *Legenda aurea* cannot have been the exclusive source of

71 See SC 44,2–4; SBOp 2:45–47; CF 7:226–28. If my suggestion is correct that SC 44 was Luther's source, then the list of unidentified sources in WA 63 and in Bell, *Divus Bernhardus,* 387, can be reduced, and the list of Luther's knowledge of the sermons on the Sg can be expanded.

72 *Legenda aurea,* 534f; *The Golden Legend* 473; Ryan 2:104; see McGuire, 'A Saint's Afterlife. Bernard in the Golden Legend and in Other Medieval Collections'. *Bernhard von Clairvaux,* Elm, ed., 197f. More on this story in Section II.8.

Luther's knowledge about Bernard's life, even though it may have been the main one. Luther appeared to have been well versed in both original Bernard texts and in other secondary sources, perhaps including the *Passional*, a thirteenth-century collection of legends based on *The Golden Legend* widely used in German-speaking lands. As Ulrich Köpf observed, numerous prints of these works shaped the Bernard image of the Reformation and early modern times.[73] Perhaps, Luther lifted them from the *Vita Bern* itself or from a vernacular version of it, circulating under the title *Leben sant Bernharts* (Life of Saint Bernard).

With regard to Luther's use of secondary source material about Bernard, one must point out that he processed relatively little from it. Luther simply was not much interested in visions and miracle stories. The *Vita Bern* mentions more than two hundred miracles performed by the saint. The *Legenda aurea*, already selective, reports only two of his miracles of healing/exorcisms. Luther followed this *tendenz* and ignored Bernard's miracles altogether. Even more selectively, he concentrated on Bernard's preaching on grace and on his Christ-centered spirituality—in contrast to the forty-six depictions of factual or legendary events shown in Carlo Garavaglia's wooden reliefs on the choir stalls in Chiaravalle Milanese. These in turn are based on Antonio Tempesta's fifty-six copper plates in a sixteenth-century book on Bernard's life and miracles, *Vita et miracula D. Bernardi Claravallensis Abbatis, incidebatur Romae 1587* (re-edited in 1990).[74] This book was meant to foster piety among the Cistercians, and most of its fifty-six illustrations were based on stories in *Vita Bern*. Three stories were added from other, later sources: (a) an encounter with Emperor Lothar; (b) the *lactatio Bernardi*; and (c) Bernard compelling the

---

73 See Köpf, 'Die Rezeptions- und Wirkungsgeschichte Bernhards von Clairvaux', *Bernhard von Clairvaux*, Elm, ed. 30.

74 P. Tiburtius Hümpfner, *Ikonographie des hl. Bernhard von Clairvaux* (Augsburg, Cologne, Vienna: Dr. Benno Filser Verlag, 1927) shows Garavaglia's forty-six scenes; see also Paffrath, *Bernhard von Clairvaux* (1984), 229–283. The modern edition of Tempesta's *Vita et miracula* came out in Benaguacil, Spain, in 1990, edited by L. Esteban.

devil to change his defective wagon wheel.[75] A comparison of these depictions of events from Bernard's life with what Luther mentions about the saint demonstrates Luther's lack of interest in all except the story of Bernard fighting temptations by jumping into ice-cold water.[76]

All in all, we may state that Luther had a substantial number of primary, secondary, and to us obscure sources about Saint Bernard at hand. His selective Bernard repertoire reveals his specific theological and spiritual interest in Bernard as the greatest preacher of the Middle Ages. It is this particular interest which found expression in the Reformer's sermon of 23 March 1538, when he told his listeners: 'I love Saint Bernard as the one who among all writers preached Christ most charmingly (*auff das aller lieblichste*). I follow him wherever he preached Christ, and I pray to Christ in the faith in which he prayed to Christ'.[77]

Luther's main job (besides lecturing at the local university) was preaching in the church at Wittenberg. In his praise of and reliance on Bernard as a great preacher, Luther was not at all original. Early on, and especially after the thirteenth century, Bernard was considered a model preacher and was often mentioned in the *Artes praedicandi* along with Augustine and Gregory the Great.[78] Luther as a preacher simply selected good examples to fulfil his assignment of proclaiming the christian message, and in this process he discovered that he shared the same central theological concerns as Bernard. Luther's interest in Bernard the preacher appears identical with that found in the medieval homiletic tradition. The Reformer brought forth a Lutheran Bernard with features characteristic of the medieval writer who preached Christ incarnate, crucified, and glorified at the right hand of the Father. In contrast, the image of

75 See Adriaan H. Bredero, 'Der heilige Bernhard von Clairvaux im Mittelalter: von der historischen Person zur Kultgestalt'. *Bernhard von Clairvaux*, Elm, ed., 157.

76 See Hümpfner, *Ikonographie des hl. Bernhard von Clairvaux*, 56, ill. 4.

77 WA 46:782, 21–24; LW 22:268.

78 Already a letter of the year 1149 praised Bernard's rhetorical skills; see Bredero, *Bernard of Clairvaux Between Cult and History*, 82f. On *Artes praedicandi*, see Jean Leclercq, 'Études sur Saint Bernard et le texte de ses écrits', ASOC 9 (1953) 183.

Bernard flourishing within the Cistercian Order of the sixteenth century appears to have been impacted mostly by the stories and miracles found in the book on the life and miracles of *Divus Bernardus* of 1587.[79]

Finally, even though we do not know which Bernard edition Luther used, this much has become clear: the works of Bernard (as of Anselm, and of Hugh and Richard of Saint Victor) were 'prominent in the libraries of the augustinian hermits,'[80] Luther's religious Order. And we do know that Luther in his early days as an augustinian friar at Erfurt had access to printed editions of the cistercian abbot's works; the following books show up in the library catalogue of the augustinian library at Erfurt:

> *De consideratione*. Augsburg: Anton Sorg, 1477 (see Plate 25).
>
> *Sermones de tempore et de sanctis*. Basel: Nikolaus Kesler, 1495.
>
> *Sermones super cantica canticorum*. Strasbourg: Martin Flach, 1497.[81]

We also know that the 1536 library catalogue of the University of Wittenberg listed Bernard's

> *Opera* (Lyon: Johannes Clein, 1515).[82]

The 1515 edition of the *Opera* included the *Vita Bern*,[83] and if Luther used this edition in his Wittenberg library, he may very well

---

79 *Ad alendam pietatem universis ordinis cisterciensis* (for the fostering of the piety of the entire cistercian Order), as found on the title page of the 1587 edition, reprint Florence 1987, as mentioned by Bredero, 157 with note 37.

80 See David Gutiérrez, 'De antiquis ordinis eremitarum sancti Augustini bibliothecis', *Analecta Augustiniana* 13 (1954) 186–307; see Constable, 'The Popularity of Twelfth-Century Spiritual Writers',10; see Köpf, 'Die Rezeptions- und Wirkungsgeschichte Bernhards von Clairvaux', *Bernhard von Clairvaux*, Elm, ed., 13; see Bell, 'Luther's Reception of Bernard of Clairvaux', 248.

81 See Matsuura, 'Restbestände', 318–26; see Köpf, 'Die Rezeptions- und Wirkungsgeschichte Bernhards', *Bernhard von Clairvaux*, Elm, ed., 13f.

82 See Sachiko Kusukawa, *A Wittenberg Library Catalogue of 1536* (Binghamton, N. Y. : Medieval & Renaissance Texts & Studies, 1995) 30.

83 See Bredero, *Bernard of Clairvaux Between Cult and History*, 164.

have read the original Bernard hagiography. The mere existence of books in a library, however, is not evidence that they were read. That he actually did read Bernard will be demonstrated in the further course of this investigation. We can discern it already from Luther's own statement: 'I hold Saint Bernard in higher esteem than any monk or priest on earth. I have not heard and *read* anybody similar to him'. [84] Elsewhere he remarked that it was a 'joy' (*lust*) for him to 'read' Bernard.[85]

There is room for further research. Luther dropped a number of hints about Bernard, but these have not yet been tracked down.[86]

84 See WA 16:400,20f; see WA 42:453, 41–454,1. Emphasis mine.

85 *das ein lust ist, quando quis legit,* WA 47:694,4f; see Posset, 'Bernhard von Clairvauxs Sermone', 116.

86 The unidentified references appear to be of minor theological significance. The rather recent index of Luther's unidentified references to Bernard in WA 63 is already out-dated. Bell, *Divus Bernhardus,* 387, presented a revised list; it can be reduced yet further and would include then the following references which so-far are not found in any (pseudo) bernardine texts:

1) On cheering up a brother (*factum ociosum*): WA 5:399,30–33 (1519–1521); according to Bell, *Divus Bernhardus,* 114, this story may be based on Div 14.4, SBOp 6–1:137. However, Bell, *Divus Bernhardus,* 387, still includes this locus in his list of unidentified references. Luther's reference appears more to be a saying about Bernard than a quotation from his works or from a pseudo-bernardine source.

2) On being a great sinner (*magnus peccator*): WA 36:205,5–7 (1532). See Bell, *Divus Bernhardus,* 353f.

3) On sitting among murderers: *Ich meinet, ich sesse im rosen garten, und weis nicht, das jch mitten unter mordern sitze,* WA 36:691,25 (1532). See Bell, *Divus Bernhardus,* 337, for the discussion of some odd possibilities regarding the origin of this saying. In contrast to all this, I propose to relate this saying to a hint about the new monastic foundation, that is Clairvaux, being located in a 'den of robbers' and that Bernard and his monks made of it 'a temple of God and a house of prayer' (metaphorically spoken, a 'rose garden'), *Vita Bern,* Book 1.5.25; Cawley 1:34.

4) On a layman in heaven (*ein fein gedichte*): WA 47:597,32- 598,34 (1539); see Posset, 'The Elder Luther on Bernard: Part I', 32f; see Bell, *Divus Bernhardus,* 292, 353.

5) A rhyme (*clamat caro . . . ego reficiam*): WA 48:274, posthumous print. See Bell, *Divus Bernhardus,* 337.

6) An enigmatic reference to the difference between what the heart acknowledges and what the mouth proclaims (*cor non agnoscit haec, quae os profert*), WA 59:290 (Advent sermon of December 21, 1533, on Jn 16:3); the student who stenographed this sermon added the editorial note: *Vide Bernardum . . . fo[lio] 83 co[lumna] 1.* Unfortunately, this

And there are numerous fifteenth-century prints of the 'Life of Saint of Bernard' in German which still need to be located in archives and their content investigated as possible sources for Luther.[87]

Bernard edition (Pseudo- Bernard?) could not be identified as of yet. It is a remarkably precise source reference by a student!

7) On Carmelite/Rosary: *Lutherus ex Bernhardi historia recitavit*, WA TR 5:683,29 (no. 6476; no date).

8) . . . *so offt habe er sich beschmitzt:* This hint which may be interpreted as Bernard being alone and not be contaminated by associating with other people may resemble a phrase in Thomas a Kempis, *On the Imitation of Christ* 1.20: WA 32:327,22 (1530- 1532), as Bell, *Divus Bernhardus*, 337 assumes. Or, if one reads this hint with the modern german wording *beschmutzt* (soiled), one could take this saying as Luther's reference to Bernard vomiting in the assembly of the monks at prayer, when he soiled himself.

87 There are several *Leben sant Bernharts*, as mentioned above in note 53. A 'Life of Saints' is known to have been edited by Johann Grüninger (Strasbourg, 1502) under the title *Heiligenleben* which includes Bernard; see Cécile Dupeux, 'Saint Bernard dans l'iconographie médiévale: l'example de la lactation'. *Vies et légendes*, 155, note 7.

Plate 5. The Crucified Embraces Saint Bernard (*Amplexus Bernardi*). Minature attributed to a dutch iconographer of the School of Bruges and Ghent, from a vernacular de luxe edition of *Seelengärtlein, Hortulus animae,* from the 1520s. *Hortulus animae* was the name given to collections of prayers for the laity. The text on this page of the 'Little Garden of the Soul' reads in translation: 'Of Saint Bernard the Abbot. O holy abbot and father Saint Bernard: You [who are] of noble birth, handsome, still young and tender . . . . ' Vienna, Österreichische Nationalbibliothek, Codex 2706, fol. 273v. Photo. Leutner Fachlabor, Vienna.

The Vita Bernardi and The Golden Legend as Sources for Luther

Vita Bernardi	Legenda aurea	Luther
Book 1		
by William of Saint Thierry	name	—
(PL 185:225–268)	mentioned	
1. 1 Bernard's Parents	mentioned	—
1. 2 Christmas vision	mentioned	—
1. 3. 5 Leaping into cold water	mentioned	(indirect)
		WA 47:326,20–23
		WA 1:495,40–496,1
1. 3. 6 Naked girl in his bed	mentioned	—
1. 3. 7 'Robbers!'	mentioned	—
1. 4.1 9f Entering Cîteaux	mentioned	—
1. 4. 23 Scripture meditation	mentioned	WA 50:519,32f
under oaks and beeches		
(see also Ep 106)		
1. 4. 24 Scripture as spring,	—	WA 50:525,24–26
with rivulets (see also		WA Br 1:602,42–46
3.6)		WA TR 4 no. 4567
		WA 10-III, WA
		7:100,25f
1. 5 At Clairvaux	mentioned	—
1. 6 Gerard	mentioned	—
1. 7. 33 raw blood/butter	mentioned	—
1. 7. 33 oil/water	mentioned	WA 43:520,24
		(oil/wine); WA
		13:662,4f
1. 8. 38 Wearing a hair shirt	mentioned	—
1. 8. 39 Bernard's spitoon	—	—
1. 8. 40 Abused body	—	WA TR 3:607,1f
		(no. 3777);
		WA 43:331,24–28
from hindsight	—	WA 12:282,28–32
		WA 10-III:376,25f
		WA 47:62,30f;
		326,23
1. 9 Miracles*		
1. 10 Miracles*		
1. 11. 49 Letter in the rain	mentioned	—
1. 11. 52 Flies story	mentioned	—

Continued

Vita Bernardi	Legenda aurea	Luther
1. 11. 55 Beer story	mentioned	—
1. 12. 57f Vision of judgment	mentioned	WA 8:332,21; 601,21f WA 34-II:441,10–23.
Vision of ship	—	—
Vision of Mary, Lawrence, and Benedict	—	—
1. 14 Miracles*		
Book 2 by Ernald	name mentioned	
Books 3–5 by Geoffrey	—	
Selections from Book 3		
3. 1 Bernard's face and body	—	—
3. 4 With the Carthusians	mentioned	—
3. 4 Along the lake at Lausanne	mentioned	—
3. 6 The whole of Scripture	mentioned	—
3. 24 Losing 600 silver marks	mentioned with embellishment	—
3. 25 Refusing a canon regular	mentioned	—
Selections from Book 4: Tallying up Miracles*	—	—
Selections from Book 5:		
5. 5f Father of more than 160 monasteries	mentioned	WA TR 5 no. 6353 WA 20:745,8 etc.
5. 22 Bernard appears to William of Montpellier	mentioned without William's name	
5. 23 Malachy	mentioned	—
Book 6 (anonymous)	—	

Book 7 (borrowings from
    ***Exordium magnum* and**
    Herbert)
	—	

7. 5 Angels' use of golden ink	—	—

Continued

Vita Bernardi	*Legenda aurea*	*Luther*
7. 7 Judas would be saved at Clairvaux	—	WA TR 4 no. 4772.
7. 8f A monk receives communion in Bernard's faith	—	WA 1:333,26–29 WA 8:451,5–9
7. 10 The Crucified embraces Bernard	—	—
7. 34 Converting an ex-monk	—	—

* The *Vita Bernardi* knows of more than 200 miracles of healing performed by Bernard (see Pierre Boglioni and André Picard, 'Miracle et thaumaturgie dans la vie de saint Bernard', *Vies et légendes de saint Bernard de Clairvaux* [Cîteaux: Commentarii Cistercienses, 1993, 59]). The Bernard story in the *Legenda aurea* mentions only two miracles of healing as exorcisms: one in Pavia, and one in Aquitaine. Luther does not mention any specific miracle stories at all, but speaks in general of Bernard and others who performed numerous miracles (see WA 34-II:441,10).

Anyone wanting to connect Luther and Bernard must first remember that four hundred years separate them, the epoch of the high and late Middle Ages, and that Luther did not read Bernard in an historical light, but came to know him over existential and theological issues. Early on, Luther differentiated between Bernard's theology and the scholastic theology shaped by aristotelian philosophy.[1] Thus, in a certain sense, Luther himself distinguished between monastic and scholastic theology, as he went looking for help in the christian tradition (*ad fontes*) in support of his renewal of theology on the basis of Scripture. We may even say that Luther is unthinkable without the monastic theology shaped by Bernard.[2]

1. *'Monastic theology'*

By monastic theology is understood the theological thinking developed and practised in monasteries, independent of the theology presented at the universities of the Middle Ages, which was a theology often taught by members of mendicant religious Orders. Monastic theology sought to articulate religious experience more than pursue speculation, and to speak to the affect as well as to the intellect. These theologians are intelligent, but not necessarily intellectuals. Monastic theology pondered the spiritual life of the cloister. It chose concrete images over abstractions. While the scholastic method of discussing problems used the *quaestio* and *disputatio*, the monastic approach relied on *meditatio*. Monastic theology deliberated in the context of meditative scriptural exposition by employing the method of 'exegetical concordance'. Persued by the believer who was in love with God, monastic theology was closely related to patristic theology; Bernardo Olivera distinguished the following features:

— It is based on *lectio divina*.

---

1 See Lohse, 'Luther und Bernhard von Clairvaux', 271–301.
2 See Heller, *Schriftauslegung und geistliche Erfahrung bei Bernhard von Clairvaux,* 197.

— Symbolism, imagination and human affectivity play an important part in it.

— Its development is essentially related to spiritual and religious experience.

— It leads to christian wisdom in daily life.

— In it, knowledge of God is inseparable from knowledge of self.

— It is deeply respectful of mystery.

— Its method of Scripture interpretation is based on the four-fold classical reading (literal, allegorical, moral/tropological, and mystical/anagogical) with preference for the moral/tropological sense.[3]

3 The notion 'monastic theology' is prominent since the publication of Leclercq's book *The Love of Learning*, 95. See also Jean Leclercq, 'Monastic and Scholastic Theology in the Reformers of the Fourteenth to Sixteenth Century', *From Cloister to Classroom: Monastic and Scholastic Approaches to Truth. The Spirituality of Western Christendom III*, E. Rozanne Elder, ed. (Kalamazoo: CP, 1986) 178–201. Olivera, 'Help in Reading St. Bernard', 12 (on Bernard as monastic theologian); Casey, *The Undivided Heart*, 4–9, 24–26 (on *lectio divina*); 93, note 17 (on the difference between 'monastic theology' and 'scholastic theology' as a switch from right-brain to left-brain thinking) with reference to his article '"Emotionally Hollow, Esthetically Meaningless and Spiritually Empty": An Inquiry into Theological Discourse', *Colloquium* 14 (1981) 54–61. Endel Kallas pointed out that 'Luther's spirituality' must be evaluated with serious regard to the monastic tradition, in: 'The Spirituality of Luther: A Reappraisal of his Contribution', *Spirituality Today* 34 (1983) 292–302. Gerard Vallée, 'Luther and Monastic Theology: Notes on *Anfechtung* and *Compunctio*', ARG 75 (1984) 290–296. Barry R. Folmar, 'Recovering Lectio Divina' (1990) as summarized in *Luther Digest: An Annual Abridgment of Luther Studies* 1993, Kenneth Hagen, ed. (Fort Wayne: Luther Academy, 1993) 50–63. R. Schwarz, 'Luther's Inalienable Inheritance of Monastic Theology', 430–450. I stress here my adherance to Schwarz's description of 'monastic theology' (which I translated into English) in response to Theo Bell, 'Bernhard von Clairvaux als Quelle Martin Luthers', 16, who lamented that I did not define this notion in my article 'Bernhard von Clairvauxs Sermone', *Lutherjahrbuch*, 93–116. My critic overlooked that I was the translator of Schwarz's essay. A more conciliatory tone is found in Bell's article 'Luther's Reception of Bernard', 265, as now Bell hesitantly joined in my (and others') approach by writing that 'perhaps understanding the young Luther and his theology as a monastic theology or as a *theologia experimentalis* offers us a valuable approach'. Ulrich Köpf, too, had indicated that the influence of monastic theology upon Luther needed to be investigated further: 'Martin Luthers Lebensgang als Mönch'. *Kloster Amelungsborn 1135–1985*, Gerhard Ruhbach and Kurt Schmidt-Clausen, eds. (Hannover: Hermannsburg, 1985) 187–208. Köpf did exactly that in his 'Monastische Theologie im 15. Jahrhundert'. *Rottenburger Jahrbuch für Kirchengeschichte* 11 (1992) 117–135. Köpf 135 noted that Luther connected himself not so much to fifteenth century monastic theology, but to Bernard's earlier monastic theology. See Casey, *Athirst for God,* 32–37.

Bernard was the greatest medieval representative of this patristic-monastic theology. And it was this same Bernard, as 'the last of the Church Fathers', whom Luther placed highest among famous teachers 'old and new'. Remarkably, Bernard and Luther shared a preference for the tropological sense of the Scriptures (as we will see, for example, in Chapter Four, on Luther's use of Bernard's 'moral' interpretation of Christ's circumcision). Furthermore, Luther declared he had learned from Saint Bernard, Saint Augustine, and other Fathers to tune in to the sounds of the Bible, to 'adapt and adjust our minds and feelings so that they are in accord with the sense of the Psalms. For since the Psalter is only a kind of school and exercise for the disposition of the heart, he sings in vain who does not sing in the spirit'. In the same lecture (on the first psalm in his *Operationes in Psalmos*), the developing Reformer asserted directly that one must pay attention to Bernard's biblical expertise:

> This I want to impress on you once more in this first psalm, so that it may not be necessary to repeat it for each individual psalm. I know that whoever becomes practiced in this will find more in the Psalter by himself than all the interpretations of other men can give him. I see that Saint Bernard was an expert in this art and drew from it all the wealth of his learning.[4]

Luther maintained that all he had done was to imitate Saint Bernard's (and Saint Augustine's) example by following the river to its source. They led him to seek the headwaters and helped him to return to the common biblical source, 'to drink the waters of life from the same source', with the same 'art' as Bernard had done. By his effort to return to fruitful biblical antiquity, Luther was sitting in the same boat as the humanists of his day who were determined to reach the headwaters of civilization (*ad fontes*). In this context, I cannot elaborate on Luther and his relationship to humanism, except to refer to the excellent study by Helmar Junghans on the young Luther and the humanists.[5]

---

4 AWA 2:63,26–27; LW 14:310–11; see WA 15:40,30–41,3; LW 45:363.

5 On Luther's and his Augustinian Order's relationship to Renaissance humanism, see Arbesmann, *Der Augustinereremitenorden und der Beginn der*

In Luther we find the monastic and the humanistic traditions joined. The monastic 'love of learning' used as its principal literary sources the patristic tradition, classical literature, and Sacred Scripture. Medieval monastic theology was basically the prolongation of the patristic pursuit of 'wisdom' (*sapientia*). With Bernard and the cistercian school the 'wisdom' which comes from experience was likened to the 'taste' for goodness; Bernard explained 'wisdom' by its supposed latin root, *sapor* (taste, savor); when wisdom is added to virtue, like seasoning to food, it imparts flavor: 'I think it would be permissible to define wisdom as a taste for goodness. We lost this taste almost from the creation of our human race. When the old serpent's poison infected the palate of our heart, because the fleshly sense prevailed, the soul began to lose its taste for goodness'.[6]

In contrast to the scholastic way of learning, the monastic distinguished itself by speaking in images borrowed from Scripture which possess both a richness and an obscurity appropriate to the mystery to be expressed. Bernard demanded that theological thinking and the interpretation of Sacred Scripture be carried out in a 'cautious and simple way', *caute et simpliciter*. He spoke in fragmentary biblical verses, giving his preaching style the biblical dialect itself. In the following short passage from SC 74, for example, each sentence is interwoven with biblical vocabulary:

> In the exposition of the holy and mystical words, let us proceed in a cautious (Eph 5:15) and simple way (cf. Prv 11:20), let us display the way of the Scripture which speaks with our words of the wisdom which is hidden in the mystery (1 Cor 2:7); while [Scripture] expresses itself figuratively it insinuates God into our affections.[7]

humanistischen Bewegung; Junghans, *Der junge Luther und die Humanisten* (1984).

6 The definition of 'wisdom' is found in SC 85, SBOp 2:312,21–27; see Odo Brooke, *Studies in Monastic Theology* (Kalamazoo: CP, 1980) 219.

7 Translation mine. Other translations differ considerably, such as the one by Irene Edmonds in vol. IV of the edition of *Bernard of Clairvaux, On the Song of Songs* (Kalamazoo: CP, 1980) 86; or the one by Gillian R. Evans, *Bernard of Clairvaux: Selected Works* (New York, Mahwah: Paulist Press, 1987) 253. Latin original in: SBOp 2:240,17–20.

Luther was drawn to this 'cautious and simple' monastic way of unlocking sacred mysteries, while he detested the scholastic way of theologizing. In his theological development, he received decisive impulses from this monastic tradition that he, too, reflected upon the experiences of the spiritual life; and he did this by means of scriptural interpretation. Even in his later theology, Luther retained some of the monastic inheritance.

That Luther as a friar learned the traditions of monasticism is beyond doubt. Basic elements of the self-understanding of monks and friars were handed down orally and are therefore difficult to demonstrate by historical research. But there are traces. The young Luther's close relationship to monastic theology shows up in his early theology and is expressed in his first lecture series on the monks' prayer book, the Psalter. Here, between 1513 and 1515, Luther processed the monastic mentality. It is therefore not surprising that he often mentioned Saint Bernard. In this course, Luther referred to the three religious vows of obedience, poverty, and chastity, as a bulwark against the three temptations people encounter in the world: haughtiness of life, concupiscence of the eyes, and concupiscence of the flesh (1 Jn 2:6). Reading Luther's deliberations on the vows, we recognize how deeply he had internalized the monastic mentality. This is also true of his ecclesiology of the spiritual Body of Christ, which he interpreted as the concrete community of the cloister.[8] Luther integrated still other elements into his lectures, mainly humanistic rhetorical annotations—this fact may simply be noted here without further describing it. Altogether, his reformation theology emerges as a specific version of a combination of 'monastic' and 'humanistic' theology. The latter had an impact on Luther mainly because of its linguistic contributions stemming from the study of the sacred languages. Our focus here and in what follows will, however, remain on the monastic theological aspects of Luther's spirituality.

8 See Schwarz, 'Luther's Inalienable Inheritance of Monastic Theology,' 434f. On Luther's concept of the Church in his early period, see Scott H. Hendrix, *Ecclesia in via: Ecclesiological Developments in the Medieval Psalms Exegesis and the Dictata super Psalterium (1513–1515) of Martin Luther* (Leiden: Brill, 1974).

2. *Spiritual development*

In fall 1508 Luther was appointed to teach moral philosophy at the newly created academy or university of Wittenberg in electoral Saxony. One year later he concluded his theological studies at Erfurt. He was then a *sententiarius* whose task it was to lecture on the *Sentences* of Peter Lombard (+1160). This he dutifully executed until the fall of 1510, when he was sent to Rome on business for his Order. As a critical marginal note to Lombard's distinction twenty-four, young Friar Martin entered into his copy of the *Libri Sententiarum* a line from Bernard: 'To stand still is to regress'. As a *literal* latin quotation the phrase cannot be found in Bernard, but what Luther quoted comes close to what can be located in Bernard's authentic works. Luther entered yet other bernardine citations. One is taken from the fourth sermon on the glories of the Mother of God; Luther abbreviated his source reference with *Super Missus est*. Another bernardine phrase, taken from SC 37.7, Luther referenced with the abbreviation *Bern.: canti*.[9] These early references give witness to Luther's initial familiarity with bernardine spiritual insights. In the following three citations I have italicized the apposite phrase.

Bernard: 'Not to progress is to regress'
      The first comes from Bernard's second sermon on the Feast of the Lord's Presentation in the Temple, on a sermon text of Ps 138:5, 'Let them sing in the ways of the Lord, for great is the glory of the Lord'. In this sermon, Bernard reflected on the Holy Family's pilgrimage to Jerusalem and simultaneously explained the cistercian custom of conducting a commemorative 'pilgrimage' in the form of a liturgical procession on that feast day. Toward the end of his brief homily he used the phrase which Luther may have memorized about 'progressing' and 'regressing' in one's development in the School of Christ:

---

9 WA 9:69,36–70,4, where Luther quoted Bernard as having said *stare est retrogredi, dicit b. Bernardus* (marginal note on Peter Lombard); see Bell, *Divus Bernhardus*, 39–42.

Let us 'sing' as I have said, 'in the ways of the Lord, for great
is the glory of the Lord' (Ps 138:5), let us 'sing to the Lord a
new canticle, because He had done wonderful things' (Ps 98:1).
But if in all these practices of devotion any of us should neglect
to advance and to 'go forward from virtue to virtue' (Ps 84:8),
let such a one know that he belongs not to the procession, but
is standing still, or rather is going back. *For on the road of life,
not to progress means to regress*, for nothing can continue in
the same condition (cf. Jb 14:11). As I remember having told
you often, the main work consists in this: that we never consider
ourselves 'as having reached the goal as yet', but that 'forgetting
the things that are behind and extending ourselves to those that
are ahead' (Phil 3:13), we strive incessantly after something
better, and keep our imperfections constantly exposed to the
eyes of divine mercy.[10]

The last few lines are a paraphrase of Phil 3:13, which Bernard
used frequently, mostly in his sermons. A similar pun on progress
and regress was employed by Bernard in the opening passage of
his *Letter* 385 to the monks of Saint Bertin:

A forward disciple is the pride of his master. Anyone who does
not advance in the school of Christ is not worthy of his teaching,
especially when we are so placed that if we do not *make progress
we must doubtlessly fall back.* Let no one say: I have had enough.
I shall stay as I am. It is good enough for me to remain the same
as I was yesterday and the day before. Anyone who thinks like
this pauses on the way and stands still on that ladder where the
patriarch saw no one but those who were going up or coming
down.[11]

10 The decisive line in the latin original is: *quoniam in via vitae non progredi
regredi est, cum nihil adhuc in eodem statu permaneat*, Pur 2.3; SBOp 4:340,11–
12; see Sommerfeldt, *The Spiritual Teachings*, 141; see Denis Farkasfalvy, 'The
Use of Paul by Saint Bernard as Illustrated by Saint Bernard's Interpretation of
Philippians 3:13', *Bernardus Magister*, 161f.

11 *Et non proficere sine dubio deficere est*, Ep 385; SBOp 8:351,14. See
also Bernard's Ep 254. A derivation of the line from Bernard's Ep 385 may be
found in Luther, WA 56:486,7 (without mention of Bernard's name); see Bell,
Divus Bernhardus, 90. See also WA 1:649,17–19 (1518). See Bernard's Abb: . . .
ut unum necesse sit e duobus, aut proficere scilicet, aut prorsus deficere, SBOp
5:290,10.

A more moralistic version is found in our cistercian abbot's *Letter* 91 to cluniac abbots:

> Let them depart from me and from you who say, 'We do not wish to be better than our fathers', proclaiming themselves sons of lax and tepid fathers whose memory is accursed because they have eaten bitter grapes and the teeth of their children have been set on edge. If they glory in the memory of good and holy fathers, then let them at least imitate their sanctity while maintaining as a law their dispensations and indulgences. Although the holy Elijah said: 'I am not better than my fathers', he did not say that he had no desire to be better. Jacob in his vision saw angels ascending and descending the ladder, but he did not see any standing still or sitting down. A fragile hanging ladder is no place for standing still or, in the uncertain conditions of this mortal life, can anyone remain fixed in one position. We have here no abiding city nor do we yet possess the one to come, but we are still seeking it. Either you must go up or you must come down. You inevitably fall if you try to stand still. It is certain that the one who does not try to be better is not even good; and when you *begin not to want to become better, then you stop also being good.*[12]

Luther: 'And Blessed Bernard says: "Standing still . . ." '

This saying was popular already in the fourteenth century when John Tauler used it in one of his sermons, perhaps in his own German translation.[13] It is impossible to decide from which bernardine source Luther took the adage. It had become a proverb and Luther could have picked it up many places. Because Luther always used the latin version of Bernard's saying, the probability that he lifted it from a latin source is greater than that he took it from the german.

When the young Luther was occupied with reading Anselm's *Opuscula*, perhaps in preparation for his first lectures on the Psalms, the bernardine adage on progress and regress entered his

---

12 Ep 91; SBOp 7:240,18f; see Gen 28:10–13 (Jacob's Ladder), 1 Kgs 19:4 (Elijah's confession); see Pennington and Katzir, *Bernard*, 88.

13 Tauler: *wan als S. Bernhardus spricht:* '*in dem wege Gotz ston, das ist hindersich gon*', as quoted by Louise Gnädiger, 'Der minnende Bernhardus', 405. Bell thought that Luther may have relied on *Sententiae*; see Bell, *Divus Bernhardus*, 73. I propose that Luther relied on a sermon such as Pur 2.

mind again, and he wrote it on the inside of the cover page of the *Opuscula*.[14] Some scholars believe that at this early point Luther did not read Bernard in the original, but encountered bernardine sayings in Bonaventure's *Meditationes Vitae Christi* in the *Opuscula parva* edition of 1495.[15] I tend to concur.

In his first Psalm Lectures (1513–15) Luther employed Bernard's adage several times. We find it in the scholium on Ps 4:2, and again in his gloss of Ps 16:5.[16] When Luther expounded Ps 119:122, he repeated Bernard's line with the extension: ' "When you start not wanting to become better, you stop being good." For there is no stopping place on God's way. Delay is itself sin'.[17] Luther's typically broad notion of sin led him to equate delay and sin. Furthermore, he used Bernard's maxim to explain personal salvation as a process: sinful believers are righteous (*iusti*) though their righteousness is not yet fully realized (*semper iustificandi*). If one stands still, one loses righteousness.

The bernardine proverb also occurred during the subsequent lectures on Rom 3:11,[18] and again on Rom 12:2, where it is found in both the gloss[19] and the lecture notes.[20] In 1518, when Luther, still an augustinian, wrote against the dominican friar, Sylvester Prierias, the official expert appointed by the pope, he again quoted Bernard (along with Augustine). This time Luther consciously used the bernardine lines as two distinct quotations: 'And Blessed Bernard says: "Standing still in the way of God and not making

14 See WA 9:107,23; also lines 28 and 108,17. See Bell, *Divus Bernhardus*, 79–80.

15 See Köpf, 'Die Rezeption- und Wirkungsgeschichte Bernhards', 14 with note 29 (referring to forthcoming studies by Jun Matsuura); Theo Bell, 'Luther's Reception of Bernard of Clairvaux', CTQ 59 (1995) 248.

16 *Quia ubi incipis nolle fieri melior . . . ait Bernhardus*, WA 55- II,1:64, 5–6 (on Ps 4:2). The original *etiam* is dropped here. *Quia secundum Bernardum . . .*, WA 55-I:124, 22f (on Ps 16:5). LW 10:53 has a wrong source reference (i.e. Ep 93); the correct one is Ep 91.3.

17 *Quia vere dicit B. Bernardus: 'Ubi incipis nolle fieri melior, desinis esse bonus. Quia non est status in via dei: ipsa mora peccatum est'*, WA 4:364,17f; LW 11:496. The second sentence is Luther's own extension which is not found in Bernard's original wording, see SBOp 7:240,18–19.

18 *Non sit standum in via Dei*, WA 56:239,22f.

19 WA 56:441,21.

20 *Unde beatus Bernardus . . .*, WA 57-I:216,12f (on Rom 12:2).

progress is falling back", and elsewhere, "when you begin not to want to become better, then you stop also being good" '.[21] And, in 1535, the last time the by then ex-friar Luther used this bernardine insight was to support his argument in a disputation over 1 Cor 13.[22]

3. Spiritual compunction

From the christian East comes the greek notion of *penthos*, which in the western latin tradition is *compunctio*. 'Compunction' means a 'clean break'; with it the spiritual journey begins. The french *componction* has connotations of 'humility' and 'contrition'. It is 'a lament over the madness of our attachments to unreal values'. The english word is defined as 'uneasiness of mind or conscience' or as 'guilt' and 'remorse'. The note of 'uneasiness' takes the original sting out of this term. Only in the equivalent 'remorse' does the biting sharpness of *compunctio* come out; similarly the german equivalent *Zerknirschung*, commonly translated with 'contrition', was originally related to the verbs, meaning 'to squash' or 'to gnash'.[23] The original latin verb, *compungere*, means to sting, to

21 *Et B. Bernhardus: Stare in via dei et non proficere est deficere, et alibi: ubi incipis nolle fieri melior, desinis esse bonus,* WA 1:649,17–19 (Against Prierias, 1518). See *Dokumente zur Causa Lutheri (1517–1521). 1. Teil,* Peter Fabisch and Erwin Iserloh, eds. (Münster: Aschendorff, 1988) 57, note 18. Luther referred to the content of Bernard's Epp 91 and 385; the latter surfaced also in WA 56:486,7 in the following version: *Et proficere, hoc est semper a nuouo incipere.*

22 *In via dei stare est regredi,* WA 59:709,1. See WA 38:568,33 (1538), where Luther combined the bernardine idea with 2 Cor 4:16: *Christianus non est in facto, sed in fieri. . . . Summa, proficiendum est, non standum et secure stertendum . . . ;* see Posset, 'The Elder Luther on Bernard: Part I', 26. Gerson has this saying in his mystical theology as follows: *in via enim dei non progredi regredi est.* See Günther Metzger, *Gelebter Glaube: Die Formierung reformatorischen Denkens in Luthers erster Psalmenvorlesung, dargestellt am Begriff des Affekts* (Göttingen: Vandenhoeck & Ruprecht, 1964) 193, note 40.

23 See *The Living Webster. Encyclopedic Dictionary of the English Language* (Chicago: The English Language Institute of America, 1977) s. v. 'compunction'. The etymological dictionary of the German Language, *Duden: Etymologie, Herkunftswörterbuch der deutschen Sprache* (Mannheim, Vienna, Zurich: Dudenverlag, 1963) s. v. '*zerknirscht*'. See Jean Leclercq, 'Essais sur L'Estétique de S. Bernard'. *Recueil d'Études sur Saint Bernard et ses Écrits* (Rome: Editioni di Storia e Letteratura, 1987) 4:43–46 (on compunction and humility); Irénée Hausherr, *Penthos: The Doctrine of Compunction in the Christian East,* Anselm Hufstader, trans. (Kalamazoo, 1982); Casey, *Athirst for God,* 120–

prick; the phrase *compunctus notis* means 'to be tattooed'. Thus, the noun *compunctio* has something to do with sting, prick, tattoo, puncture; we may perhaps be allowed to speak here of 'spiritual acupuncture'. The old monks put a high value on the 'tears of compunction' which they considered a divine gift. Compunction in the monastic sense leads the creature to the recognition of its true position before God. Our two great representatives of western spirituality can help us further clarify the meaning of it.

Bernard: Compunction of the heart

Compunctio as a technical monastic term occurs in the Rule of Saint Benedict, which speaks of the 'compunction of tears' and the 'compunction of the heart'.[24] Bernard used the expression 'compunction of tears' in his *On Conversion, A Sermon to Clerics* to describe the initial phase of conversion.[25] In interpreting the Benedictine Rule, Saint Bernard said that humility feeds on the 'bread of sorrow' and drinks the 'wine of compunction'. He used the Vulgate Ps 126:2 and Ps 59:5 in his description of the elementary grade in the 'school of humility' (no. 21) on the path toward the contemplation of the Truth.[26]

The concept of compunction also turned up in Bernard's *On Consideration*, a book Luther greatly appreciated, and therefore we are on safe ground in claiming Luther's familiarity with it. At one point, Bernard spoke of the lack of compunction as part of his definition of a 'hard heart':

No one with a hard heart has ever attained salvation, as the Prophet says, unless God in his mercy has taken from him a heart of stone and given him a heart of flesh (Ez 36:26). Now what is

---

129; Casey, 'Mindfulness of God in the Monastic Tradition', CSQ 17 (1982) 111–26; reprinted in *The Undivided Heart,* 61–77; see Casey on compunction according to Gregory: *The Undivided Heart,* 50–53; M. Basil Pennington, 'Thomas Merton and Byzantine Spirituality', ABR 38 (1987) 263.

24 *The Rule of Saint Benedict,* Adalbert de Vogüé, ed. CS 54 (Kalamazoo: CP, 1983). Terrence Kardong, *The Benedictines* (Wilmington: Michael Glazier, 1988) 84; Casey, 'Saint Benedict's Approach to Prayer'. *The Undivided Heart,* 18–34.

25 See Conv 33, SBOp 4:110–111.

26 See Hum 4, SBOp 3:19,1–21.

a hard heart? One that is not torn by compunction, softened by piety, or moved by entreaty.[27]

Compunction, then, is a means to producing a softened heart, the opposite of the hardened heart; compunction is the precondition of the process of conversion and spiritual healing.

In SC 22 we discover Bernard's monastic concept of compunction interwoven with the theme of justification by faith alone: 'Someone therefore who always suffers compunction because of his sins and hungers and thirsts for righteousness, let him believe in you who justifies the impious (Rom 4:5), and justified by faith alone, he will have peace with God' (Rom 5:1).[28] Luther may have been inspired by this sermon, as he was by Bernard's *First Sermon on the Annunciation*,[29] as we shall see in greater detail in Chapter Two.

At the end of his SC 15, on the name of Jesus, Bernard beautifully summed up his notion of compunction:

> What else is the death of the body than to be deprived of life and feeling? Sin, which is the death of the soul, took from me the feeling of compunction, hushed my prayers of praise; I was dead. Then he who forgives sin came down, restored my senses again and said: 'I am your deliverer' (Ps 34:3). Why wonder that death should yield when he who is life comes down? 'For a man believes with his heart and so is justified, and he confesses with his lips and so is saved' (Rom 10:10).[30]

The monastic concept of compunction was nurtured by the psalm-

27 SBOp 3:396,11–14. On Luther's knowledge of Bernard's Csi, see my article 'Recommendations by Martin Luther of St Bernard's *On Consideration*', CSQ 25 (1990) 25–36. Luther was familiar with Bernard's definition of a 'hard heart', but interestingly Luther regularly deleted the notion of compunction when he referred to the 'hard heart' as he circumscribed it with other words: *Bernardus: 'Durum cor dicitur, quod nec mollitur pietate, non cedit minis, flagellis etiam magis duratur'*, *sicut Iudei*, WA 56:19, 26–27; LW 25:17; see WA 56:192,28–30; LW 25:176; see WA 57-I:23,5–7 (gloss); see WA 43:36,2–3; LW 3:225.

28 SC 22.8; SBOp 1:134, 5–17; CF 7:20.

29 See Franz Posset, '*Bernardus Redivivus:* The *Wirkungsgeschichte* of a Medieval Sermon in the Reformation of the Sixteenth Century', CSQ 22 (1987) 239–249.

30 SC 15.8; SBOp 1:88,11–16; CF 4:112.

ist's strophe: 'O God, do not refuse a humble and contrite heart' (Ps 51:19), which was one of Bernard's favorite lines. We find it whenever he deals with compunction.[31]

Even if Luther had missed, for some reason, all the passages in the sermons on the Song which deal with compunction, he would have encountered it in other texts of Bernard he knew; for instance the section previously mentioned from *On Consideration* about the 'hard heart', or the *First Sermon on the Annunciation* for which Luther had high regard. In the latter, Bernard says after discussing justification by faith and grace alone: 'When a man begins to feel compunction for his sins, that is an effect of the divine mercy by which he is already prevented. But it does not enter his heart until it is met by the truth of his confession. "I have sinned against the Lord" '.[32]

Luther: In and out of the state of compunction

There are no direct references to Bernard's notion of compunction in Luther's works. The concept was probably generally known and thus familiar to the young friar Martin. In his first course on the Psalms, when he lectured on contrition and compunction, the negative result of compunction dominated; he pointed out that those who feel compunction may end up in despair and thus be thrown into hell. Luther's focus on the despairing aspect of compunction was not quite in agreement with the bernardine concept, which always included hope in God's mercy. According to Luther, one could be in and out of the state of compunction, and he admitted that at one particular point he was 'outside compunction' (*extra compunctionem*). Because it was therefore difficult for him to put the experience of compunction adequately into words, it was practically impossible for him to expound on Psalm 77.[33]

31 SC 28.12; SBOp 1:200,22–24; CF 7:99.
32 Ann 1; SBOp 5:3–29.
33 WA 3:169,28–34 (on Ps 31); WA 3:540,9–19 (on Ps 77); WA 3:549,30–33; see also WA 4:88,6–12 (on Ps 93:4) and WA 4:152,25 (on Ps 102:5). Luther used the notion *compunctio* altogether about one hundred times in all of his works, see Vallée, 'Luther and Monastic Theology', 290–97.

4. 'Wall of sensuality'

Bernard: 'Our flesh is the wall'

In SC 56, Bernard dealt with the 'wall' of Sg 2: 9, and with the Bridegroom standing behind it:

> Our flesh is the wall, and the Bridegroom's approach is the incarnation of the Word. The windows and lattices through which he is said to gaze can be understood, I think, as the bodily senses. . . . And for each one of us who desire his coming he also stands behind the wall as long as this body of ours, which is certainly sinful, hides his face from us and shuts out his presence. . . . Not because we are embodied, but because we are in this body which is after all from sin (*de peccato*), and is not without sin. So you may know that it is not our bodies but our sins that stand in the way. . . . How I wish that the body's wall were the only obstacle, that I should suffer only that single barrier of fleshly sin and not the many fences of vice that intervene! I have added a host of sins to that which my nature inherits, and by them I set the Bridegroom at too great a distance from me, so that if I am to speak the truth I must confess that to me he stands not behind a wall but behind walls.[34]

Luther: 'Cursed impediment of the flesh'

Towards the end of his life, in 1543/44, Luther used bernardine and augustinian ideas in his exposition of Is 9. In interpreting the beginning verses of that chapter, he first reminded readers of Saint Paul's utterance in Rom 8:32 and 7:23 that God had given us the Son and that man is such a 'prisoner of the law of sin' that he cannot (even if he wanted to) enjoy the sweetness of the Lord because of the body. At this point Luther introduced Bernard's thoughts from the rather mystical Sermons 31 and 56 on the Canticle. From SC 31, apparently used only this once by him, Luther had learned how Bernard had tasted the sweetness of the Word's visitation to

34 SC 56; SBOp 2:114–16; CF 4:87–94. On the significance of SC 56 ('our flesh is the wall') for cistercian architecture, see Stiegman, 'The Light Imagery of Saint Bernard's Spirituality and Its Evidence in Cistercian Architecture', Elder, ed., *The Joy of Learning,* 367.

the soul. The experience had filled him with incredible joy, but had necessarily to be brief because of the impediment of the flesh.[35] A few lines later, Luther made an explicit reference to the monastic tradition of 'pious monks' who had described this phenomenon of the cursed impediment of the flesh as what he called the 'wall of sensuality'.[36] The older Luther understood this expression clearly as a concept drawn from the monastic tradition and developed in Saint Bernard's sermons.

Even though the sermons do not contain it *expressis verbis*, what Bernard described was aptly summarized by the notion of the 'wall of sensuality'. Not content with referring to this concept once, Luther took it up two more times in the same immediate context. He continued with a quotation from 2 Pt 3:18 about 'growing in grace and in the cognition of the Lord and Saviour Jesus Christ'. Then Luther invited everyone to exercise spiritually and meditate diligently and industriously in order to grow in this cognition toward 'absolute insight' (*absoluta cognitio*), because outside meditation there is no increase in this knowledge. Simply to learn that the Son of God is born for me is not enough, he says, as he repeats that 'this wall of sensuality impedes'. 'But when we are liberated from this wall of sensuality, from this mud and dirt of our flesh, we reach eternal life. . . .'[37]

35 *Bernhardus fatetur . . .* , WA 40-III:652,20–23.

36 WA 40-III:652,24–25. One does not need to seek Luther's respective source in the pseudo-bernardine text *De contemplando deo* (as the index in WA 63:95 suggests, and as Bell's list has it in *Divus Bernhardus,* 386), if one takes Luther's familiarity with SC 31 and SC 56 into serious consideration as we do here. Since Bell, *Divus Bernhardus,* 336, neglected SC 31 (which is not found in his list), he may not have realized that Bernard spoke in SC 31 about the 'various ways of seeing God', which may be the reason for Luther's mention of Bernard having a beautiful view, *visio,* on this subject; see WA 36:6. The monastic concept of the 'wall of sensuality' as used by Luther is discussed in Posset, 'The Elder Luther on Bernard: Part I', ABR 42 (1991) 34–36. Luther spoke of this topic several times during the 1530s (this late date is surprising!), see WA 36:6,2 and 19 (1532); WA 37:474,22–24 and 475,3f (1534). In a table talk of March 1532, Luther said that this wall is like a huge mountain that prevents us from seeing our salvation, WA TR 1:81,1f (no. 178). Luther mentioned Augustine, Bernard, and Bonaventure in one breath. Luther probably quoted *De septem itineribus aeternitatis* (6.5) which was attributed to Bonaventure, but originally written by the franciscan mystic Rudolf of Biberach. See also WA 46:328,4 and 10; WA 46:524 (1538).

37 *Murus ille sensualitatis impedit . . .* , WA 40-III:653,10–23.

Clearly, there is an explicit monastic heritage in this text by the older Luther, but it was lop-sidedly processed. Luther's concept of the 'wall of sensuality' was more pejorative than Bernard's: in Luther's use the emphasis which Saint Bernard had placed on the distinction between 'our bodies' and 'our sins' was deleted. Bernard wanted everyone to realize 'that it is not our bodies but our sins that stand in the way'. Luther dropped this significant distinction (at least here). As a result, man's entire bodily existence appeared to him as sinful flesh, mud, and dirt. Luther's concept of flesh and sin is complex and needs further clarification which cannot be attempted here. But it seems fairly obvious that the two theologians differed in their concept of sin and flesh; they seem identical only if one disregards Bernard's cautiousness. What Luther picked up here from the monastic tradition was a concept of man's bodily existence which over the centuries had taken on a pejorative overtone not found in Bernard's original sermon. On this particular point it appears that Luther relied more on the later monastic tradition, which coined the term of the 'wall of sensuality', than he did on the original texts of Bernard's sermons, where the phrase does not occur.

5. *Penance*

Bernard: 'No need of penance'?

According to liturgical tradition, the season of Advent is a time of penance. It was quite natural that Bernard would preach about penance then, as he did in his second sermon *In vigilia nativitatis*:

> Whoever, therefore, does not ardently desire penance appears by his actions to be saying either that he has no need of penance, in which case he does not confess his fault, or that penance can be of no use to him, in which case he does not acknowledge the goodness of God.[38]

38 V Nat 2; SBOp 4:204,8–11.

Luther: 'He who does not constantly hasten to repentence . . .'

A reference to Bernard on penance shows up in Luther's first Psalm lectures: 'He who does not constantly hasten to repentance declares in deed that he does not need repentance'.[39] It emerged again in his interpretation of Rom 13:11, during his famous lectures on the *Letter to the Romans* in 1515/16, when he cited the beginning of this bernardine phrase and summarized the rest.[40]

6. *Tears of Devotion*

Bernard: 'Tears of devotion'

Bernard's affective monastic spirituality never confused 'tears of devotion' with tears of compunction. The former are sweet and stem from meditation on God's benevolence and sweetness.[41] They well up when the spirit of adoption descends into one's heart and when the Holy Spirit gives testimony to the human heart that one is a child of God. Bernard talked about these tears in his third sermon for Epiphany: 'These are the tears of devotion in which not the forgiveness of sins, but the benevolence of God the Father is being sought, as the spirit of adoption as sons descends into us, giving testimony to our spirit that we are sons of God'.[42]

Luther: 'Tears of devotion and hope'

Luther was familiar with this affective spirituality and he specifically mentioned Bernard as experienced in this area, along with Bonaventure and Hugh of Saint Victor. To Luther it was incredible how 'refreshing for the soul are the tears of devotion

---

39 WA 55-II:119,8–10; LW 10:106. Both, the critical edition WA and the american translation LW, indicate a wrong source reference by referring to a non-existing sermon *in virg nativ serm 2*; there is only one sermon on the birth of the Virgin, the famous 'aqueduct' sermon; the correct reference is to the second Christmas Eve sermon: V Nat 2; SBOp 4:204,8–11.

40 WA 56:486,1–2; LW 25:478 (on Rom).

41 See Leclercq, *The Love of Learning,* 58f; McGuire, *The Difficult Saint,* 133–51 (on Monks and Tears).

42 *Lacrimae devotionis*, Epi 3.8; SBOp 4:309,13f.

and hope', of which these experts spoke.[43] Luther added 'hope' to Bernard's expression as a legitimate amplification, because this monastic piety is hope-filled (and thus also faith-filled); these tears are signs not of sadness, but of hope-filled desire to enjoy some day the sweetness of God.[44]

When Luther lectured on the Vulgate expression *gustate* (taste) in Psalm 33:9, and about tasting the sweetness of the Lord, he observed that it was Bernard who had indeed experienced the sweetness of the Lord. 'If someone had Bernard's soul', Luther said, he would well 'taste' the meaning of this particular verse.[45] We will return to this topic at the end of Chapter One.

7. 'On Precept and Dispensation'

Bernard: Writing for benedictine monks

In the fall of 1521, when he was hidden at the Wartburg Castle incognito and when several fellow friars left their cloister at Wittenberg, Luther began to rethink the theological foundations of the monastic vows. He mentioned this in a letter to Philip Melanchthon: 'For he who is free can, just like the Apostle Paul, submit himself to all laws, and to the dominion of all men, in the same way in which Saint Bernard and others who were monks in the truest sense of the word surrendered themselves to [living under] a vow'.[46]

Perhaps the example of Bernard made Luther hesitant to break his vows. It took him several years to make up his mind. This

43 *Incredibile enim est, quantum reficiant animam lachryme deuotionis et spei, vt dicunt experti Bernardus, Bonauentura, Hugo,* WA 55-I:352 (WA 3:233, 22f). Bell, *Divus Bernhardus,* 57 has a more convincing source reference: *Hae sunt lacrimae devotionis . . .* (Epi 3.8; SBOp 4:309,13) than what the new *Dictata* edition (1993) indicates with SC 18.5 and SC 30.3 ['penitential tears'], WA 55-I:353.

44 See Leclercq, *The Love of Learning,* 58f.

45 WA 55-I:301 (WA 3:186,34).

46 WA Br 2:383,29–30 (no. 428; September 9, 1521, to Melanchthon); LW 48:298. See Bernhard Lohse, 'Die Kritik am Mönchtum bei Luther und Melanchthon'. *Evangelium in der Geschichte. Studien zu Luther und der Reformation* (Göttingen: Vandenhoeck & Ruprecht, 1988) 94; see Bell, *Divus Bernhardus,* 201.

rethinking led to a publication in Latin (*De votis monasticis*) in February 1522. He had no immediate intention of leaving the religious state, even though his confrères in the Order of Saint Augustine decided at a chapter meeting early in 1522 to let every member go who so wished. Luther did not leave the religious life behind until he married in 1525. From his personal experience as an obedient friar and later as a subprior and district vicar of ten friaries, Luther was familiar with problems of interpreting monastic rules and relationships between superior and subordinate. From an expert's background, he evaluated the vows, and in doing so he drew on Bernard, saying that the cistercian abbot 'asserts that a monk is not obliged to be obedient to his abbot if he commands him other than his rule allows'. And he quite agreed with Bernard 'that man is saved by faith'. 'We can see the divine work in Bernard and men like him'. Luther complained that 'nobody vows to live in the spirit in which Bernard lived'. 'If there were men of Bernard's caliber in the monasteries they could be tolerated. . . .' In this connection, Luther quoted 1 Tim 4:16, 'Watch yourself and watch your teaching. . . . By doing so you will bring to salvation yourself and all who hear you'.[47]

It should therefore come as no surprise that Luther's critical appraisal of the religious vows was influenced by Bernard's book *On Precept and Dispensation*, even though Luther would not have read the original and not in its entirety, but in mediated form, perhaps by way of ideas taken from Jean Gerson. Bernard had written it for the benedictine monks at Chartres, to answer a question about the power of an abbot and the monks' freedom of conscience. Here is what Luther had to say on this issue:

> It is everywhere agreed that Bernard, in his book *On Dispensation* argues that every part of the rule is in the hands of the superior, who may grant dispensation to those set under him, not only if it is impossible or if a danger arises, but even if in his judgment it seems appropriate or convenient. This means that

---

47 WA 8:622,28–32; see WA 8:612,27–30; Bernard was under the vows without the vows: *sub voto sine voto,* WA 8:617,32; see Bell, *Divus Bernhardus,* 216–219.

these particular rules sometimes hold good and sometimes do not hold good.[48]

Luther had in mind the section where Bernard wrote on charity as the norm for all decisions. An abbot is not above the Rule, he argued, for he himself once freely placed himself under it. There is only one power which we admit above the Rule of Saint Benedict, and that is God's rule, charity. The freedom of the superior is further circumscribed in that the subject promised not unqualified obedience, but specifically obedience according to a Rule, and no Rule other than that of Saint Benedict. If, once one had made such profession, the abbot attempted to impose something which was not according to the benedictine Rule, and also not in accord with the Rules of Saints Basil, Augustine, or Pachomius, did one have to conform, he asked; and he responded: 'I can be obliged to perform only that which I have promised'.

In addition to Luther's use of the bernardine interpretation of the vows, we find a phrase from the conclusion of that same treatise already in his earlier lectures on Romans and on Hebrews. It is a proverbial phrase which occurred as he dealt with Saint Paul's words of Phil 3:20, 'Our conversation is in heaven', and of 2 Cor 5:6, 'So long as we remain in the body, we are exiled from the Lord'. Saint Bernard declared:

> One may also connect the words 'Our conversation is in heaven', with that other saying of the Apostle, 'We are saved by hope' (Phil 3:20). Therefore it is hope which allows us to dwell already in heaven, while our bodies are yet in exile. Again one might say that we are bound partly to our bodies and partly to the Lord: bound to our bodies by bonds of life and feeling, and bound to the Lord by faith and love. Yes, love, for *the soul is*

48 See *De votis monasticis Martini Lutheri iudicium*, WA 8:573–669, with the direct reference to Bernard's Pre 9 and 10 in WA 8:634,1–5; LW 44:343; SBOp 3:243–295 (no. 9–10). Still other references to Bernard are found in WA 8:586,18–19; 600,26–29; 601,20–24; 628,24–25; 640,32–33. Luther's further statement on Bernard: *Sanctus Bernhardus et quicunque sancti religiosi vota sua libere servaverunt*, WA 8:331,13–15 (*Themata de votis*, 1521). See Bernhard Lohse, *Mönchtum und Reformation: Luthers Auseinandersetzung mit dem Mönchsideal des Mittelalters* (Göttingen: Vandenhoeck and Ruprecht, 1963) 356–362; see Bell, *Divus Bernhardus*, 200–238.

not more present where it animates than where it loves, unless perhaps unwilling necessity is considered a stronger bond than free and ardent choice. Indeed, 'Where your treasure is, there also is your heart'.[49]

Luther: 'The soul is not more present where it animates than where it loves'

Luther was fascinated with the idea that the soul abides no less in what it loves than in what it animates. He was, however, unaware that he quoted this line from Bernard. This likely indicates that he had not read the original, but took his insights from secondary literature. Evidently, Luther trusted a tradition which attributed this utterance to Augustine, as did Tauler, whom Luther esteemed highly. In his Lectures on Romans, Luther quoted the phrase freely (if not directly) by sayings, 'the soul is more where it loves than where it animates',[50] leaving the word-play on the latin *animare*

49 *Neque enim praesentior spiritus noster est ubi animat, quam ubi amat*, Pre 60; SBOp 3:292, 24–25.

50 *Secundum illud B. Augustini: 'Anima plus est, Vbi amat, quam vbi animat'* (Lecture on Rom), WA 56:374,10f (with note), where the point is made that Tauler thought of this phrase as originating from Augustine. See WA 57-I:192,12f, where the phrase *anima plus est . . .* is taken as Augustine's and interpreted with Mt 6: *Ubi est thezaurus tuus, ibi et cor tuum erit.* See Bell, *Divus Bernhardus,* 91 and 333. Luther always quoted the phrase in latin, using *anima* or the bernardine *animus* (see below, WA 43:184,4), although the phrase was handed down also in the vernacular by Tauler and Rudolf von Biberach. In one of the sermons of Meister Eckhart this line was quoted as an augustinian sentence: 'Saint Augustine says: "When the soul loves, it is more properly itself than when it gives life" '. I follow the translation in *Light from Light: An Anthology of Christian Mysticism*, Louis Dupre and James A. Wiseman, eds. (New York and Mahwah: Paulist Press, 1988) 157 with note 2. The Dominicans, Eckhart and Tauler, thought of the sentence as an augustinian one. The english hermit and mystic Richard Rolle also used the phrase, but without any source reference, see 'The Love of God'. *The Cell of Self-knowledge: Early English Mystical Treatises*, John Griffiths, ed. (New York: Crossroad, 1981) 114. The Franciscan Rudolf von Biberach (living in the first half of the fourteenth century; Pseudo-Bonaventure) gave the correct source reference: *Sicut dicit Bernardus: 'Non est praesentior noster spiritus ubi animat, quam ubi amat'*, *S. Bonaventurae Opera omnia* (Paris 1864–1871) 8:447. The Augustinian Johann von Paltz (+1511) attributed it to Hugh of Saint Victor: . . . *quia anima secundum Hugonem de Sancto Victore ibi plus est ubi amat, quam ubi animat, Coelifodina* 1:132,9–10, as it has a remote resemblance to Hugh, PL 176:970B. The Augustinian Johann von Altenstaig (Luther's contemporary) mentioned it in his theological dictionary as Augustine's adage under the entry *'voluntas'*, *Lexikon theologicum* (Cologne 1619, reprint: Hildesheim and New York: Olms, 1974). Luther may have followed his confrère Altenstaig in this.

(to animate) and *amare* (to love) intact. In his Lectures on Hebrews Luther also quoted this line, but without mentioning any author's name.[51] Even as late as his last Lectures on Genesis (on Gen 21:19), Luther remembered this saying. Quoting a character in a comedy by Terence as saying that he is so angry he cannot apply his mind to thinking, Luther continued, still believing he quoted Augustine, 'But if anger upsets the mind to this extent, what would be the effect of the stupor and the distractions which an awareness of God's anger and of eternal damnation brings with it? "The heart", says Augustine, "is where it loves rather than where it lives".'[52]

When we add up these echoes of originally bernardine proverbial sayings, which he thought to be augustinian, Luther appears to have been even more influenced by Bernard than he himself realized.

8. *On prayer*

Bernard makes a wager
In *The Golden Legend* we read the following story about Bernard and a 'countryman' making a bet about attentiveness at prayer:

> Once when blessed Bernard was riding along a road, he met a countryman, to whom he spoke sadly about a matter that was on his mind, namely, the instability of the human heart at prayer. The peasant, hearing this, immediately formed a low opinion of him and said that in his own prayer he always kept his heart firm and stable. Bernard wished to change the man's mind and temper his bold overconfidence, so he said to him: 'Go aside a little way, and, with all the attention you can bring to it, begin to pray the Lord's Prayer; and if you are able to finish it without any distraction or wandering of the heart, the beast I'm riding will be yours without doubt or question. But you must give me your word that if any other thought come

---

51 WA 57-III:215,9f (on Heb 9:23) without mention of any name).

52 *Animus, inquit Augustinus, magis est, ubi amat, quam ubi animat*, WA 43:184, 4. In 1540, in the printed version of the exposition of the Gradual Psalm 130, the aging Reformer again referred to this proverbial saying, WA 40-III:354,22–24.

Plate 6: *Bernard and a Rustic Make a Wager on Attentive Prayer.* Sixteenth-century glass window, originally from the cistercian monastery of Altenberg, Germany; today at Saint Mary's Church, Shrewsbury, England.

to you, you won't hide it from me'. Happy with the offer, and
feeling that he already owned the animal, the man withdrew,
recollected himself, and began to recite the Our Father. He was
not halfway through the prayer when a distracting thought stole
into his heart: 'The saddle . . . will I get the saddle with the
mount or not?' Becoming aware of his distraction, he hurried
back to Bernard, told him the selfish thought that had come to
him as he prayed, and from then on was not so rashly sure of
himself.[53]

This story must have been popular at the beginning of the
sixteenth century, when it was depicted in a glass window of
the cistercian monastery at Altenberg (Plate 6), part of a series
of sixty-eight windows illustrating the life of Saint Bernard. For
some unknown reason, this particular window ended up in the
north window of Saint Mary's Church at Shrewsbury, England; it
is one of the very rare iconographic witnesses to this story. The
latin caption in the window is taken straight out of the *Legenda
aurea*: 'Once when blessed Bernard was riding along a road, he
met a countryman . . .'. The banderole issuing from the rustic's
mouth paraphrases the latin words of the legend: 'I always have
a heart firm and stable . . .'. Bernard's words to the peasant are
found in the four lines of the inscription close to the saint's head:
'Go aside a little way, and, with all the attention you can bring to
it, begin to pray the Lord's Prayer; and if you can finish it without
any distraction or wandering of the heart, the beast I'm riding
will be yours without doubt or question'. The window shows the
moment the bet was struck; both men are ready to shake hands,
Bernard still riding his horse. In the upper right corner we see
the peasant kneeling, trying to pray attentively. The latin text of
his attempt at prayer plays with the words *in caelis* (in heaven)
and *sella* (saddle) by contracting both into *in cellis* (in the storage
room), thus producing a confused prayer: 'Our Father that I will
have who art in the storage room (saddle)'.[54]

---

53 *Legenda aurea*, 534f; *The Golden Legend,* 473; Ryan 104.
54 See Paffrath, *Bernhard von Clairvaux* (1984), 211f, illustration 62, and
note 579, which includes the latin captions and banderoles in transcription. The
confused prayer text reads as follows in latin: *Pater noster (utique habebo), qui*

Luther and this lore

This story surfaced three times in Luther's later career. First, Luther made a brief but distinct reference to it in his sermon on Jn 16 of 6 May 1526, saying: 'As Saint Bernard [has it] who said that he himself never prayed the *Pater Noster* without another thought entering his mind'. Apparently, Luther found this story helpful in conveying his message about the difficulties with attentive prayer. It emerged again in Luther's sermon of 8 August 1528.[55] Here Luther revealed himself as an expert on prayer and a great orator who appreciated a good story and knew how to use it. Evidently he did not mind at all that his source was a legend. On the contrary, the experienced preacher and teacher even went so far as to write (in his preface to a new edition of pious stories published by his friend Lazarus Spengler) that 'next to the Bible there is not a more useful book than the legends, if they are pure and upright'.[56] This condition was obviously met by the story about Saint Bernard as it was handed down in *The Golden Legend*. A third time Luther found this story helpful in commenting on Isaac's prayer (Gen 25:20) during his last great exegetical project, his lectures on Genesis: 'A prayer of this kind is praised in the case of the man who had made a bet with Bernard that he would say the Lord's Prayer without any wandering thoughts'.[57] Luther liked not only this story, but also another statement on prayer Bernard made in a lenten sermon; to this we turn our attention now.

Bernard: Prayer 'is written in His book'

One other aspect in Bernard's teaching on prayer fascinated Luther, and this is connected to Mk 11:24, 'I give you my word, if you are ready to believe that you will receive whatever you ask

---

es in cellis (sellam). Paffrath 212 has the differing opinion that the window would show the moment when the boor returned to Bernard to tell him what thoughts came to his mind while he was praying. But this interpretation would conflict with the words given in the banderoles which assume the beginning and not the conclusion of the story.

55 WA 20:380,1f (1526), and WA 38:313,1–19 (1535).

56 WA 28:77,4–6 and 12–14 (1528). On L. Spengler, see Berndt Hamm, *Lazarus Spengler: Schriften* (Gütersloh: Gütersloher Verlagshaus, 1995).

57 See WA 43:382,30–34; LW 4:342 has a deluding reference to Bernard. See Posset, 'The Elder Luther on Bernard: Part II', 186; see Bell, *Divus Bernhardus,* 307. The index in WA 63:98 listed it as unidentified.

for in prayer, it shall be done for you'. On the basis of this text, Bernard advised his brethren not to consider their prayer worthless precisely because God to whom the prayer is directed does not hold it in low esteem: 'Before it [prayer] has left our mouth, he himself commands that it be written in his book'.[58]

Luther: 'Saint Bernard . . . admonishes . . . not to despise their prayers'

This bernardine idea became one of Luther's favorite references, although the Reformer was mistaken about its origin. He opined he had read it in one of the sermons on the Song of Songs, as he indicated in his lecture on Heb 9:24 in 1517/18. In fact, he paraphrased Bernard's lenten sermon:

> Saint Bernard somewhere in a sermon on the Song of Songs admonishes his brothers not to despise their prayers in any way but to believe that they are written and have been written in heaven before they are completed, and that they should expect with the greatest certainty that their wish, namely, that their prayers, have either been heard and are to be fulfilled in their own good time or that it is better if they are not fulfilled.[59]

The content of Luther's reference points unmistakably to Bernard's lenten sermon and not to any of his sermons on the Song of Songs, which do not contain an equivalent passage. Bernard's concept of prayer was so much an element of Luther's thought that in later years he brought it to the attention of his readers. In 1520 Luther clarified his position on 'good works' in the treatise of this name. In it the Reformer included his thoughts on prayers, and in this context he mentioned Bernard's phrase in the lenten sermon: 'We should pray not as we do now, by turning over many pages and counting many beads'. Instead, people should exercise their faith and put their confidence in God along the lines of Bernard's teaching on prayer:

58 Quad 5; SBOp 4:374,22–375,4.
59 *Inde beatus Bernhardus . . .* , WA 57-III:216,16–19; LW 29:218.

This is how Saint Bernard instructs his brethren and says: 'Dear brethren, you shall by no means despise your prayer as if it were in vain, for indeed I tell you that before you have uttered the words, the prayer is already written in heaven; and you shall confidently expect from God one of two things: either that your prayer will be granted, or that if it is not granted this is because to fulfil it would not have been a good and useful thing'.[60]

In addition to the passage just quoted from the *Treatise on Good Works*, Luther spoke of Bernard's notion of prayer in his course on John's first epistle in 1527. As he expounded on 1 Jn 5:14 (prayer for sinners) Luther declared in the spirit of Bernard:

I have prayed and I know you have heard me; you will give, when, where, and through whom you want, and in a better way than I ask for, because some ask for life and he gives something better. . . . Bernard [says]: 'Be not contempt of prayers because whenever you pray, it is written down in heaven'. Our prayers should not be held in contempt because neither God nor his angels despise the Church; they [prayers] are ordered by God, therefore they please him.[61]

Here Luther integrated into his lecture what he had learned from Bernard. And while he was elaborating on his own personal prayer life and experience, he was reminded of the verse in Is 65:24 ('before they call, I will answer'), which helped him to expound the text of 1 Jn 5:14.[62] The same associations of thought occurred some time later, when Luther arrived at the same verse, Is 65:24, in his commentary on this prophet (1527–1530). Here again he introduced the bernardine teaching on prayer. He called this verse 'the most beautiful promise' because it is a most necessary promise and stimulates our hearts to pray. Luther saw Saint John as an interpreter of this verse from Isaiah; by this he probably meant

60 *Also leret sanct Bernhardt seine bruder,* WA 6:232,16–21; LW 44:58.
61 See WA 20:793,6–16.
62 See WA 20:794,5. Bernard, too, referred to Is 65:24 in one of his sermons: *De Diversis*; SBOp 6–1:380,25–381,1.

1 Jn 5:14 which he saw in relation to the prophetic text.[63] Here one can see the 'energy' of prayer, according to Luther. Human beings tend to forget that prayers are written down in God's sight before they are even uttered. The prayer of the just person is heard before it is finished. Luther added to his exposition of the prophetic text Bernard's admonition to his brethren that they should know that prayers are written down in heaven. If what one asks is not granted, then it is not good for the person praying. At this point, the Reformer exclaimed: 'This statement of Bernard comes from the Holy Spirit'.[64] In his course on Isaiah Luther spoke about the *energia* of prayer, and the stenographer of these lectures wrote on the margin that this idea stemmed from Saint Bernard: *dictum Bernhardi de oracionis energia.*[65]

In his interpretation of Ps 130:4, written down in 1532/ 1533, Luther praised the praying and trusting Bernard as a 'beautiful teacher' who ascribed everything to Christ.[66] In his sermon of 16 August 1534, Luther again presented to his audience the typical bernardine idea about our prayers being recorded in heaven.[67] In a table talk of October 1538, Luther brought up Bernard's view on prayer yet again.[68] In Luther's german sermons on Jn 16, delivered about the same time as the table talk was recorded, Bernard's insight on prayer was mentioned twice. First, the Reformer corroborated the abbot's teaching from his own personal experience. He observed that Bernard was taking great pains in admonishing his people that they not go to church with doubts about their prayers to God.[69] Later, he repeated his praise of Bernard's advice by calling him 'a fine man' who has had 'christian thoughts' in telling his

63 WA 31-II:566,6–9. The editors of WA do not take the reference to 1 Jn 5:14 into account; in their marginal note at this place they suspect Luther is referring perhaps to Jn 15: 7. See WA 46:79,15–20; 86,34–39.

64 *Haec sentencia Bernhardi est ex spiritu sancto*, WA 31- II:566,30f; LW 17:393; see WA 25:390,10–17.

65 WA 31-II:566, note to line 27–28.

66 WA 40-III:354,3–5 (stenographer's notes); 354,16–24 (printed version, 1540).

67 WA 59:306,37 (sermon of August 16, 1534).

68 WA TR 4:119,1–3 (no. 4076).

69 See WA 46:79,15–20; LW 24:386. See Bach, 'Bernhard von Clairvaux und Martin Luther', 40f; see Soeur Eva, 'La prière chez Luther', Coll 45 (1983) 303–316; see Posset, 'The Elder Luther on Bernard: Part II', 182–86.

brethren to have no doubts when they pray, because 'as soon as one begins to pray, the individual words are already counted and written down in heaven'.[70]

While the ageing Luther was working on his commentary on Genesis, Saint Bernard's teaching on prayer surfaced again. In the context of Gen 19:21f, Lot praying to the Lord, Luther introduced it: 'Therefore Bernard admonishes his brothers not to esteem their prayers lightly but to know that their prayers are written in heaven before they themselves have finished them. The holy man observed the faint-heartedness in praying with which we all are commonly plagued'.[71] Luther mentioned Bernard's teaching as well when he expounded Gen 24, the chapter in which Abraham's servant prays for a favorable outcome of his search for a potential wife for Isaac: 'Thus in one place Bernard has stated excellently that as soon as you begin to pray, your prayer is read and written down at once in the presence of the Divine Majesty.[72]

Not only in edifying sermons and expositions did Luther draw on the venerated teacher's insights, but also in an academic disputation. On 28 February 1540, Luther compared the praying Bernard with the apostles Peter and Paul. Prior to saying that, however, in speaking about the correct interpretation of the church fathers, Luther passed one of his severest judgments on his otherwise beloved Bernard: that at times he talked 'just as if he were a heretic'.[73] Luther hastened to mitigate his criticism by adding his admiration for Bernard, saying that when Bernard was 'speaking with God', he may be compared to the apostles Peter and Paul. Luther's fascination with Bernard's prayer life overrode his criticism.

Our review of Luther's references to Bernard's understanding of prayer leads to this conclusion: the Reformer became demonstrably aware of texts on Bernard's prayer life during his Lectures on Hebrews (1517/18), and again in his reformational writing on good

70 *Darumb ist S. Bernhard des halb ein feiner man gewest,* WA 46:86, 34–39; LW 24:395. (= SBOp 4:374,22–375,4).

71 WA 43:83,30–33; LW 3:291.

72 WA 43:326f; LW 4:67; see Bell, *Divus Bernhardus,* 201f.

73 *Sic Bernhardus aliquando incommodissime et impropriissime loquitur, ac si esset haereticus . . . ,* WA 39-II:112,4f.

works (1520), i. e. at the high point of his challenges to the Church. In the following years, Luther did not hesitate to refer repeatedly to the medieval saint in this regard. Especially after 1526, he made use of Bernard's idea from the lenten sermon and from *The Golden Legend*, as can be adduced from his lectures and sermons on both the Old Testament and New, namely on John, Isaiah, Psalm 130, and Genesis. Not only in lectures and in a disputation, but also in preaching and in conversation at table Bernard's teaching on prayer was present to Luther's mind, and he was always ready to burst into praise of Bernard, the 'fine man', the 'holy man', the 'wonderful man', or the 'beautiful teacher'.

9. *Warped soul – Warped man*

Bernard and Luther were intimate with the Word of God in Scripture. It is no surprise then that biblical concepts emerge in similar ways in the works of both theologians. One such concept is the curvedness of the soul, which both discuss in relation to sin and freedom of the will. It is worth our while to reflect on it, even though we were unable to find any texts in which Luther referred to Bernard in this regard.

Bernard: 'Bent out of shape' (*anima curva*)

According to Bernard human freedom of choice (*libertas*) is held captive because of human existence under flesh and spirit, under inherited original sin. Christ is the only one who by his grace can set the human's will in order, i. e. to straighten a soul 'bent out of shape' into a soul 'in shape,' or 'shaped' into the form it was originally intended to have by its Creator. This imagery of the soul is rooted in biblical language. The psalmist (in the Vulgate version) speaks of being 'warped' (*curvatus*), bent out of shape. In Ps 38:7, in the prayer of an afflicted sinner we find: 'I am stooped and bowed down to the earth, all day I go in sadness'. This psalm lies behind the concept of 'man bent out of shape' (*homo curvatus*) of whom Bernard spoke in terms of 'soul out of shape' (*anima curva*).

Meditation on Sg 1:3 inspired Bernard to speak about the upright and the warped soul. His latin bible text gave him the verse in the following version: 'The righteous love you'; modern translations render it as 'the maidens love you'. Therefore, the medieval preacher, who did not question his latin text, preached about 'the righteous' in his Sermon 24; 'spiritual righteousness' is meant here, not physical perfection of the body. The soul is created upright (*rectus*) by God, who formed everyone to his own image and likeness (Gen 1:26), and God is *rectus*, righteous. There is no wrong in him—here Bernard is borrowing words from Ps 92:16. God made man righteous like himself, without iniquity. Then the mellifluous teacher makes a statement perhaps surprising to some people: 'Iniquity is a fault in the heart, not in the flesh'.[74] Evil stems not from the body but from the human heart from which a 'pestilent virus' comes forth.[75] According to Bernard, the likeness of God is to be restored in the human *spirit*, 'not in his body of gross clay'. God gave man an upright body so that this bodily uprightness might prompt the soul to cherish spiritual uprightness. The beauty of the body may rebuke the warped mind/soul. The great rhetorician cast this thought into the form of a dispute between the body and the soul. The body in rectitude tells the soul to be ashamed of herself. The upright body reprimands the soul by saying:

> Look on me, my soul, and blush for shame. . . . Blush that despite your heavenly origin you now wallow in filth. Created upright and in your Creator's likeness, you received me as a helper like to yourself, at least in bodily uprightness. . . . Now, every help you received from me you have turned into disgrace: you abused my subordination to you, you dwell unworthily in this human body, you are a brutish and bestial spirit. Those whose souls are warped (*animae curvae*) in this way cannot love the Bridegroom.[76]

Souls bent out of shape cannot be the Bridegroom's girlfriends because they belong to the world. Their worldliness makes them

---

74 *Deus hominem rectum fecit*, SC 24.5; SBOp 1:56,13; CF 7:46. See SBOp 1:157,1–9. See Casey, *Athirst*, 145 and 207, and his most informative footnote 8 on the notion *anima* (67f). See Sommerfeldt, *The Spiritual Teachings*, 3–41.

75 *Pestiferum virus*; see Bernhard Stoeckle, 'Amor carnis – abusus amoris: Das Verständnis von der Kupiszenz bei Bernhard von Clairvaux und Alred von Rieval', *Analecta Monastica* 7, SAn 54 (Rome: Herder, 1965) 147–74.

76 *Curvae animae*, SC 24.6f; SBOp 1:158,4–159,9; CF 7:47.

bent over to the ground; in their curvedness (*curvitas*) they seek and taste what is on the ground, while uprightness (*rectitudo*) means meditating on and desiring what is above.

The concept of the 'warped soul' was also woven into SC 80, a philosophical, theological, and philological tract on God's righteousness/ uprightness. Only indirectly relating his sermon to the text of Sg 3:1, the preacher hammered against what he considered the heretical speculations of Gilbert of Poitiers. He defended the catholic doctrine of God by calling on Augustine, Boethius, Fulgentius, and the Council of Reims, which failed in 1148 to silence the bishop of Poitiers. After having complained about the difficulty of penetrating the 'obscurity of these allegories', he attempted to explain the 'moral meaning' of the text. He started with the creation of man made in God's image, and with Christ as the Image of God. The Image, the Word, is righteousness from righteousness, wisdom from wisdom, truth from truth, and (in an allusion to the Creed) God from God. In contrast, the soul is none of these, for it is not the Image. It is capable of them and yearns for them. The capacity for the eternal is there, but the soul clings to earthly things and is bent down, out of shape. These souls are not upright, but are curved by sin. It is at this point of his sermon that Bernard brings in the image from Psalm 38:7, 'I am warped' (*curvatus sum*).[77]

Using this verse the gifted speaker developed his theological insights into God's righteousness and human likeness to God. Bernard unfolded the psalm verse 38:7 in his own rhetorical style. He showed human iniquity not as 'carnal' but as 'cordial', stemming not from the flesh (*caro*) but from the heart (*cor*). He presented the human spirit as brutish (*brutus*) and beastial (*bestialis*) while living in the body. The soul is totally bent out of shape by the sins which come from the heart. The curvature of the soul is

---

77 *Anima . . . capax aeternorum . . . non plane recta, sed curva. . . .'Miser factus sum et curvatus sum usque in finem, tota die contristatus ingrediebar'* (Ps 38:7), SC 80.3; SBOp 2:279,3–280,1; CF 40:148. See M. Pia Schindele, 'Rectitudo und Puritas. Die Bedeutung beider Begriffe in den Gründungsdokumenten von Cîteaux und ihre Auswirkungen in der Lehre des hl. Bernhard von Clairvaux', *Zisterziensische Spiritualität*, 53–73, here 62. Bernard employed this concept, *anima curva,* in a similar way also in his letter to the Carthusians: Ep 11.5; SBOp 7:56,14f.

understood as a curvature into oneself, a sort of 'narcissism'. The man sighs, bent into himself, under his own willfulness.[78]

Luther: 'Curved onto himself' (*homo curvatus*)

This concept of sinfulness as curvature into oneself especially impressed Luther. One expert on the history of christian spirituality opines that *homo curvatus* is a classic concept in the history of christian mysticism and is found in such writers as Augustine, Bernard, and Luther.[79] Here we have described only Bernard's view of the *anima curva*. This is not the place to scrutinize Augustine's concept, but it is important to find out how the augustinian friar Martin Luther handled the biblical notion.

As a Scripture professor Luther was, of course, familiar with the biblical anthropology which views human being as 'bent out of shape'. In his first course on the Psalms he spoke of it in connection with the gospel message of the cross, and from this gospel viewpoint distinctions in regard to 'sin' become less important; even the doctrinal differentiation between original sin and actual sin looses significance for Luther. The Reformer picked up this concept of man curved into himself in his lecture on Rom 8:3, 'The law was powerless because of its weakening by the flesh. Then God sent his Son in the likeness of sinful flesh as a sin offering, thereby condemning sin in the flesh'. Lecturing that the Scriptures clearly speak of man bent out of shape to the degree that he inflects into himself not only corporal but also spiritual goods, and that in everything he seeks himself, Luther does not give any precise biblical references, but appears to draw a general conclusion from his Bible studies. When one examines the latin text of Luther's lectures, one cannot fail to notice that, unlike Bernard who balanced uprightness and curvedness and taught about the soul's capacity for the eternal, Luther stressed only one aspect: man is warped,

78 See Bernardin Schellenberger, 'Bernhard von Clairvaux'. *Grosse Mystiker: Leben und Wirken*, Gerhard Ruhbach and Josef Sudbrack, eds. (Munich: Beck, 1984) 114f.

79 See Josef Sudbrack, 'Christliche Mystik – Vorüberlegungen'. *Grosse Mystiker*, 9; see Walther von Loewenich, *Martin Luther: Der Mann und das Werk* (Munich: List, 1982) 70, where the author declared that Luther identified *concupiscentia* and egotism with original sin.

curved toward himself in a narcissistic way: *incurvatus in se*.[80] Luther, used a biblical and bernardine concept, but gave it his own lop-sided emphasis.

Bernard also spoke of willfulness, *propria voluntas*, in contrast to *communis voluntas*, which is charity.[81] Self-centredness is the essence of the *curvatio* of the warped soul. In this regard Bernard and Luther thought alike. According to Bernard, we remember, evil stems not from the body, but from the heart. This idea may also have rubbed off on Luther. In his lecture on 1 Jn 1:10, he spoke of human beings as carrying 'a monster in our flesh',[82] which may echo the bernardine *brutus* and *bestialis spiritus*. In the context of this johannine lecture, Luther declared that we are weakened, not only by fleshly sins, not only by the fervor of *libido*, wrath, false wisdom, but also by the carnal affect which flees hope and faith; and that we are always inclined to wrath, which is a graver sin than any in the flesh. Furthermore, he said, people have the tendency to seek a remedy on their own, while only the Word of God provides real medicine. Luther claimed that only a few of the church fathers reported those more sublime forces of sin. And one of Luther's students indicated in his lecture notes that here Luther was referring to Bernard.[83] From the fact that Bernard's name came up in this context one may assume that he had Bernard's teaching in mind.

It is not unlikely that Luther was thinking of Bernard's SC 82, where the abbot reflected on whether man resembles more God or a beast (even though one cannot demonstrate that Luther had actually read this sermon). Certain passages of Scripture seem to say that God's image in man is destroyed by sin, while the tradition held that it must be regarded as darkened and confused. The biblical

---

80 *Et hoc consonat Scripturae, Quae hominem describit incurvatum in se adeo,* WA 56:356,4–6. See George Yule, *Luther: Theologian for Catholics and Protestants,* 9. In regard to Luther's use of this notion in his first lectures on the Psalms, see Metzger, *Gelebter Glaube,* 149f, where unfortunately the author did not make any connection to Bernard whatsoever. He was occupied with showing the contrast or the relationship between Augustine, Peter Lombard, Biel, and Luther.

81 Res 2.8; SBOp 5:98,19–24.

82 *Monstrum portamus in carne nostra,* WA 20:628,16 (on 1 Jn).

83 See Probst's notes, WA 20:628.

references Bernard had in mind were Psalm 49, verses 13 and 21, 'Man, for all his splendor, if he has no prudence, resembles the beasts', and Psalm 105:20, 'They changed their glory into the likeness of a calf who eats hay'.[84] The metaphor of beasts bent to the ground feeding, of course, is applied to a soul bent out of shape. But this does not mean that the image of God in man is destroyed completely, as the abbot continuously stressed.

More likely, Luther was hinting at another passage in SC 82 which speaks of turning to the Word of God for rescue when we are faced with the discrepancy between the condition of our utter sinfulness and the original nature of man: 'When the soul perceives this great disparity within itself, it is torn between hope and despair. . . . There is no difficulty in finding grounds for hope: the soul must convert to the Word' (cf. Sg 7:1).[85]

Equally probably, Luther may have been reminded of Bernard's SC 3 (a sermon he had read, as he elsewhere indicated) about the heavenly physician who comes with speed to the soul's aid, because 'his word runs swiftly', and this word surely is 'a medicine strong and pungent, testing the mind and the heart'.[86] Whatever the exact passage Luther referred to in his lecture, it had a bernardine origin.

10. *Devil's sin – Diabolic sin*

Bernard: 'Devil's sin'

Bernard viewed man as 'constantly tending to sin',[87] a phrase we encounter in Bernard's *First Sermon on the Annunciation*. In another passage of that same significant sermon, Bernard blamed the misery of human sinfulness on Eve.[88] The concept of inherited sin as original sin was familiar to Bernard, who stood within the augustinian tradition. In describing in SC 56 how people erect walls

---

84 SC 82.2; SBOp 2:293,5–8; CF 40:172.
85 *ad Verbum est conversio eius*, SC 82.7; SBOp 2:297,1–11; CF 40:178.
86 SC 3.2; SBOp 1:15,9–11; CF 4:17.
87 See SBOp 5:14,7.
88 See SBOp 5:14,7.

between themselves and the Bridegroom, Bernard asserted that man has a body which has a sinful lineage and therefore is 'never without sin'. He remembered Rom 7:24 and 1 Jn 2:16, where in Latin we meet the 'concupiscence of the flesh' (*concupiscentia carnis*) which cannot possibly be avoided while one lives on earth. Man adds to this inherited concupiscent nature a host of sins, thus erecting additional walls.[89] At the end of SC 37, Bernard spoke, in connection with the problem of lacking self-knowledge, of the 'devil's sin' as the 'original' sin of pride and rebellion:

> See how great the evil that springs from our want of self-knowledge; nothing less than the devil's sin and the beginning of every sin, pride (Sir 10:15). . . . For the present it suffices that each one has been warned about want of self-knowledge, not only by means of my sermon but also by the goodness of the Bridegroom of the Church, our Lord Jesus Christ, who is God, blessed for ever. Amen.[90]

The 'devil's sin' is rebellious pride, and in this bernardine sense it re-surfaced in Luther, along with the conviction that all humans are essentially sinners.

Luther: 'Diabolic sin' fights grace

Throughout his life, as augustinian friar and ex-friar, Luther held a consistent position on original sin. What is traditionally called 'concupiscence' Luther used synonymously with 'sin' (*peccatum*). This identical usage points to Luther's concept of original sin more as 'inherited' than original. Following Augustine, Luther saw in concupiscence the reason why human beings are sinners. Luther's formula *simul iustus et peccator* must be understood to imply both actual sin and original sin.[91] He, like Saint Bernard, had

89 SC 56.3–5 (referring to Rom 7 and 1 Jn 2); SBOp 2:116,3–117,21; CF 31:98–92.

90 SC 37.7; SBOp 2:13,24–26; CF 7:186.

91 This section of my investigation is indebted especially to Manns' essay in *Thesaurus Lutheri*, 90–104, and to Ebeling, *Lutherstudien*, 3:74–98. A thorough study of the concept of sin according to Bernard and Luther would require a separate monograph. What can be said here must remain rather fragmentary. Such a study would have to take into consideration Luther's reflections on the differentiating terminology of *peccare* and *peccatum habere* on which he lectured in his johannine lectures in 1527, a text which is neglected in Luther research.

no problem viewing fallen man as 'constantly tending to sin', and 'never without sin', and the justified sinner as the 'holy sinner'.

In his course on 1 Jn in 1527, Luther lectured on the same combination of thoughts Bernard had used in his *First Sermon on the Annunciation*; here the johannine 'world' stands for 'concupiscence'. Luther said: 'Here you see what the world is, clearly [it is] concupiscence, of course. Here he [John] describes what the world is. It is "concupiscence of the flesh". . . . It is bad concupiscence. . . . This is the world, fie!'[92]

Luther's lectures on 1 Jn contain rich materials which help us uncover at least some aspects of Luther's complex notion of sin. He spoke of interpreters who took 1 Jn 5:16 ('deadly sin') to mean 'natural and great sin' (*peccatum naturale et grande*),[93] without at first illuminating his students as to what he himself meant by it. We may assume that he meant the great 'original sin' which he elsewhere called 'nature sin' (*natursund*).[94] In his johannine lectures he referred to other authorities who from this verse (1 Jn 5:16) drew distinctions among the 'seven mortal sins'. Again, he did not further clarify what he meant. Luther then introduced a revealing biblical example to illustrate his own understanding: 'I understand this as deadly sin which was the sin of Korah; this example seems to me of value to be proposed'. The 'sin of Korah' hints at Num 16:1–24, which served as an explanation for his concept of 'deadly sin': rebellion against God's will that leads to death. 'The nature of this sin is to fight against grace'.

Luther continued his lecture by applying this idea to his contemporary situation. There are sins unto death, *peccata ad mortem*, which happen under the guise of piety among hardened heretics. 'It is a sin without remission, *contra remissionem*'. When heretics are obstinate and maliciously pertinacious, they evince diabolic sin

92 WA 20:664f, where Luther embellished his exposition with typical humanistic references to classical literature (Horace's *Satires* I.1.12 or a reference to Alexander the Great).

93 This is Luther's concluding lecture on 1 Jn, WA 20:794–799. During the lecture, he quoted a certain Bishop Malachias who had published a book on sin, *Liber de veneno peccatorum* (Paris 1518). On the nature of the sin unto death as the fight against grace, see WA 20:795,9.

94 See Ebeling, *Lutherstudien,* 3: 82–88.

(*diabolicum peccatum*), which is basically the rebellious 'pride' which does not admit to being wrong. This is 'sin against the Holy Spirit'. The similarity between Bernard's notion of the 'devil's sin' and Luther's 'diabolic sin' as 'deadly sin' is striking. Whereas Luther referred to it as the fate of Korah, Bernard did not use this example from Num 16.

In the further course of his johannine lectures, Luther concluded that he could not pray for the Swiss reformers Zwingli and Oecolampadius because they persisted in defending what he saw as their heretical position; all he could do was to pray that they might be led to acknowledge their sin. Only after they had, 'can I also pray for remission'. This was so because infidelity/unbelief does not receive remisssion of sins. In this same lecture, at verse 16b—God is love, which he called 'simple but grand words'—he moved to his famous theological theme of 'law and gospel'. When sin is acknowledged, miserable conscience is produced. 'Death, sin, and law, those three run to each other' (*die 3 lauffen auff einander*). This expression resembles a metaphor in Bernard's first Annunciation sermon, the image of a 'threefold cord' of 'curiosity, pleasure, and vanity', 'a three-ply cord not easily broken', drawn from Qoheleth 4:12.[95] The law demonstrates sin, and after that demonstration people are frightened to death and close to despair. They are told that their sins are forgiven and that life is promised to them. To illustrate his doctrine, Luther pointed to contemporary enthusiasts who 'do not feel the law, sin, death, wrath of God', but invent the mere mercy of God. It is better to feel remorse (*in peccato conscientiarum*) than to be so hardened as not sense the sin. The devil cooperates by troubling people with real and ficticious sins and he 'makes them a hundred times bigger and he makes death more horrible, and he does this in order to take away faith and confidence in God, which is sin unto death. . . . He is such a great artist in frightening the consciences. . . . Therefore, in the Church the remission of sins and consolation are necessary'.[96]

95 *Funiculus triplex difficile rumpitur*, Ann 1.8; SBOp 5:20,14f.
96 *Sola infidelitas non habet remissionem*, WA 20:716,23.

Bernard could have said the same thing. And in speaking of the 'sin against the Holy Spirit', which Luther used here and also in his interpretation of 1 Jn 2:1, Luther spoke Bernard's language. Luther insisted that we first acknowledge that we are sinners. This alone is salvific thinking and stands in contrast to 'presumption', 'the sin against the Holy Spirit'.[97]

Unlike Bernard however, the Reformer took the expression 'natural sin' (*peccatum naturale*) also as personal sin (*peccatum personale*). In Luther's vocabulary both serve for 'original sin', being equivalent to *peccatum originale, radicale, capitale, principale, substantiale, mortale, diabolicum*. All these variations of Luther's terminology may be summed up in a statement from his last lecture on 1 Jn, again against Erasmus in his *Bondage of the Will*: that the basic sin is 'not to believe in Christ'.[98] Since all human existence in this world is under 'sin', Luther could include sinful man's good works under 'sin' and even call them 'sins', as he did in his lecture on Romans. Or, from another angle, he could lecture that 'knowledge of God' is fear of God, 'which leads me to say that all good works are sins'.[99] Thus, when Luther subsumed every human action under the notion of sin (*peccatum*), he turned sin into a synonym for 'human being' and 'human nature' after the Fall. From this sinful 'nature', due to the 'alien sin' which is handed down to man and by which he is damned (*ut alieno peccato damnari*),[100] man cannot redeem himself. Alien sin (*pecccatum alienum*) needs to be overcome by the alien righteousness (*aliena iusticia*), i. e. Christ's, by which alone we are saved. The cursed, sinful world needs the 'Saviour of the World' who is sent not to the 'righteous' (*iusti*), but to sinners. Luther maintained that it is 'inevitable' that we be damned first, so that we can be 'saved by

97 WA 20:798,1ff.

98 See WA 20:633,9–11.

99 WA 18:782,13–15. See WA 56:289,14–21 (lectures on Rom, 1515–1516). See Ebeling, *Lutherstudien,* 3:74–107. Unfortunately, Ebeling and many other lutheran Luther scholars are preoccupied with emphasizing the contrast between Luther and scholastic theology, and thus do not bring Bernard's monastic theology into play.

100 WA 20:739,10f.

Christ'. Luther called his audience's attention to 1 Jn 4:14 ('Saviour of the World') and declared in Christ's own words: 'I have come to call, not the self-righteous, but the sinners (Mt 9:13). Therefore, sin belongs to the whole world'. Luther concludes: 'The greatest article [of faith]' is 'to be saved by alien righteousness'.[101]

The backdrop of Luther's theology was the johannine 'world' concept and the message that Christ is the Saviour of that world. In this 'damned world' Luther included all that we mean by 'reason, free will, willing, wisdom, virtue, works'. All these need the Saviour: *quia indiget salvator*.[102]

Although no direct quotations from Bernard can be found in Luther's writings on sin and concupiscence, there are explicit parallels in Bernard's sermons on general ('natural') human sinfulness. Both theologians shared the notion of 'diabolical sin'. They did not shy away from calling people to recognize themselves as sinners precisely because both of them knew Christ as the 'Saviour of the World'. In Luther, more than in any other author, we observe the tendency to amplify sin for the purpose of magnifying the divine work of justification. He readily admitted this in a disputation on Rom 3:28 in the 1530s,[103] and it consequently showed up in a thesis in 1543, that 'every sin by its nature is mortal'.[104]

Both theologians were familiar with the Adam-Christ parallel of Saint Paul. Bernard insisted on the doctrine of original sin; and since sin came through the old Adam, salvation must come through the new Adam, Christ. Adam has made us sinners by his semen (*in semine*), Christ makes us righteous by his blood (*in sanguine*). We are tied to Adam through the flesh (*per carnem*), but to Christ through faith (*per fidem*). As we are infected by 'original concupiscence', so we are healed by Christ's grace, as Bernard stated in his polemic against Abelard's errors. In both sin and salvation the causation is an alien one. Righteousness comes from outside the human person, just as original guilt stems from

---

101 WA 20:751,22.

102 WA 20:751,21; see WA 20:707,9f ('alien righteousness').

103 *Ut ergo iustificatio, quantum potest fieri, magnificetur, peccatum est valde magnificandum et amplificandum,* as quoted in Ebeling, *Lutherstudien,* 3:276 (no. 28).

104 *Omne peccatum sua natura est mortale,* WA 39-II:225,7.

Adam. Someone other than me made me a sinner, and someone else needs to make me a saint.[105]

---

105 . . . *et si infectus ex illo originali concupiscentia, etiam Christi gratia spirituali perfusus sum*, Abael 6.15–16. It appears that Bernard used the notion 'original sin' interchangeably with 'original concupiscence'. On Bernard versus Abelard see, for instance, E. Little, 'Bernard and Abelard at the Council of Sens, 1140', *Bernard of Clairvaux. Studies Presented to Dom Jean Leclercq* CS 23 (Kalamazoo: CP, 1973) 55–71; Jacques Verger and Jean Lolivet, *Bernard – Abélard, ou le cloître et l'école* (Paris 1982); Gerhard B. Winkler, 'Bernhard und Abälard. Oder: Das Ärgernis am Ursprung der westlichen Theologie', *Weisheit Gottes – Weisheit der Welt*. Festschrift für Joseph Kardinal Ratzinger zum 60. Geburtstag, Walter Baier et al., eds. (St. Ottilien: EOS Verlag, 1984) vol. 1:729–38; Lawrence Braceland, 'Bernard and Abelard on Humility and Obedience'. *Erudition at God's Service: Studies in Medieval Cistercian History*, John R. Sommerfeldt, ed. (Kalamazoo: CP, 1987) 149–59.

Plate 7: *Saint Bernard Under Trees in the Company of Biblical Authorities and Students of the Scriptures. The latin caption refers to the story of Bernard meditating in the woods.*

Another glass window at Altenberg (Plate 7) depicts Saint Bernard under trees in the illustrious company of Moses, holding the two tablets of the law, King David with a crown holding the psalter, while his harp has dropped to the ground in front of Jerome (lower right-hand corner); in the background we see Saints Peter and Paul, perhaps Saint John the Evangelist, and other students of Scripture. Bernard as one of them is totally dedicated to learning from the great biblical authorities and interpreters of the 'sacred page'. The latin banderole which issues from Bernard's mouth reads: 'How I loved your law, o Lord; all day long it is my meditation'. Saint Jerome's banderole is a quotation from Ps 119:2: 'Happy are they who search his testimony'. The entire scene is supervised by the Holy Spirit who hovers above the group, surrounded by a banderole which says simply: 'Search the Scripture'.

This glass window aptly expresses the sixteenth-century perception of the centrality the study of Scripture had for Bernard. Although the hermeneutical principle 'Scripture alone' is not explicitly articulated here, the glass window obviously shows the abbot as an eminent biblical scholar and a scripturally-based preacher. In its caption this glass window makes explicit mention of the trees beneath which Bernard meditated, just as Luther does in his *On the Councils and the Church* to which we will refer later in this section. Both this window and Luther's text are probably based upon the same Bernard story in *The Golden Legend* (based on Vita Bern): 'He confessed that whatever he knew about the Scriptures he had learned while meditating and praying in the woods and the fields, and he sometimes said that among his friends he had no teachers except the oaks and the beeches'.[1]

---

1 *The Golden Legend*, Ryan 101. The window caption begins with the words from the *Legenda aurea*: *Confessus in silvis. . . .* See Paffrath, *Bernhard von Clairvaux* (1984), illustration 64. See Jean Leclercq, *Bernard of Clairvaux and the Cistercian Spirit* (Kalamazoo: CP, 1976) 129. As to *Doctor mellifluus*, which is one of the traditional honorific titles for Bernard, one must know that Luther seems to have used it not for Bernard as the doctor of the Scriptures, but for Bernard as the marian teacher, see Franz Posset, *Luther's Catholic Christology According to His Johannine Lectures of 1527* (Milwaukee: Northwestern Publishing House, 1988) 121 with reference to WA 20:637,24–638,2. Originally, Bernard was called *Doctor egregius*. This title is found, for instance, in a prayer book of 1494: *Oratio*

In a similar way, the study of theology meant for friar Martin Luther the study of God's Word, theo-logy. God is to be listened to in Sacred Scripture, the 'sacred page' (*sacra pagina*) precisely because it comes from God. Luther as a reformer continued the monastic approach to the Bible within a 'catholic context'. He took an approach to theology that had been shaped by patristic, non-scholastic authorities. In the monastic tradition 'theology was practiced, prayed, sung, proclaimed, worked, copied, and edited'.[2] Luther elaborated on this approach in his preface to the 1539 edition of his german writings. This may be considered the summary statement of his life-long involvement with the Bible as a professor and preacher at Wittenberg and should have more authority than any of his previous statements.[3]

Previously, I characterized Luther's approach as 'orational', related to the monastic theological tradition.[4] This adjective, not found in Webster's Dictionary, requires an explanatory note: *oratio* in ecclesiastical Latin means 'prayer', in classical Latin 'speech' (oration). In his 1539 preface, Luther used *oratio* in the sense of 'prayer'. When Luther advised a prayerful approach to the Bible, he was thinking at the same time of two other dimensions involved in the study and the understanding of the Bible: meditation and the experience of spiritual temptations (*tentatio*). In fact, Luther spoke of a 'three-fold' rule of interpreting the Scriptures, *drey Regel*:[5] *oratio, meditatio, tentatio*. These three elements of his 'orational' approach were interwoven in the one monastic or 'orational' method of Scripture interpretation. It is difficult to say whether he intentionally wanted to depart from the well-known monastic scheme: *lectio, oratio, meditatio, contemplatio*.

---

de sancto Bernardo clarevallensi et doctore egregie, which is mentioned by McGuire, *The Difficult Saint*, 240.

2 See Hagen, *Luther's Approach to Scripture*, 17f, 35, 82–86. A brief historical survey of the authority of the Scriptures in the medieval Church is given by Hagen et al., *The Bible in the Churches: How Different Christians Interpret the Scriptures* (New York, Mahwah: Paulist Press, 1985) especially 18–23.

3 WA 50:657–661; LW 34:279–88. It is noteworthy that Gerhard Ebeling in his book *What Is Theology* (Philadelphia: Fortress Press, 1972) provided a complete translation of Luther's preface in order to stress its importance for his theology.

4 See Posset, *Luther's Catholic Christology*, 153–157.

5 WA 50:659, 3.

1. *Oratio*

In this preface to his german works Luther contrasted prayer and
reason. He saw a fundamental dichotomy between *o-ratio* (prayer)
and *ratio*; only the 'orational', not the 'rational', access is per-
mitted when one approaches the Word of God. Therefore, Luther
advocated letting go of one's own reasoning when interpreting the
Bible, since human *ratio* not only cannot achieve anything in divine
matters, but will cause one to fall into hell like Lucifer. Luther's
'orational' approach was essentially grounded in the fear of God;
humility was the beginning point in understanding the Word of
God. Therefore, Luther advised, in place of the rational approach
one should retreat into one's private chamber, according to Mt 6:6,
kneel down there, and pray to God 'with the right humility and
earnestness'. One is to pray that God may send through his dear
Son the Holy Spirit who may illuminate and guide the person who
prays. The Spirit is the only master who gives *verstand* (reason,
insight). Apparently, then, only the Spirit-enlightened 'reason' is
ready to read and understand theo-logy, the Word of God. Such
understanding can come only by reading the Word of God medita-
tively 'with closed eyes'.[6] This does not mean that Luther dismissed
the God-given gift of mental capacity, as his pejorative use of *ratio*
may imply.

Luther insisted on a distinction between the interpretation of
the Word of God and the exposition of secular texts, such as the

6 See Franz Posset, 'Bible Reading 'With Closed Eyes' in the Monastic
Tradition: An Overlooked Aspect of Martin Luther's Hermeneutics', ABR 38
(1987) 293–306. Studies of Luther's concept of *ratio* are provided by Bernhard
Lohse, *Ratio und Fides: Eine Untersuchung über die ratio in der Theologie
Luthers* (Göttingen: Vandenhoeck & Ruprecht, 1958); Brian A. Gerrish, *Grace
and Reason: A Study in the Theology of Luther* (Oxford University Press, 1962);
Gerhard Ebeling, 'Fides occidit rationem: Ein Aspekt der theologia crucis in
Luthers Auslegung von Gal 3,6'. *Lutherstudien* 3:181–222; Jerry K. Robbins,
'Luther on Reason: A Reappraisal', *Word & World* 13 (1993) 191–202; Karl-
Heinz zur Mühlen, 'Der Begriff *ratio* im Werk Martin Luthers'. *Reformatorisches
Profil: Studien zum Weg Martin Luthers und der Reformation* (Göttingen: Vandenhoeck & Ruprecht, 1995) 154–173. These studies point to the phenomenon that
for Luther the problem of faith and reason was primarily a soteriological, not an
epistomological issue. Most recently, an investigation of Bernard's critical view
of reason was provided by Otto Langer, 'Affekt und Ratio. Rationalitätskritische
Aspekte in der Mystik Bernhards von Clairvaux', *Zisterziensische Spiritualität*,
33–52.

popular story books to which he refers in his preface, *Marcolfus, Aesop's Fables,* or Livy's history.[7] Luther believed his approach followed 'David's rule'. As David prays in Psalm 119, so Luther recommended we pray: 'Teach me your statutes, make me understand the way of your precepts. . . . Instruct me, O Lord, in the way of your statutes' (verses 27, 33). David does not want to become his own teacher by listening to his own reasoning. Saint Jerome, in the window mentioned above, quotes the same Psalm. Luther was afraid that those who fail to use this 'orational' approach subject the divine Scriptures to human reasoning, while according to his own approach, the Scriptures remain in command. Anyone who approaches Scripture solely in terms of human reasoning considers it nothing but another piece of literature, 'as if it were *Marcolfus,* or *Aesop's Fables'*. For understanding such literature the Holy Spirit is not needed and thus no prayer, no 'orational' approach, would be called for.[8] The Bible as the Word of God is, so to speak, a unique, exclusive 'literary category'. One needs the Holy Spirit to understand it. In modern terms, Luther felt that the scholarly, historical-critical method would not be adequate to reach the genuine understanding of the Bible as the Word *of God.* In saying this, I do not mean to imply that Luther's prayerful approach must necessarily run contrary to modern biblical scholarship. Rather, Luther was unhappy with what he considered the deficient humanistic scholarship of an Erasmus. He wanted to do more than just linguistic and literary studies or even 'sacred philology'. One understands Luther's approach best if one views him as an expositor who wanted to do both humanistic and spiritual exegesis, to be up-to-date with contemporary biblical scholarship while remaining within the monastic context of prayer and meditation on the Word of God as he has been trained to do. He kept this approach even after he left the friary. The preface which most clearly expresses his 'orational' approach was written by the elderly Reformer long after he had left the 'religious life' behind. Throughout his career he understood the Bible as *the* Word of God, not as a piece of ancient

7 WA 50:659,10–20.
8 WA 50:659,13–660,7–21.

literature subject to human, arbitrary interpretation. The Reformer followed in the footsteps of Bernard who, too, was critical of any purely rationalistic approach to theology. Luther is best understood if placed in the context of the monastic tradition in which one meditates on the mysteries of the Word of God with the heart rather than with the head ('reason').

Luther's 'orational' approach was unthinkable without the element of 'humility' as he himself pointed out in his preface to his german works. True humility lay at the center of Luther's approach to understanding the Word of God and thus also of his spirituality, from the moment of his entry into the friary at Erfurt until his death. His last spoken words were taken from the monks' latin Compline: 'Into your hands, I commend my spirit (Lk 23:46). You have redeemed me, God of truth'.[9] Humility was also a concern of Bernard, who wrote an entire book about it, *The Steps of Humility and Pride,*[10] but not one from which Luther ever quoted.

2. *Meditatio*

One has to 'meditate' on the Scriptures, Luther insisted; otherwise one will never become a good theologian. Those who do not meditate will be like green apples fallen from the tree before they are even half ripe.[11] Meditation on the Word of God was so important to Luther that he felt compelled to define it: '[to meditate] is always to propel and rub the word in the Book; not only in the heart, but also externally by reciting it orally and literally; to read and read again, with industrious concentration and deliberation on what the Holy Spirit means by it'.[12] Luther's definition has a monastic provenance. In monastic vocabulary, *meditatio* meant the slow, reflective, and in the Middle Ages

---

9 See Peter Manns, *Martin Luther: An Illustrated Biography* (New Popular Edition, New York: Crossroad, 1983) 119. On humility, see Rudolf Damerau, *Die Demut in der Theologie Luthers* (Giessen: Wilhelm Schmitz Verlag, 1967) 303.

10 Hum; SBOp 3:13–59.

11 WA 50:659,28–29.

12 WA 50:659,22–25.

semi-audible, repetition of Scripture texts.[13] What Luther described here as 'reciting' may surely be understood as monastic *meditatio* or rumination of the Word in the bernardine way.[14] In this context Luther warned not to become tired of what one reads, or to think that if one has read the text once or twice, heard it, or spoken it, one has understood it in all its depth.[15] This advice makes special sense when understood in a monastic context, where one is led from meditation to contemplation, the spiritual enjoyment of the Word of God. His advice to study the Bible thoroughly for preaching purposes may also very well have come from Bernard, who spoke about his prayerful, meditative approach to Scripture and encountering God in SC 69:

> If I feel that my eyes are opened to understand the Scriptures, so that I am enlightened from above to preach the word of wisdom from the heart or reveal the mysteries of God, or if riches from on high are showered upon me so that in my soul fruits of meditation are produced, I have no doubt that the Bridegroom is with me. . . .
>
> And so it is: the love of God gives birth to the love of the soul for God, and his surpassing affection fills the soul with affection, and his concern evokes concern. . . . So God must appear to you as you have appeared to God; 'with the holy he will be holy, and with the innocent man he will be innocent' (Ps 17:26). Why not

13 See Leclercq, *Love of Learning*; his older study features 'contemplation': *Otia monastica. Études sur le vocabulaire de la contemplation au moyen âge* (Rome: Orbis Catholicus, Herder, 1963).

14 See Hans Wolter, 'Meditation bei Bernhard von Clairvaux', *Geist und Leben* 29 (1956) 206–18; J. MacCandless, "Meditation' in Saint Bernard', Coll 26 (1964) 277–93; Fidelis Ruppert, 'Meditatio – Ruminatio: Zu einem Grundbegriff christlicher Meditation', *Erbe und Auftrag* 53 (1977) 83–93; Ruppert, 'Meditatio-Ruminatio', Coll 39 (1977) 81–93; Sommerfeldt, *The Spiritual Teachings*, 66–79; Bernard McGinn, *The Growth of Mysticism* (New York: Crossroad, 1994) 132–138 (on *lectio/meditatio*), 138–146 (on *oratio/contemplatio*).

15 WA 50:659,24–27. Elsewhere, Luther recommended the rumination of the Word of God before going to sleep so that one may fall asleep while ruminating like a pure animal which falls asleep; see Ruppert, 'Meditatio – Ruminatio', 90f; Martin Nicol, *Meditation bei Luther* (Göttingen: Vandenhoeck & Ruprecht, 1984) 57–60; John W. Kleinig, 'The Kindred Heart: Luther on Meditation', *Lutheran Theological Journal* 20 (1986) 142–54; Erdei, *Auf dem Wege zu sich selbst*, 76–85 (on Luther); Edith Scholl, 'Pondering the Word: *Meditare* and *Ruminare*', CSQ 28 (1993) 303–310.

also loving with the loving, eager with the eager, and concerned with those who are concerned?[16]

While Bernardine meditation as rumination and illumination from above is the same as Luther's meditation under the assistance of the Holy Spirit, Luther also pointed out that meditation in the heart is not enough. He advised readers not only to meditate in their heart but 'to rub' the words of the Bible externally until they produced insight. Here another influence appears to be at work. When Luther included external oral speech, *eusserlich die muendliche rede* in his definition of meditation, he may have been mindful of the ancient rhetorician, Quintilian (whom he esteemed highly) and his concept of *meditatio* as the *exercitatio* of a rhetor's oration.[17]

In Luther's concept of *meditatio,* two traditions meshed: the monastic and the humanistic. This should come as no surprise. The young Luther was in close contact with humanistic philologists at Erfurt and he may be considered a 'humanist' in his own right. He looks like a 'biblical humanist' here because of his return to the biblical sources (*ad fontes*), here the psalm which calls for the exclusive adherence to the Word of God.[18]

In his preface Luther dealt with yet another problem. Increasingly he had become concerned with the propaganda of contemporary enthusiasts who wanted to rely on inner illumination alone. Luther felt compelled to stress, in an anti-enthusiastic polemic, that God gives his Spirit not without the external word which is found in the Scriptures.[19] Because God has given this external word, man should not neglect it, but read and meditate on it, as

16 SC 69.6; SBOp 2:205,27–206,1; CF 40:33. Luther quoted from SC 69.7, where Ps 17:26 is used, in his *Dictata* on Ps 17:26, WA 3:126,10ff; 127,8ff. SC 69.7 was handed down as a saying of Augustine, see Bell, *Divus Bernhardus,* 65, note 176.

17 On Luther's high esteem of Quintilian, see Ulrich Nembach, *Predigt des Evangeliums: Luther als Prediger, Pädagoge und Rhetor* (Neukirchen-Vluyn, 1972) 130–174. On Luther and the classical rhetorical tradition, see Knut Alfsvag, 'Language and Reality: Luther's relation to classic rhetoric in *Rationis Latomianae*', *Studia Theologica* 41 (1987) 85–126; see Junghans, *Der junge Luther und die Humanisten,* 81–83.

18 WA 50:659,32.

19 WA 50:659,33–35.

David did in Psalm 119, where 'meditation' occurs several times. Thus Luther wanted to 'walk with the Word of God' through all life's tributations (which he called *tentationes*).

3. *Tentatio*

Spiritual trials are part of life, especially in the monastery. Luther called these attacks, in German, his *Anfechtung;* in his latin texts he wrote of *tentatio*, a term he used in his 1539 preface.[20] Throughout his life he suffered these trials, better called 'attacks' since the german etymological root of *Anfechtung* is *fechten*, 'to fence', 'to fight'. This experience is the touchstone of the spiritual life and has the function of teaching a theologian not only to know and to understand, but also to experience (*erfaren*) how right, truthful, sweet, lovely, mighty, and consoling God's Word is: wisdom over all wisdom, as Luther said. Here he echoed Saint Bernard's joyful encounter with the Word of God, and also the bernardine insight that temptations necessarily follow, as Luther could have read in Bernard's SC 64, where Mt 18:7 is referred to: 'Now it is necessary that temptations come, for who shall receive a crown of victory unless he has contended according to the rules? . . . When you come to serve God, then, stand in awe and prepare your soul for temptation. . . .'[21] If Luther had not read or did not remember this particular passage, his mentor, Johannes von Staupitz, may have pointed out to him the positive function of temptations. Staupitz once told Luther that temptations were good for him since the devil never disturbed the tranquility of people who were already safely in his pockets.[22] In this regard Luther in his preface again quoted Palm 119, here verses 72, 98–100:

20 WA 50:660,1. Should the spiritual 'attacks'/temptations simply be identified with 'depressions' or 'acute anxiety', as David C. Steinmetz, *Luther in Context* (Bloomington: Indiana University Press, 1986) 1 ('Luther against Luther') insinuated? On prayer and temptation in Luther's spirituality, see David P. Scaer, 'Luther on Prayer', CTQ 47 (1983) 305–316.

21 SC 64.1; SBOp 2:166,15–167,6; CF 31:169.

22 See *Dokumente zu Luthers Entwicklung*, Otto Scheel, ed. (Tübingen 1929) 138, 207, 209, 210; Steinmetz, *Luther in Context*, 9.

> The law of your mouth is to me more precious than thousand
> of gold and silver pieces. . . . Your command has made me
> wiser than my enemies, for it is ever with me. I have more
> understanding than all my teachers (when your decrees are my
> meditation). I have more discernment than the leaders, because
> I observe your precepts.[23]

Once one has experienced the power of the Word of God, prayed
for it, meditated on and exercised it, then one realizes how dull,
flat, and foul other books taste—one's own books included, Luther
wrote self-critically.[24] There is no question that the friar and the ex-
friar Martin was permeated with Scripture and with the monastic,
'orational' approach to it, or that he had been tested through
spiritual trials and attacks. He read the Sacred Scriptures as a
'book of experience', as the monastic tradition with Bernard read it.
The Cistercian usually expressed his own and the general human
experiences in biblical vocabulary. This interweaving of human
experience and biblical wording may be operative in the introductory phrase of Bernard's third sermon on the first verse of the
Canticle: 'Today we read in the book of experience. You must turn
toward yourselves, each one must take note of his own particular
awareness (*conscientia*) of the things I am about to discuss'.[25] I
suggest that we understand the expression 'book of experience'
in a two-fold sense: (1) Scriptures which speak of the human
experience of God, and (2) the book of one's own experience.[26]

23 WA 50:660,17–23.

24 WA 50:660,23–26.

25 SC 3.1; SBOp 1:14,7; CF 4:16. See Dorette Sabersky-Bascho, *Studien zur Paronomasie bei Bernhard von Clairvaux* (Freiburg/Schweiz: Universitätsverlag, 1979) 28; Dorette Sabersky, ' "Affectum Confessus sum, et non Negavi". Reflec-tions on the Expression of Affect in the 26th Sermon on the Song of Songs of Bernard of Clairvaux'. *The Joy of Learning*, Elder, ed.,187–216. On 'religious experience', see Johannes Schuck, *Das religiöse Erlebnis beim hl. Bernhard von Clairvaux* (Würzburg: C. J. Becker, 1922); Köpf, *Religiöse Erfahrung,* 136–143 (on *affectus*).

26 SBOp 5:151,19–21. See Ulrich Köpf, 'Ein Modell religiöser Erfahrung in der monastischen Theologie: Bernhard von Clairvaux', *Religiöse Erfahrung: Historische Modelle in christlicher Tradition,* Walter Haug and Dietmar Mieth, eds. (Munich: Wilhelm Fink Verlag, 1992) 109–123, here 122. McGinn has the felicious expression 'coherence of the book of experience and the book of scripture', *The Growth of Mysticism*, 210. Pierre Miquel, *Le Vocabulaire Latin*

For Bernard, the spiritual reading of Scripture was a religious experience guided by the Holy Spirit; Luther envisioned it in the same way when he advised readers to pray for the Spirit before reading the sacred text. Bernard's and Luther's theological experiences were fundamentally biblical experiences; the main object for both was not a rational understanding of, but the discovery of their own experiences expressed in, the inspired Word.

In his early period Luther had spoken primarily of *compunctio* and meditation as preconditions to the understanding of certain scriptural passages. He did so in his First Lectures on the Psalms, where he went so far as to say that if one has not experienced *compunctio,* one could not expound Psalm 77.[27] Now, in this late preface, he preferred to speak of *tentatio* as an essential experience in his 'orational' approach. All three elements—prayer, meditation, and temptation/life experience—were united in Luther's single approach to the study of the Word of God. This approach pointed back to the monastic tradition by which the friar had daily been nurtured for almost two decades. Although Luther was not a member of the Cistercian Order, he seemed to have shared much of that Order's spirituality of *lectio divina.* According to this custom, Scripture reading is to lead to prayer and further rumination on the readings. The sacred texts must be so internalized as to make the experiences out of which they were written the personal experiences of the reader.[28] One may rightly conclude that Luther set spiritual 'experience' in the context of prayer and Bible meditation through his close familiarity with monastic practices, especially

---

de l'Expérience Spirituelle dans la Tradition Monastique et Canoniale de 1050 à 1250 (Paris: Beauchesne, 1989) 106, pointed out that the notion ('book of experience') may be found also in Aelred of Rievaulx, Isaac of Stella, and Guigo II.

27 See WA 3:549f (with reference to Augustine, not to Bernard); see WA 4:152. See Otto Scheel, *Martin Luther: Vom Katholizismus zur Reformation* (Tübingen, 1930, fourth printing) 2:252–54; Emmanuel Hirsch, *Lutherstudien* 1 (Gütersloh 1954) 130; Leclercq, *The Love of Learning,* 37–40; Damerau, *Die Demut in der Theologie Luthers,* 37. On the paronomasia in regard to *compungere,* see Sabersky-Bascho, *Studien zur Paronomasie,* 56.

28 See G. R. Evans, 'The Classical Education of Bernard of Clairvaux.' *Cîteaux* 33 (1982) 121–134, especially 127–130; G. R. Evans, *The Mind of St. Bernard of Clairvaux* (Oxford: Clarendon Press, 1983) 47.

through the texts of our cistercian abbot.[29] He was very much a disciple of Bernard without belonging to his Order. He was greatly indebted to the *sacra pagina* approach which developed within the wider monastic / religious tradition in which he came of age as a Reformer. Luther learned a lot of his experiential or 'existential' theology from the monastic theology shaped by Bernard.

From this perspective it is easily understandable that in a treatise with the title *On the Councils and the Church*, written in 1539, the same year as the preface under analysis here, Luther called upon Saint Bernard and Saint Augustine as the real masters who lead us to the true sources, i. e. to biblical theology: Saint Augustine because he wanted to see Scripture as the master and judge of everything; and Saint Bernard because he 'learned his wisdom from the trees . . . that is, he conceived his ideas from Scripture and pondered them under the trees'.[30] This widespread view of Bernard studying under the trees stemmed perhaps from a collation of bernardine passages such as his letter to his friend Henry Murdac: 'Believe me who has experience, you will find much more laboring under the trees than you ever will from books. Woods and stones will teach you what you can never hear from any master'. In the letter Bernard spoke of the study of Scripture and of the central importance of Christ as the fountain from whom 'clear water' springs, in contrast to the 'dark waters' of the prophetic

29 Köpf, *Religiöse Erfahrung in der Theologie Bernhards von Clairvaux*, 235f. A very enlightening essay on Bernard's concept of 'experience' is found in the article by Brian Stock, 'Experience, Praxis, Work, and Planning in Bernard of Clairvaux: Observations on the *Sermones in Cantica*'. *The Cultural Context of Medieval Learning: Proceedings of the First International Colloquium on Philosophy, Science, and Theology in the Middle Ages – September 1973,* John Emery Murdoch and Edith Dudley Sylla, eds. (Dordrecht-Holland and Boston: D. Reidel Publishing Company, 1975) 219–268.

30 Luther on Bernard: WA 50:519,32–520,10; LW 41:20–27 (1539); WA Br 1:602,42–46 (no. 235, to Hieronymus Dungersheim of Ochsenfurt, December 1519); WA 7:100,25f (1520/21). Bell, *Divus Bernhardus*, 165–67; see Jacques-Noël Pérès, 'Où il est question de source et de rivière: saint Bernard et Martin Luther à propos du rapport de l'Église à l'Écriture', Coll 52 (1990) 299–306; however, the author makes no effort to locate this image in Bernard's *opus*. As to Luther's hint at Augustine in this regard, no such metaphor (spring/rivers) is found in Augustine; see Theobald Freudenberger, *Hieronymus Dungersheim von Ochsenfurt am Main 1465–1540, Theologieprofessor in Leipzig: Leben und Schriften* (Münster: Aschendorff, 1988) 141, note 88.

texts. This passage has some similarity with SC 22.2, where we
read about drawing spiritual waters from the open streams of the
Scriptures. Luther processed the imagery of source and streams,
when in his *On the Councils and the Church*, he once more
hinted at Bernard, 'that oaks and pines were his masters' and that
he would rather let the brooks run their course, but drink from
the spring'.[31] Luther may have lifted this from the *Vita Bern*, to
explain the relationship between the original Bible text (spring)
and the derived expositions of the Fathers (rivulets). He pictured
Bernard outdoors, under 'oaks and pines'; not to portray Bernard
as a lover or a philosopher of nature, but to present him as an
eager student of the Scriptures in the open air. In processing this
image of Bernard studying outdoors, Luther may have followed the
humanists who ever since Petrarch treated Bernard as an example
of the solitary life. Petrarch paraphrased the respective passage
from the Bernard hagiography and added that he could say the same
thing of himself.[32] The renaissance artists in Italy, too, understood
Bernard as having studied and meditated outdoors and that it was
on that occasion that the Virgin Mary appeared to him.[33] Luther

31 . . . *das die Eichen und Tannen seine meister gewest sind, wolle lieber
aus der Quelle trinken, weder aus den Bechlin. . . .* [Bernard] *lesst die Bechlin
fliessen und trinckt aus der Quelle*, WA 50:525,23–30 (1539); Ep 106, to Henry
Murdac; SBOp 7:266f. See *Vita Bern*, Book 1.4,23f; PL 185:240f; Cawley 32. See
also SC 22.2: *dulcius ea bibitur aqua, quae ab exiguo licet alveo fontis hauritur*,
PL 185:302; CF 7:15. Theo Bell, *Divus Bernhardus*, 166, doubts that Luther lifted
it from *Vita Bern* directly. Bell did not pursue the issue of the origin of this saying
within Bernard's own works (such as perhaps SC 22.2), nor did he examine the
letter to Murdac as a possible source for the image of the spring and the rivers; see
Divus Bernhardus, 165–69, 326, 358f. One may also suppose that Luther melded
Bernard and Jerome who writes in his Ep 20.2: *omissis opinionum rivulis ad
ipsum fontem, unde ab evangelistis sumptum est, recurramus*, CSEL 54:104,14f.

32 See Petrarca, *De Vita Solitaria,* as based on *Vita Bern* 1:4.23; PL 185:240,
as quoted by Alison Luchs, 'Saint Bernard in the Wilderness', *Mélanges à la
mémoire du Père Anselme Dimier*, Benoit Chauvin, ed. (Arbois: Pupillin, 1984)
349–54, here notes 3 and 11.

33 For example: (1) Master of the Rinuccini Chapel with his *Vision of
Saint Bernard* (Galleria dell' Accademia, Florence, fourteenth century); three
trees are featured which make up the background of this picture; Mary and two
angels hover over the ground in front of Bernard kneeling by his desk ready to
write something down; see Steven Janke, 'The Vision of St. Bernard: A Study
in Florentine Iconography' *Hortulus imaginum. Essays in Western Art*, eds. R.
Enggass and S. Stokstad (Lawrence, Kansas: 1974) 45–50, with illustration 28.
(2) The Scuola Florentina produced a series of six paintings of Bernard's life,
one of which shows Bernard reading outdoors, with a tree in the background

apparently viewed Bernard in this renaissance perspective and did not understand Bernard as a despiser of scholarship, as the bernardine statement to Murdac was at times misunderstood to mean that Bernard found his wisdom more in the forest than in books.[34]

Furthermore, Luther's metaphor of 'clear water' for Scripture may evoke in any Luther scholar the question of the 'clarity of the Scriptures', which had become a hotly debated issue by the time of the early Reformation, especially between Erasmus and Luther. Over the course of time it degenerated into denominational quarrels as the problem of 'Scripture and Tradition(s)', culminating in the debates at the Council of Trent, with its aftermath.

For Bernard this problem had not been posed in the intense way it was in the sixteenth century, when the question of ecclesiastical authority in relation to scriptural interpretation heated up. Bernard's (and the monastic) method of Bible meditation meant interpreting Scripture with Scripture (the so-called 'exegetical concordance' method), a method which the renaissance humanists and Luther aggressively advocated under the slogan 'Scripture

---

to the left, as the Virgin appears to him from above to the right, accompanied by two figures (now in Bode Museum, Gemäldegalerie, Berlin, inv. 1066); see Laura Dal Prà, *Iconografia di San Bernardo di Clairvaux in Italia. II.1 La Vita* (Rome: Editiones Cistercienses, 1991) 14 with illustration 8. (3) In Filippino Lippi's *Vision of Saint Bernard* (now in the Badia in Florence, approximately 1481 to 1486) Bernard is placed into a rocky landscape ('wilderness'), but the artist did not feature trees; yet, he may have alluded to the 'stones' which 'will teach you what you can never learn from any master' (Ep 106); the text of Luke 1 (*Missus est*) is shown in a book leaning prominently against the rocks; on this painting, see David L. Clark, 'Filippino Lippi's The Virgin Inspiring St. Bernard and Florentine Humanism', *Studies in Iconography* (1981–82) 175–187. (4) The *Sforza Hours* show a similar placement on some sort of a terrace (now in the British Library, approximately 1490); see Mark Evans, *The Sforza Hours* (New York: New Amsterdam Books, 1992) 17–45 with illustration 54 (Saint Bernard, fol. 200v). (5) Fra Bartolommeo's *The Madonna Appearing to Saint Bernard* does not feature trees, but the artist situated the scene on a veranda outdoors (now in the Uffizi in Florence, approximately 1507). The common denominator of these renaissance paintings is that Bernard is not enclosed in a monastic cell, but outdoors or at least on a terrace, where he reads the Bible and other books, where he meditates and receives inspirations, as at times he is shown with a pen in his hand ready to write.

34 *Experto crede: aliquid amplius invenies in silvis, quam in libris*, Ep. 106, SBOp 7:266f. It is not difficult to see that this phrase can easily be misinterpreted; see Anselme Dimier, 'A propos d'un mot célèbre de saint Bernard: "Les chênes et les hêtres, mes maîtres . . .",' Coll 33 (1971) 283–286.

alone'. 'Scripture interprets Scripture' was not the Reformer's hermeneutical invention.[35]

Without exaggeration we may say that Luther's place in the history of exegesis is best located within the tradition of monastic Scripture study. But to stop there would be misleading, because an equally strong influence came from the linguistic approach of renaissance humanists. Their approach need not be seen in total contrast to the monastic approach, since there was a widespread phenomenon of what may be called 'monastic humanism' (*Klosterhumanismus*) in Italy and north of the Alps. Monasticism and humanism appeared happily joined at least for a time around the turn of the sixteenth century. The augustinian friaries at Wittenberg and Nuremberg were very much part of a progressive 'monastic humanism'.[36] This intellectual climate contributed to the

35 On this hermeneutical issue, see Leclercq, *Love of Learning,* 95 (on 'exegetical concordance'). As to Luther's hermeneutics, see Gerhard Ebeling, *Evangelische Evangelienauslegung. Eine Untersuchung zu Luthers Hermeneutik* (reprint Darmstadt: Wissenschaftliche Buchgesellschaft, 1962; first printing 1942); Ebeling, *The Word of God and Tradition: Historical Studies Interpreting the Divisions of Christianity,* S. H. Hooke, trans. (Philadelphia: Fortress Press 1964) 102–147 (on 'Scripture alone'); Ebeling, 'The Beginnings of Luther's Hermeneutics', *Lutheran Quarterly* 7 (1993) 129–158, 315–338, 451–468; Friedrich Beisser, *Claritas Scripturae bei Martin Luther* (Göttingen: Vandenhoeck & Ruprecht, 1966); Walter Mostert, 'Scriptura sacra sui ipsius interpres. Bemerkungen zum Verständnis der Heiligen Schrift durch Luther'. *Lutherjahrbuch* 46 (1979) 60–96; Otto Hermann Pesch, *Hinführung zu Luther* (Mainz: Matthias Grünewald Verlag, 1983) 68. Otto Hof, *Schriftauslegung und Rechtfertigungslehre: Aufsätze zur Theologie Luthers* (Karlsruhe: Evangelischer Presseverband für Baden e. V., 1982) 109–110.

36 See Posset, 'Bible Reading 'With Closed Eyes', 299–306. On 'monastic humanism,' see Richard Newald, *Probleme und Gestalten des deutschen Humanismus: Studien* (Berlin: Walter de Gruyter and Co. 1963) 82–102. Newald described the monastic humanism in the augustinian friaries (and benedictine monasteries) where the new spirit of the Renaissance found entry; see Machilek, 'Klosterhumanismus in Nürnberg um 1500', 32f (on the augustinian friars). Furthermore, on Luther's contemporary, the benedictine Johannes Tritheim, see Klaus Arnold, *Johannes Trithemius (1462–1516), Quellen und Forschungen zur Geschichte des Bistums und Hochstifts Würzburg* (Würzburg: Schöningh, 1971); Klaus Ganzer, 'Zur monastischen Theologie des Johannes Trithemius'. *Historisches Jahrbuch* 101 (1981) 385–421; Noel L. Brann, *The Abbot Trithemius (1462–1516): The Renaissance of Monastic Humanism* (Leiden: Brill 1981) 228–236, and 355; Barry Collett, *Italian Benedictine Scholars and the Reformation: The Congregation of Santa Giustina of Padua* (Oxford: Oxford University Press, 1985); Leclercq, 'Monastic and Scholastic Theology in the Reformers of the Fourteenth to Sixteenth Century,' 178–201; Lewis W. Spitz, 'Luther and Humanism'. *Luther and Learning. The Wittenberg University Luther Symposium,* Marilyn J.

breakdown of scholasticism and helped create what some scholars call 'evangelical humanism' which all the chief reformers appear to have shared. 'The lines of development are sometimes tantalizingly close. Erasmus, Luther, Zwingli, Calvin, and Ignatius all started from a belief in the spiritual power of the fusion of evangelicalism and humanism, traditions which, until Erasmus joined them, had been often in conflict and never entirely joined.'[37]

To summarize the particular congeniality of Bernard and Luther, one may observe in them both a tendency to concentrate on Scripture interpretation. Luther reduced the traditional four-fold Bible interpretation to 'a two-dimensionality of *littera occidens* and *spiritus vivificans*'.[38] And he did this within the context of his 'orational' approach to the *sacra pagina*—something important to him and to Bernard.[39]

Luther by-passed the scholastics and returned to Bernard because he believed he had discovered in contemporary (late) scholastic theology a disrespect for Scriptures, and in Bernard a love for them. Luther judged the school men harshly in a table talk of summer 1540: 'They had no understanding at all of Christ because

---

Harran, ed. (Selinsgrove, London, and Toronto: Susquehanna University Press and Associated University Presses, 1985) 69–94. On the specifics of humanism at Erfurt and Wittenberg in Luther's days, see Grossmann, *Humanism in Wittenberg 1485–1517*; Junghans, *Der junge Luther und die Humanisten*, 11–239. Leif Grane, 'Luther und der Deutsche Humanismus'. *Martin Luther 'Reformator und Vater im Glauben'*. Referate aus der Vortragsreihe des Instituts für europäische Geschichte Mainz, Peter Manns, ed. (Stuttgart: Franz Steiner Verlag Wiesbaden GMBH, 1985) 106–117. Morimichi Watanabe, 'Martin Luther's Relations with Italian Humanists'. *Lutherjahrbuch* 54 (1987) 23–47.

37 A. H. T. Levi, 'The Breakdown of Scholasticism and the Significance of Evangelical Humanism'. *The Philosophical Assessment of Theology: Essays in honour of Frederick C. Copleston*, Gerard J. Hughes, ed. (Kent and Washington: Search Press; Georgetown University Press, 1987) 101–128.

38 Mikka Ruokanen, *Hermeneutics as an Ecumenical Method in the Theology of Gerhard Ebeling* (Helsinki: Vammala, 1982) 150, with note 2. See Metzger, *Gelebter Glaube*, 200–217.

39 See SBOp 3:493,24–25; and Csi; SBOp 5:14,32. On *oratio* as prerequisite for better understanding, see the conclusions of SCs 29 and 32. See Gertrud Frischmuth, *Die paulinische Konzeption in der Frömmigkeit Bernhards von Clairvaux* (Gütersloh: Bertelsmann, 1933) 27. On the Bible as 'sacred page' according to Bernard, see Pranger, *Bernard of Clairvaux and the Shape of Monastic Thought*, 275, and his quotation of SC 52.2. where Pranger unjustifiedly insinuated that Bernard had spoken of 'sacred page'. However, the latin original only has *pagina*; Pranger mistakenly referred to Walsh as the translator of this text as having translated it with 'sacred page', which he has not.

they despised the Bible and because nobody read the Bible for the
sake of meditation but only for the sake of knowledge, as one would
read a historical work'.[40] Clearly, this statement indicates that in
retrospect the ageing Luther placed himself into the tradition of
monastic Scripture meditation. He felt disgust at such scholastic
theologians as Thomas Aquinas, whom he viewed primarily as
abstracting statements from the Bible and then concluding 'that
Aristotle says so–and–so and he interprets Scripture according to
Aristotle'.[41] Whether or not Luther's evaluation of Thomas was
fair is an issue which we cannot pursue here. This much is clear:
Luther's aversion to those who neglected the study of the Bible had
increased in the hot-bed of the monastic tradition, and was rooted
in Bernard and in Luther's own augustinian Order. There concentration on reading the Sacred Scriptures was emphasized. They
were cultivated as books on monastic life, as it was understood, for
example, by the augustinian friar Conrad von Zenn (d. 1460). This
spiritual leader taught that one had to know the Sacred Scriptures if
one wanted to know Christ.[42] Luther himself reminisced in a table
talk of 1538 about his early encounter with the Bible within his
religious Order. He had found the Bible in the library and began
reading it to the 'greatest admiration of Dr Staupitz',[43] the leading
officer of the Reformed Augustinian Hermits in Germany.

In concluding this section, let us note, first of all, that Luther's
'orational', meditative approach to the study of the Scriptures is
still significant today. So eminent a modern theologian as Gerhard
Ebeling included it as the 'postscript' in his introduction to the
study of theology.[44] And secondly, Luther used the fairly typically

40 WA TR 4:679–80 (no. 5135, August 1540).

41 WA TR 1:117–118 (no. 280). See G. R. Evans, *The Language and Logic
of the Bible: The Road to Reformation* (Cambridge etc: Cambridge University
Press, 1985) 140.

42 See Hellmut Zschoch, *Klosterreform und monastische Spiritualität im 15.
Jahrhundert: Conrad von Zenn OESA (+1460) und sein Liber de vita monastica*
(Tübingen: J. C. B. Mohr [Paul Siebeck], 1988) 169, note 216.

43 WA TR 3:598,13–15 (no. 3767, February 1538).

44 Gerhard Ebeling, *The Study of Theology*, Duane A. Priebe, trans. (Philadelphia: Fortress Press, 1978) 167–169. See Oswald Bayer, 'Oratio, Meditatio,
Tentatio. Eine Besinnung auf Luthers Theologieverständnis'. *Lutherjahrbuch*
55 (1988) 7–59; Theo Bell, 'Pater Bernardus: Bernard de Clairvaux vu par
Martin Luther', *Cîteaux* 41 (1990) 233–255, here 236f; Johannes Jürgen Sieg-

monastic 'exegetical concordance' approach to the interpretation of the Bible. Needless to say, 'exegesis' is a term neither Bernard nor Luther used in or for their works; nevertheless they constantly expounded biblical texts. Theirs would be an *eisegesis* if we approach Bernard and Luther in terms of modern exegesis, and we might lament, as Ceslas Spicq did, that Bernard *ne composa aucune oeuvre exegetique*.[45] With Leclercq and in following him with Bertrand de Margerie, one has to respond that Bernard did neither exegesis nor dogmatics, but mainly wanted to express his faith and contemplation.[46]

The same we may say of Luther, about whom Ulrich Köpf wrote: 'The greatest monastic theologian from the early sixteenth century who helped this type of theology achieve new historical power—the augustinian hermit Martin Luther—did not link up with the monastic theology of the fifteenth century, but on his own went back to Bernard's [monastic theology]'.[47] Reformation research in the past usually missed this point and ascribed great importance to Luther's study of scholastic theology during his formative years; his indebtedness to the monastic theological tradition was largely ignored.

All in all, it was the primacy of the Scriptures in Bernard's work which attracted Luther and which was noticed already in the fourteenth century by Robert of Basevorn in his book on preaching:

> Now about Saint Bernard. . . . He more than the rest stresses Scripture in all his sayings, so that scarcely one statement is his own which does not depend on an authority in the Bible or on a

mund, 'Bernhard von Clairvaux und Martin Luther', 95f; Robert A. Kelly, '*Oratio, Meditatio, Tentatio Faciunt Theologum:* Luther's Piety and the Formation of Theologians', *Consensus: A Canadian Lutheran Journal of Theology* 19 (1993) 9–27. Jos E. Vercruysse, 'Eine rechte Weise in der Theologia zu studirn. Oratio – Meditatio – Tentatio. Luthers Vorrede von 1539'. *Denkender Glaube in Geschichte und Gegenwart. Festschrift aus Anlaß der Gründung der Universität Erfurt vor 600 Jahren und aus Anlaß des 40jährigen Bestehens des Philosophisch–Theologischen Studiums Erfurt*, Wilhelm Ernst and Konrad Feiereis, eds. (Leipzig: Benno Verlag, 1992) 297–307.

45 Ceslas Spicq, *Esquisse d'une histoire de l'exégèse latine au moyen age* (Paris: J. Vrin, 1944) 119.

46 See Bertrand de Margerie, *Introduction à Histoire de l'Exégèse. L'occident latin de Léon le Grand à Bernard de Clairvaux* (Paris: Cerf, 1990) 265.

47 See Köpf, 'Monastische Theologie im 15. Jahrhundert,' 135.

multitude of authorities. His procedure is always devout, always artful. . . . Using every rhetorical color so that the whole work shines with a double glow, earthly and heavenly.[48]

Not only the primacy of the Scriptures is involved here, but also the way in which they are treated and accepted. Peter Damian's famous sentence on the servant role the arts played to their mistress, the *sacra pagina*, applied as well to Bernard and Luther. For all of them the priority of the 'sacred page' concerned not only the priority of biblical theology, but 'life performance of the monastic theatre'.[49]

Bernard, in his fourth homily on the glories of the virgin mother, expressed his understanding of the use of the Word of God as *sacra pagina* so eloquently that the new *Catechism of the Catholic Church* quotes from it: 'Christianity is the religion of the "Word" of God, "not a written and mute word, but incarnate and living" '. The passage from Bernard's sermon reads in full:

Let him become to me not an audible word which sounds in the ear, but a visible Word that my eyes may see him, a tangible Word that my hands may hold him, a portable Word that I may carry him in my arms. And let Him become for me not a written and mute word, but incarnate and living: that is to say, not a word inscribed in dumb characters upon dead parchment, but the Word of God in human form impressed upon the living page of my chaste bosom, impressed, I say, not by the agency of mortal hand, but by the operation of the Holy Spirit.[50]

---

48 Robert of Basevorn, *De forma praedicandi* (1322), as quoted in Pranger, *Bernard of Clairvaux and the Shape of Monastic Thought*, 11.

49 Pranger, *Bernard of Clairvaux and the Shape of Monastic Thought*, 275.

50 Miss 4.11; SBOp 4:57. The *Catechism* has it in Part One, article 3, no. 108, on Sacred Scripture.

1. *Bernard: 'Taste and see that the Lord is sweet'*

Among the early cistercians, it was Saint Bernard who made explicit use of the notion 'sweetness of Christ' (*Christi suavitas*). 'If the sweetness of Christ is present', he wrote to Hugh, 'the inedible meal of the Prophet (2 Kgs 4: 41) will be savored with sauce'.[1] Bernard did not use the expressions 'sweetness of God' (*dulcedo dei* or *suavitas dei*), and in this he resembles Augustine.[2] He did, however, reflect extensively on the content of the concept even without using these expressions. He knew the divine Father's sweet name;[3] he spoke of the 'sweetness of the Lord' (*dulcedo Domini*), and of the 'sweet Lord' who is more sweet than sublime. Like Cassiodorus and William of Saint Thierry, Bernard explained that the Lord's sweetness comes from his breasts: 'If you feel the sting of temptation, look upon the bronze serpent raised on the staff (Num 21:8f) and drink not only from the wounds but from the breasts of the Crucified. For he will be a mother to you'.[4]

The concept of the sweetness of God in Christ, expressed either by *Christi dulcedo* or *Christi suavitas*, was inspired by the christological reading of the psalms; 'the Lord' of the psalms is identified with Christ. It is above of all in the psalter where the monastic authors found the sweetness of Christ[5] on the palate of

1 See Ep 322.2f; SBOp 8:257; see John R. Sommerfeldt, 'The Monk and Monastic Life in the Thought of Bernard of Clairvaux'. *Word and Spirit. A Monastic Review* 12 (1990) 46f.

2 See Posset, 'The Sweetness of God', ABR 44 (1993) 143–178, here 147–155 (on Augustine); see Edith Scholl, 'The Sweetness of the Lord: *Dulcis* and *Suavis*', CSQ 27 (1992) 359–366.

3 See SC 15.2; SBOp 1:83; CF 4:106; see Renée H. Bennett, 'The Song of Wisdom in Bernard's *Sermones Super Cantica Canticorum*', CSQ 30 (1995) 147–178; on sweetness: 170–172.

4 See Franz Posset, '*Christi Dulcedo*: 'The Sweetness of Christ' in Western Christian Spirituality', CSQ 30 (1995) 245–265, here 249–251.

5 See Joseph Ziegler, *Dulcedo Dei: Ein Beitrag zur Theologie der griechischen und lateinischen Bibel* (Münster: Aschendorff, 1937). See Posset, '*Christi Dulcedo*', 246.

152   Luther's Indebtedness to the Monastic Tradition

the heart.[6] In his sermons on the Canticle alone, Bernard several times made use especially of the Vulgate version of Psalm 33:9, 'taste and see that the Lord is sweet'. In English, the psalter, and therefore SC 61.3, have 'good' in place of 'sweet': 'I can taste and see that the Lord is good'.[7] We prefer the literal translation of *suavis*, 'sweet'. Bernard may alternate the conjunction: At times he says 'that' (*quoniam*) the Lord is sweet; at other times he speaks of tasting 'how' (*quam*) sweet the Lord is. The adjective *suavis* remains unaltered, however, as does the first verb, *gustare*; the second verb (*videre*) of this verse is sometimes replaced by *sentire, sapere,* or *spectare*.

The original 'Taste and see that the Lord is sweet' is found in SC 37, where Bernard speaks of man 'seeing God'. The person who sees God is the person who has tasted, and so now sees that the Lord is sweet, 'for how could one not see God when one tasted him and is seeing that he is sweet?' Bernard goes on to say that a person experiences (*sentit*) how sweet the Lord Jesus is in the forgiveness of sins. Clearly, 'sweetness' carries the notion of salvation for him. Experiencing forgiveness means tasting the sweetness of the Lord.[8] Bernard may use yet a third verb, *spectare,* as a synonym: 'And *to behold* is to taste and to see that the Lord is sweet'.[9] In SC 19, Bernard changes the verb to *sentire*: 'Taste and experience (sense, feel) how sweet the Lord is'.[10] Originally, *sentire* referred to the physical experience of tasting food. But Bernard had no difficulty saying—on the basis of his synonymous use of the notions 'sweetness' and 'grace' (see below)—that the soul 'feels grace', *sentit gratiam*.[11] In SC 50.4 Bernard uses *sapere* (to savor, experience that the Lord is sweet).[12] *Sapere* and *sapientia* share

6 On the spiritual palate and related subjects, see Robert Thomas, 'Saint Bernard and the Psalms', *Liturgy OCSO* 29 (1995) 63–72 and Franz Posset, 'Sensing God with the "Palate of the Heart" According to Augustine and Other Spiritual Authors', ABR 49 (1998) 356–386.

7 SC 61.4; CF 31:143.

8 SC 37.4; SBOp 2:11,9–12; CF 7:183.

9 SC 67.6; SBOp 2:192,10–11. The american edition gives the translation: 'And to see is to taste, and to know how gracious the Lord is', CF 40:9f.

10 SC 19.7; SBOp 2:112,14–15; CF 4:144.

11 *Sentit gratiam,* SC 74.2; SBOp 2:240,25f; CF 40:87.

12 SC 50.4; SBOp 2:80,15f; CF 31:33. See Köpf, 'Ein Modell religiöser Erfahrung', 115.

the same root. The verb may mean 'to taste' or 'to have insight'. Bernard wanted to say: 'Taste and gain the insight that the Lord is sweet'. Elsewhere he says of this experiential wisdom that the 'seasoning salt of wisdom' fills the mind with the 'multitude of the sweetness of the Lord'.[13] The verb *sapere* is used also in SC 85.8, where he speaks about the 'palate of the heart':

> When wisdom enters, while it dulls the carnal taste, it purifies the understanding, heals and prepares the palate of the heart. Thus, with a sane palate one soon *tastes* the good, wisdom itself tastes, as there is nothing better among the good things.[14]

Thus, he used a broad spectrum of verbs to interpret the phrase in Ps 33:9 'taste and see' the sweetness of the Lord: *scire, probari, sentire, spectare, videre,* and *sapere* (to know, to discover, to experience, to behold, to see, and to savor); and this usage fits squarely into Bernard's concept of 'wisdom' as 'taste' (*sapientia— sapor*). As he explains in SC 85.8: 'And perhaps wisdom is derived from taste . . . I think it would be permissible to define wisdom as a taste for what is good'.[15] This insight led him to add: 'For in nothing is the victory of wisdom over malice more evident than when the taste for evil . . . is purged away, and the mind's inmost task senses that it is occupied with total sweetness . . . . To taste and see that the Lord is sweet—that is wisdom'.[16]

Bernard's integration of this psalm verse into his sermons allowed a variety of virtually synonymous verbs. But the verb *gustare* is never altered. Nor, as we saw, is the adjective *suavis,* which also has a broad meaning reaching from physically 'sweet' or 'good' to theologically 'gracious'. The tasting of the sweetness of God means the possession of saving wisdom. When one finds

---

13 SC 50.4 (speaking with Ps 30:20); SBOp 2:80,19f; CF 31:33. This affection becomes 'rich and sweet', *pinguis et suavis est,* SBOp 2:80,17.

14 SC 85.8; SBOp 2:313,5–7; CF 40:204. In his Dil, Bernard made use of yet another combination, i. e. with *probari,* which is translated with 'discover': 'to taste and discover how sweet the Lord is'. At this point Bernard insisted that we love God 'for we have tasted and know how sweet the Lord is', whereby he introduced yet another verb to interpret the 'tasting', namely *scire,* 'to know': SBOp 3:141,3-12; CF 13b:28.

15 SC 85.8; SBOp 2:312,21–24; CF 40:204.

16 SC 85.9; SBOp 2:313,18–22; CF 40:205.

oneself 'locked in the arms of Wisdom', one will experience 'the sweetness of holy love being infused'.[17]

'Sweetness' provided the central category for Bernard's applied, mystical, experiential soteriology. It came from his reading of the psalms, especially psalm 33, about which he observed, in another sermon, that like the psalmist who successfully strove to experience the sweetness of God, so he, too, had the same desire to taste and see that the Lord is sweet.[18] When Bernard meditated on the verse 'Blessed is the fruit of your womb', he reflected on the sweetness of that fruit, who is Christ, and to do so he employed the Vulgate vocabulary of Ps 33:9 and 1 Pt 2:3:

> Blessed is his odor, blessed is his savor, and blessed is his beauty. Long ago [the Patriarch Isaac] inhaled the perfume of this fragrant Fruit, when he cried out: 'Behold the smell of my Son is as the smell of a plentiful field which the Lord has blessed' . . . And concerning the flavor of the Fruit, the Psalmist after enjoying it, broke into song and said, 'Oh, taste and see that the Lord is sweet' (*suavis*, Ps 33:9), and, 'Oh, how great is the multitude of your sweetness (*dulcedinis*) O Lord, which you have hidden for those who fear you!' (Ps 30:20). And to the same [the Apostle Peter] thus refers, 'If only you have tasted that the Lord is sweet' *(dulcis,* 1 Pt 2:3). The Fruit himself, inviting us to him, declares, 'They who eat me shall yet hunger; and they who drink me shall yet thirst' (Si 24:29). He speaks thus, no doubt, on account of the sweetness of his taste (*saporis dulcedinis*), which, when once experienced, excites rather than appeases the appetite.[19]

The desire for the sweetness of the Lord is hard to endure. And so Bernard asked, with the Bride: 'How long must I be satisfied with what you offered in the words, "Taste and see that the Lord is sweet" (Ps 33: 9)?' And he commented: 'Your fruit, nevertheless, is sweet to the palate and sweet to the taste, so that even for this much the Spouse had good reason to break forth in the voice of

17 SC 32.2; SBOp 1:227,9–11; CF 7:135; see Casey, *Athirst*, 86f.
18 SBOp 6–1:363,5ff.
19 Miss 3.6; SBOp 4:39,10–17.

thanksgiving and praise'.[20] This is not the place further to extend the investigation of the 'sweetness of the Lord' in Bernard's spirituality and theology. What has been said will serve as the foundation for a demonstration of what Luther was talking about when he referred to Bernard's insights in his interpretation of verse 33:9.

2. Luther: 'Bernard admitted that whoever once has tasted the sweetness of this knowledge. . . .'

To illustrate Luther's life-long indebtedness to the monastic spiritual vocabulary, and his awareness of it (which may constitute dependency), two texts shall be presented here: one from his *Dictata*, from the beginning of his career as an expositor, and one from the end of his life. When, in his *Dictata*, the young interpreter of the psalms arrived at Ps 33 (Vulgate), he first of all classified it as an *Alphabetarius*, an alphabetic psalm in which each verse in the original Hebrew begins with a new hebrew letter, in alphabetical order. Soon he talked about the righteous person as his own accuser before God so that confession of sin is identical with praise of God. Here he sounds like Augustine and Bernard (and Staupitz) without, however, mentioning any names. On verse nine he commented, faithful to the monastic tradition and in contrast to the scholastics, that the psalmist said 'taste' because the affect makes a person more learned than the intellect. 'Seeing' means 'understanding'. When the psalmist said 'for the Lord is sweet', he meant that He is 'good'. As a humanistic philologist, Luther worked here with the hebrew psalter. In his latin lectures he rendered the verse with *bonus* ('good') even though the Vulgate has *suavis* ('sweet'). Luther explained further:

> From this verse we learn that we may see God's power and wisdom without the taste of his goodness, yet nobody can see and correctly believe in his goodness except someone who has somehow experienced it and has tasted it. If someone had the soul of Bernard, he would understand this verse well'.[21]

---

20 Nat BVM; SBOp 5:276,8–12, using Sg 2:3 (' . . . sweet to my palate').

21 . . . *Si quis animam Bernhardi haberet, hic versum istum bene caperet,* WA 55-I:298–301, here 301 (WA 3:186,31–34). Bell, *Divus Bernhardus,* 56, uses

From this comment one may discern that Luther was as well versed in bernardine spirituality as he was in humanistic scholarship. As late as 1543/44, in expounding the Christmas text Isaiah 9:5, Luther mentioned that Bernard and Augustine spoke of the sweetness of the Lord. He went on to make clear that his insights had been decisively shaped by his humanistic study of the biblical hebrew. To achieve a better understanding of the Isaiah text, he interpreted it by a New Testament text, presenting the definition of the greek notion *chrestós/chrestótes* from Titus 3:4, the traditional lesson for Christmas. Mindful of his studies on Titus in 1527, he associated the original greek version of Titus 3:4 (*chrestótes*) with the latin expression *summa suavitas*,[22] although the familiar Vulgate version does not use the concept of 'sweetness' at this point, but has instead *benignitas et humanitas*. Luther practised the 'exegetical concordance' method here and retrieved the familiar latin notion *suavitas* from the monastic theological tradition, and he used it here to bring out his understanding of Isaiah 9:5. A little later, Luther explicitly connected the spiritual authorities he cherished most: Bernard and Augustine:

> Bernard made it known that whoever once has tasted the sweetness of this insight is refilled with incredible joy, he greatly deplores then that this taste does not last long because of the impediment of the flesh. Augustine deplores the same thing.[23]

---

the german word *Geist* for the latin *anima*. Bell did not mention Bernard's Conv 13.25 as a possible source, while the new edition of the *Dictata* in WA 55-I:301 (1993) refers to Conv 13.25 (SBOp 4:9,8; CF 25:61) where Bernard used the expression *suavitas domini* and Ps 33:9. This should not, however be understood to mean that Luther had actually read Bernard's Conv. Only a similarity of thought can be implied here, because nowhere did Luther indicate that he was familiar with this particular bernardine sermon. For this reason I have opted to refer here to the more obvious texts, such as the passages in Bernard's SC, in which Ps 33:9 was used explicitly, because Luther made it known through his own source references that he was familiar with Bernard's SCs.

22 WA 40-III:650–57.

23 WA 40-III:652,20–25 (on Is 9, 1546). Luther probably meant Augustine's *De agone Christiano*.

In 1545, the ageing Scripture professor at Wittenberg complained in his last lectures, on Genesis, about the church fathers' ways of interpreting the Scriptures, especially about Augustine, who, he observed, was 'playing with allegories'.[1] Luther wanted instead to elaborate on the original and grammatical sense of a text first; only after that is one not hindered (*nihil obstat*) from also seeking in it a figurative or allegorical meaning. As another example of such a 'playful' method Luther pointed to Bernard's artistry with words. As he lectured on Gen 47:31, he pointed out in a critical, and simultaneously admiring observation:

> And Bernard is a wonderful artist in [working with] catachreses. For he often connects a passage which should be referred to some specific image with some general meaning. In this manner, of course, it is permissible to resort to a catachresis and transfer a text to something else. This meaning is also good. Nevertheless, one must not do violence to simple grammar.[2]

The greek word *catachresis* is rendered in latin by *abusio* (unusual, inappropriate use); it is this of which Luther spoke here, not of *abusus* ('abuse'). After this remark, Luther noted that even 'the author of the Epistle to the Hebrews' worked with the rhetorical concept of catachresis.[3] According to the Reformer's own definition, catachresis is an *abusiuus* way of speaking, a misapplication.[4] The latin adjective *abusiuus* stems from the verb *abuti*, 'to use up' or 'to consume', which may also, at times, mean 'to misuse' and 'to use not literally' or 'not properly'. Thus Bernard was using Scripture texts 'not literally', *abusiuus*. Luther's remark about Bernard is supported by the meaning of the latin noun *abusio*, which he also employed in this passage;[5] it meant the non-literal or inappropriate use of words taken out of their original context.

---

1 WA 44:686,14.
2 *Bernardus mirabilis artifex est in Catachresibus*, WA 44:686,25f.
3 WA 44:686,30–33.
4 WA 30-II:381,23f (1530).
5 WA 44:686,27–29.

Catachresis, according to Luther's definition, meant 'borrowing a statement from Scripture and playing around with it, but
without harming the text and its proper meaning'.[6] Luther thought
that a strained teasing with words is done without damage to the
text and its correct meaning, but it nevertheless yields an incorrect
understanding (*misverstand*). Catachresis, essentially an improper
playing with the words, was associated in Luther's mind with
Augustine 'playing with allegories' and Bernard toying master-
fully with *catachreses*. Earlier in these same lectures, on Gen
18:2–5, Luther commented that sometimes these *catachreses* are
acceptable.[7] The rhetorically trained Reformer had no objections
to this use of the Scriptures, which he observed in the church
fathers' works, and actually admired Bernard for it. Already in
his commentary on Galatians (published in 1535), Luther praised
Bernard's Bible interpretation as beautiful (*pulchre*) catachresis.[8]

Luther's concern was with the correct understanding of the
original meaning of the Word of God. He wanted to make sure that
no one did 'violence to simple grammar' or 'harm the text and its
proper meaning'. Catachresis as embellishment, the way Bernard
practised it, was fine with him; but Luther was always anxious
to find the proper meaning of the revealed word. His struggle for
the correct understanding manifested itself most visibly during the
notorious academic debate at Leipzig in the summer of 1519, when
Dr Eck and Dr Luther waged a war of words over the correct use
and interpretation of the Bible. At Leipzig, Bernard's name was
entered into the debate by Eck, who referred to Bernard's use of
John 5:19 in *De consideratione*, Book Three. Eck claimed that
Bernard spoke about the form of the Church as of divine right.[9]
Luther maintained that Bernard treated the johannine verse 'in
another sense',[10] by which he meant the non-literal, allegorical

6 WA 30-II:381,24–27.
7 See WA 43:12,13f.
8 WA 40-II:53,36–54,11 (printed version).
9 *De consideratione ad Eugenium,* WA 59:441,267–280.
10 *Bernardus alio sensu tractat hoc verbum Christi,* WA 59:445,410f; 446,
422.

sense. For the first time in public, Luther was forced by Eck to admit his difference from Bernard.

Later in the debate, Eck adduced from *De consideratione*, Book Two, a passage allegorically interpreting the 'sea' as the 'world' on which Saint Peter walked (Mt 14:29).[11] Luther rejected this interpretation as a proof-text supporting the institution of the petrine office by divine right. Luther maintained that this was a meaning 'alien' to Scripture,[12] and exclaimed that 'Bernard tortures the text about Peter'.[13] This judgment was possible only if Bernard's utterance was taken at the level of allegorical interpretation, as it was meant. All kinds of interpretations are allowed because they were not considered binding. It was in this sense, that Luther dared to accuse Bernard of torturing the text. As a literal and thus binding interpretation the application made of the story of Peter walking on water he could not accept.

In emphasizing grammatical and literal interpretation, Luther thought he was following Augustine and Bernard, despite their allegorizations. By this he hoped to find the simple, solid sense of the Scriptures, as he wrote in a letter while looking back at the Leipzig Disputation. He objected to weakening the words of Scripture by interpreting them with opinions of the church fathers. In contrast, he pointed out, he was used to following Augustine and Bernard from the brooks to the spring, so that he and other theologians would be well armed against Satan.[14] Luther was apparently not aware that he also followed Thomas Aquinas, who in the tracks of Augustine adhered to the same hermeneutical

11 *Per mare interpretatur mundus*, WA 59:454, 688f.

12 *Alieno sensu scripturae*, WA 59:464,986 and 994; 521,2741.

13 *Et Bernardum credo torquere textum de Petro ambulante super mare,* WA 59:525, 2850f, referring to Csi 2.16. On the controversial interpretation of Bernard by Eck and Luther, see Köhler, *Luther und die Kirchengeschichte*, 314–318; Bell, *Divus Bernhardus*, 150–165. Lohse, 'Luther und Bernhard von Clairvaux', 293f. Lohse sees in the Leipzig Debate a turning point in Luther's view of Bernard, which I cannot see that clearly at all, especially not when one takes Luther's life-long positive utilization of bernardine texts into consideration – before and after the Leipzig Debate.

14 See WA Br 1:602, 42–46 (no. 235). See Otto Hermann Pesch, *Hinführung zu Luther* (Mainz: Matthias-Grünewald-Verlag 1982) 65f, with note 4; Bell, *Divus Bernardus*, 165; Lohse, 'Luther und Bernhard von Clairvaux', 294.

principle. There is no confusion if one takes the literal sense as one's basis of interpretation.[15]

His focus on the binding literal sense did not prevent the Reformer from occasionally distancing himself from the esteemed Augustine and admired Bernard, especially when they 'played with allegories', or when they practiced catachresis or produced centos, that is, compositions made up from bits of biblical sources. Bernard was especially good at this and displayed an incomparable virtuosity in speaking the dialect of the Bible.

Here I want to draw attention to the fact that Bernard's interpretation of the Bible had become an issue during the Reformation era. In this climate Luther appraised Bernard for his artistry of catachreses, but also for his torturing of the text. It should become clear, then, that Luther's development in his own hermeneutics suffered neither a gradual nor an abrupt shift from the medieval allegorical, fourfold interpretation toward 'the simple' interpretation. Instead he oscillated back and forth, to and from allegorical interpretations. His tendency, however, was always to give preference to the original meaning of the text, which to him was essentially christological.[16] This having been said, one needs to be well aware that the hermeneutics of Luther (or of Bernard) have not been treated exhaustively. There is room for further study in this regard, including the investigation, which cannot be pursued here, of the phenomenon of catachresis in Bernard's texts to which Luther alerted us. Still further research is needed, similar to studies done in recent years on paronomasia ('puns') in the works of Bernard,[17] and research on Luther's own strong inclination toward puns and paronomasia. From an other than theological perspective, one might perhaps be able to explain further the great admiration which Luther, the linguist, had for

---

15 See Pesch, *Hinführung zu Luther*, 65f, with note 46.

16 See Pesch, *Hinführung zu Luther*, 60.

17 Recent scholarship pointed out Bernard's play with words, i. e. *paronomasia*, but not his *catachreses*; see Saberski-Bascho, *Studien zur Paronomasie bei Bernhard von Clairvaux* (1979); see Henri Rochais and Jean Figuet, 'Le jeu biblique de Bernard', Coll 47 (1985) 119–128.

Bernard, who remained in his eyes the great medieval mentor and the 'last of the fathers'.[18]

Finally, we must realize that Luther shared with the humanistic scholarship of his time the evaluation of Bernard's use of the Sacred Scriptures. Erasmus, the philologist, observed that Bernard used the Bible inappropriately, and counted him among the *abusores sacrae scripturae*.[19] Perhaps Luther followed Erasmus in this. Despite his criticism, Luther maintained in dispute with Eck that he 'venerated' Saint Bernard.[20] Interestingly, when, in his *preface* to the publication of his *Operationes* in 1519, he listed those expositors who were occasionally quite removed from the literal sense in their interpretations such as Augustine, Jerome, Athanasius, Hilary, and Cassiodorus, he did not include Bernard. Instead, in his *Operatio* on Psalm 1, Luther referred readers very pointedly to 'Saint Bernard' as an outstanding interpreter who drew all his 'erudition' from the Bible.[21]

In Chapter One, we have come to see how close Bernard's monastic theology was to the theological axiom 'Scripture alone' for which Luther is the champion. Yet in Bernard we never encounter the slogan *sola scriptura*. We do, however, find him speaking of 'grace alone' and 'faith alone' and to these we turn in Chapters Two and Three.

18 See INTRODUCTION.

19 See Erasmus' *Ratio verae theologiae* (1518; which is also his preface of his 1519 edition of the greek New Testament). The Cistercian George Schirn objected to it; see his letter to Erasmus (Ep 1142); see Posset, 'Saint Bernard of Clairvaux in the Devotion, Theology, and Art of the First Half of the Sixteenth Century', *Lutheran Quarterly* 11 (1997) 308–352, here 323.

20 *Divum Bernhardum veneror . . .* , WA 59:441–45.

21 See AWA 2:63,26–28. The most recent study on Luther's *Operationes* appears to have overlooked this important aspect, Hubertus Blaumeiser, *Martin Luthers Kreuzestheologie. Schlüssel zu seiner Deutung von Mensch und Wirklichkeit. Eine Untersuchung anhand der Operationes in Psalmos (1519–1521)* (Paderborn: Bonifatius Verlag, 1995).

Plate 8: *Bernard Preaches to his Monks on God's Mercy.* Glass window, early sixteenth-century, originally from the cistercian monastery of Altenberg, Germany; today in Schnütgen Museum, Cologne. Rheinisches Bildarchiv, Cologne. The inscription in black is a quotation from the Third Sermon for the Feast of Saints Peter and Paul; this source reference is given in red letters as part of the inscription: *In sermone III° de apostolis petro et paulo.*

2

Grace Alone

N CHAPTER TWO, Bernard's and Luther's theology of grace come into focus. Another glass window from Altenberg (Plate 8) may help us understand the sixteenth-century perception of Saint Bernard as the preacher of God's mercy. In the window he is depicted with a halo, an open Bible on his lap and the abbatial staff in his right hand. The throne on which he sits before his assembled monks is slightly lifted off the floor by two angels. The monks surrounding the preacher are shown with happy faces as they receive their abbot's consoling message. The inscription to the left of Bernard's head is a quotation from his third sermon for the solemn feast of the Apostles Peter and Paul (PP 3). Citing Sirach 44:10 the preacher called the two apostles 'men of mercy', not because they were themselves merciful, but because they received rich mercy. The sermon is introduced with the words: 'You have heard how our Apostles received mercy, so that now none of you need be unnecessarily confounded about past sins or pricked by them on the bed of conscience'. The inscription in the glass window reads:

> Why not? Perhaps you sinned in the world, but did you sin more extensively than Paul? If you have sinned in the religious life, did you sin more than Peter? Yet by doing penance with all their heart they received not only salvation, but also holiness;

they even attained both the *ministerium* of salvation and the *magisterium* of holiness. Do likewise then.[1]

This paragraph of the sermon concludes with these words: 'Because Scripture says for your benefit that these were men of mercy. Undoubtedly this was because of the great mercy they were worthy of receiving'. Bernard is pictured here as the comforting preacher of God's mercy. Luther emulated him in this regard, even though, most likely, he had never read any of these three sermons for the feast of the Apostles, for he never, not even remotely, referred to them in any way.[2] Yet, the congeniality of Bernard and Luther over the message of divine mercy contained in this particular sermon is striking.

In what follows, we will look at a bernardine sermon which impressed Luther perhaps more than any other. In this case we have definite proof that Luther had read it, for he quoted it extensively, as we shall see. The message again is God's mercy on sinners. After we have investigated this bernardine sermon on the Annunciation (Ann 1), we will proceed to the issues of grace and free choice, and of salvation by faith alone. Here we will discover Bernard using the phrase 'salvation by faith alone', and will have the opportunity of finding out what Bernard and Luther taught about faith and good works, and about the necessity of faith and baptism. We will investigate how progress in faith is to be made, and what Bernard understood by 'holy sinner' and Luther by 'saint and sinner at the same time'. We will reflect on their understanding of

1 The picture is found also in Paffrath, *Bernhard von Clairvaux* (1984), 204, illustration 60. The text is found in SBOp 5:200,12–15. I follow the translation in *Bernard of Clairvaux: Sermons for the Summer Season. Liturgical Sermons from Rogationtide and Pentecost,* Beverly Mayne Kienzle, trans. (Kalamazoo: CP, 1991) 112, except for the word play *ministerium – magisterium.*

2 Luther also never appears to refer to Bernard's response to Abelard, in which the concept of forensic justification is expressed ('Why should I not have someone else's righteousness since I have someone else's guilt?'), nor to Ep 190.16 where the *extra nos* aspect is talked about, see Abael 6.15; SBOp 8:29f. *Cur non aliunde iustitia . . .* : 'Why would not justice come from elsewhere, when the culprit comes from elsewhere? It is one person who established sin and another who frees from sin. The one in seed, the other in blood. Or is sin in the seed of the sinner, but justice not in the blood of Christ?' Ep 190.16; SBOp 8:30; as translated in Pranger, *Bernard of Clairvaux and the Shape of Monastic Thought,* 270.

humility and humiliation; their shared view of the interrelatedness of 'knowledge of self' and 'knowledge of God'; and their thoughts on Christ dwelling in the heart of the believer (Chapter Three).

I. THREE CONVICTIONS: GOD'S MERCY, GRACE, AND FREE GIFT

1. *Saint Bernard's message of grace in his 'First Sermon on the Annunciation'*

Exactly nine months before Christmas—on March 25th—the Church celebrates the feast of the annunciation, when Mary learned that she would become the Mother of Christ. On this feast Bernard preached to his monks about the 'glory dwelling in our land', a phrase which is taken from Ps 84:10f (in the Vulgate version: *Ut inhabitet gloria in terra nostra*). The full biblical text reads: 'Near indeed is his salvation to those who fear him, glory dwelling in our land. Kindness and truth shall meet; justice and peace shall kiss' (Ps 84:1f). The homilist combined this psalm verse with 2 Cor 1:12, 'Conscience gives testimony to the boast', or more literally and closer to the Latin: 'this is our glory: the testimony of our conscience' (*Nam gloria nostra haec est*). The key word relating the psalm verse to the pauline text is *gloria*. Bernard interpreted the 'glory in our land' by the 'testimony of our conscience', interpreting one biblical verse with another, following the 'methods of 'exegetical concordance'. The preacher went on to explain that this testimony was not like that of the pharisee who prayed with unbowed head in Luke 18. Thus, an additional Bible passage was employed in the effort to proclaim the message. Before Bernard actually presented the 'testimony' which he made the topic of his homily, he interwove yet three more verses from Scripture. Two are taken from John's Gospel and one from Paul's letter to the Romans: Jn 5:31, Jn 8:13f,[3] and Rom 8:16 (on 'testimony').[4] There are, he wrote, three truths of faith:

---

3 SBOp 5:1,4–6; 13,8.
4 SBOp 5:13,9.

First of all, we ought to believe that we cannot have forgiveness of our sins other than through God's indulgence; secondly, that we are powerless to do any good work whatever except by his grace; thirdly, that by no works of ours can we merit eternal life, unless it too is given to us freely. . . . Undoubtedly, that which has been done can never be undone: yet if God wills not to impute it, it shall be as if it had not been. The Prophet (Psalm 31:2) had this in mind when he exclaimed, 'Blessed is the man to whom the Lord imputes no sin'.[5]

Bernard preached here the exclusivess of grace (*sola gratia*), for no human merit can win eternal salvation: (1) God's mercy alone brings remission of sins; (2) one's own good works are given by God; (3) eternal life cannot be earned (*promereri*), because it, too, is a free gift. The notion of 'imputation' he used, following the wording of the Latin Psalm 31:2 and the pauline quotation from Rom 8:16, must be kept in mind during the investigation of Luther's texts that follows.

Bernard used Rom 8:16 in his introduction to the sermon, as we just saw. In the body of the sermon, he continued with verse 18: we know that the sufferings of the present time are nothing compared with the glory that is to be revealed. He concluded that all our merits are God's gift (*merita omnia Dei sunt dona*),[6] interweaving the words of Acts 13:22 and Ps 143:2, about a man like David who is formed after God's heart and who prays to God: 'And enter not into judgment with your servant, for before you no living man is just'.[7] To these quotations Bernard linked the warning from Luke 14:31: 'Let nobody deceive himself; for if he considers carefully, he will undoubtedly discover that even with ten thousand soldiers he cannot stand up against the Lord who comes at him with twenty thousand'.[8] Bernard advised: 'But add to this

5 SBOp 5:13,10–13. In the famous *Aqueduct Sermon*, Bernard preached even more concisely: 'For it is by grace alone that we shall be saved', *Nimirum sola est gratia, qua salvamur*, SBOp 5:279,26–27. When Luther criticized Bernard's marian sermons, he hardly could have had this sermon in mind since it contains the message of grace which Luther wanted to proclaim.

6 SBOp 5:14,11–12.

7 SBOp 5:14,15–16.

8 SBOp 5:14,16–18.

that you also believe that through him your sins are forgiven. This is the testimony which the Holy Spirit brings to your heart, saying "your sins are forgiven you", for thus the Apostle concluded that a man is freely justified by faith.'[9] Here he used Rom 3:24 and 3:28, about justification by faith, and in his next sentence he quoted Jn 15:26, on the Spirit of Truth, emphasizing that we must also believe that our merits are God-given.[10] When Bernard explained the remission of sins by grace and faith alone, he relied primarily on the two biblical theologians, John and Paul, whom Luther called the 'high commanders' (*duces*) of theology.[11] Bernard continued by reflecting on Ephesians 3:17 (Christ dwelling in the heart by faith), and eventually spoke of the loss generated by Adam and Eve, 'our cruel mother':

> When she began to burn with so fierce a fire of concupiscence that she spared neither herself nor her husband nor her offspring-to-be, but doomed all alike to the chastisement of a terrible curse and inevitable death. . . . Here we have a threefold cord of curiosity, pleasure, and vanity: and 'a threefold cord is not easily broken' (Qo 4:12). Such things alone are offered by the world: 'The concupiscence of the flesh, and the concupiscence of the eyes, and the pride of life' (1 Jn 2:16).[12]

2. Luther: 'There is no better phrase in all of Bernard'

We do not possess any marginal notes by Luther on any of Bernard's sermons, as we do his notes on Peter Lombard and Augustine.[13] Nor do we know at what exact time Luther was reading Bernard's first sermon on the Annunciation. We do, however, find Luther quoting this sermon several times over the years. Certainly he had come into contact with Bernard's sermons by 1513–1515, when

9 SBOp 5:14,22–15,2.

10 SBOp 5:14,23–15,4.

11 WA 18:757, 9–10; LW 33:241.

12 SBOp 5:20,9–17. On the use of Eph 3:17 in Ann and other bernardine texts, see Robert O'Brien, 'St. Bernard's Use of Sacred Scripture', *Word and Spirit: A Monastic Review* 12 (1990) 162–171, here 166.

13 See WA 9:5–27 (on Augustine); WA 9:29–94 (on Peter Lombard).

he lectured on the psalms.[14] That there was an earlier point of contact we know from Luther's dear friend, Philip Melanchthon, who in his preface to the second volume of Luther's works, published at Wittenberg in 1546, mentioned Luther's first awareness of Bernard's sermon. There is no reason to question the validity of Melanchthon's reminiscence. The younger friend gives us the biographical detail that an unknown senior augustinian friar of the 'College of Erfurt' had taught Luther truly to believe in the forgivenenss of sins proclaimed in the Creed: 'I believe in the forgiveness of sins'. In this connection the older friar made the consternated young Luther aware of Bernard's *dictum* in Ann 1 (Melanchton quoting Bernard): 'But add to this that you also believe this, that through him *your* sins are forgiven. This is the testimony which the Holy Spirit brings in your heart, saying "your sins are forgiven you", for thus the Apostle concluded that a man is freely justified by faith.'[15] The emphasis on 'your' sins is indicated in Melanchthon's text by capitalization: *TIBI*.

Luther: 'As Bernard meditates beautifully in a certain sermon' (On the Psalms, 1513–1515)

After having been introduced to the insights of Ann 1 at an early date at Erfurt, Luther from then on remembered the essential content of this sermon, especially the wording of Vulgate Psalm 31:2 on God's non-imputation of sin; but he did not, apparently, recall its exact locus within the bernardine sermon collection. In 1513, when Luther started his first course on the psalms and arrived at the exposition of that crucial verse (31:2), he remembered that Bernard had used it in one of his sermons. Luther did not remember at that moment which sermon it was. He referred to Bernard by

14 See Maurer, 'Cisterciensische Reform und reformatorischer Glaube', 6.

15 See *Corpus Reformatorum*, Carolus Gottlieb Bretschneider, ed. (Halle: C. A. Schwetschke, 1834) 6:159. See Stephen Strehle, *The Catholic Roots of the Protestant Gospel: Encounter Between the Middle Ages and the Reformation* (Leiden: Brill, 1995) 18–22; Strehle 21 wrote as if there was only one sermon by Bernard for the feast of the Annunciation; he did not quote from the standard critical edition SBOp. Melanchthon's Luther biography of 1549 is found in English translation in *Hymns of the Reformation by Dr. Martin Luther, and others, from the German, To which is added, His Life, translated from the original latin of Philip Melancthon* [sic] (London: Charles Gilpin, 1845).

name and to 'a certain sermon' of his. And he paid Bernard the
fine compliment that he was 'meditating beautifully' and that 'the
world' does not know this mystery of the faith; the world fought
against the Apostles who preached it; the world rejected Christ
who proclaimed it:

> ... as Bernard meditates on it beautifully in a certain sermon.
> Hence he says: 'Blessed are they whose iniquities are forgiven',
> and then: 'Blessed is he to whom the Lord does not impute sin'
> (Ps 31:2), because it is not enough that we impute nothing to
> ourselves or that we are not aware. . . . For no one is without
> iniquity. And there is no one who has no iniquities, but there are
> only some whose iniquities are forgiven, etc. And this is what
> the title of the psalm has in mind when it is called the 'erudition
> of David'. For we are taught by the understanding through faith,
> and not by feeling or reason.[16]

By quoting Bernard's 'certain sermon', in a positive way,
Luther made clear his congeniality with Bernard's thought.

Luther: 'Thus [says] Blessed Bernard in Sermon One on the Annunciation' (On *Romans*, 1516)

By 1515, Luther had finished his *Dictata* and proceeded to
the other text which Bernard also valued highly, the *Letter to the
Romans*. In Paul's letter, at Rom 4:7–8, Psalm 31:2 is quoted, but
at this point Luther did not bring in his insights from Bernard's
Ann 1. The occasion arose during his exposition of Rom 8:16, a
verse which Bernard used in the introduction to his Annunciation
sermon.[17] Luther's mental associations connected the latin Bible
version of Rom 8:16, *ipse enim Spiritus testimonium reddit spiritui
nostro*, with Bernard's latin sermon which incorporated it. This

16 WA 3:175,34–38; see LW 10:147. In my 'Monastic Influence on Luther'
(1988) I assumed that Luther had SC 22 in mind, while Bell, *Bernhardus Dixit*
(1989), 61, thought it was SC 23. In 1990, at the international Bernard congress
in Kalamazoo, I revised my position and suggested Ann 1 as the text which
Luther may have meant most likely, see my 'Divus Bernhardus: Saint Bernard
as Spiritual and Theological Mentor of the Reformer Martin Luther', *Bernardus
Magister*, 520f. In 1993, Bell joined me in this opinion in his revised german
edition *Divus Bernhardus*, 66f.

17 See SBOp 5:13,9.

scriptural line must have been stored in Luther's memory and associated with Bernard's use of it in Ann 1, because at this point Luther processed all the essential passages of Bernard's homily both in his scholium and in his gloss on Rom 8:16. In his gloss he explicitly mentioned Bernard: 'For he who trusts with strong faith and hope to be a son of God, is indeed a son of God, which nobody can be without the Spirit. Thus Blessed Bernard in sermon one on the Annunciation'.[18] In his scholium he quoted Bernard's homily extensively. In his opinion, Bernard had explained the subject under discussion 'very clearly' (*preclarissime*), and was an expositor filled 'with this same Spirit'.[19] Luther continued his 'exploitation' of Bernard's Ann 1 by quoting word for word the three aspects of Bernard's introduction to the sermon.[20] Luther also lifted from the main part of that sermon a passage which reads: 'But add this: That you also believe this, not that you could; but it is necessary that the Spirit causes you believe this'.[21] This is the same quotation Melanchthon gives in his preface of 1546. Luther continued citing Bernard in a passage on the forgiveness of sins.[22] At this point, however, Luther deleted Bernard's original statement, including the words of the Vulgate version of Rom 3:24 that justification is *gratis*. It seems that Bernard had taught the 'reformation' doctrine of justification more radically than Luther did in his lecture!

18 *Quia qui confidit forti fide et spe se esse filium Dei, Ipse est filius Dei, Quod sine spiritu nemo potest. Vnde B. Bernardus ser. 1 de annunciatione Dominica*, WA 56:79,15–17 (gloss). See Posset, '*Bernardus Redivivus*', 239–249.

19 *Quod testimonium istud sit ipsa fiducia cordis in Deum, preclarissime ostendit B. Bernardus, plenus eodem spiritu, sermone de annunciatione 1. dicens*, WA 56:369,28–29. See Kleineidam, 'Ursprung und Gegenstand', 235f; Posset, '*Bernardus Redivivus*', 244, with note 26; Posset, 'Divus Bernhardus', *Bernardus Magister*, 521–23; Bell, *Divus Bernhardus*, 93f and 377; Lohse, 'Luther und Bernhard von Clairvaux', 276f.

20 WA 56:370,1–6 = SBOp 5:13,9–13.

21 The editor of WA did not recognize this phrase as a direct quotation from Bernard's sermon since the quotation marks in WA are missing. A simple text comparison produced the identity of this phrase from Luther's scholium with Bernard's sermon: *Sed adde adhuc: vt et hoc credas*, [= SBOp 5:14,22] *non quod possis tu, Sed necesse est, vt spiritus faciat te hoc credere*, WA 56:370,8f.

22 WA 56:370:9–12. Bernard's original has the stylistic difference of *tibi peccata donantur*, while Luther wrote *peccata tibi donantur*.

Luther adopted Bernard's vocabulary, copying his verb *per-hibet*,[23] even though the Vulgate text of Rom 8:16 has *reddit*. This means that Luther followed Bernard's wording rather than the Bible's. Here we have clear evidence that by the time of his lectures on Romans, Luther had actually looked up the text of Bernard's sermon. He was no longer satisfied with referring his audience to 'a certain sermon', as he had done in the earlier course on the psalms. In addition, Luther definitely wanted to point out that this bernardine doctrine stemmed from Paul, his favorite 'Apostle'.[24] Luther quoted yet another phrase from Ann 1, the subsequent sentence about human merits also being gifts of God as revealed by the Spirit's testimony.[25]

Luther's final quotation from Ann 1 was also taken from the central part of the sermon, which deals with 'eternal life'. His reference to the source differs only in style, mainly in the sequence of the words, with Luther adding an extra line for clarification.[26] Thus Luther confirmed the value he put on Bernard's sermon in his own interpretation of Paul's Letter to the Romans. For further corroboration of his position, he added two more pauline references, Rom 8:33 and 8:38–39.[27]

What Luther did here was typical of the monastic-humanistic exegesis of his time: he interpreted one biblical passage with others and he did all of this under the guidance of a church father's interpretation.[28] Simultaneously, Luther critically evaluated Bernard's scriptural foundation and came to the conclusion that Bernard was in agreement with Saint Paul. Or, in other words, Bernard's Ann 1 was of decisive help to Luther in interpreting Paul's Letter to the Romans.[29]

23 SBOp 5:14,23 = WA 56:370,9.

24 SBOp 5:15,1 = WA 56:370,2.

25 WA 56:370,14–16. Bernard's original is only slightly different: SBOp 5:15,2–4.

26 SBOp 5: 5:4f, quoted by Luther, WA 56:370,20–23. See Posset, 'Divus Bernhardus', 517–532.

27 WA 56:370:24–29.

28 See Junghans, *Der junge Luther und die Humanisten,* 108–92.

29 See Bell, *Divus Bernhardus,* 83–99.

Luther: 'Blessed Bernard in a certain sermon on the Annunciation' (On *Hebrews*, 1517)

Luther also referred to Bernard's Ann 1 in his scholium on
Heb 5:1: 'Every high priest is taken from among men and made
their representative before God . . .' (*pro hominibus constituitur*).[30]
He clearly indicated his source: 'Blessed Bernard in a sermon
on the Annunciation',[31] and to leave no room for mistake, he
immediately added the exact title of that sermon: *cuius thema est:
'Ut inhabitet gloria in terra nostra'*,[32] Bernard's *thema,* taken from
Psalm 84:10f, is used in the headline of Ann 1. After having referred
to the exact source, Luther presented the quotation *sentencialiter*,[33]
i. e. quoting the 'sense' without using the identical wording.[34] This
suggests that Luther did not have an edition of Bernard's sermon at
hand at that very moment and could not copy out the exact wording.
That he was able to quote Bernard from memory suggests that this
sermon had impressed him so decisively that he remembered the
precise content, which he repeated as follows: 'It is necessary that
you believe that God can forgive you your sins, that he confers
grace and gives glory'.[35] This is a fairly accurate rendition of
Bernard's text.[36] Luther even refers to the same biblical quotations
which Bernard had used.[37] He continued in conscious dependence
on Bernard by saying: 'as Blessed Bernard says'.[38] Here, Luther,
with Saint Bernard, interpreted Saint Paul in an anti-pelagian way.
Decisive for Luther was the emphasis on the personal conviction
of the remission of one's sins. It is not sufficient to believe only

30 WA 57-III:169,10–23; see WA 57-I:189, 23–190,14.

31 . . . *sic B. Bernhardus in sermone quodam de Annunciacione* [sic], *cuius
theme est . . . ,* WA 57-III:169,13–14. On Luther's handling of source references
and cross references, see Junghans, *Der junge Luther und die Humanisten*, 115–
21.

32 WA 57-III:169,14; see WA 57-I:189,23–190,14.

33 WA 57-III:169,15.

34 See note to line 15 in WA 57-III:169, and WA 31-II:465,13.

35 WA 57-III:169,15f.

36 SBOp 5:13,5.

37 2 Cor 1:[12], WA 57-III:169,19f; Luther also employed Rom 8:16 as
Bernard did, see WA 57-III:169,18; Bernard in SBOp 5:13,9.

38 *Non enim testimonium consciencie [sic] eiusmodi, ut B. Bernhardus ait,
intelligitur . . . ,* WA 57-III:169,20–23; see Posset, *'Bernardus Redivivus'*, 245;
Bell, *Divus Bernhardus,* 101.

in a general remission, he declared, but that '*to you* your sins are remitted' (*tibi remissa peccata*).[39] The accent in the latin is on *tibi* ('to you') as the latin word-order indicates. Luther simply picked up Bernard's phrase, which is rendered in the critical edition in capital letters: *DIMISSA SUNT TIBI PECCATA TUA.*[40] We may assume that this emphasis was already in the Bernard edition which Luther used. In Melanchthon's preface a similar emphasis is found, but highlighting a different sentence within Bernard's sermon.

How much Luther's *pro me* matched its bernardine matrix remains striking. What was thought to be typical of Luther, i. e. his emphasis on 'for me' (*pro me*) had actually already been expressed by Bernard even more directly than by Luther himself. Bernard explicitly used the pronoun 'for you' (*tibi*), which Luther did not, although Luther elsewhere emphasized strongly an existential, personal faith in Christ who died for us. What should be recognized in this connection is that Luther, with his stress on *pro me*, wrote within the bernardine tradition.[41]

Luther argues with insights from his '*Divus Bernhardus*' (1518)

Luther was so permeated by Bernard's message that he remembered Ann 1 not only in his academic lectures on Scripture, but also during his interrogation by Cardinal Cajetan at the meeting in Augsburg, on 14 October 1518. At Augsburg, the thomistic tradition clashed with the augustinian/bernardine tradition. Luther quoted the now familiar passage from Bernard's Ann 1, by which he was assured that the Holy Spirit says: 'Your sins are forgiven you', and that the apostle teaches justification by faith *gratis*.[42] The essential bernardine phrases recur here in Luther's emphatic

39 See WA 57-III:169,17; see WA 57-I:189,23–190,14.

40 See above note 9; WA 57-III:169,16–18.

41 I contest the thesis that the emphasis on *pro me* had its roots in the late Middle Ages or in Tauler's mysticism, as Pesch maintained, *Hinführung zu Luther*, 88f. However, I concur with Pesch against Paul Hacker's thesis that this emphasis would incorporate heterodoxy. If Luther is interpreted in the light of the bernardine monastic theology, Hacker's thesis turns out to be ridiculous.

42 *Et Bernhardus sermone de annunctiatione i.,* WA 2:15,35–16,3 (*Acta Augustana*, 1518); see Kleineidam, 'Ursprung und Gegenstand', 239f; Posset, '*Bernardus Redivivus*', 246f; Bell, *Divus Bernhardus*, 133–137; Lohse, *Luthers Theologie*, 13. Lohse in his 'Luther und Bernhard von Clairvaux', 278, stressed that Luther relied also on Augustine next to Bernard.

defense against the roman delegate's accusation that he had created a 'new theology'. Luther did not hesitate to mention Bernard by name in this context. He boldly declared that *'Divus Bernhardus* with the universal Church' admired this exemplary faith based on the pauline teaching on justification. Luther concluded his argument with the words: 'These and many other authorities lead me, compel me, captivate me in the opinion (*sententia*) I have stated'.[43]

In his commentary *On Galatians*, of 1519, Luther may also have alluded to Ann 1, but he did not mention it by name. In his gloss and scholium on Gal 1:4f, 'who gave himself for our sins, to rescue us from the present evil age, as our God and Father willed— to him be glory for endless ages. Amen', Luther pointed out: 'This is the faith that justifies, that Christ lives in you. . . . This is the testimony of the Spirit which he gives our spirit, that we are sons of God', and made reference to Rom 8:16.[44]

Luther: 'There is no better phrase in all of Bernard. Another one is in the Sermon on the Annunciation' (On *1 John*, 1527)

At roughly the time when the tenth anniversary of the 'Reformation' was to be commemorated at Wittenberg,[45] Luther again spoke explicitly of Bernard's Ann 1, this time during his lectures on the *First Letter of John*. It was on 9 October 1527, when the verse 'not that we have loved God, but that he has loved us and has sent his Son as an offering for our sins' (1 Jn 4:10), triggered his memory of Bernard's insights. This johannine verse, one of the cistercian preacher's favorite Bible passages,[46] best expressed the priority of grace. Luther declared: 'I myself have paid attention

43 *Unde fidem eius* [Mary] *miratur divus Bernhardus et universa Ecclesia,* WA 2:15,18. Luther used the insight from Ann 1 also in WA 1:543,23 without mentioning Bernard, see Bell, *Divus Bernhardus,* 103. On the humanists' use of *divus,* see PART ONE, I with note 4.

44 See WA 2:458,20–26 (1519). See Manns, 'Zum Gespräch zwischen M. Luther und der katholischen Theologie', 144f.

45 'We drank in memory of them [indulgences] in this hour and consoled one another', WA Br 4:275,25–27 (no. 1164).

46 In Bernard's SCs, the verse 1 Jn 4:10 was quoted several times: SC 20.2; 39.10; 50.6; 57.6; 67.10; 71.10; 84.5. On the 'absolute primacy' and the 'all-pervading presence of divine grace' as Bernard's theological basis, see Casey, *Athirst,* 55.

to no holier monk than Bernard; I rank him higher than Gregory, Benedict. . . . "My life is wasted and achieves nothing". There is no better phrase in all of Bernard; another one is in the sermon on the Annunciation.'[47]

Evidently, even after many years of struggle inside and outside the monastic milieu, Luther had not forgotten the liberating effect which Bernard and his monastic theology had had on him. Both Luther[48] and Bernard[49] contrasted true christian faith with 'pharisaic righteousness', corroborating our argument that Luther indeed had Bernard's Ann 1 in mind. Bernard's Ann 1 became the theological matrix of Luther's reformation theology. Luther's return to this bernardine 'source'—in the fashion of the humanists' return to the original sources of the faith, *ad fontes*—made him confident that he was teaching orthodox catholic doctrine. It is not far-fetched to connect Luther's high esteem for Bernard with this particular sermon and to the sermons of the author of whom he said: 'Bernard with his sermons excels all other teachers, even Augustine himself'.[50]

47 *Non est melior locus in toto Bernardo, alter in sermone de Annunciatione*, WA 20:746,13–18. See Posset, *Luther's Catholic Christology,* 116–126, 201–221.

48 See WA 20:744,15–19.

49 SBOp 5:13,7.

50 *Bernhardus in suis praedicationibus excellit omnes alios doctores vel ipsum etiam Augustinum*, WA TR 3:295,6f (no. 3370). My article '*Bernardus Redivivus*', 248, note 51, has a printing mistake as to this source reference which is thus to be corrected.

1. *Bernard: 'Free Choice Makes Us Willers; Grace, Willers of the Good'*

In 1128, at the age of about thirty-eight, Bernard wrote a treatise *On Grace and Free Choice* (*De gratia et libero arbitrio*). Luther was about forty-two years old when he quarreled with Erasmus of Rotterdam over the 'bondage of the will' (*De servo arbitrio*). In this controversy Bernard's treatise played no role.

Bernard's treatise may be considered as his commentary on Paul's Letter to the Romans: 'We trust the reader may be pleased to find that we have never strayed far from the Apostle's meaning', he wrote and referred to Paul's letter eighteen times explicitly and twenty-five times implicitly.[1] Bernard's *leitmotif* was the rhetorical question he posed at the beginning: 'What part do you play . . . if it is all God's work?'[2] More precisely he asked: 'What part, then, does free choice play?' He gave the answer in one passive verb: *salvatur*, it (free choice) is saved. Thus the answer was: It plays no part whatsoever:

> Take away free choice and there is nothing to be saved. Take away grace and there is no means of saving . . . . God is the author of salvation, the free choice is merely capable of receiving it: None but God can give it, nothing but free choice receive it.[3]

He continued:

> For to consent is to be saved.[4] Where you have consent, there

1 See *On Grace and Free Choice: De gratia et libero arbitrio*; CF 19a (Kalamazoo: CP, 1988) 5, note 13. See Sr Marie-Bernard Saïd, 'The Doctrine of Grace in St Bernard', CSQ 16 (1981) 15–29.

2 Gra 1.2; SBOp 3:165,17–19; CF 19a:54. Interestingly, Luther's opponent, Hieronymus Dungersheim of Ochsenfurt, quoted Gra 1 with its source references to Rom 3:24f and Tit 3:5, in order to point out to Luther that famous theologians such as Thomas Aquinas (*Summa contra gentiles* 3.149), Augustine (*De fide et operibus* 14.21), and Bernard always taught justification by God's grace: Dungersheim, *Widerlegung* 21v, as quoted by Freudenberger, *Hieronymus Dungersheim*, 300.

3 Gra 1.2; SBOp 3:166,19–20; CF 19a:54.

4 Gra 1.2; SBOp 3:167,2; CF 19a:55.

also is the will (*voluntas*). But where the will is, there is freedom. And this is what I understand by the term 'free choice'.[5]

According to Bernard's crucial Chapter Six, even freedom of choice (*libertas*) is held captive because humans exist as flesh and spirit, as Paul says in Gal 5:17, 'You do not do what your will intends'. Bernard then reflected:

> To will indeed lies in our power as a result of free choice, but not to carry out what we will. I am not saying to will the good or to will the bad, but simply to will. For to will the good indicates an achievement; and to will the bad, a defect; whereas simply to will denotes the subject itself which does either the achieving or the failing. To this subject, however, creating grace has given existence. Saving grace gives it the achievement. But when it fails, it is to blame for its own failure. Free choice, accordingly, makes us willers; grace willers of the good. Because of the former [the willing faculty], we are able to will; because of the latter [saving grace], we are able to will the good.[6]

Christ alone can set the human will in order; Jesus—according to Luke 12:5—said, 'I will show you whom you should fear'. Furthermore, Christ taught his disciples how to set their wills in order. When, at the beginning of his passion, he prayed that the cup might pass from him, he immediately prayed that the Father's will be done (Mt 26:39). After giving these biblical references, Bernard concluded: 'Thus we have received from God as part of our natural condition how to will, how to fear and how to love. In this we are creatures. But how to will the good, and how to fear God, and how to love God, we receive by the visitation of grace, so that in this we are creatures of God.'[7]

Since we are created to a certain extent with our own free will (*in liberam voluntatem*), we become God's, as it were, by good will. Moreover, God who made it free also makes the will

5 Gra 1.2; SBOp 3:167,17–19; CF 19a:56.

6 Gra 6.16; SBOp 3:177,22–178,5; CF 19a:72; see Sommerfeldt, *The Spiritual Teachings*, 49–51; Bernard follows Augustine here, see Bell, *Divus Bernhardus*, 276–278.

7 Gra 6.17; SBOp 3:178,13–179,3; O'Donovan translated the latin expression *in visitatione gratiae* rather liberally with 'grace's touch', CF 19a:73.

good. He makes it good to the end: that we may be the first fruits of his creatures. It would have been better for us never to have existed than to remain always our own. For those who wished to belong to themselves became indeed like gods, knowing good and evil; but then they were not merely their own but the devil's, declared the abbot, alluding to Gen 3:5.[8] Thus, the free will (*libera voluntas*) makes us our own; bad will makes us the devil's, and good will God's.[9] This is because (quoting Mt 6:24) 'no one can serve two masters':

> It is our own will that enslaves us to the devil, not his power; whereas God's grace subjects us to God, not our own will (*voluntas*). . . . Finally, the Apostle, feeling what he really was by nature and what he hoped to be by grace, said: 'I can will what is right, but I cannot do it' (Rom 7:18). He realized that to will was possible to him as a result of free choice, but that for this will to be perfect he stood in need of grace.[10]

The best thing humans can do is to be wise and to convert their will to the good, and to act powerfully, confirmed in what is good. These two, wisdom and fortitude, are needed for our perfection, and they are the 'two-fold gift of grace'.[11]

Bernard made it clear that 'salvation is from the Lord (Ps 3:9), not from free choice', giving references to Ps 35:3 and Jn 14:6: 'Are we to say, then, that the entire function and the sole merit of free choice lie in its consent? Assuredly. Not that this consent, in which all merit consists is its own doing, since we are unable even to think anything of ourselves; which is less than to consent.'[12] It is not as if grace did half the work and free choice the other, he clarified; each does the whole work, according to its own peculiar contribution, with this one qualification: 'Whereas the whole is done in free choice, so is the whole done of grace', referring to Rom 9:16, 'it

8 Gra 6.18; SBOp 3:179,4–9; CF 19a:74.

9 Gra 6.18; SBOp 3:179,10–11; CF 19a:74.

10 Gra 6.18; SBOp 3:179,15–180,1; CF 19a:74f.

11 Gra 6.19; on the difficulty with the translation, see CF 19A:75, n. 16.

12 Gra 14.46; SBOp 3:199,1–5; CF 19a: 105. See Gra 13.43; SBOp 3:197,5–7; CF 19a:101 (on the mentioned scriptural reference).

is not a question of human willing or doing but of God's grace'.[13]
Bernard continued that anyone who justifies himself ignores the
justice (righteousness) of God, and thinks that his merits come
from elsewhere than from grace.[14] He concluded his treatise by
glossing Rom 8:30 in these words:

> God is, in consequence, the author of merit, who both applies
> the will to the work, and supplies the work to the will. Besides,
> if the merits which we refer to as ours are rightly so called,
> then they are seed-beds of hope, incentives to love, portents of
> a hidden predestination, harbingers of happiness, the road to
> the kingdom, not a motive for playing the king. In one word:
> it is those whom he made righteous, not those whom he found
> [already] righteous, that he has magnified.[15]

In one of his final sermons on the Song of Songs (SC 81.7), the
elderly Bernard returned to the issue of 'free choice' in discussing
the dignity of the soul and its resemblance to the Word. Free choice
is clearly something divine (*plane divinum*) 'which shines forth
in the soul like a jewel set in gold'.[16] The soul has the power
of judgment and the ability to choose between good and evil.
This faculty is called free choice (*liberum arbitrium*) because it is
exercised out of the freedom of will (*arbitrio voluntatis*) by which a
person can acquire merit.[17] Yet sin intervenes and dominates human
beings who were born with freedom. By sin the corruptible body
oppresses the soul. Although the soul fell of itself, it cannot rise of
itself, because the will is weak and powerless. The will cannot free
itself from this 'condition' (*necessitas*).[18] People brought this evil

13 Gra 14.48; SBOp 3:200,5–10; CF 19a:106.
14 Gra 14.48; SBOp 3:201,1–3; CF 19a:108.
15 Gra 14.51; SBOp 3:203,14–19; CF 19a:111.
16 SC 81.6; SBOp 2:287,15–18; CF 40:162.
17 SC 81.6; SBOp 2:287,24f; CF 40:162.
18 SC 81.7; SBOp 2:288,6–15; CF 40:163f. Bernard's notion of *necessitas* is complex; see Klaus Schreiner, 'Puritas Regulae, caritas und necessitas. Leitbegriffe der Regelauslegung in der monastischen Theologie Bernhards
von Clairvaux'. *Zisterziensische Spiritualität. Theologische Grundlagen, funktionale Voraussetzungen und bildhafte Ausprägungen im Mittelalter*, Clemens
Kasper and Klaus Schreiner, eds. (St. Ottilien: EOS, 1994) 75–100; Glauco Maria
Cantarella, 'Dalla *necessitas* alla *dispensatio*: un'indagine sul lessico in Bernardo

on themselves by themselves; Bernard cites Is 38:15, 'For I myself have done this evil'. Thus for Bernard 'voluntary servitude' has brought this yoke on man. Because it is servitude, he is miserable, yet because it was voluntary, it is inexcusable. For the will, although created free, by consenting to sin became a slave to sin. Yet by its voluntary servitude the will holds itself in subjection to sin.[19] The soul is both enslaved and free, because Christ has set us free (Gal 4:31 and 2 Cor 3:17).[20] In the conclusion of this sermon Bernard referred to his earlier treatise *On Grace and Free Choice*.[21]

2. Luther: 'We are able to will, but not to will well'

Did Luther read Bernard's treatise *On Grace and Free Choice*? Probably not. Detesting 'disputations', Luther favored 'sermons'. In 1518, in his vernacular booklet on the Lord's Prayer, Luther referred to an obscure sermon which he attributed to Bernard, although the remark he made sounded very much like a line from Bernard's treatise. Luther wrote:

> Thus says Saint Bernard about the gospel of Mary Magdalen: We are able to will, but not to will well (*Wir konnen wollen, aber nicht wol wollen*). Because willing well is making things perfect, which is God's doing alone. Willing the bad is our doing. . . . Here, Bernard throws down the teaching of *Arestotles* [sic], who says that a man is the lord of all his works, from beginning to end. . . . Therefore, nobody can act well and will well except through sanctifying grace alone.[22]

di Clairvaux'. *Studia in Honorem Eminentissii Cardinalis Alphonsi M. Stickler*, R. S. Castillo Lara, ed. (Rome: Pontificia studiorum universitas Salesiana Facultas Iuris Canonici) 37–50.

19 SC 81.7; SBOp 2:288,23–28; CF 40:164.

20 SC 81.9; SBOp 2:289,17f; CF 40:165.

21 SC 81.11; SBOp 2:291,13–17; CF 40:168. The passage Gra 9.28–35 (which Bernard had second thoughts about) dealt with image and likeness, see SBOp 3:185–191.

22 *Darumb sagt der heylige Bernhart uber das ewangelium van Marien Magdalenen: Wir konnen wollen, aber nicht wol wollen. Dan wol wollen ist volkommen machen, das allein gottes ist, ubel wollen ist gebruch leyden, das ist unser. . . . Hye wirfft darnydder Bernhardus dye lere Arestotelis*, WA 9:137,19–23 (*On the Lord's Prayer*, 1518); see Bell, *Divus Bernhardus*, 276–278.

I could not find any sermon of 'Saint Bernard about the gospel of Mary Magdalen' and there is no sermon text which matches the quotation. What Luther unknowingly incorporated into his booklet at this point is Bernard's phrase from Chapter Six in *On Grace and Free Choice* in a german paraphrase: 'We are able to will, but not to will well'. Luther wrote that by nature human beings have will power ('we are able to will'), but not the power to will what is good ('but not to will well'), stating negatively in German what Bernard said positively in Latin: 'Free choice, accordingly constitutes us willers; grace, willers of the good'.[23] The paraphrase in German (whether by Luther himself or by somebody before him) was so ingenious that Bernard's original latin word play was preserved in the vernacular version:

Bernard:	Luther:
volentes – benevolos	*wollen – wol wollen.*
velle – bonum velle.	

Without knowing it, Luther based his insight on Bernard's treatise. How could Luther incorporate a line from a bernardine treatise he had most likely never studied? This remains an open question. If Luther had not read this treatise, then his sympathetic hint at Bernard's position 'against the free will'—a very general observation to which we will return shortly—may stem from his knowledge of other bernardine texts, namely his sermons, which contain the clear message 'grace alone'.

At this point, it is crucial that we recall what we stated in the Introduction about distinguishing two different categories of bernardine works: 'sermons'; and 'writings'/'treatises'. Luther praised Bernard as 'golden' when he preached, but not when he engaged in 'disputation'. Writing on Luther and his attitude toward 'disputations', Peter Manns observed with right: 'It looks like the mere reading of its title [Bernard's *De gratia et libero arbitrio*] was, as it seems, sufficient to adduce a negative evaluation of it. The actual study of this tract could have convinced Luther that his own concept as expressed in *De servo arbitrio* in no way contradicts

---

23 *Liberum arbitrium nos facit volentes, gratia benevolos. Ex ipso nobis est velle, ex ipsa bonum velle*, Gra 6.16; SBOp 3:177,22–178,5; CF 19a:72.

principally the positions of Bernard'.[24] However, Luther in a table talk allegedly said something to the contrary: 'Bernard loves Jesus very much; there is nothing but Jesus with him; but there is no Jesus in disputations such as on free will'.[25] There is a problem with this table talk: If we take Luther at his word that he thought there is 'no Jesus' in Bernard's treatise, we must conclude that Luther did not read that text, because Jesus is in it. And we must acknowledge that this table talk openly contradicts a sentence which Luther uttered at the time of his controversy with Erasmus on 'free will' (1525): 'Bernard [is] against the free will' (*Bernardum contra liberum arbitrium*),[26] which is found in his commentary on Deuteronomy (Dt 16:20).

I suggest that we discredit this table talk, because whenever one is in doubt as to which Lutheran source to favor, one must give preference to Luther's own texts over recordings by others of his talks at table. We conclude that Luther did not read any bernardine 'disputations' and thus need not charge him of making false statements about a text such as Bernard's treatise *On Grace and Free Choice*. There is no cogent proof that Luther studied this bernardine treatise; he never referred to it (except in this dubious table talk). If he had read it, he would have had to agree with it.

My interpretation of the sources relies on authentic Luther texts, and not on sometimes faulty table talks. My interpretation has the further advantage of no longer having to accuse Luther of superficially reading Bernard's treatise. If he had read it and understood it, he certainly would have used it as ammunition against Erasmus, which he did not do; nor did Erasmus.[27] In his *Bondage of the Will* Luther made reference to Bernard only once[28]

24 See Manns, 'Zum Gespräch zwischen M. Luther und der katholischen Theologie', 105f.

25 *Bernardo ist der Jesus so lieb; es ist eitel Jesus mit im, aber in disputationibus ut de libero arbitrio, da ist kein Jesus*, WA TR 5:154,6f (no. 5439a). See Bell, *Divus Bernhardus*, 345–347, who appears to be reluctant to dismiss this table talk as unreliable.

26 WA 14:667,16–26; LW 9:164.

27 See Winkler, 'Die Bernhardrezeption bei Erasmus von Rotterdam', 262.

28 See WA 18:644, 8f. In 1537 Luther touched upon the issue once more in his *Articles of Christian Doctrine* (see *The Book of Concord. The Confessions of the Evangelical Lutheran Church,* Theodore G. Tappert, trans. and ed. (Philadel-

and then not to his treatise on this subject, as one would expect in that context. Rather, he mentioned something the abbot said about his wasted life which Luther had probably found in *The Golden Legend*. That Luther nevertheless and unknowingly quoted a phrase from the bernardine treatise (although in a vernacular version), can be explained without insisting on Luther having read the treatise. The fact that he quoted it in German and not in Latin may hint that he picked it up from an unknown vernacular text, perhaps a pseudo-bernardine sermon, such as the unidentifiable sermon 'on the gospel about Mary Magdalen' which he gave as his source reference in this regard.

Others recognized Luther's congeniality with Bernard on the subject of grace and free choice. Some fathers of the Council of Trent did so. The bishop of Cava, for example, presented a direct quotation from Bernard's treatise *On Grace and Free Choice* in support of his position that 'faith alone' justifies.[29]

---

phia: Fortress Press, 1981, fourteenth printing, 306). The bernardine idea, which Luther might have had in mind, could be the one in SBOp 3:173,2–11, where Bernard gave the example of a person who complained about not having a good will. Bernard stated that this example in no way argues against the freedom of which he was speaking, but rather that this person is witnessing to the fact that he lacks that freedom which is called freedom from sin. 'Because, whoever wants to have a good will proves thereby that he has a will'. All this meant that his 'will is oppressed, though not suppressed'.

29 Gra 14, SBOp 3:199,1–5, as quoted in *Concilium Tridentinum,* Societas Goerresiana, ed. (Freiburg: Herder, 1950–1967) 5:295,44–47.

3

𝔉𝔞𝔦𝔱𝔥 𝔄𝔩𝔬𝔫𝔢

N CHAPTER THREE, we will reflect on Bernard's axiom 'faith alone' and on his understanding of faith indwelling the heart, as well as on the related issues of faith and good works, faith and baptism, gratitude, humility, knowledge of self and of God, and on the way in which Luther dealt with them.

I. THE PRIORITY OF FAITH

1. *Bernard: Salvation 'by faith alone'*

Bernard's spirituality and theology are grounded in his faith in Christ as the Redeemer and God-man. His faith was born of deep conviction, held with an affection which expressed his trust in the Christ who is the center of the biblical message of salvation. He began to work on his sermons on the Song of Songs in 1135 and finished the last one, SC 86, shortly before his death in 1153. In Sermon 2 he proclaimed that because Christ died for us and rose again we are 'justified by faith and have peace with God'.[1] In SC 22 he talked about the various perfumes the bridegroom, Christ, presents to his Bride (Sg 1:3). Within this picturesque context he preached explicitly on justification 'by faith alone' (*solam per fidem*):

1 See SC 2.8; SBOp 1:13,19f; CF 4:14f.

Take note therefore of the fourfold anointing. . . . He came down
to you in your prison, not to torture you but to liberate you from
the power of darkness. . . . By the 'righteousness that comes of
faith' (Rom 9:30), he looses the bonds of sin, justifying sinners
by his free gift (cf. Rom 3:24). . . . Utterly generous, for not
a mere drop but a wave of blood flowed unchecked from the
five wounds of his body. . . . [Speaking to God] As for your
justice, so great is the fragrance it diffuses that you are called not
only just but even justice itself, the justice that makes men just.
Your power to make men just is measured by your generosity
in forgiving. Therefore the man who through sorrow for sin
hungers and thirsts for justice, let him trust in the One who
changes the sinner into a just man, and judged *righteous in terms
of faith alone,* he will have peace with God (Rom 5:1). . . . When
our wisdom lets us down, when our righteousness falls short,
when the merits of our holiness founder, your Passion becomes
our support. Who would presume that his own wisdom, or
righteousness or holiness suffices for salvation? . . . 'Remember
not the sins of my youth, or my transgressions' (Ps 24:7), and
then I am righteous. . . . He [the pharisee of Lk 7:39] did not
realize that righteousness or holiness is a gift of God, not the fruit
of man's effort, and that the man 'to whom the Lord imputes no
iniquity' (Ps 31:2) is not only just but blessed.[2]

This passage makes clear that the sixteenth-century Reformer's
axiom 'faith alone' was not at all unique to him. Bernard and
Luther shared this decisive conviction. This justification is imputed
by God, declared Bernard, using the notion of imputation which
Luther favored so much. The pharisee of the gospel story did not
realize that righeousness or holiness is a gift from God, not the
fruit of human effort, and that anyone 'to whom the Lord imputes
no sin' (Ps 31:2) is 'not only just but blessed'.

2 . . . Solam *iustificatus* per fidem, *pacem habebit ad Deum* . . . , (emphasis
added), SC 22.7–9; SBOp 1:133, 2–135,22; CF 7:18–22. With Richard D. Balge
one must note that (in contrast to Bernard, as shown here) Augustine did not
explicitly speak of 'by faith *alone*': 'Martin Luther, Augustinian'. *Luther Lives.
Essays in Commemoration of the 500th Anniversary of Martin Luther's Birth,*
Edward C. Fredrich, Siegbert W. Becker, David P. Kruske, eds. (Milwaukee:
Northwestern Publishing House, 1983) 7–20, here 12. This means that on this
issue Luther is theologically closer to Bernard than to Augustine.

In the following sermon, SC 23, Bernard took up this theme of God's righteousness and explained it in pauline and johannine terms, referring to Rom 3:23, 8:33, and 1 Jn 5:18. The heavenly birth is the eternal predestination by which God loves his chosen ones.[3] In the subsequent sermon, SC 24, Bernard interpreted Sg 1:3, 'the righteous love you', and stressed the unity of faith and love: 'The state of the invisible soul is made known by one's faith and action. You may consider a man upright if you prove him Catholic by faith and just by [his] work . . .'. He then quoted Jas 2:20, 'faith without good works is dead', and continued: 'The gift you offer to God is dead. For if devotion is the soul of faith, what is faith that does not work through love (Gal 5:6) but a lifeless cadaver? Can you pay due honor to God with a gift that stinks?'[4] In SC 71 he reiterated: 'They may be justified by grace and become righteousness in him' (2 Cor 5:21 and Rom 3:24).[5] And in SC 73 he concluded: 'Therefore even the saints have need to ask pardon for their sins, that they may be saved by mercy, not trusting in their own righteousness. For all have sinned (Rom 3:23), and all need mercy'.[6]

The medieval monastic teacher unfolded his ideas and exposed his emotions about Christ as the center of the faith as well in his SC 27, to which Luther explicitly referred. Bernard declared the Bride to be the residence of God; as the heavens are God's residence so also is the Church or the individual soul; and as the sun, moon, and stars shine in the skies so does the soul as God's residence. Therefore, the saintly soul is the heaven; it has the intellect as its sun, faith as its moon, and the virtues as its stars.[7]

The bride's form must be understood in a spiritual sense. . . . Finally the Apostle says explicitly that 'Christ dwells by faith in our hearts' (Eph 3:17). . . . No need to be surprised that the Lord Jesus should be pleased to dwell in this heaven, which he not only called into being by his word like the other creatures,

---

3 SC 23.15; SBOp 1:148,25–149,4; CF 7:39.
4 SC 24.7; SBOp 1:159,5–7; CF 7:47.
5 SC 71.11; SBOp 2:222,13; CF 40:58.
6 SC 73.4; SBOp 2:235,27–29; CF 40:78.
7 SC 27.8; SBOp 1:187,15f; CF 7:81f.

but fought to acquire and died to redeem. . . . Do you not now see what heavens the Church possesses within her, and that she herself, in her universality, is an immense heaven, stretching out 'from sea to sea, and from the river to the ends of the earth' (Ps 71:8). Consider therefore, to what you may compare her in this respect, provided you do not forget what I mentioned a short while ago concerning the heaven of heaven and heavens of heavens. Just like our mother above (Gal 4:26), this one, though still a pilgrim (2 Cor 5:6) has her own heaven: spiritual men outstanding in their lives and reputations, men of genuine faith, unshaken hope, generous love, men raised to the heights of contemplation. These men rain down God's saving work like showers, reprove with a voice of thunder, shine with a splendor of miracles. They proclaim the glory of God (Ps 18:1), and stretched out like curtains over all the earth (Ps 103: 2) make known the law of life and knowledge (Si 45:6) written by God's finger into their own lives (Ex 31:18) 'to give knowledge of salvation to his people' (Lk 1:77). They show forth the gospel of peace (Eph 6:15), because they are the curtain of Solomon.[8]

2. Luther: 'Saint Bernard is . . . a true and sincere Christian in his belief'

Luther did not refer in any direct way to the bernardine Sermons on the Canticle 2, 22, 23, 73, which were quoted above, even though they contain some of Luther's central teachings. We may assume, however, that Luther had knowledge of them, for on one occasion he explicitly quoted several sentences from the neighboring SC 27 when, during his first Lectures on the Psalms, he treated Ps 8:4. At that point he indicated that he drew insights from *ser. 27 super Can.*[9]

---

8 SC 27.12; SBOp 1:190,18 and 24–28; CF 7:85.

9 'Habet Ecclesia celos suos, homines spirituales, vita et opinione con-spicuos, fide puros, spe firmos, latos charitate, contemplatione suspensos. Et hii pluentes pluviam verbi salutarem tonant increpationibus, choruscant mira-culis, enarrant gloriam dei. Hi extenti sicut pelles super omnem terram', as quoted by Luther on Ps 8:4; WA 55-II,1,1:101,13–19; LW 10:88. The critical edition of Bernard's works differs only slightly (in regard to punctuation and orthography) from the critical edition of Luther's works. A scholar once counted more than a dozen explicit Bernard quotations in Luther's first exegetical course

Spiritual men are models of pure faith, solid in hope, persevering in love and contemplation. Luther and Bernard agreed on this ideal type which the medieval master had expressed in his flourishing style. To Bernard the Bride meant both the individual soul and the Church, and in a single sermon, SC 27, he could switch from 'soul' to 'Church'. The beauty of the Church consists in *homines spirituales*, who are the heavens within the Church. This idea has something to do with Bernard's affective Christocentrism which was nurtured by Eph 3:17, 'may Christ dwell in your hearts through faith, and may charity be the root and foundation of your life', a passage employed by Bernard twice in this sermon.[10]

The message of the sinner's justification by faith found full acceptance in Bernard's piety, as we have seen in the sermon texts already quoted. In this regard Luther always considered Bernard to be the true witness to the gospel and his 'father' in the faith. Luther may have had in mind one of these particular sermons when he praised Bernard and his beautiful meditation. But since Luther referred so explicitly and repeatedly to Bernard's first Annunciation sermon, as we have seen, it is safer to assume that he meant Ann 1. In any case, it was in Bernard's theology that Luther encountered the passive concept of the righeousness of God, *iustitia dei*, which is thought to be an important element of the so-called reformation discovery, namely, the belief that the sinner receives righteousness from God through his faith in Christ as his Saviour.[11]

These or similar words of Bernard on salvific faith in Christ, on the passive concept of God's righteousness, and on the non-

---

on the Psalter: Erich Vogelsang, *Die Anfänge von Luthers Christologie nach der ersten Psalmenvorlesung insbesondere in ihren exegetischen und systematischen Zusammenhängen mit Augustin und der Scholastik dargestellt* (Berlin and Leipzig: Verlag von Walter de Gruyter & Co., 1929) 66, note 4; see Stange, *Bernhard von Clairvaux: Studien der Luther Akademie*, 8; see also Ernst Benz, Luther und Bernhard', *Eckhart* 23 (1953/54) 60–64. It is striking that Theo Bell did not include this comparatively lengthy quotation in his *Divus Bernhardus*, 75; he only referred to SC 27 in passing, quoting a line other than the lengthy quotation given here.

10 See SC 27.3 and 8; SBOp 1:184,2f, and 188,6f; CF 7:77 and 82.

11 See Bernhard Lohse, ed., *Der Durchbruch der Reformatorischen Erkenntnis bei Luther – Neuere Untersuchungen* (Stuttgart: Franz Steiner Verlag Wiesbaden GMBH, 1988) 1–13 (B. Lohse) and 167–211 (M. Brecht).

imputation of sins [as well as the impressive text of Ann 1], may
have been on Luther's mind during the culminating years of the
Reformation. And when, probably in 1521, in his reflections on
monastic vows he mentioned Bernard's teaching about justification
by faith alone, and when in 1530 he commented: 'I have observed
this in Saint Bernard', he could conclude, 'whenever he begins to
speak of Christ, it is a pure pleasure to follow'.[12] Toward the end of
the Reformer's life we find him again praising Bernard's Christ-
centered faith and referring to Bernard's numerous testimonies:
'Thus Saint Bernard is a monk in his vocation but a true and sincere
Christian in his belief, who does not depend, insist, and rely on his
cowl and his Order, as the majority do, but builds solely on the
mercy of Jesus Christ, as he himself often testifies.'[13]

3. *Faith and Good Works*

Bernard: 'Flower as faith, fruit as action'
    Not only had Bernard in his Ann 1 clarified the central im-
portance of God's mercy and his non-imputation of sins, but he
had also underscored the significance of good works, teaching that
'with regard to good works, it is absolutely certain that no one
can perform them of himself'.[14] Furthermore, he explained in his
SC 51 on Sg 2:5 that, as Luther would also say later on, 'faith
ought to come before good works' and that 'there is neither fruit
without flower nor a good work without faith', as he employed the
allegorical interpretation of 'flower' and 'fruit':

> If however, you want to attribute both of these, the flowers
> and the fruit, to the one person according to their moral sense,
> understand the flower as faith, the fruit as action. Nor do I think
> that this will seem wrong to you, if, just as the flower by necessity

---

12 See WA 8:601,7–31; LW 44:290f (*On Monastic Vows*, 1521). *Ich habs
jnn Sanct Bernhard auch gesehen, Wenn der selbige man beginnet von Christo
zu reden, So gehet daher das lust ist, Wenn er aber ausser diesem stueck ist und
von regeln oder wercken redet, so ists nicht mehr S. Bernhard*, WA 31:25,29–32
(on Ps 117, 1530); LW 14:38.
    13 WA 54:85 (on 1 Sam 23:1–7); LW 15:335.
    14 SBOp 5:14,1–2.

precedes the fruit, so faith ought to come before good works. Without faith, moreover, it is impossible to please God, as Paul attests. And he even teaches that 'whatever does not proceed from faith is sin'. Hence there is neither fruit without a flower nor a good work without faith. But then, faith without good works is dead, just as a flower seems vain where no fruit follows.[15]

Bernard continued to preach on Sg 2:6 in the second part of SC 51. He first felt compelled, however, to refer the reader to his previous work on this text of Sg 2:5f, his book *On Loving God:* 'This too I remember having discussed elaborately in the work mentioned'. He then carried on as follows:

It is clear that the bridegroom has returned for the purpose of comforting the distressed bride by his presence. . . . And because he found that during his absence she had been faithful in good works and eager for gain, in that she had ordered that flowers and fruits be given to her, of course, he returns this time with an even richer reward of grace. As she lies back he cushions her head on one of his arms, embracing her with the other, to cherish her at his bosom. Happy the soul who reclines on the breast of Christ, and rests between the arms of the Word![16]

This passage, too, perfectly mirrors Bernard's affective christo-centric spirituality.

Bernard's important metaphor of good works as 'fruit' emerged also in SC 63: 'Only of the wise man, who possesses life, can it then be said that he has, or better is, a vineyard. He is a fruitful tree in God's house. . . . He does live, but by faith. The wise man is a just man, and the just man lives by faith'. As much as the abbot of Clairvaux emphasized 'faith alone', he did not lose sight of good works performed in love; in SC 24 he axiomatically stated that separation from charity would mean the 'death of faith': *Mors fidei est separatio caritatis.*[17]

15 SC 51.2; SBOp 2:84,22–85,2; CF 31:41.
16 SC 51.4; SBOp 2:85,15–87,10; CF 31:44.
17 SC 63.3; SBOp 2:162,27–163,1; CF 31:163. SC 24.8; SBOp 1:161,3–162,4; CF 7:48f.

Do you believe in Christ? Do the works of Christ so that your faith will live; love will animate your faith, action will reveal it. . . . You see then that right faith (*fides recta*) will not make a right man (*hominem rectum*) unless it is enlivened by love. . . . Deeds, however right they may be, cannot make the heart righteous without faith.[18]

Luther: 'You can tell a tree by its fruit'

Luther's spirituality followed bernardine thought patterns. Early on he may have encountered this bernardine teaching in Ann 1, where Bernard wrote: 'With regard to good works, it is absolutely certain that no one can perform them of himself'.[19] Bernard's words on faith and action could have come straight from Luther's mouth. It would be totally lop-sided to understand Luther's emphasis on 'faith alone' as neglect of 'good works'. In 1527, for instance, when Luther lectured on 1 Jn 3:10, he clearly understood faith and love as the two-fold essence of Christianity (Luther spoke of 'parts' or 'articles'), not unlike Bernard in his sermons. In this context he declared 'works' to be the 'signs of the faith and of the word';[20] by them Christians bear witness to the world that they are sons of God.[21] In his commentary on 1 Jn 2:29 he used the metaphor 'tree' and its 'fruits', as had Bernard in SC 63 and 51: 'The tree is not idle when Christ makes the tree a good one. . . . He is truly born of God who does justice, who serves his neighbors'.[22] At this point Luther repeated the concept of the two-fold christian doctrine: part one is grace, part two is the call to do good works, to bear fruit.[23] On 1 Jn 3:23 Luther emphasized, in the footsteps of Bernard, that

18 SC 24.8; SBOp 1:161f; CF 7:48f.

19 Ann 1; SBOp 5:14,1f.

20 *Quae sint signa fidei et verbi*, WA 20:708,1. See WA 20:707,6–13. And again: *Nam Christina doctrina consistit in his duobus* (i. e. faith and love), WA 20:714,15. When Luther lectured on 1 John 3:20, he implied that on the Day of Judgment one should appear with good works; but if someone does not have them, he must have at least faith in God, by which he implied a faith in the merciful judge who does not reject a miserable sinner who dares to come without good works; see WA 20:716,29 (Probst's lecture notes).

21 The stenographer, Rörer, has written *testi* above the word *signa*, see note 1 in WA 20:708.

22 WA 20:691,14–692,7.

23 WA 20:691,11–13.

one has to believe in Christ's name and to love.[24] And on 1 Jn 4:21 he lectured that one must remain in faith and in love because these 'two articles' cannot be taught enough. He repeated in his tract *On Good Works* in 1520 that he had always wanted to teach 'the good works of faith'.[25] In *On Christian Liberty* he very expressly spoke of faith and works in terms of 'good tree' and 'good fruits' in the way Bernard did. Luther declared that one may derive good fruits (works) from a good tree but not in the reverse. So-called good works may stem from egotism or self-righteousness. Therefore, one must make the tree a good one and thus one will produce good fruits. When you want to do good works, you should start not with the works but with the person who does good works. The person will not be good except by faith alone (*Glaube*); and a person is bad by 'un-faith' (*Unglaube*). In support of his teaching Luther referred to Mt 7:20: 'You can tell a tree by its fruit'.[26]

The parallels demonstrated here sufficiently indicate the congeniality of Bernard and Luther on the relationship of faith and works. Both their theologies were undergirded and structured around the center, Jesus Christ. Faith in Christ leads to good works. This is not an abstract belief but an existential faith active in love. As we have pointed out, Bernard said in SC 24 that separating love from faith would be the death of faith. Similarly, Luther spoke of the intrinsic connection of the 'two articles', i. e. faith and good works. After having made these remarks during his johannine lectures of 1527, Luther went so far as to say, in 1528, that if somebody taught that faith could exist without works, he would be teaching a new doctrine (*novum dogma*).[27]

---

24 WA 20:721,21–23.

25 WA 20:763,**14–15. See *On Good Works*, WA 6:206,33–207,14.

26 See WA 7:32,4–33,14 (german version of *On Christian Liberty*). See also Luther's expression of 'the good tree which a Christian is', in his sermon on 1 Pt 4:8ff in 1539, WA 47:757–771. See Werner Wolbert on Luther: 'Ein guter Baum bringt gute Früchte: Konsekutives und finales Verständnis von Moralität im ökumenischen Gespräch', *Catholica* 39 (1985) 52–68. Bernard, too, used the image of the good tree with blossoms and fruits, see Sommerfeldt, *The Spiritual Teachings*, 184.

27 See Hans-Günter Leder, 'Luthers Beziehungen zu seinen Wittenberger Freunden'. *Leben und Werk Martin Luthers von 1526 bis 1546. Festgabe zu seinem 500. Geburtstag*, Helmar Junghans, ed. (Göttingen: Vandenhoeck & Ruprecht, 1983) 422. John Agricola was meant here and the antinomian con-

At this point, we must stress that catholic sermons of the fourteenth and fifteenth centuries display no essential differences from what our twelfth and sixteenth century theologians taught. The homiletic tradition of the late medieval Church, so far as it is traceable today, always preached the insufficiency of human works for salvation, particularly under the influence of Bernard.[28]

4. Gratitude

Bernard: 'Ingratitude . . . dries up the source of love'
The soul rests in the arms of Christ, Bernard preached in SC 51. Special grace provokes the soul's gratitude in the form of good works. This caused the abbot to give further advice in the same sermon:

> Learn not to be tardy or sluggish in offering thanks, learn to offer thanks for each and every gift. Take careful note, Scripture advises, of what is set before you (Prov 23:1), so that no gift of God, be it great or mediocre or small, will be deprived of due thanksgiving. We are even commanded to gather up the fragments, lest they be lost (Jn 6:12), which means that we are not to forget even the smallest benefits. Is that surely not lost which is given to an ingrate?[29]

---

troversy (on Law and Gospel). On the issue of faith and works, see Peter Manns, 'Fides absoluta-Fides incarnata: Zur Rechtfertigungslehre Luthers im Grossen Galaterkommentar'. *Reformata Reformanda: Festgabe für Hubert Jedin,* Erwin Iserloh and Konrad Repgen, eds. (Münster: Aschendorff, 1965) 1:247–264, as referred to by Pesch, *Hinführung zu Luther,* 162–68. See Rolf Schäfer, 'Glaube und Werke nach Luther', *Luther* 58 (1987) 75–85. Tuomo Mannermaa, 'Das Verhältnis von Glaube und Liebe in der Theologie Luthers'. *Luther in Finnland. Der Einfluß der Theologie Martin Luthers in Finnland und finnische Beiträge zur Lutherforschung,* Mikka Ruokanen, ed. (Helsinki: Luther-Agricola-Society, 1984) 99–110.

28 See Adolar Zumkeller, 'Das Ungenügen der menschlichen Werke bei den deutschen Predigern des Spätmittelalters', *Zeitschrift für Katholische Theologie* 81 (1959) 265–305. Ian D. K. Siggins, 'Luther and the Catholic Preachers of His Youth' in Yule, ed., *Luther: Theologian for Catholics and Protestants,* 59–74. Siggins pointed out that the pastoral message at that time often was justification by true contrition alone (65), and by faith alone (70).

29 SC 51.6; SBOp 2:87,13–17; CF 31:44f; see SC 24 on separating faith and works which results in the death of faith.

Having posed this rhetorical question, Bernard declared that 'ingratitude is the soul's enemy, a voiding of merits, dissipation of the virtues, wastage of benefits'. With great eloquence he described ingratitude as 'a burning wind that dries up the source of love, the dew of mercy, the streams of grace'.[30] Already in SC 13, Bernard had called ingratitude an 'abominable vice'.[31]

Luther: 'And Bernard says: "No vice is more pernicious than ingratitude" '

Luther must have been quite impressed by this metaphor in Bernard's meditation on faith and good works. Yet it was not the young Luther who remembered it, but the ageing preacher who in October 1537 began to quote it: 'Ingratitude', he said, is like 'an evil, dry wind which dries up and makes disappear all the founts of grace and goodness with God and the people'. And again: Ingratitude is like a wind 'which dries up all founts of goodness'.[32] When the Reformer gave his Christmas sermon in 1540, and again when he expounded the book of Genesis at about the same time, the bernardine metaphor turned up. In the lectures on Genesis it shows up in two places, on Gen 39:7–10 and Gen 40:20–23; the former in dealing with handsome Joseph and his master's seductive wife, the latter in dealing with his dreams: 'And Bernard says: "No vice is more pernicious than ingratitude because it dries up the fount of goodness" '. Shortly afterwards, he repeated himself with an addition: 'And Bernard says: "No vice is more pernicious than ingratitude because it dries up the fount of goodness", that is, human goodness, not God's and that of the sons of God, whose kindness is inexhaustible'.[33] Apparently, Bernard's

30 SC 51.6; SBOp 2:87,18–20; CF 31:45. See Posset, 'The Elder Luther on Bernard: Part II: Last Exegetical Work', ABR 42 (1991) 193f; Sommerfeldt, *The Spiritual Teachings,* 202.

31 See SC 13; SBOp 1:74,26–28; CF 31:95.

32 WA 22:355,19f (1537); *Bernardus: Ist so ein holer wind, der austrocken alle brune der gutigkeit,* WA 45:196,16f (October 28, 1537); see Bell, *Divus Bernhardus,* 334.

33 WA 49:178,30f (1540); WA 44:361,20–24 (on Joseph in Egypt); see LW 7: 83, where the translation has 'voice' instead of 'vice', evidently a printing mistake. WA 44: 390,35–37; LW 7:124. Also on Joseph in Egypt, see Bernard: SC 13.4, SBOp 1:70,27–71,19; CF 4:90. It it noteworthy that in his last major

spirituality influenced Luther to such a degree that phrases like this were stored in his mind and soul as a repertoire where they were available for use whenever he deemed them appropriate.

5. Faith and Baptism

Bernard: 'People can be saved by faith alone'
About the year 1125, Bernard was asked by Hugh of Saint Victor to share with him his opinion on 'faith and baptism'. Bernard's response, preserved in his Ep 77 is also called Bernard's treatise *On Baptism.* In it Bernard employed insights from Ambrose and Augustine and related them to Mk 16:16:

> Believe me, it will be difficult to separate me from these two pillars, by which I refer to Augustine and Ambrose. I confess that with them I am either right or wrong in believing that people can be saved by faith alone and the desire to receive the sacrament, even if untimely death or some other insuperable force keep them from fulfilling their pious desire. Notice also that the Saviour said 'Whoever believes and is baptized will be saved', but only 'Whoever does not believe will be condemned' (Mk 16:1). This intimated that for a time faith alone would suffice for salvation, and that without it, nothing would be sufficient.[34]

Luther: 'Saint Bernard has noticed it: he who believes and is not baptized may nevertheless be saved'
Luther was well aware of Bernard's teaching on faith and baptism. In 1522 he dealt with it as Bernard had done, but without mentioning his name: 'Somebody may have faith, even if he is

exegetical work, on Gen, Luther referred to Bernard at least twenty times, see WA volumes 42–44 (LW volumes 2–8). In my article 'The Elder Luther on Bernard: Part II', 193f, I incorrectly stated that Luther referred to the bernardine metaphor of the dry wind exclusively in his commentary on Genesis, while I also hinted at Luther's Christmas sermon of 1540. However, with Bell, *Divus Bernhardus*, 334, one must point out that Luther referred to it several times after 1537.

34 *Credens et ipse sola fide hominem posse salvari,* Bapt 2.8; SBOp 7:190. I follow Hugh Feiss' translation as found in 'Bernard of Clairvaux, Letter 77'. *Bernardus Magister,* 366f. For a more elaborate explanation of Bernard's concept of faith, see Sommerfeldt, 'Bernard of Clairvaux On the Truth Accessible Through Faith', *The Joy of Learning,* Elder, ed., 239–251.

not baptized'.[35] Fourteen years later, Luther treated this subject again, on Ascension Day 1536; in preaching on Mk 1, he referred to Bernard explicitly:

Saint Bernard has noticed it: He who believes but is not baptized may nevertheless be saved, because Christ does not add anything on baptism of desire, because a case can be made that a catechumen could die suddenly from a stomach ache. But from the given text one may conclude that he is saved. But this is a matter that can be debated, whereby [one should keep in mind] that the baptized people are to be righteous, as he taught in Mt (28:20), to do everything he has commanded.[36]

35 *Es kan auch ainer glauben, wenn er gleich nit getaufftt ist,* WA 10-III:142,18–20.

36 *Ex hoc textu sequitur, ut alibi Christus in Joh 4 proponens, quidem baptisati et salvantur. S. Bernhardus hats gemerckt, qui credit et non baptisatus, tamen salvaret,* WA 41:594,29–36; see Posset, 'The Elder Luther on Bernard: Part I', 26f; Bell, *Divus Bernhardus,* 335.

II. KISSING THE FEET, HAND, AND MOUTH

1. The three kisses

Bernard: 'You have made a beginning by kissing the feet'
 Bernard devoted his first eight sermons on the Song of Songs
to unfolding the meaning of the 'kiss' in the first verse, 'Let him
kiss me with the kiss of his mouth'. 'How shall I explain so abrupt
a beginning?'[1] he asked, and began by interpreting the kiss as
Christ's living, active word:

> The mouth that kisses signifies the Word who assumes human
> nature; the nature assumed receives the kiss; the kiss, however,
> that takes its being both from the giver and the receiver, is the
> person (persona) that is formed by both, none other than 'the
> one mediator between God and mankind, himself a man, Christ
> Jesus' (1 Tim 2:5).[2]

The kiss is the uniting of God and man.[3] Since God has become
man, there is no more fear or distrust, the cistercian preacher
explained in his second sermon:

> When I come to recognize that he is truly mine, then I shall feel
> secure in welcoming the Son of God as mediator. Not even a
> shadow of mistrust can then exist, for after all he is my brother,
> and my own flesh. It is impossible that I should be spurned by
> him who is bone from my bones, and flesh from my flesh.[4]

1 SC 1.5; SBOp 1:5:3–5; CF 4:3. On the three kisses according to Bernard,
see Pennington, 'Saint Bernard of Clairvaux'. *The Last of the Fathers,* 83.
 2 SC 2.2f; SBOp 1:9,17–10,3; CF 4:8–10. The encounter with the traditional
christology which found its expression in the doctrine of the two natures (as
mirrored also in SC 2) is probably the reason for the young Luther's turning
away from the unorthodox occamist thinking; Luther was 'assisted' by Augustine
and Bernard, as Reinhard Schwarz indicated in his essay, 'Gott ist Mensch: Zur
Lehre von der Person Christi bei den Ockhamisten und bei Luther', *Zeitschrift
für Theologie und Kirche* 63 (1966) 345–49. See Ulrich Asendorf, *Die Theologie
Martin Luthers nach seinen Predigten* (Göttingen: Vandenhoeck & Ruprecht,
1988) 201.
 3 See SC 2.3; SBOp 1:10,6f; CF 4:10.
 4 SC 2.6; SBOp 1:11,28–12,2; CF 4:12.

Bernard picked up his train of thought on 'the kiss of the Lord's feet, hands and mouth' after he had summarized his second sermon in the following words:

> It would seem that this holy kiss was of necessity bestowed on the world for two reasons. Without it the faith of those who wavered would not have been strengthened, nor the desires of the fervent appeased. Moreover, this kiss is no other than the Mediator between God and man, himself a man, Christ Jesus, who with the Father and the Holy Spirit lives and reigns as God for ever and ever. Amen.[5]

At the beginning of his third sermon on the kiss, the abbot pointed out that few people actually experience the 'spiritual kiss'. But there is hope for those who do not, including Bernard himself. They are on their way to salvation. Yet they have to start from the bottom and work their way up:

> They may not rashly aspire to the lips of the most benign Bridegroom, but let them prostrate themselves with me in fear at the feet of the most severe Lord. . . . All you who are conscious of sin, do not regard as unworthy and despicable that position where the holy sinner (*sancta peccatrix*) laid down her sins (cf. Jer 13:23).[6]

As long as sinners repent and the evil that inflamed their passions is cleansed away, the 'heavenly physician' will come to them with his medicine. 'Prostrate yourself on the ground, take hold of his feet, soothe them with kisses, sprinkle them with your tears and so wash not them but yourself'. He continued:

---

5 SC 2.9; SBOp 1:13,27–14,3;CF 4:15.

6 SC 3.1f; SBOp 1:14,7–15,5; CF 4:16f. On the rare experience of the kiss of the mouth, see SC 8.1; SBOp 1:36,15; CF 4:45. On the cultural context of the kiss of the mouth, see Klaus Schreiner, ' "Er küsse mich mit dem Kuß seines Mundes" (*Osculetur me osculo oris sui*, Cant 1,1). Metaphorik, kommunikative und herrschaftliche Funktionen einer symbolischen Handlung', *Höfische Repräsentation. Das Zeremoniell und die Zeichen*, Hedda Ragotzky and Horst Wenzel, eds. (Tübingen: Max Niemeyer Verlag, 1990) 89–132. Yannick Carré, *Le Baiser sur la Bouche au Moyen Âge. Rites, symboles, mentalités, à travers les textes et les images, XIe-XVe siècles* (Paris: Editions Le Léopard d'Or, 1992), especially 316–322 (on Bernard). See below, pp. 203ff.

> Though you have made a beginning by kissing the feet, you may not presume to rise at once by impulse to the kiss of the mouth; there is a step to be surmounted in between, an intervening kiss on the hand. . . . It is a long and formidable leap from the foot to the mouth. . . . Consider for a moment: still tarnished as you are with the dust of sin, would you dare touch those sacred lips? Yesterday you were lifted from the mud, today you wish to encounter the glory of his face? No, his hand must be your guide to that end.[7]

Once one has had this twofold *experimentum* of divine benevolence in these two kisses, one need no longer hold back. Growth in this grace brings confidence as well: 'First we cast ourselves at his feet, we weep before the Lord who made us. . . . Secondly, we reach out for the hand that will lift us up, that will steady our trembling knees. And finally, when we shall have obtained all this . . . we humbly dare to raise our eyes to his mouth . . . to receive its kiss.'[8]

Luther: 'Concerning this threefold kiss, read Bernard at the beginning of the Song of Songs'

When Luther preached on Psalm 110 on the Saturday after the Feast of the Ascension, 8 May 1535, he had Bernard's sermons on the mystery of the God-Man and the incarnation in mind. Reflecting on the verse, 'The Lord said to my Lord: "Sit at my right hand" ', the ageing Reformer explained it as an utterance about Christ, born of the Virgin Mary, flesh and blood of David, but true God. Of him the angels said to the shepherds in the field of Bethlehem: 'To you is born Christ, the Lord' (Lk 2:4). Christ is true God and true man, Luther emphasized, and 'he has not taken on the form of angels', but 'our flesh and blood'; he even calls us his brothers.[9] At this point in his sermon the Reformer referred to the second bernardine

---

7 SC 3.2–4; SBOp 1:15,5–16,20; CF 4:17–19. The theme of kissing the 'spiritual feet of God' is discussed further in SBOp 1:28,25–26; see SC 6.6–8; 29,13–30,8; CF 4:35–37.

8 SC 3.5; SBOp 1:17,1–11; CF 4:19f.

9 See WA 41:87–97 (Rörer); LW 13:245 (on Ps 110).

sermon: 'He even calls us brothers. As Bernard says although he is a monk: "Why should I despair? My flesh and blood is sitting above. I hope that he does not spurn me, who is of my flesh and bone". This is a good, heavenly, spiritual thought.'[10]

The three kisses may represent also the three stages of the soul's progress: the first is the sign of a genuine *conversio* of life, the second is accorded to those making progress, the third is the experience of only a few, *rara perfectio*.[11] It is difficult to determine at what date Luther came to know the bernardine spirituality and theology of the three kisses. When he spoke of the 'kiss' in giving his first course on the psalms, starting in 1513, he did not mention Bernard by name in his treatment of Psalm 2:1. Luther also did not pick up on the mystical experience which Bernard mentions in his sermons. In this context Luther referred only to Jerome:

> And the meaning is: 'Receive Christ, the Son of God, with all reverence and humility as king and Lord, as they do who pay homage'. In summary let us say that 'to kiss' is, first, a sign of the highest reverence and adoration. Therefore blessed Jerome has 'worship purely'. Second, it is the most perfect sign of friendship and love. Therefore our translation reads 'receive'. Third, it is the closest adhesion and joining of mouth to mouth, face to face; therefore it expresses the most perfect and most friendly union. . . . But since 'kiss the son' is here put absolutely, not mentioning hand, foot, and mouth, it is proper to take 'kiss' in the broadest sense.[12]

Several years later, in 1519, the Reformer worked on the psalms a second time. He now encouraged his students to read more about those three kisses and referred them to 'Bernard at the beginning of the Canticle'. Simultaneously he summarized his and Bernard's thoughts by writing:

> Since he does not mention feet, hand, or face, it is right to understand the kiss in its broadest meaning. Thus we may worship

10 WA 41:97,1–98,1; see LW 13:245.
11 SC 4.1; SBOp 1:18,5–11; CF 4:21f.
12 WA 3:34,3–15; LW 10:38f.

Christ as the Son of God and the true God by kissing His feet. By kissing his hand we accept Him as our rightful Lord, our eternal Helper and Saviour. And by kissing his eyes and face we embrace him as our most beloved Brother and Friend, and the Bridegroom of our soul. Concerning this threefold kiss read Bernard at the beginning of the Song of Songs to find this interpretation: 'Kiss the Son', that is, worship Christ as God with the greatest reverence; subject yourselves to Christ the Lord with the greatest humility; and cling to Christ, the Bridegroom, with the greatest love. Behold, love and fear, with humility as the measure and midpoint of both—this is the most perfect worship of God.[13]

In this second work on the psalms, Luther did not hesitate to use mystical language, and he explicitly referred to Bernard. He also recommended Bernard's art of interpretation, which he also saw at work by such other Church Fathers as Augustine whose teachings he also mentioned:

We should adapt and adjust our minds and feelings so that they are in accord with the sense of the psalms. For since the psalter is only a kind of school and exercise for the disposition of the heart, he sings in vain who does not sing in the spirit. . . . First practice on one psalm, even one little verse of the psalm. You will progress enough if you learn to make only one verse a day, or even one a week live and breathe in your heart. After this beginning is made, everything else will follow, and you will have a rich treasury of understanding and affection. . . . This I want to impress on you once more in this first psalm, so that it may not be necessary to repeat it for each individual psalm. I know that whoever becomes practiced in this will find more by himself in the psalter than all the interpretations of other men can give him. I see that Saint Bernard was an expert in this art and drew from it all the wealth of his learning. I have sensed this also in Saint Augustine and others. Therefore we must drink the waters of life from the same source (*fons*), so that the ridicule of the prophet Amos may not apply to us.[14]

13 AWA 2:113,18–22; LW 14:347.
14 AWA 2:63,26f; LW 14:310f.

2. 'Holy Sinner' – 'Saint and Sinner'

Bernard: 'Slave and free at the same time'

One aspect of Bernard's sermons on the kiss of the feet remains to be taken into consideration. It is his expression 'holy sinner' (*sancta peccatrix*). This paradoxical notion anticipated by almost half a millennium the famous lutheran formula, saint and sinner at the same time (*simul iustus et peccator*). Bernard spoke of the 'holy sinner' in the context of the initial stage of the soul's progress toward salvation, it consists in laying down one's sins and putting 'on the garment of holiness'.[15] He clearly meant a change from sinfulness to holiness, as the ethiopian woman changed her skin from dark to bright,[16] and as she was restored to a new shine. He called this person also a 'blessed penitent' who would not dare to look up until receiving absolution: 'Your sins are forgiven' as in Lk 7:48.[17] The congeniality of Bernard's teaching and Luther's formula is evident, especially since Luther also declared that the believer is a real sinner but imputed with forgiveness, thus 'holy'.

On the subject of 'saint and sinner', another bernardine passage from the final phase of his sermon series on the Song of Songs is revealing. His SC 81 also sounds like an anticipation of Luther's concept of being 'saint and sinner at the same time'. Bernard included references to Gal 4 and at least ten references to Rom 7, which were *loci* also dear to Luther. Bernard had this to say:

> [The soul] is enslaved and free at the same time; enslaved through bondage, free because of its will. . . . Unhappy man that I am, who will deliver me from the shame of this bondage? (Rom 7:24). I admit I am not good, because there is no good in me. But I shall find comfort in the word of the saint: 'I know that in me there is no good' (Rom 7:18).[18]

15 *Ubi sancta peccatrix peccata deposuit, induit sanctitatem*, SC 3.2; SBOp 1:15,3f; CF 4:17.

16 SC 3.2; SBOp 1:15,4f; CF 4:17.

17 See SC 3.2; SBOp 1:15,14–19; CF 4:17.

18 SC 81.9; SBOp 2:289,17–22; CF 40:165. On the rhetorical aspects of this text (paronomasia of *mirum/miserum*), see Sabersky-Bascho, *Studien zur Paronomasie bei Bernhard von Clairvaux*, 45f.

We see, then, that at the beginning and at the end of his sermons on the first two chapters of the Canticle, Bernard worked with the concept of 'sinner and saint'. We may therefore take this as one of the basic insights he gained from his meditation on the Scriptures. This fundamental bernardine idea that the justified person is 'saint and sinner' was treated by Luther in the sixteenth century in his own way.

Luther: 'Saint and sinner at the same time'

Luther's controversial concept of the believer as simultaneously saint and sinner[19] may be best viewed from the perspective of the monastic tradition. It is a view normally not taken in Luther research, but the one which we suggest here and which is neccessary because it helps us understand the historical Luther within the wider monastic and specifically bernardine tradition. The concept of the 'holy sinner' belongs primarily to the realm of spirituality and less to that of systematic/dogmatic theology. Simultaneity should therefore not be turned into an axiomatic, dogmatic principle. It would be more profitable to interpret Luther's concept primarily as one of piety, and to view it from a bernardine perspective. Luther, too, meant a change from sinfulness to sainthood. He also spoke of being partly righteous and partly sinner (*partim iustus, partim peccator*) and of being a 'sinner in reality, [but] righteous in hope' (*peccator in re, iustus in spe*).[20] We shall take up this issue in the following Section on Christ as resident in the heart of the believer; saint and sinner cannot stand together (*non stant simul*).

For Luther, 'reason, free will, willing, wisdom, virtue, works', come under 'sin' and 'slavery', all of which need the divine Saviour. This need was expressed in Bernard's advice to turn to the 'Word' and 'Bridegroom', a moving counsel given virtually as his last testament in one of his final sermons on the Canticle. There Bernard indicated that he had been talking about the relationship of the soul to the Word 'for the last three days', and that 'there is

19 The literature on this issue is enormous; see for instance, K. O. Nilsson, *Simul: Das Miteinander von Göttlichem und Menschlichem in Luthers Theologie* (Göttingen: Vandenhoeck & Ruprecht, 1966).
20 WA 56:260,23; 269,30; 271,30; 272,17ff; 343,1; 442,21.

no difficulty in finding grounds for hope: the soul must turn to the Word'.[21] The 'Word' is the 'Bridegroom' who stands by 'my side' as he had said in SC 23, where he had explained the non-imputation of sins in a way Luther must surely have liked:

> If he [Word, the Bridegroom] decrees that a sin is not to be imputed to me, it is as if it never existed. Inability to sin constitutes God's righteousness; God's forgivenness constitutes man's. When I grasped this I understood the truth of the words: 'We know that anyone who has been begotten by God does not sin, because a heavenly birth protects him (1 Jn 5:18).[22]

In disclosing these parallels between Bernard and Luther, I believe I have emphasized some basic similarities of theological thought. I do not claim that Bernard and Luther always put the same weight on the same theological concepts, or that they structured their theology in identical ways. But without doubt, both men of God were shaped more by their common reliance on pauline and johannine theological perspectives than by differences due to their historical distance of several centuries. At times, Luther radicalized what he picked up from the pre-scholastic theology and processed it within his own theology of grace, sin, and his concept of the human person. All in all, we come to the conclusion that Luther's Christ-centered thinking was similar to that of Bernard.[23] Around this center everything else is structured.

21 SC 82.7; SBOp 2:297,1–10; CF 40:178.

22 SC 23.15; SBOp 1:148,29–149,4; CF 7:39.

23 See Karl Barth, *Church Dogmatics*, as referred to by Ebeling, *Luther-studien* 3:463. Compared with Calvin, one finds in Luther's theology more the johannine than the synoptic matrix; see Posset, *Luther's Catholic Christology*, 131.

III. 'CHRIST DWELLING IN OUR HEART THROUGH FAITH'

1. *Faith as 'making room'*

Bernard: 'Making sufficient room' for the Word

In his first Easter sermon Bernard presented the Lord as the victorious Lion of Judah and as the Wisdom who, in striking forcefully out and ordering all things sweetly for us, has conquered malice. In his second Easter sermon and in other sermons in the Easter cycle, he concentrated on the pauline concept of Christ dwelling in the heart of the believer and he occasionally used the johannine verse 'Everyone begotten of God conquers the world . . .' (1 John 5:4). Here is what he had to say about faith in his second Easter sermon:

> We have learned from the Apostle that it is through faith that Christ dwells in our hearts (Eph 3:17). Consequently, it does not seem wide off the mark if one takes this to mean that Christ lives in us as long as faith is alive. . . . Not does it seem incongruent with this state of affairs to hold that faith is dead in itself when it is without works. Just as we know the life of this body from its movements, so we know the life of faith from good works.[1]

In SC 27 Bernard again spoke in the words of 'the Apostle' (Eph 3:17) about 'Christ dwelling in our heart, not in any and every way, but particularly by faith'. A little later in the same sermon he repeated Eph 3:17. Still later, he again described faith as 'making sufficient room' for the Word:

> What a capacity this soul has, how privileged its merits, that it is found worthy not only to receive the divine presence, but to be able to make sufficient room! What can I say of her who can provide avenues spacious enough for the God of majesty to walk in! . . . She cannot be enslaved by gluttony and sensual pleasures, by the lust of the eyes, the ambition to rule, or by pride in the possession of power. . . . The soul must grow and expand, that it may be roomy enough for God. Its width is its love, if we accept what the Apostle says: 'Widen your hearts in

1 Res 1.1; SBOp 5:80f; Res 2.1; SBOp 5:95; see Pranger, *Bernard of Clairvaux and the Shape of Monastic Thought,* 295–304.

love' (2 Cor 6:13). . . . Eventually it becomes 'a holy temple in the Lord' (Eph 2:21).[2]

Luther: 'Believing' means 'making room'

In his first lectures on the psalms (1513), though, in some other regard, Luther made explicit reference to Bernard's third sermon on Easter, and we may therefore assume that he had also come across the second Easter sermon. We may therefore take this sermon—along with Bernard's SC 27, to which he also referred in these same first lectures—to be the bernardine matrix of his deliberations on Christ as resident in the heart. As it turns out, the same concept, that faith 'makes room' for Christ, is found in his 1527 lectures on 1 Jn 5:4.

It may be a coincidence that both Bernard and Luther connected Eph 3:17 and 1 John 5:4, or it may have been the result of their shared monastic theological method ('exegetical concordance'). It is, however, not surprising that during his johannine lectures of 1527, Luther referred to Bernard several times. In using the metaphor of 'making room' for the Word as the definition of 'faith', Luther took 'sin' to be the opposite, i. e. making room for the devil. Thus, Luther expounded the johannine 'being born of God', as meaning that Christ, the Word of God and the *semen* of God, takes up residence in the believer's heart and consequently, sin has to cede to the presence of Christ.[3]

2. *Cleansing the soul room*

Bernard: 'This fire has consumed every stain of sin'

Bernard wrote in SC 57, with reference to 1 Jn 4:10, that God loved us first. Of God Scripture says that 'fire goes before him'

2 SC 27.3,8 and 10, SBOp 1:183–189; CF 7:76f, 81f, 83f; see also SC 58.7 and 76.6. See Claudio Stercal, *Il 'Medius Adventus': Saggio di lettura degli scrifti di Bernardo di Clairvaux* (Rome: Editiones Cistercienses, 1992), 111–124.

3 See Posset, *Luther's Catholic Christology*, 216–219; see Raymond E. Brown, *The Epistles of John: Translated with Introduction, Notes, and Commentary*, The Anchor Bible (Garden City: Doubleday & Company, Inc., 1982) 410. On Bernard's use of Eph 3:17 and 1 John 5:4f, see O'Brien, 'St. Bernard's Use of Sacred Scripture', 164–167.

(Ps 96:3), and that the Lord is close to those who are brokenhearted (Ps 33:19). 'The fire that is God does indeed devour. . . . It is a coal of desolating fire but a fire that rages against vices only to produce a healing unction in the soul'. The preacher explained further that 'this fire has consumed every stain of sin and the rust of evil habits'; the conscience has been cleansed and tranquillized.[4] This is the result of the 'divine rescue mission' in the spiritual struggle over the 'custody of the heart'.[5]

Luther: 'Sin is grilled on the spit'

Bernard's message in SC 57, in metaphors of 'devouring' and 'burning' sin away, emerged in Luther's lecture on 1 Jn in the same surprising imagery. Luther's graduate student George Rörer (an outstanding stenographer) kept the following literal lecture notes:

> What should I say? To sum it up: We Christians are born [of God] so that there is no make-up (*fucus*), no nice-looking piety, but the real thing, the essence. Therefore, if one is born [of God], one does not commit sin (*non facere peccatum*) because being born of God cleanses sin away, crucifies and burns sin [an alternative reading would be: 'He bites sin off'], thus he cannot give in [to sin]; sin is grilled on the spit.[6]

The final image evokes a comparison between sin and a german sausage or a pig being roasted on the spit; it is preserved in lecture notes in Rörer's hand in a mixture of German-Latin: *in veru peccatum steckts*. Another one of Luther's students preserved this phrase entirely in German: *Da wird die sunde am brand spiess gesteckt*. 'Here sin is put on a spit'. Sin is burned away. In any case

4 SC 57.6–8; SBOp 2:123,1–124,18; CF 31:101–03; see SC 31.4; SBOp 1:221,27–30; CF 7:127. On the fire of love which consumes every stain of sin, according to Bernard, see Casey, *Athirst*, 76; Sommerfeldt, *The Spiritual Teachings*, 118.

5 Bernard Bonowitz, 'Custody of the Heart in the 'Sermons on Diverse Subjects', *Word & Spirit* 12 (1990) 137. Bonowitz's observations are valuable for our purposes here, even though it is fairly certain that Luther did not read Bernard's 'Sermons on Diverse Subjects'. Even without establishing any direct dependence of Luther on Bernard's Div, their congeniality is striking.

6 See WA 20:705,18f (Rörer's macaronic notes); see Posset, *Luther's Catholic Christology*, 192–210; see WA 20:706,25f (Probst's notes).

sin is not present where God's *semen/sperma* is present. Grilling produces the genuine christian believer.

Although Luther did not indicate any direct source here, the image of fire is strikingly similar to Bernard's; and in light of the fact that Luther at other places during his johannine lectures made direct references to Bernard's sermons on the Canticle, it is likely that Luther was influenced by this section of Bernard's SC 57 as he sought a solution to the problems he had in interpreting 1 John.

In his johannine lecture of 1527, the professor in passing identified God's *semen* as *verbum,* following patristic tradition. The Reformer interpreted John by Peter and in doing so he concurred with Augustine's commentary on 1 Jn that God's *semen* means the Word of God, *Semen Dei, id est verbum Dei.*[7] Luther interpreted 1 Jn 3:9 by using 1 Pt 1:23, lecturing: 'Your rebirth has come, not from a destructible but from an indestructible *semen,* through the living and enduring Word of God'. Luther elaborated: 'God's word remains, it is eternal *semen*'.[8] However, Luther did not make any explicit reference here to Augustine's commentary on the *First Letter of John*, as one might expect; instead he referred to 1 Pt 1:23, true to the monastic exegetical concordance method according to which Scripture interpets itself through Scripture. Luther attributed the impossibility of sinning to the eternal 'seed', mentioned in 1 Pt 1:23. Because of the divine seed, the faithful person stands tall and cannot be confused; indeed he cannot even sin: *stat, non potest exturbari. Imo non potest peccare.*[9] This is because Christ's presence takes up the entire space of the heart, so that there is no room for sin, at least not as long as Christ reigns in it. Sin is dominated (*peccatum regnatum*), as Luther said elsewhere.[10]

Since Luther's hermeneutic was essentially christological, his solution rested in a christological interpretation of 1 Jn 3:9: Christ is resident in the heart. This reminds us of Luther's own statement

7 PL 35:2016.

8 See WA 20:705,21–706,1.

9 WA 20:706,1. It seems to me that for Luther's lectures on 1 Jn the background reading was not so much Augustine's commentary on 1 Jn but his *Perfection of Man*.

10 See WA 8:96,18 (Antilatomus, 1521).

concerning Scripture interpretation: 'Scripture must not be interpreted in any other way except that man is nothing and Christ alone is everything'.[11]

Christ is so powerful that he makes it possible that the Christian 'cannot sin', as 1 Jn 3:9 claims. The puzzled Luther asked: 'Why, my John?' And he answered: 'For they contradict each other: to be a sinner and to be born of God. [If] one can send away the birth of God, then one is able to sin'.[12] But when Christ is in the heart, sin cannot simultaneously be present. Luther admitted: 'We neglected these verses; we did not understand [them]. It is [now however] the simplest sentence', *sententia simplicissima*:[13]

> God's seed in us does not tolerate any sin at all in us, because Christ is the purger of sins (*purgator peccatorum*) who is sitting in the heart by faith, and he says: 'Brother, here you began to be concupiscent, unworthy of honor; your [Christian] name is affected by disgrace'. So he obeys; thus sin does not reign. The sin, of course, murmurs, but Christ bites it to death with his teeth.[14]

'Christ's teeth', a very rare metaphor in the christian tradition, becomes Luther's solution to the problem. As far as I know, it appears only once in Bernard's Canticle sermons. Since Luther was familiar with them, he may have picked it up there, i. e. from SC 72, where, in interpreting Sg 2:14–17, Bernard spoke of the Bridegroom as feeding in the midst of lilies. Sinners have to be masticated by Christ's teeth in suffering in order to be incorporated into his mystical body.[15]

Both Bernard's SC 72 and Luther's johannine lecture contain the ideas that Christ is the purger of sin in the believer's heart and that Christ shows his teeth. Given the rarity of the images,

---

11 *Scriptura non debet aliter gedeut werden, quam quod homo nihil sit et solus Christus omnia,* WA 15:527,35–37 (Sermon on Easter Monday, 1524).

12 WA 20:706,2–4. On this quotation see also Bengt Hägglund 'Rechtfertigung – Wiedergeburt – Erneuerung in der nachreformatorischen Theologie', *Kerygma und Dogma* 5 (1959) 323–24.

13 WA 20:706, 5f.

14 WA 20:706, 6–9.

15 SC 72.2–3; SBOp 2:226,11–13 and 227,8; CF 40:64f.

Luther's dependence upon Bernard's sermon is very likely, even though Luther makes no direct reference to Bernard. Since these bernardine sermons were quoted by Luther in other instances and thus exercised an undeniable influence on him, we consider it not far-fetched to assume Bernard's influence on this point.

Luther continued his lectures on 1 Jn as follows: ' . . . If someone sins and fullfills sin, he is not of God *etc.* because "being of God" is contradictory [to sin]; having said this, [I find this saying] useful to me now. This has been said about fulfilling sin so that we do not lose consolation'.[16] By his emphasis on fulfilling sin, the Reformer left some room for his concept that the Christian is simultaneously in sin and in righteousness, just as Bernard also used the paradoxical concept of the 'holy sinner' who develops from sinfulness to sainthood,[17] as we have shown above.

Luther concluded his lecture of 24 September 1527, by saying: 'Now sin solicits and murmers against us, but we are under grace, *sub gratia*'.[18] Nevertheless, Luther knew that we cannot live without struggle. The *Semen Dei*, the 'mystical' Christ who is the belligerent resident in the believer's heart, where he purges, burns and bites sin away, under 'protest' from sin, cannot and does not want to coexist with sin. Christ as *Semen Dei* is stronger than sin and sin and the devil must cede to him.

In the lecture of 30 September 1527, Luther returned to 1 Jn 3:8f. ' "Everyone who is born of God, does not commit sin", as those two fight each other, that someone is born of God and that he sins'.[19] At this point Luther called on Rom 6:2 and, again following the monastic exegetical concordance method, he related this johannine text to the Epistle to the Romans: 'The Apostles [Paul and John] solve it: "We are justified by alien justice . . ."; elsewhere: "How can we live in sin, when we died to it," *etc.*' (Rom

16 WA 20:706,11–13. There is no need to emend the Rörer text as the editor of WA suggested at this point, i. e. to read *repugnant hec duo* in place of *hoc dicto utitur*. What Luther seemed to express here is this: He did not understand John previously, but now he can make sense of John's *dictum*: If 'being born of God' is understood as struggle against sin, then it is a consolation.

17 SC 3.2; SBOp 1:15,3–4; CF 4:17; see Sommerfeldt, *The Spiritual Teachings*,122f.

18 WA 20:706,13–15.

19 WA 20:707,6–8.

6:2). They are not present at the same time (*non stant simul*): to
commit sin and to be born of God.'[20]

By focusing on 1 Jn 3:9 and Rom 6:2, Luther appears here
to have negated his own previous theological statement, that the
Christian is *simul iustus et peccator*, which he saw formulated in
Rom 7 and 1 Jn 1. And he confirmed further: 'Thus there remain
[only] the débris and *feces* of sin, but the matter as such is this: when
we stay in the state of being born of God, sin does not follow'.[21] By
the power of God's seed, Christ himself reigning in the heart, sin
is reduced to left-overs which have burnt up; sin has become the
excrement which Christ purged and expelled from the believer's
heart.

Going on to expound 1 Jn 3:10, which he considered the conclusion of the argumentation, Luther declared once more that faith
and love are the two essentials of Christianity.[22] Still struggling to
understand the verse, 1 Jn 3:9, he returned to it at the end of his
lectures, on 7 November 1527. He drew his conclusion from 1 Jn
5:18 (*generatio Dei conservat eum*) which, according to Luther, is
the evangelist's own 'conclusion, and high point and brief recapit-
ulation' (*Conclusio et Epiphonema et brevis recapitulatio*). Those
two fight each other: sinning and being born of God. Reminded
again of Rom 7, Luther declared: 'Double is the Christian: as long
as he lives in faith he does not sin'; but whenever a person is
preoccupied with 'fervor' so that the flesh dominates and seduces,
then the *generatio Dei* is not in control.[23]

When Luther looked at the Christian's existence in this 'world'
(in John's sense), he saw a person situated in this double existence
of being *simul iustus et peccator*. But when he took the other
perspective, looking at the *Semen Dei* as the mighty Christ baring
his teeth in the believer's heart, he could not but declare that there
can be no compromise, no simultaneity of sin and *semen*. Thus
it depends on his christological and anthropological perspective
whether Luther saw the sinner and saint as either *simul* or *non*

20 *Non stant simul peccare et nasci ex deo*, WA 20:707,9f.
21 WA 20:707,10f.
22 WA 20:707,11–13.
23 WA 20:798,17–19.

simul. In his lectures on 1 Jn, the christological perspective was dominant. Luther as the exegete of John was led to conclude:

> But in as much as he is born [of God], it is impossible that he sins. He has that which conserves him. What [is it]? It is the birth [of God, *nativitas*]. 'And the evil one' (1 Jn 5:18b), be it Satan or the world ['cannot touch him']. How is that?. . . . A Christian can be tempted, but he cannot be conquered. If he ever falls, the birth [of God] returns [him] to faith. . . . Therefore, let us be eager to remain in the faith, and in the birth of God and then we will be without sin, and we are clean and we cannot sin.[24]

How can the Christian have God's seed in his heart? A believer receives Christ by opening his heart to the *Semen Dei* which comes as the Word of God through preaching.[25] Bernard and Luther shared an axiom from Rom 10:17: 'faith comes from hearing' (*fides ex auditu*). *Semen Dei*, Christ, the johannine *Logos* of God, is the divine gift to the heart of the believer who makes room for Christ who purges sin. The heart is cleansed by his grace alone, not by one's own works and personal zeal.[26] Anyone who attempts self-purgation is an ignoramus who does not know Christ, and such *ignorantia* plays into the devil's reign.[27] The sign of knowing Christ is loving one's neighbor; and this knowledge of Christ is salvation: *cognitio est salus*, as Luther said in lecturing on 1 Jn 2:3.[28] This *cognitio* is identical with faith.[29] Bernard spoke similarly of knowledge and faith.

After the Wittenberg professor had made it perfectly clear that the presence of Christ tolerates no sin in the believer's soul, he painted a picture of the Christian in the likeness of Christ. The Christian, too, is supposed to show his teeth; Christ with his spiritual teeth is the *exemplum* for the believer. He, too, must use his spiritual teeth to fight and bite in order to keep sin from his heart:

24 WA 20:798,19–799, 6.
25 WA 20:772,20f.
26 WA 20:656,6f (on 1 Jn 2:12).
27 WA 20:640,21.
28 WA 20:641,18.
29 WA 20:756,1 (on 1 Jn 4:16).

> The Christian mortifies the flesh, as in Gal 5. He does not let sin
> reign, but he detests it and immediately begins to bite it with his
> spiritual teeth. Let us see to it that we are found among those
> who take away sins and serve our neighbors.[30]

Those who are born of God's seed 'acquire the nature of God',
Luther declared. He continued: 'Therefore, . . . we are born [of
God] as Christians so that we who before were bad are now
by *natura* good'.[31] Clearly, there is no simultaneity here. Rather,
there is a change from bad-then to good-now. The sinner becomes
the *sancta peccatrix* of Bernard's sermon. That this is so Luther
explained with yet other comparisons. Because Christ is the 'War
Lord', he liberates us from all sin.[32] The concept of the 'joyous
exchange' is also at work here: 'Through him I put all my mischief
on him, and he puts all good things on me'.[33] The faithful are prepared for the Day of Judgment; they have confidence (*parrhesia*,
1 Jn 4:17), because then 'we will be similar to but not identical
with God, who is life and justice', and it will become apparent
'that we are saints'.[34] We become divine because we are in the
Father, in God. 'We are made gods (*dii*), i. e. priests and kings, as
in 1 Pt 2 [:9]'.[35]

Ultimately it is 'Christ alone' who reigns in the true believer's heart, and therefore simultaneity must change into non-
simultaneity because being born of God's *semen* and sinning 'cannot stand at the same time' (*non stant simul*). This 'either/or'
thought pattern was not unusual for Luther, who already in his
first Lectures on the Psalms had said that 'pure truth' cannot stand

30 *Pugnant illa duo: 'Manere in Christo' et 'peccare'. Ratio: ubi est Christus, tollit peccatum*, WA 20:702,16–18 (on 1 Jn 3:5); see 702,18–703,1 (on 1 Jn
3:6); see Posset, *Luther's Catholic Christology*, 222.

31 WA 20:692,4–6 (on 1 Jn 2:29).

32 WA 20:692,2f. The proof for being born of God is found in those who do
justice and serve their neighbors, WA 20:692,7. He who does not love his neighbor
is not of God, see lines 8f. Luther had used 'War Lord' as a christological title
elsewhere in his lecture on 1 Jn: WA 20:773,14–16.

33 WA 20:677,3–7.

34 WA 20:698,12–15 (on 1 Jn 3:2).

35 WA 20:687,2f (on 1 Jn 2:24). See Franz Posset, ' "Deification" in the
German Spirituality of the Late Middle Ages and in Luther: An Ecumenical
Historical Perspective', ARG 84 (1993) 103–26, here 122.

simultaneously with 'haughtiness of heart'. And in his late disputation on Rom 3:28 (1538) he formulated it somewhat differently, saying that 'the nature of man cannot be understood as corrupt and whole at the same time'.[36]

3. Lying on the 'bed of conscience' in the room of faith

Bernard: 'The bed of conscience'

By viewing the theme 'Christ dwelling in our heart by faith' from yet another angle, another similarity between Bernard and Luther emerges. We turn to Bernard's sermons 46 and 47, where he speaks of 'conscience'. In sermon 46 he exegetes Sg 1:15f, 'our bed is covered with flowers. . . .' On this bed the Groom is invited to repose. The Bride 'entices him [Christ] to be the guest of her soul, compels him to spend the night with her'. The spiritual meaning of 'bed' is cloisters and monasteries. 'This bed is seen to be adorned with flowers', which in this sermon take on the meaning of good works (while elsewhere they are taken to mean faith). 'You must take care to surround your [bed] with the flowers of good works, with the practice of virtues that precede holy contemplation as the flower precedes the fruit'. Bernard perceived the 'bed' as the 'bed of conscience' which needs cleaning. 'Then you may confidently invite the Bridegroom because when you lead him in you also can truly say: "Our bed is covered with flowers", since the conscience undeniably breathes forth affection, peace, meekness, righteousness, obedience, joyfulness, humility'. In concluding sermon 46, he elaborated on making the soul room pretty by emphasizing the adornment of the room. One's conscience is 'a room that is always adorned' for Christ, its 'guest' who reposes on the 'bed of conscience' which is decorated with 'flowers' of good works.[37]

36 *Quia non potest pura veritas simul stare cum superbia cordis*, WA 3:514,23–25. *Non enim potest natura simul corrupta et integra intellegi*, WA 39-I (theses on Rom 3:28, 1538).

37 *Lectulus noster floridus*: SC 46; SBOp 2:56–61, especially 59,13f; CF 7:245f; Jean Leclercq, '*Lectulus*. Variazioni su un tema biblico nella tradizione monastica'. *Biblia e Spiritualità* (Rome, 1967) 417–36; reprinted in Leclercq, *Chances de la spiritualité occidentale* (Paris: Cerf, 1966).

This theme was so important to Bernard that he spoke of it again in the following sermon, SC 47, where he pointed out that the 'flowers' have to be renewed regularly:

> A flower grows both in field and garden, but in a room never. It brightens and perfumes it, not by standing upright as in the garden or field, but by lying prone because it is brought from without, not sprung from within. So it is they must be frequently renewed, fresher blooms must always be added, because they soon lose their scent and beauty. And if, as I have stated in another sermon, the bed bedecked with flowers is the conscience laden with good works, you must certainly see that it is by no means enough to do a good deed once or twice if the likeness is to be preserved; you must unceasingly add new ones to the former, so that sowing bountifully you may reap bountifully (2 Cor 9:6). Otherwise the flower of good works withers where it lies, and all its brilliance and freshness are swiftly destroyed if it is not renewed continually by more and more acts of love. So it is in the room.[38]

Of importance for our considerations here is Bernard's notion of the 'bed of conscience' which is decorated with 'good works' which, we remember, are the fruits of faith. Christ comes to the heart as a 'guest' and expects a heart of faith to be active in love. The good works have a decorative function; faith is the essential foundation. At this point, we focus, however, on the 'bed'.

Luther: 'Conscience has its spouse, marriage bed'

Luther followed the same line of thought as Bernard when he lectured on faith active in love on the occasion of expounding 1 Jn 3:19: 'Faith itself is being stabilized by [bringing forth] fruit, by application, by practice, because otherwise faith is very weak'.[39] In the further course of his johannine lectures Luther spoke of the duty of the conscience to clean all its corners, a metaphor which echoed Bernard's notion of conscience and its renewal. Sharply

---

38 SC 47.2; SBOp 2:62,19–63,7; CF 31:4.

39 In latin-german mix: *Stabilitur fides ipsa fructu, usu, exercitio, alioqui fides est seer schwach*, WA 20:716,3f.

differing from Bernard, however, is Luther's predominant use of 'conscience' as primarily 'bad conscience', which he called a 'bad beast'.[40] But congenial is Luther's idea that 'faith is nothing but a good conscience',[41] 'faith' being understood here as active in love. The good works are the flowers on the 'bed of conscience', which is then a good conscience.

In these johannine lectures, no direct reference is found to Bernard's sermons on the Canticle, just as any such reference was missing from Luther's exposition of Psalm 45 in 1532, when he used the vocabulary of bridal mysticism in speaking on conscience. But the evidence of literary dependency suggests that Luther was echoing the language and imagery of Bernard's sermons. Luther's 1532 statement on Psalm 45 is best understood, therefore, when interpreted from the bernardine matrix: 'Conscience has its spouse, [conscience is the] marriage bed, where Christ alone must reign'.[42] Christ is the sole reigning resident and lover in the believer's heart. He does not tolerate sin in his presence. Expressing himself in the language of bridal mysticism, Luther claimed that 'conscience' (or heart) is the unpolluted marriage bed of the divine Bridegroom. Bernard envisioned it as covered with the beautiful 'flowers' of good works which have grown out of faith. However, Luther no longer took into consideration the fact that Bernard in his sermon 46 on the Song had been speaking of monasteries as symbols for the bed of Christ.

40 *Conscientia mala bestia*, WA 20:718,11. *Conscientia est mala bestia, quae facit hominem stare contra se ipsum*, WA 44:545,16; *pessima et infernalis bestia*, 546,32. See Ernst Wolf, 'Vom Problem des Gewissens in reformatorischer Sicht'. *Peregrinatio: Studien zur reformatorischen Theologie und zum Kirchenproblem* (second edition, Munich: Kaiser Verlag, 1962) 90–94; Ebeling, *Lutherstudien* 3:108–125.

41 *Fides nihil aliud est quam bona conscientia*, WA 20:718,19f.

42 WA 40-II:585,5 (1532). Theo Bell pointed out that Luther also in *De votis* (WA 8:610,1) talked about Christ and the spouse's conscience. However, Bell brought into play only Bernard's SC 23.9–16 as a possible source for Luther at that point (*Divus Bernhardus*, 232). Although, this connection to SC 23 is not impossible, the more likely source is SC 46 which in the tradition is well known as the sermon *Lectulus noster floridus*, which we took into consideration here as Luther's more probable source (together with the subsequent SC 47, in which Bernard carried on with this theme).

We realize that Luther dropped the narrow monastic, allegorical interpretation of the cloister as the 'bed'. But he unequivocally lived off the monastic matrix when he employed the concepts of faith as 'making room' for the 'seed of God' and of Christ as the resident in the believer's heart who does not tolerate any coexistence with sin and the devil.

1. *The Virtue of Humility*

'Humility' is a prominent subject in monastic theology, ranking as highest among monastic virtues. Sometime before 1124 Bernard wrote a book on it with the title *The Steps of Humility and Pride*. Luther was either unaware of it or chose to ignore it, and there is no evidence that he studied it. There is no traceable impact of it on Luther's work. One may suspect that Luther had an aversion to anything that did not seem to him useful for preaching. Therefore, we must look not to treatises but primarily to bernardine sermons for his spirituality of humility, and to discover whether the preacher Luther made use of them.

Bernard: 'O humility, virtue of Christ'

In the first of three sermons for the Feast of the Epiphany (Epi) Bernard meditated on the humility of Christ as a lesson for us all:

> O humility, virtue of Christ, how much you confound the haughtiness of our vanity. All too little do I know, and when I seem to know a little more I soon find myself unable to shut up, being impudently and imprudently pushy and showing off, eager to talk, quick to lecture, slow to listen. And Christ, for how long a time was he silent and lived unnoticed; was it because he was perhaps concerned about inane glory?[1]

Luther copied Bernard's entire passage

Perhaps during his preparations for his first lectures on the psalms (1513–1515), young friar Martin copied almost literally into his desk copy of Anselm's *Opuscula* these three sentences from Bernard's Epi 1.[2] The reason Luther copied them is unknown;

1 Epi 1; SBOp 4:299,14–18. See Sommerfeldt, *The Spiritual Teachings,* 53–63, where, however, our text is not quoted.

2 Luther's wording is slightly different: *O humilitas, virtus Christi, quantum confundis superbiam meae vanitatis. Parum aliquid scio vel magis scire mihi videor et jam silere nescio. Nam impudenter et imprudenter me ingerens et ostentans promptulus ad loquendum, velox ad docendum, tardus ad audiendum. Et Christus tanto tempore tacebat . . . ,* WA 9:108,28–30. See Bell, *Divus Bern-*

he never quoted this particular passage again. But its message remained with him. In his first course on the psalms, bernardine spirituality shone through when he spoke of the justifying force of humility. In his gloss on Psalm 36 he declared that the saints persevere in the Church because of their humility. And on Psalm 109, by intimately connecting 'faith' and 'humility', he could state that 'nobody is justified by faith unless he first confesses through humility that he is not justified'.[3] Here there came into play the theme of self-accusation, which will be taken up later.

2. The proud

Bernard: 'But the proud man answers: since you will not give it to me I will seize it'

Another passage about humility and pride is found in yet another bernardine sermon, his fourth for Christmas. The proud person is juxtaposed to the humble. Humility is the only attitude possible in the face of divine majesty. This is so because 'the proud man, in so far as it is possible, dishonors God. The Lord says: I will not give my glory to another; but the proud man answers: since you [God] will not give it to me I will seize it'.[4]

Luther: 'As Saint Bernard says, I will seize it'

Luther was inspired by Bernard's fictional speech of the proud person, and in 1519 he made use of it in his sermon on 'Two Kinds of Righteousness'. Yet, he did so in a christological context: 'That

hardus, 79. There is reason to believe that Luther relied on a source like *Flores seu sententiae*, PL 183:1204. Luther also utilized at that point a thought from Miss 4.9, that the virtue of humility is always close to divine grace: *Semper solet esse gratiae divinae familiaris virtus humilitas*, SBOp 4:54,26, which he quoted with a change of the word sequence and a change to the genetive case in WA 9:107,29: *Semper solet esse divinae gratiae familiaris virtus humilitatis.*

3 WA 3:208,33–36 (Ps 36); WA 3:345,29f (on Ps109). With Regin Prenter (against E. Bizer) I hold that Luther's notion of *humilitas* should not be interpreted as preparatory 'work' for grace. Furthermore, humility is not to be separated from faith, see Regin Prenter, *Der barmherzige Richter: Iustitia dei passiva in Luthers Dictata super Psalterium 1513–1515* (Kopenhagen: Universitetsforlaget Aarhus, 1961) 129.

4 Nat 4.2; SBOp 4:265,8–10.

Christ did not count himself equal to God means that he did not wish to be equal to him as do those who presumptuously grasp for equality and say to God, "If you [God] would not give me your glory (as Saint Bernard says), I shall seize it" '.[5] When the Reformer worked on his *Operationes in Psalmos* (1519–1521), he was still equally impressed by Bernard's insights and again referred to him, as we shall now see.

3. Absolute Humility, not Humiliation

Bernard: 'I say humility and not humiliation'
    In reflecting on 'true humility' in SC 34, the great cistercian theologian made a distinction between *humiliatio* and *humilitas*. The Bride seems to demand a very special concession, and for this she is rebuffed with a response that is meant, however, to be helpful. Everyone is to strive toward the spiritual heights but must keep a 'lowly opinion of himself'. Only when one is in a lowly position can one look up for grace. Bernard pointed out: 'I say humility and not humiliation. How many are humiliated who are not humble!' From the biblical base of Psalm 118:71 in the Vulgate version, 'It is good for me that you have humiliated me that I may learn your justifications',[6] he declared that humility makes a person righteous and, he continued, 'it is joyful and absolute humility that alone merits grace which precedes [it]'.[7] What Bernard meant by 'joyful and absolute humility' is probably best interpreted with 'faith'.[8] Grace precedes in any case; humility in humiliation/lowliness prepares one for this grace and thus one receives righteousness. However, the preparation itself is also grace:

> To receive grace one must be humiliated willingly. You may take as a general rule that everyone who humbles himself will be

---

5 'Si non dederis (ut ait B. Bernhardus) mihi gloriam tuam, ipsemet mihi usurpabo', WA 2:148,28–29 (*On Two Kinds of Righteousness*). The index in WA 63 does not know this connection; see Bell, *Divus Bernhardus*, 267f.

6 SC 34.3; SBOp 1:246,29–247,2; CF 7:162.

7 . . . *absoluta humilitas*, SC 34.3; SBOp 1:247,16f; see CF 7:162.

8 A translator rendered *absoluta humilitas* (weakly, in my opinion) with 'genuine humility', CF 7:162.

exalted (Lk 14:11). It is significant that not every kind of humility
is to be exalted, but only that which the will (*de voluntate*)
embraces, and not from sadness (*ex tristitia*) or necessity (*ex
necessitate*).[9]

In SC 42 the bernardine distinction emerged again. The occasion was provided in Sg 1:12 by the word 'nard', which was
understood as an insignificant herb and therefore a fitting symbol
for humility. With his christocentric focus on Phil 2:7 (and his use
of Rom 12:16 in this instance) Bernard declared that 'necessity
compels the former [humiliation], [while] the latter [humility] is
of free choice . . . and so he [Christ] gave us a pattern of humility.
He emptied himself, he humbled himself, not under the constraint
of an assessment of himself but inspired by love for us'.[10] Here
again Bernard's affective Christocentrism was at work, when he
explained 'humility' with Phil 2:7.

Luther: 'Bernard calls it *humiliatio* and not *humilitas*'
Since Luther had found the quotation on the anger of God
in SC 42, there is a good chance that he also had this same
sermon in mind when he dealt in his *Operationes* with humility
and humiliation. How did Luther take up the bernardine distinction
between humility and humiliation? Trained in humanistic 'sacred
philology', he spoke of it during his exposition of the verse Ps
21:22 (*salva me ex ore leonis et de cornibus unicornium exaudi
me*), and trained in the monastic 'exegetical concordance' method
he combined it with Rom 12:16, 'Have the same attitude toward
all. Put away ambitious thoughts and associate with those who are
lowly'. Then he added Ps 9:14, 'I am afflicted by my foes'. Using
this monastic method, Luther had no problem in interpreting Ps
21:22, and in utilizing Bernard's distinction and Paul's original
concept of *tapeinophrosyne* (he may have encountered this hint
in Erasmus' Greek New Testament). And so Luther interpreted
humility/lowliness in his *Operationes* as:

9 SC 34.4; see CF 7:163.
10 See SC 42.7; SBOp 2:37,17–19; CF 7:215; see Sommerfeldt, *The Spiritual Teachings*, 53–65. Strangely, Bell, *Divus Bernhardus*, 118, did not take SC
42 into consideration at this point.

the *affectus* which knows what is lowly (*humilia*) as in Rom 12 [:16], and not what is exalted, but which knows affliction and oppression and altogether this form of *humilitas* in which this virtue *tapinophrosyne* [sic] is exercised, which Bernard calls *humiliatio* and not *humilitas*, about which is said in Ps 9[:14]: 'See the affliction (*humilitatem*) stemming from my foes'.[11]

This passage illustrates Luther's great expertise in spiritual exegesis and affective meditation. He combines several biblical verses and weaves into them one of his favorite authorities, in this case Bernard. He undergirds all these insights with his humanistic expertise in philology by working with the Greek original *tapeinós* of Rom 12:16 in interpreting the Vulgate term *humilitas*. Luther proved himself a biblical humanist who had come of age in the monastic tradition. What had happened by this point in his lecture? Luther interpreted Paul's Rom 12:16 through Bernard's distinction between humility and humiliation. With the pauline verse interpreted in this way, he then expounded on Ps 21:22 along with Ps 9:14. What a tightly knit argumentation! One may rightly conclude that Luther had so completely internalized Bernard's thoughts, as well as his biblical and philological insights, that he could come up with the interpretation he displayed here. In this process Luther had to disregard the latin version of Rom 12:16 which speaks of the 'humble' (*humiles*), and to use instead the greek original, *tapeinói*, 'the lowly'. It appears that Luther, the humanistic exegete, was put on this track by Bernard's distinction and what he found in Erasmus' Greek New Testament. Bernard helped him overcome the unfortunate latin translation which did not make this distinction between humility and humiliation; the latin version simply speaks of 'humility' (*humilitas*) at Ps 21:22 and Ps 9:14, and at Rom 12:16 of the 'humble' (*humiles*).

11 . . . *quam Bernhardus humiliationem, non humilitatem appellat . . .*, WA 5:656,24–29, where the spelling *tapinophrosyne* is found, which should be *tapeinophrosyne*. Luther may have relied on Erasmus' distinction of humility and humiliation; see Bell, *Divus Bernhardus*, 117–121. With right, Bell distanced himself from interpretations which want to see a great difference between Luther's and Bernard's concept of humility. See Luther, *Magnificat*, WA 7:559,29–560,37; LW 21:312.

1. *The Two Belong Together*

Bernard: 'True knowledge of self'

According to the cistercian father, 'humility is the virtue by which man has a low opinion of himself on the basis of an utterly true knowledge of self'.[1] This self-knowledge is the humbling insight into one's sinfulness and is the necessary first step to salvation. It brings personal shame, but at the same time it allows for the awareness that one has ben created in the image of God. From this double insight (into the divine aspect of God the Creator and the Redeemer on the one side and into the human aspect of being a sinner who needs to acknowledge in humility his own sinfulness on the other side) results the virtual identification of humility as faith; with this insight all salvific knowledge begins, declares Bernard. We acknowledge in humble faith or in trusting humility that we are sinners before God and the world. In a way, self-knowledge evokes humility and thus trust and faith that God will redeem us.

Bernard in SC 37 and SC 38 continues to explain the relatedness of one's knowledge of self and knowledge of God: 'No one is saved without knowledge of self, since it is the source of that humility on which salvation depends, and of the fear of the Lord that is the beginning of salvation as much as of wisdom. No one, I repeat, is saved without that knowledge'.[2] He continued: 'Knowledge of God and of self are basic and must come first; they are essential for salvation'.[3] He argued for this position with such rhetorical questions as these: 'But if we are ignorant of God how

1 Hum 1.2; SBOp 3:17,21f. See Csi 2.6: 'If you do not know yourself, you are like a building without a foundation; you raise not a structure but ruins. . . . Therefore, let your consideration begin and end with yourself'. See Gilson, *The Mystical Theology of Saint Bernard*, 70–72; Heinrich G. J. Storm, *Die Begründung der Erkenntnis nach Bernhard von Clairvaux* (Frankfurt am Main, Bern, Las Vegas: Peter Lang, 1977) 116–270; Marie-Madeleine Davy, *Bernard de Clairvaux* (Paris: Éditions du Félin, 1990) 104–111 (on knowledge of self), 140–157 (on knowledge of God).

2 See SC 37.1–2; SBOp 2:9,9–10,1; CF 7:181f.

3 SC 37.5; SBOp 2:12,1–3, CF 7:184.

can we hope in one we do not know? If ignorant about ourselves, how can we be humble, thinking ourselves to be something when we are really nothing?' Then he made the statement (SC 37.6) which had an impact on Luther:

> Just as the fear of the Lord is the beginning of wisdom, so pride is the beginning of all sin; and just as the love of God is the way to the beginning of wisdom, so despair leads to the committing of every sin. And as the fear of God springs up within you from knowledge of self and love of God from the knowledge of God, so on the contrary, pride comes from want of self-knowledge and despair from want of knowledge of God.[4]

Bernard continued with this subject in his introduction to the next sermon, SC 38: 'Thus despair, the greatest evil of all, follows on ignorance of God.' Bernard was well aware of the socratic origin of the classical axiom 'know thyself' which he cited and which he interpreted immediately with a psalm verse: 'I am more concerned to know myself, as the greek motto advises, so that with the Prophet 'I may know what is wanting to me (Ps 39:5)'.[5] In these words, he combined the classical and the biblical traditions in one breath. He was thus the prototype of a monastic, biblical humanist we meet several hundred years later in Luther.

Luther: 'According to Bernard, knowledge of self without knowledge of God leads to despair . . .'

In his second series of lectures on the monks' prayerbook, i. e. in his *Operationes in psalmos*,[6] Luther referred to the two stirring passages from SC 37 and SC 38 just quoted, which present great insights from the monastic meditative tradition. During his exposition of Ps 18:13 the friar of Wittenberg explicitly called on the abbot of Clairvaux: 'For just as, according to Bernard, knowledge of self

---

4 SC 37.6; SBOp 2:12,12–14; CF 7:185.
5 SC 38.1; SBOp 2:15,5–7; CF 7:188.
6 The dissertation on the *Operationes* by Hubertus Blaumeiser, *Martin Luthers Kreuzestheologie: Schlüssel zu seiner Deutung von Mensch und Wirklichkeit. Eine Untersuchung anhand der Operationes in Psalmos (1519–1521)* (Paderborn: Bonifatius Verlag, 1995) makes no effort to identify the quoted Bernard texts in the critical edition SBOp.

without the knowledge of God leads to despair, so knowledge of
God without the knowledge of self leads to presumption'.[7] This
monastic mind-set encouraged the search for the knowledge of
God and of self and recognized man's nothingness, his need for
salvation, and his dependence on God's mercy, all of which are included in the mystery of the incarnation, passion, and resurrection
of Christ.[8]

Luther's piety was decisively nurtured by this monastic theological matrix. Bernard's concept of the two-fold knowledge of
God and of self shone through Luther's *Meditation on Christ's
Passion*, published in 1519. There he wrote that through such
meditation man recognizes his sinfulness, on one side, and God
as his redeemer through the passion of his Son, on the other.[9]
This bernardine spirituality never ceased to influence Luther. We
see its impact on him again in mid-career, after he had taken off
his cowl. When he gave his course on 1 John, he returned to the
bernardine topic of the 'salvific knowledge' of self and of God,
specifically to the insight that man is a sinner and in need of prayer
for the forgiveness of sins and deliverance from evil; this means, in
Luther's own words in these lectures 'that we learn to understand
ourselves. This thought (*cogitatio*) is very salvific. Someone who
with an honest heart speaks like the publican has the promise: "To
the humble he gives grace" (1 Pt 5:5). Presumption, however, is
the sin against the Holy Spirit.'[10]

Luther continued his interpretation of 1 Jn 2:1 by saying
that knowledge of one's own sinfulness must not lead to despair,
since that would deny trust in God's mercy. The devil would
love to see despair, since 'he wants to trouble one's heart and to
carry God's mercy away. He is much concerned with seeing the
heart being either presumptuous or desperate'.[11] Although Bernard

---

7 *Sicut enim (ut Bernhardus ait) Cognitio sui sine cognitione dei despera-
tionem, ita cognitio dei sine cognitione sui praesumptionem operatur . . . ,* WA
5:508,23–26; see Schwarz, 'Martin Luther'. *Grosse Mystiker,* 376, note 3; Bell,
Divus Bernhardus, 115f; Blaumeiser 401.

8 See WA 2:137,10–141,7; LW 42:3–14. See Nicol, *Meditation bei Luther,*
126.

9 WA 20:633,9–11 (on 1 Jn 2:1).

10 WA 20:633,21–634,3.

11 SC 23.9; SBOp 1:144,20–22; CF 7:33.

was not mentioned by name at this point in Luther's lecture, the bernardine pattern of knowledge of self and of God is clearly recognizable; and the expression 'this thought is very salvific' exactly echoed Bernard's axiom that nobody is saved without 'self-knowledge', and that 'knowledge of God and of self are basic and must come first'.

2. Happy self-judgment

Bernard forcefully stressed the need for humble self-accusation and contrition. In SC 20 he wrote: 'I have been living miserably (*perdite vixi*) because I have been wasting my time. All I know is that you, O God, will not reject a contrite and humble heart' (Ps 50:19). Bernard drew his concept of self-accusation from 1 Cor 11:31, 'If we were to judge ourselves, we would not be falling under judgment'[12], and perhaps also from Augustine.[13] As we shall see, Luther was influenced on this point not so much by Augustine as by Bernard, as he tells us in his own words.

Bernard: 'God loves the soul that . . . judges itself'

Nurtured in the pauline-augustinian tradition, Bernard made use of the concept of self-condemnation or self-accusation several times, usually in the context of his deliberations on humility and knowledge of self. He explicitly quoted Augustine's sermon 354 on pride in his tract *On Humility and Pride*: 'For what else is pride but, as a saint [Augustine] has defined it, the love of one's own excellence. We may define humility as the opposite: contempt of one's own excellence.' The divine Word and Wisdom delegated to human reason the power of judging, making it an accuser of self (*sui accusatrix*). Bernard continued: 'To judge is the proper act of Truth, and in this it shared when, out of reverence for the Word to which it is joined, it became the accuser, witness, and judge

---

12 SC 20; SBOp 1:14,14–19. Vulgate version of 1 Cor 11:31: *Quod si nosmetipsos diiudicaremus, non utique iudicaremur.*

13 Augustine: *Quia qui confitetur peccata sua, et accusat peccata sua, iam cum Deo facit (In Joannis Evangelium* 12.13; PL 35:1491).

against itself. Humility had been born from the union of the Word with human reason'.[14]

The humble person knows that he is a sinner. He therefore accuses himself: 'The haughty excuses his sin, the humble accuses [himself], knowing that God will not judge him a second time, and that if we have judged ourselves, we will indeed escape judgment'.[15] Bernard explained further that a person wanting to gain complete self-knowledge will have first to take the beam of pride out of the own eye first (Mt 7:5) in order to reach the humbling truth that man is a liar (Ps 115:11). And, with Ps 118:75, he said that God has humiliated man in truth, and by adhering to that truth man accuses himself, realizing that he is impotent at achieving his salvation by his own power.[16]

Bernard preached on salvific self-accusation also in his third Advent sermon: 'For [God] loves the soul which before his eyes and without ceasing reflects upon itself and without dissimulation judges itself'. God brings this judgment out from us for our own good because 'if we have judged ourselves, we will not be judged'—another echo of 1 Cor 11:31.[17]

Luther: 'Blessed Bernard in a sermon on Advent: "O happy soul which always judges itself"'

The concept of self-judgment was alive and active in the late-medieval augustinian tradition. We see it represented in the augustinian preacher and german vicar general, Johann von Staupitz, Luther's superior in the Order.[18] Thus it is not surprising that Luther

14 Hum 7.21; SBOp 3:27,7–32,8; see Augustine: *Amor excellentiae, superbia vocatur*, S 354.6.6; PL 39:1565.

15 *Superbus excusat peccatum suum, humilis accusat . . . et quod si nosmetipsos iudicaverimus, non utique iudicabimur* (1 Cor 11:31, using the Vulgate version), SBOp 3:227,13–15. See Sommerfeldt, *The Spiritual Teachings*, 58, who however did not take 1 Cor 11:31 into consideration.

16 '*Omnis homo mendax.*' . . . *In illo . . . seipsum diiudicat . . . omnis homo miser et impotens, qui nec se, nec alium possit salvare*, SBOp 3:28,21–26.

17 *Diligit enim [deus] animam, quae in conspectu eius et sine intermissione considerat, et sine dissimulatione diiudicat semetipsam. Idque iudicium non nisi propter nos a nobis exigit, quia si nosmetipsos iudicaverimus, non utique iudicabimur* (1 Cor 11:31), Adv 3.7; SBOp 4:181,4–7.

18 See Staupitz's Tübingen sermons of 1498: S 20 and S 22; critical edition: *Johann von Staupitz. Sämtliche Schriften*, Lothar Graf zu Dohna and Richard

also took this concept into his own spirituality and his teaching on justification. He integrated the monastic version of the doctrine of justification into his first lectures on the psalter (on Ps 105 and on Ps 109). At that time he already taught (on Ps 109) that nobody is 'justified by faith' unless he has first confessed in humility that he is not yet justified.[19] This statement rephrases the bernardine concept of humble self-accusation. That Luther knew all of the bernardine passages on this concept is doubtful, but he mentioned one bernardine source in his early lecture on Ps 105: Bernard's third Advent sermon with its use of 1 Cor 11:31. Luther indicated that, when he spoke of the 'happy soul', he meant it in Bernard's sense: 'So, blessed Bernard in a sermon on Advent expresses this idea with different words as follows: "O happy soul which always judges itself before the eyes of God and accuses itself. Because if we judge ourselves, we will not be judged by God".'[20]

Aware that he was unable to produce the precise wording of the text, Luther clearly (and correctly) remembered that it was an

Wetzel, eds., *Lateinische Schriften 1. Tübinger Predigten* (Berlin and New York, Walter de Gruyter, 1987) 319 and 348. Also: Staupitz's Advent sermons (1516) in german: *Er hat got fur sich, und wer mag im widerstreben? Er hat keinen anklager, wann inen got selbst rechtfertigt; er kan nit haben einen verteilenden richter, dann er hat Christum zu einem fursprecher*; latin: *Non habet accusatorem, quia deus ipse iustificat* (no. 238); german: *das der gerecht zuvorderst sein selbst ankleger ist;* latin: *quod iustus in principio accusator sui est* (no. 242), *Johann von Staupitz. Sämtliche Schriften,* 286f and 290f. And again in *John Staupitz On God's Gracious Love,* Chapter XXI, John Joseph Stoudt, trans., *Lutheran Quarterly* 8 (Gettysburg 1956) 243. Staupitz's Lenten sermon 5 of 1520 also contains the concept of self-accusation, see Rudolf K. Markwald, *A Mystic's Passion: The Spirituality of Johannes von Staupitz in his 1520 Lenten Sermons. Translation and Commentary* (New York etc: Peter Lang, 1990) 135–137.

19 *Quia nemo per fidem iustificatur, nisi prius per humilitatem sese iniustum confiteatur,* WA 3:345,29f. See Pranger, *Bernard of Clairvaux and the Shape of Monastic Thought,* 23–26, touched upon the reception of this theme in Luther's thought. Pranger, however, made no clear connection to Luther's central theological doctrine of justification. He instead wrote of monastic 'self-justification' in this connection.

20 *Vnde b. Bernardus sermone de aduentu istum versum aliis verbis sic exprimit: 'O felix anima, que in conspectu Dei seipsam semper Iudicat et accusat . . .* (on Ps 105:3), WA 55-I:704 (WA 4:198,19–21). See on Ps 36: WA 55-I:324 (WA 3:208,33–36). See *Adnotationes Quincuplici Psalterio adscriptae* (on Ps 1, in 1513), WA 4:469,16–17; see WA 55-I:300 (WA 3:185,6); WA 3:288,31–33; WA 55-I:463 (WA 3:370,18) as dealt with by Prenter, *Der barmherzige Richter,* 133–140. See WA 3:292,1. See Bell, *Divus Bernhardus,* 63f; I fully agree with Bell on his evaluation of the mistaken interpretation of this topic by lutheran scholars.

Advent sermon. In subsequent years, this pauline, augustinian, and bernardine concept of self-accusation appeared several more times in Luther's works. We find it, significantly enough, in his lectures on Romans (1515–1516), especially in the section on Rom 4:6f. Luther's scholion is extensive in this regard. He pointed out that the righteous always have their own sinfulness before their eyes, and because they judge themselves as sinners, God does not impute their sin to condemnation. In the actual lecture Luther dictated to his students: 'Thus the righteous person in principle is a self-accuser'. Already at Rom 2 he had mentioned the same thought. In both instances he referred to Prov 18:17, which in the Vulgate version speaks of self-accusation. In his concluding remarks on Rom 4:6f, Luther insisted that the knowledge of self as sinner is the precondition for God's salvific action of the non-imputation of one's sins.[21] We encounter the concept again in the disputation theses of Bartholomew Bernhardi in September 1516.[22] The concept also appeared in his famous *Heidelberg Disputation* of May 1518 (no. 4), here again with reference to 1 Cor 11:31:

> As 1 Cor 11 says, 'If we judged ourselves truly, we should not be judged' by the Lord. Dt 3[:36] also states, 'The Lord will vindicate his people and have compassion on his servants'. In this way, consequently, the unattractive works which God does in us, that is, those which are humble and devout, are really eternal, for humility and fear of God are our merit.[23]

Later in that same disputation, in no. 12, he affirmed: 'For as much as we accuse ourselves, so much God pardons us, according to the verse, "Confess your misdeed so that you will be justified" ' (Is 43:26).[24] Apparently Luther had become aware of the concept

21 *Sic Iustus in principio est accusator sui*, WA 56:270,6f (lectures); *quod sibi ipsis imputant, a Deo non imputatur*, WA 57-I:164,9–11; on Rom 2: *iustificator – accusator*, WA 56:17,19–21 (gloss); WA 57-I:21,14–16 (lecture); Gabriele Schmidt-Lauber, *Luthers Vorlesung über den Römerbrief 1515/16: Ein Vergleich zwischen Luthers Manuskript und den studentischen Nachschriften* (Cologne, Weimar, Vienna: Böhlau Verlag, 1994) 99–112. Bell neglected to trace the concept of self-accusation back to Bernard in Luther's lectures on Rom.

22 WA 1:145,28.

23 *Heidelberg Disputation*, no. 4, WA 1:357,13–15.

24 *Heidelberg Disputation*, no. 12: *Patet satis ex dictis, quia quantum nos accusamus, tantum Deus excusat, Iuxta illud: Dic iniquitates tuas, ut iustificeris.*

of self-judgment first from reading Bernard's third Advent sermon; once he had internalized it and realized the biblical origin of it, he dropped the reference to Bernard and stayed with the scriptural references, as happened here. All in all, it remains significant that Luther had learned from Bernard (and not from Augustine) that God loves the soul that accuses and judges herself as a sinner.

VI. ECHOS OF BERNARD'S SPIRITUALITY
IN LUTHER'S 'MAGNIFICAT'

The impact of Bernard's understanding of humility and knowledge of self and God was felt not only in Luther's second course on the psalter (1519–1521) and in his meditation on Christ's passion of 1519, but also in his 1521 booklet on the *Magnificat*. There he analyzed the lowliness of the 'Mother of God'. To Luther the Song of Mary testified to the experience of God's workings with man. This experience taught humankind that God raises the lowly and deposes the mighty. In reading Luther on man's typical way of 'looking up' to God, one is reminded of Bernard's introductory sermons on the Song of Songs. The sinner is lowly 'stinking dust' (SC 13) and must begin by kissing the feet, and from there work his way up to the face of Christ. According to Luther, Christians learn to be lowly by pondering Mary's lowly position.

After these remarks Luther described man's praise of God as God's work alone, not man's. He spoke of God's sweetness that is to be 'tasted' and also 'seen' by those who believe and who are thus led to full knowledge.[1] This is monastic language. Further along in his exposition of the *Magnificat*, Luther showed his readers the central meaning of lowliness when he analyzed the Vulgate's notion of *humilitas*. He suggested that it be rendered with the german word *nichtickeyt* (modern german: *Nichtigkeit*), 'despicable being', and not with *Demut*, 'humility'. When he continued the exposition of Luke 1:48, he explicitly introduced the distinction between humility and humiliation which he also used in his second psalm lectures, where he brought Bernard's insights into play. He adduced again Paul's greek term *tapeinophrosyne* (Rom 12:16), and he repeated that 'humility' is to be understood in the sense in which the latin language uses *affectus vilitatis* or *sensus humilium rerum*, i.e. the will to or sense for neglected matters.[2] Apparently

---

1 WA 7:550,7–18.

2 WA 7:559,29–560,37. Vulgate: *humilitas;* the german *Biblia Menteliana* (dated 1466) has *demutigkeit*; Luther in 1521: *nichtickeyt* (modern german: *Nichtigkeit* [nothingness]); Luther in 1522: *nydrickeyt* (modern german: *Niedrigkeit* [lowliness]); Luther in 1521: *geringe magd* (little maid); Luther in 1545/1546: *elende Magd* (miserable maid). A detailed linguistic analysis and review is

Luther was led to interpret *tapeinosis* (= Vulgate *humilitas*) of verse
1:48 with the pauline concept in Rom 12:16 by following Bernard's
example, as he had done also in his *Operationes in psalmos*.
All the elements of Bernard's sermons on humility are present
in Luther's *Magnificat*. But the saint's name was not mentioned;
nor are any other authorities referred to by name, except Augustine.
The Reformer moved in the tracks of monastic theology also in
insisting that, by closing one's eyes to everything else, one may
'feel' the sweetness of God being infused. What Mary expressed
in her song can be experienced by the believer, Luther declared,
because the person who trusts in God will experience in himself
the working of God. The blessedness of 'experiential sweetness'
leads to full understanding. What happens to a person infused
with 'divine sweetness' is inexpressible: '[He] feels more than can
be expressed'.[3] Luther's observations closely resemble Bernard's
statement about feeling the sweet burden of Christ's yoke, which
is sweet 'only to him who feels it, who has experience of it'.[4]

Also quite in line with the monastic tradition was Luther's
assertion that God wants to be recognized by faith. The senses
and reason must be shut out; if they intervene, they should be torn
out, on the advice of Mk 9:47, to tear out 'the eyes of reason'.
'Closing one's eyes' and ignoring purely human thoughts was
Luther's way of emphasizing his theological principles of 'faith
alone' and 'Christ alone'; he used the expression 'closing one's
eyes' when he preached about adhering exclusively to the word of
Christ. He repeated this in one of his last sermons in 1546, and on
numerous other occasions.[5]

found in Edgar Papp, 'Luthers Übersetzungen des 'Magnificat'. Textphilologische
und übersetzungstheoretische Untersuchungen'. *Martin Luther. Annäherungen
und Anfragen,* Willigis Eckermann and Edgar Papp, eds. (Vechta: Vechtaer
Druckerei und Verlag GmbH & Co., 1985) 118–144, especially 134–136, 140–
141. However, Papp did not take any influence from Bernard on Luther into
consideration.

3 WA 7: 550,7–18; see Posset, 'The Sweetness of God', 143–178; Posset,
'*Christi Dulcedo*', 245–265.

4 QH 15; SBOp 5:476:1–5. However, Luther did probably not depend on
QH directly.

5 WA 7:587,17f. See WA 51:194,29–34; see Posset, 'Bible Reading "With
Closed Eyes"', 293–306.

Luther's traditional, monastic theology in his *Magnificat*
greatly impressed Pope Leo X, who expressed his admiration for
this booklet without knowing who its author was. Ironically (or
tragic-comically), this pope had its author condemned at about the
same time the *Magnificat* hit the book market in Germany. Unaware
of Luther's authorship, Leo reportedly exclaimed: 'Blessed are the
hands that have written it!'[6] This papal praise can be explained
only by the fact that there was nothing wrong with the monastic
matrix on which Luther's reformation theology had grown and
which to a large degree was rooted in the 'happy self-accusation'
which Luther learned from Bernard's teaching on knowledge of
self and of God.[7]

Even Luther's later, mature definition of 'theology' mirrored
bernardine insights to a considerable degree. Luther declared in
1532 that the knowledge of God and of man means divine wisdom
and is theological in the proper sense. By this he meant knowledge
of God as the justifying God and knowledge of man as sinner
to be justified. The proper subject of theology is sinful man and
saving God. Anything discussed outside this topic is declared by
Luther to be erroneous and vain.[8] Overwhelmed by Bernard's
wisdom, Luther declared at one point: 'Bernard had great faith
and knowledge of God'.[9]

---

6 Quoted after Albert Brandenburg's introduction to the modern German
edition of Luther's *Das Magnificat* (Freiburg: Herder, 1964) 9.

7 *Sündenbekenntnis und Selbstgericht kennzeichnen den Wurzelboden und
Quellort der Reformation,* writes Otto Rodenberg, 'Gottes Gnade unter seinem
Zorn: Anmerkungen zu den Bußpsalmen im Anschluß an Martin Luthers Ausle-
gungen', *Theologische Beiträge* 21 (1990) 307–318, here 307.

8 See WA 40-II:327,11–328,3 (on Ps 51:2 in 1532); see WA 55-II, 1,2:136,8–
11 (*Dictata*); see Lohse, *Luthers Theologie*, 52–54, where the congeniality between Luther, Augustine, and Bernard is stressed.

9 *Magnam fidem habuit et cognitionem de deo*, WA 15:608,27 (1524).

4

Christ Alone

Christ alone, 'the Wisdom of God' (1 Cor 1:24), is 'the tree of life' (Gen 2:9), he alone the 'living bread which comes down from heaven' (Jn 6:51) and gives life to the world. . . . There is only one 'author of life' (Acts 3:5), 'one mediator between God and men, the man Christ Jesus' (1 Tim 2:5). *Bernard*[1]

IN THIS PASSAGE from Sermon 48 on the Canticle, Bernard expressed his characteristic christocentrism in his idiosyncratic, biblical way. We have now arrived at the center of christian spirituality: Christ. In an introductory section we will first review Bernard's role in the history of christian piety, assisted by iconographic examples; then we will investigate Bernard's and Luther's theology of the cross and of the Incarnation.

I. AFFECTIVE CHRISTOCENTRISM

Before the turn of the first millennium, the divinity of Christ was very much to the fore in christian piety. By the middle of the eleventh century, the humanity of Christ has been rediscovered, as we know from such meditational works of the time as Pseudo-Augustine and the meditations of Anselm of Canterbury.

1 SC 48.6; SBOp 2:70.

Tenderness and compassion for the sufferings and helplessness of the Saviour was probably born in the monasteries of the eleventh century, and every century since then has paid tribute to its monastic inspiration by adding some new development to the theme. Connected to the medieval theology of the cross is a concentration on the incarnation of Christ which in turn gave rise to expressions of homage to the Virgin Mary in new and more intense forms. The spirituality of the twelfth century, in which Bernard lived, does not represent a sudden turn, but stands on the shoulders of the previous practices of meditation.[2] One must also keep in mind that the crusaders were bringing home their own personal impressions, visions, and images of Christ, along with relics, from the Holy Land.

At that same time, the romanesque image of Christ the divine King or *Christus Dominator*—shown at times as the Crucified with a royal crown—gradually gave way to the gothic depiction of the suffering Christ, shown without any crown (Plates 8–11), or, later, with the crown of thorns. One of the earliest surviving depictions of Christ's crucifixion dates to the sixth century: it shows Christ crucified between the two criminals. Christ is dressed in some sort of tunic, standing (not hanging) on the cross as his dead body is pierced by the spear of the legendary soldier Longinus. Although Scripture reports that this happened after he died, Christ is shown with wide open eyes to indicate that although Christ's humanity is mortal, Christ's divinity is not. The artists of the time wanted to express Christ Crucified in his humanity and divinity: the *Logos* on the cross.[3]

    2 See R. W. Southern, *The Making of the Middle Ages* (New Haven and London: Yale University Press, 1977, 23rd printing) 232; Amatus van den Bosch, 'The Christology of St Bernard: A Review of Recent Work', *Cîteaux* 8 (1957) 245–251; Richard Kieckhefer, 'Major Currents in Late Medieval Devotion'. *Christian Spirituality: High Middle Ages and Reformation*, Jill Raitt, ed. (New York: Crossroad, 1987) 95f. The best investigation in this regard is Erdei's *Auf dem Wege zu sich selbst*, 16–36.
    3 Aloys Grillmeier, *Der Logos am Kreuz: Zur christologischen Symbolik der älteren Kreuzigungsdarstellung* (Munich: Max Hueber Verlag, 1956), illus. 1 (Rabulas Codex, Florence, 586 AD) and ill. no 2 (The Painted Panel of *Sancta Sanctorum*, 6th century); Grillmeier appreciated and challenged the interpretation of René-Jean Hesbert, *Le problème de la transfixion du Christ dans les traditions: biblique, patristique, iconographique, liturgique et musicale* (Paris, Tournai,

Plate 9: Crucifix with royal crown, ca. 1125–1150. Originally from the cistercian monastery of Maulbronn. Württembergisches Landesmuseum, Stuttgart, Germany.

Plate 10: Crucifix without crown, ca. 1200. Originally from the cistercian monastery of Maulbronn. Württembergisches Landesmuseum, Stuttgart, Germany.

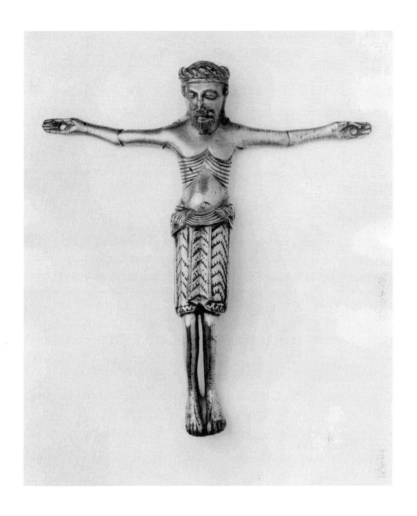

Plate 11: Crucifix with headband (crown filed off). Saint Clare's nunnery, Meran, Italy; first half of the twelfth century. Private possession. Württembergisches Landesmuseum, Stuttgart, Germany.

Plate 12: Detail of Crucifix. Württembergisches Landesmuseum, Stuttgart, Germany.

A picture from the eleventh century, closer to Bernard's time, shows the Crucified with Mary and John. Christ is seen in a loin cloth, standing on the *suppedaneum* (foot rest); blood is squirting from his side wound, hands, and feet; his eyes are still wide open, his head turned slightly.[4] By the time Bernard's career reached its zenith or of his death in the middle of the twelfth century, crucifixes seem more often than not to be shown without the royal crown. Increasingly, Christ became the suffering Jesus, with closed eyes and occasionally with bleeding wounds. In romanesque art, closed eyes signify the dead Christ (*Christus mortuus*). By comparison, Christ's side wound is rarely shown in bronze crucifixes of the romanesque period, and, normally, there are no nail marks on his feet.

A brief look at some representations of Christ's head may illustrate our point concerning the changes in spirituality and art in Bernard's day. In the former german cistercian monastery at Maulbronn (founded in 1147; declared a World Cultural Heritage by the UNESCO in 1993) a crucifix was unearthed which had been cast in the second quarter of the twelfth century (Plate 9). Made of bronze, it shows Christ the King with a royal crown and closed eyes, thus representing the romanesque imagery of the Crucified. There are numerous doublettes of this particular sculpture. A younger Maulbronn crucifix (Plate 10), which was at first dated at about 1150, but now at about 1200, also of bronze,

---

Rome, 1940). Elisabeth Roth, *Der volkreiche Kalvarienberg in Literatur und Kunst des Spätmittelalters* (Berlin: Erich Schmidt Verlag, 1958) 11–13. Jean Leclercq, 'From the Tender Heart of Christ to his Glorified Body'. *Word and Spirit: A Monastic Review* 12 (1990) 80–91. As to the royal crown in the Middle Ages, based on Rv 14:14, see Jean Leclercq, *L'idée de la royauté du Christ au moyen âge* (Paris: Cerf, 1959). With Elisabeth Roth, *Der volkreiche Kalvarienberg*, 20, one must say that Bernard represents the change with a *neuen theologia crucis*. With Peter Dinzelbacher, *Christliche Mystik im Abendland* (Paderborn: Schöningh, 1994), 117f, one must concur that the changes in christian art from romanesque to gothic were based on the changes in spirituality as shaped by Bernard. Erich Pattis and Eduard Syndicus, *Christus Dominator: Vorgotische Grosskreuze* (Innsbruck, Vienna, Munich: Tyrolia-Verlag, 1964) 13, stated that the representation of the Crucified with only a loin-cloth (dated ca. 600) caused a scandal at that time. With observations like that in mind, one can appreciate the breakthrough toward the depictions of the truely human Christ who is suffering on the cross, later in the Middle Ages, as fostered by Bernard's spirituality.

4 Grillmeier, *Der Logos am Kreuz*, illus. 4 (Crucifixion, cod. brev. 98, fol 8v, Stuttgart: Landesbibliothek).

differs decisively in that Christ no longer wears the romanesque royal crown. He wears no crown at all. At one and the same cistercian monastery within a very short period of time religious and artistic conventions developed from displaying the crucified Christ wearing the royal crown to Christ wearing no crown at all. In both crucifixes from Maulbronn, Christ's eyes are closed, so this is not a distinctive mark.

Even more striking is a romanesque crucifix from about 1130; the Crucified had originally worn a royal crown. However, the points of the crown have been filed off to accomodate the new gothic taste which emphasized no longer Christ's kingship, but his suffering (Plates 11 and 12).[5] Today only a rope-like headband is visible where once there was a royal crown.

This coincidence of Bernard's career and the dramatic changes in iconography probably did not occur incidentally. The artistic change took place because of a changing spirituality which was to a large degree shaped and promoted by Bernard. After all, he was the decisive religious figure of his era. He helped to give this new focus on the humanity of Christ a strong, affective, and effective literary expression, saying that the contemplation of Christ in his equality with the Father, the king seated in beauty upon the cherubim, on a lofty throne, is the prerogative of the angels, while he, Bernard, as a human being must describe Christ to human beings according to his human form, 'made lower than the angels' (Psalm 8:5; Heb 2:9):

---

5 The two crucifixes of the former cistercian monastery at Maulbronn are preserved in Württembergisches Landesmuseum, Stuttgart, Germany: Inventory no. 1898–11233 (with royal crown, second quarter of the twelfth century) and Inventory no. 1967–47 (without crown, appr. 1200), see *Suevia Sacra: Frühe Kunst in Schwaben* (exhibition catalogue; Augsburg: H. Mühlberger, 1973) illus. 65 and 76. The crucifix of Meran (today in the possession of the Poor Clares at Meran, Italy) has the Inventory no. L 1984–92 (Christ's head is shown with a filed off crown), see Heribert Meurer, 'Triumph und Passion. Zur Entwicklung des Kruzifixes', *Christus im Leiden: Kruzifixe. Passionsdarstellungen aus 800 Jahren*, Württembergisches Landesmuseum Stuttgart in Verbindung mit der Diözese Rottenburg-Stuttgart, eds. (Ulm: Süddeutsche Verlagsgesellschaft Ulm, 1986) 21–32 with ill. 6 (Meran crucifix); see Peter Bloch, *Romanische Bronzekruzifixe* (Berlin: Deutscher Verlag für Kunstwissenschaft, 1992) 72 with ill. I C 4 (Maulbronn, middle of twelfth century); 322 with ill. X C 2 (Maulbronn, approx. 1200); 138f with ill. I M 6 (Meran crucifix). I am grateful to Dr. Heribert Meurer of the Landesmuseum Stuttgart, Germany, for detailed information and for permission to use the museum's photographs.

I present him as attractive rather than sublime as God's appointed servant and not a remote deity, as the one whom the Spirit of the Lord anointed and sent 'to bring good news to the poor, to bind up hearts that are broken, to proclaim liberty to captives, freedom to those in prison; to proclaim a year favorable to the Lord'.[6]

Bernard as a venerator of the cross guided western christianity toward the contemplation of Christ's wounds. After Bernard's spiritual focus prevailed, later medieval mysticism always concentrated on the passion of the Lord. Bernardine piety, with its emphasis on Christ's humanity, included meditations not only on Christ's suffering and death but also on his incarnation. Yet the passion is preponderant in Bernard's Sermons on the Canticle, which he wrote over a period of about two decades, beginning in about 1135 and ending with the last nine sermons produced shortly before his death. His affective christocentrism was concerned, however, not only with the humanity of Jesus but also with Christ as God. Bernard never separated the two natures of Christ from each other (nor did Luther).[7] Accordingly, Bernard states:

For when I name Jesus I set before me a man who is meek and humble of heart, kind, prudent, chaste, merciful, flawlessly upright and holy in the eyes of all; and this man is the all-powerful God whose way of life heals me, whose support is my strength. All these re-echo for me at the hearing of Jesus' name. Because he is man I strive to imitate him; because of his divine power I lean upon him. The examples of his human life gather like medicinal herbs; with the aid of his power I blend them, and the result is a compound like no pharmacist can produce. . . . Hidden as in a vase, in this name of Jesus, you, my soul, possess a salutary remedy against which no spiritual illness will be proof. Carry it always close to your heart, always in your hand, and ensure that all your affections, all your actions, are directed to Jesus.[8]

6 SC 22.3; SBOp 1:130,25–131,13; CF 7:15f. See OS 5; SBOp 5:361–370.

7 On Bernard, see Jaques Hourlier, 'The Medieval Masters', in Malatesta, ed., *Jesus in Christian Devotion and Contemplation,* 41.

8 SC15.6f; SBOp 1:87,6–17, CF 4:110; SC 43.2; SBOp 2:42; CF 7:222; see Kurt Knotzinger, 'Hoheslied und bräutliche Christusliebe bei Bernhard von Clairvaux'. *Jahrbuch für mystische Theologie* 7 (1961) 7–88. Bernhardin Schel-

This passage, together with the famous *fasciculus myrrhae* (Bernard's Sermon on the Canticle 43, see below), may serve to describe what we mean by 'affective christocentrism'. It is not so much an expression of theoretical Christ-centered theology, but rather an emotional/affective utterance, emphasizing the personal relationship between Christ and the believer who yearns to be healed, helped, and held by the Saviour, the God-man. Contemplation of Christ's humanity and divinity helps to orient the soul toward its ultimate goal, the beatific vision, which is of course not achieved in this life. We can trace this affective christocentrism throughout Bernard's sermons on the Bride and the Groom, who represent the individual soul (or the Church) and Christ the Word of God. In meditating on this marriage song, 'it is not the words which are to be pondered, but the affections behind them', since the subject of this canticle is the sacred love which cannot be described 'in the words of any language': 'By divine inspiration [Solomon] sang the praises of Christ and the Church, the grace of holy love, the sacrament of eternal marriage; and at the same time he expressed the desire of the holy soul, the love song of marriage, exulting in the spirit, poured forth in figurative language pregnant with delight.'[9]

The Germans called this affective christocentrism *Jesusminne*, the loving contemplation, the memory, of Jesus. The medieval germanic term *minne* stems from the word group *mahnen*, to remind, and it took on the meaning of loving consideration, inclination, and finally the equivalent of love. Thus, affective christocentrism means love for Jesus. Bernard is the chief *minnesinger*, praising Jesus, commemorating and celebrating him as the heavenly Bridegroom of the individual soul (and of the Church): 'Jesus is honey in

lenberger, 'Bernhard von Clairvaux'. *Grosse Mystiker,* 110, see 107–121. Luc Bresard, 'Bernard et Origene commentent le Cantique', Coll 44 (1982) 111–130, 183–209, 293–308. Stanislas Breton, 'Saint Bernard et la Cantique des Cantiques', Coll 47 (1985) 110–118. Raffaele Fassetta, 'Le Mariage spirituel dans les Sermons de saint Bernard sur le Cantique', Coll 48 (1986) 155–180, 251–265. Marsha L. Dutton, 'The Face and the Feet of God: The Humanity of Christ in Bernard of Clairvaux and Aelred of Rievaulx', *Bernardus Magister,* 203–223, here 211. Dorette Sabersky, ' "Affectum Confessus sum, et non Negavi". Reflections on the Expression of Affect in the 26th Sermon on the Song of Songs of Bernard of Clairvaux'. *The Joy of Learning*, Elder, ed., 187–216.

9 SC 1.8 (my own translation); SBOp 1:6,13–16; see CF 4:5. See SC 79.1; SBOp 2:272,14–16; CF 40:138.

the mouth, melody in the ear, gladness in the heart'. His spirituality begins 'with sentiment, grows through imitation, and reaches its culmination . . . in union with the Christ'.[10]

---

10 SC 15.6; SBOp 1:86,18f; CF 4:110. Casey, *Athirst*, 204f (on devotion to Christ in his humanity and divinity); Dutton, 'The Face and the Feet of God', 203–223. See Webster's *Encyclopedic Dictionary of the English Language*, s. v. 'minnesinger'.

Plate 13: The Crucified Embraces Bernard (*Amplexus Bernardi*). Nuremberg Altar of the Reformed Augustinians. Painting by Michael Wolgemut, 1487. Photo: Bayerische Staatsgemäldesammlungen, Munich.

Bernard: 'To know Jesus and him crucified'

About fifteen different times Bernard uses 1 Cor 2:2 in speaking about meditation on Christ crucified: 'To know Jesus and him crucified'.[1] He did this in particular in his SC 43 on Sg 1:12, where he meditated on the sufferings of Christ: 'Because myrrh is a bitter herb it symbolizes the burdensome harshness of afflictions'; he wrote, pointing out how aptly the word 'little bundle' (*fasciculus*) not 'bundle' (*fascis*), was chosen, 'for he is born to us an infant'. He referred back to one of his previous sermons (SC 10.2) before continuing his meditation:

> The breasts of the bride signified a sharing in joy (*congratulatio*) and a sympathy in suffering (*compassio*), like the pauline prescription to rejoice with those who rejoice and to weep with those who weep (Rom 12:15). . . . You too, if you are wise, will imitate the prudence of the bride, and never permit even for an hour that this precious bunch of myrrh should be removed from your bosom. Preserve without fail the memory of all those bitter things he endured for you, persevere in meditating on him and you in turn will be able to say: 'my beloved is to me a little bunch of myrrh that lies between my breasts'.[2]

Bernard then hinted at his own experiences:

> As for me, dear brothers, from the early days of my conversion, conscious of my grave lack of merits, I made sure to gather for myself this little bunch of myrrh and place it between my breasts. It was culled from all the anxious hours and bitter experiences of my Lord; first from the privations of his infancy, then from the hardships he endured in preaching, the fatigues of his journeys,

---

1 Gertrud Frischmuth, *Die paulinische Konzeption in der Frömmigkeit Bernhards von Clairvaux* (Gütersloh: Bertelsmann, 1933) 61f, gathered from Bernard's *opus* numerous references to this pauline axiom; see also Köpf, 'Schriftauslegung als Ort der Kreuzestheologie Bernhards von Clairvaux', *Bernhard von Clairvaux und der Beginn der Moderne*, Dieter R. Bauer and Gotthard Fuchs, eds. (Innsbruck and Vienna: Tyrolia, 1996) 1:94–213, here 196.

2 SC 43.1f; SBOp 2:41,10–15; 42,7–17; CF 7:221.

the long watches in prayer, the temptations when he fasted, his tears of compassion, the heckling . . . , the insults, the spitting, the blows, the mockery, the scorn, the nails and similar torments that are multiplied in the Gospels, like trees in the forest, and all for the salvation of our race. Among the teeming little branches of this perfumed myrrh I feel we must not forget the myrrh which he drank upon the cross and used upon his anointing at his burial. In the first of these he took upon himself the bitterness of my sins, in the second he affirmed the future incorruption of my body. . . . I have reaped the myrrh that they had planted. This life-giving bunch has been reserved for me; no one will take it away from me, it shall lie between my breasts.[3]

Bernard insisted that these mysteries must be pondered, for they are the source of perfect righteousness, of the fullness of knowledge, of the efficacious graces, and of abundant merits. They provide safe guidance for anyone traveling on God's royal road and win the favor of him who is the world's judge. They reveal him, despite his awesome powers, as one who is gentle and humble. 'They are a familiar theme in my writings, as is evident', he declared. At this point, he enunciated his christocentric 'philosophy' by using the words of 1 Cor 2:2:

This is my philosophy, one more refined and interior, to know Jesus and him crucified. I do not ask, as the bride did, where he takes his rest at noon, because my joy is to hold him fast where he lies between my breasts. I do not ask where he rests at noon for I see him on the cross as my Savior.[4]

The abbot took up this theme again in his subsequent sermon (SC 45) on Sg 1:14, 'behold, how beautiful you are, my dearest. . . .' First he explained this verse as an expression of admiration for innocence and humility, and then continued with a quotation from Juvenal's *Satires*: ' "This is a rare bird on earth", where neither innocence is lost nor humility excluded by innocence'. As Bernard reflected on the soul's sinfulness, he let the Bride proclaim: 'My beloved is to me a little bundle of myrrh that lies between my breasts', by which she meant: 'It is enough for me; I desire to

3 SC 43.3; SBOp 2:43,8f and 9–27; CF 7:221f.
4 SC 43.4; SBOp 2:43,16–18; CF 7:223.

know nothing more than Jesus and him crucified (1 Cor 2:2). What great humility! Though in fact innocent she adopts the attitude of the penitent'.[5]

Bernard: The hidden God

In SC 56, on Sg 2:9 about the Groom hidden behind the wall, Bernard preached on Christ as the 'hidden God' and called up Is 45:15: *vere tu es Deus absconditus Deus Israel salvator*: 'His standing behind the wall then means that his prostrate weakness was manifested in the flesh, while that which stood erect in him was as it were hidden behind the flesh: the "manifest man" and "the hidden God" are indeed one and the same'.[6] According to Bernard, God is hidden within or beneath the crucified Christ. While broken in body, he stands upright as God by the power of his divinity. This theological concept of the God-man Christ found artistic expression in romanesque art; Christ stands upright on the cross, he does not yet *hang* from it. And Christ is wearing a *royal* crown, not yet one of thorns. Bernard put into precious words what artists of his time portrayed visually. This concept of Christ crucified as the 'hidden God' was readily taken up by Luther in his 1518 disputation at Heidelberg, as we shall see.

In SC 61 Bernard explained 'the clefts of the rocks' (Sg 2:14) as the wounds of Christ, following Gregory the Great and others before him. To describe them he used the words of Ps 83:4 ('the sparrow finds a home, and the swallow a nest'), Ps 103:18 ('the cliffs are a refuge . . .'), and Is 53:5 ('He was pierced for our transgressions'). Mingled with these scriptural references is Bernard's decisive, rhetorical question: 'And indeed where do the weak find secure and firm rest, if not in the Saviour's wounds?' The rock, of course, is Christ on whom one must rely. The clefts in the rock are Christ's wounds. Here follows an illustrative section from SC 61.4:

The world rages, the body presses, the devil lays his snares: I do not fall because I am founded on the rock. I have sinned

5 *Haec mea subtilior, interior philosophia, scire Iesum, et hunc cruci-fixum . . .* , SC 45.3; SBOp 2:51,9–20; CF 7:234.

6 . . . *sane unus idemque homo manifestus, et Deus absconditus*, SC 56.2; SBOp 2:115,29–116,2;CF 31:89.

gravely, my conscience is disturbed, but not perturbed, because in my heart I shall remember (*recordabor*) the wounds of the Lord. For 'he was wounded for our transgressions' (Is 53:5). What sin is so 'deadly' (*ad mortem*) that it cannot be forgiven in the death of Christ. If therefore a medication so powerful and efficacious finds entrance to my mind, no disease, however virulent, can frighten me. . . . Whatever is lacking in my own resources I usurp for myself from the heart of the Lord (*ex visceribus Domini*), which overflows with mercy. And there is no lack of clefts by which they are poured out. They pierced his hands and his feet, they gored his side with a lance, and through these fissures I can suck honey from the rock.[7]

Bernard: 'Sweet on the cross'

Having praised the grace of God who has covered the multitude of sins, he continued with a quotation of Ex 33:22f, about 'Moses in the cleft' who was allowed to see God's back. In this context he spoke of Christ being 'sweet on the cross':

This contemplation of his back is no small favor, not to be despised. . . . For this view of the Lord's back holds something that delights. . . . May he meet us with the blessings of sweetness. . . . One day he will show his face in its dignity and glory, now let him show 'the back' of his gracious concern. He is great in his kingdom, but sweet (*suavis*) on the cross. In this vision may he come to meet me, in the other may he fill me full. . . . Each is salutary and sweet, the one on high and in splendor, the other in lowliness and in paleness.[8]

At first it may sound odd that Christ was called 'sweet on the cross'. To call the cross and the wounds of the crucified Lord 'sweet'

7 SC 61.3; SBOp 2:149,20–150,22; CF 31:142–144; see Bell, *Divus Bernhardus,* 58–60, 231, 247, 253, 260, 333, 352f. On the five wounds of Christ see also Bernard's Nat 1; SBOp 4:250,15–20. On the rhetorical aspects of this text, see Sabersky-Bascho, *Studien zur Paronomasie bei Bernhard*, 43–44, see 62. This author did not point out, however, the other paronomasia which is included in the given text, i. e. *turbabitur/ perturbabitur* which impressed Luther so much. Christ's side wound is so deep that the soul of the believer can find shelter deep down in Jesus' viscera (*in visceribus Jesu*): 'Of course in security, of course in the rock, of course in the bowels of Jesus, where it has entered, indeed, through the open wounds', SBOp 2:153,9–10 (SC 61.8).

8 *Sed suavis in cruce*, SC 61.6; SBOp 2:152,1–14; CF 31:146.

challenges our modern concept of both 'cross' and 'sweetness'. The latin originals, *suavitas* and *dulcedo* certainly need to be read in their original patristic and monastic contexts. The modern english translation of *suavis* by 'gentle' does not bring out the theological connotations of this word. Once one realizes that 'sweetness' is a patristic and monastic theological notion, i. e. an expression of salvation, this strangeness may dissipate.[9]

In SC 62 Bernard again recommended with 1 Cor 2: 'Let him place before him Jesus and him crucified, that without effort on his part he may dwell in those clefts of the rock at whose hollowing he has not labored'. A little later in his sermon he asked: 'What greater cure for the wounds of conscience and for purifying the mind's acuity [is there] than to persevere in meditation on the wounds of Christ?'[10]

Late Medieval Passion Piety

Bernard's Sermon 43 on the Canticle received more attention than any other of this sermon cycle and was handed down under the title *fasciculus myrrhae*, taken from the latin of verse Cant 1:12, which the sermon interpreted: 'a little bundle of myrrh is my beloved who lies between my breasts'. Later spiritual masters translated this sermon into the vernacular and/or adopted it into their prayers and writings, as did Saint Birgitta of Sweden in the fourteenth century.[11] Martin Elze has pointed out that the influential works of Ludolf of Saxony, Bonaventure, Henry Suso, Mauburnus, and Gabriel Biel relied heavily on Bernard's passion meditations.[12] One of these authors, Suso, explicitly praised *sant Bernart* and the 'little bundle of myrrh' in his South-German dialect, referring to Bernard's *mirrenbuschelli*.[13]

9 On the soteriological meaning of the 'sweetness of God' in patristic and monastic texts which make up the matrix for Bernard and Luther, see Franz Posset, 'The Sweetness of God', ABR 44 (1993) 143–178; Posset, '*Christi Dulcedo*: "The Sweetness of Christ" in Western Christian Spirituality', CSQ 30 (1995) 245–265.

10 SC 62.6–7; SBOp 2:159,11–12,24–26; CF 31:157f.

11 See Gerhard Eis, 'Fasciculus myrrhae', *Leuvensche Bijdragen* 49 (1960) 90–96; Martin Elze, 'Züge spätmittelalterlicher Frömmigkeit in Luthers Theologie', *Zeitschrift für Theologie und Kirche* 62 (1965) 381–402.

12 See Elze, 'Züge spätmittelalterlicher Frömmigkeit in Luthers Theologie', 396f.

13 As quoted by Gnädiger, 'Der minnende Bernhardus', 307–409.

Within the augustinian-bernardine tradition, Luther's Order of the Hermits of Saint Augustine was committed to this late medieval practice of meditating on Christ's passion. As the catalogues of the augustinian libraries of the fourteenth and fifteenth centuries indicate, Bernard was a very prominent author within the Order.[14] In the works of Johann von Paltz (d. 1511), a leader of the reformed augustinian friars to which Luther belonged, one finds sixty Bernard citations.[15] Not only Paltz, but also Johann von Staupitz (d. 1524) dealt elaborately with Christ's passion. For our discussion here, paragraph 44 of Staupitz's book on predestination is significant. He declared that our good works are ultimately God's works, something Bernard had already taught. Only Christ's works are meritorious; they alone gain us 'the right' to the eternal kingdom. This was a concept originally found in bernardine hagiography, a concept to which we will return in a later section. Staupitz followed bernardine thought patterns, and expressly quoted Canticle 2:13, on the dove in the clefts of the rock, which he interpreted as Bernard had done in SC 61, without however mentioning his name.[16] The motif of reaching the heart of God through meditation on Christ's side-wound is also found in Staupitz's sermons.[17] Staupitz appeared to have been quite in-

14 See David Gutiérrez, 'De antiquis ordinis eremitarum sancti Augustini bibliothecis', *Analecta Augustiniana* 23 (1954) 186–307, as quoted by Constable, 'The Popularity of Twelfth-Century Spiritual Writers in the Late Middle Ages', 10; see Adolar Zumkeller, 'The Spirituality of the Augustinians'. *Christian Spirituality: High Middle Ages and Reformation*, Jill Raitt, ed., 67–72. Already in 1900, Köhler had pointed out that the high appreciation of Saint Bernard within Luther's Order must have been of influence on Luther, *Luther und die Kirchengeschichte*, 324. Köhler pointed to Paltz, Staupitz, and Linck, who all were augustinian friars. A recent study confirmed the thesis that within the Augustinian Order, Bernard was the most popular author next to Augustine, see Zschoch, *Klosterreform*, 90; Franz Posset, 'Saint Bernard in the Devotion, Theology, and Art of the Sixteenth Century', *Lutheran Quarterly* 11 (1997) 325–36.

15 Especially 'Die Himlische Funtgrub', as prepared by Horst Laubner, Wolfgang Urban an others, in: *Johannes von Paltz: Opuscula*, Christoph Burger et al., eds. (Berlin and New York: Walter de Gruyter, 1989) 201–253. See Robert Fischer, 'Paltz und Luther', *Lutherjahrbuch* 37 (1970) 9–36; Posset, 'Saint Bernard in the Devotion, Theology, and Art. . . .', 325–28.

16 *Merita igitur Christi ius ad regnum aeternum conferunt* (no. 44), *Libellus de Exsecutione Aeternae Praedestinationis*, Johann von Staupitz, *Sämtliche Schriften, Abhandlungen, Predigten, Zeugnisse*, Lothar Graf zu Dohna and Richard Wetzel, eds. (Berlin: Walter de Gruyter, 1979) 126.

17 See Staupitz's sermons of Salzburg in 1512: . . . *du mugst wol dadurch eintringen zu der sel und durch die sel zu der gothait. Da soltu smecken und*

fluenced by bernardine christocentrism and, as Luther's teacher
and superior in the Order he may very well have passed it on to
friar Martin, who acknowledged the impact of Staupitz's pastoral
care on him. Luther testified: 'My good Staupitz said, "one must
keep one's eyes fixed on that man who is called Christ" '. And, 'I
have everything from Doctor Staupitz'.[18] Staupitz and his Order's
tradition mediated the bernardine passion piety to Luther, who
then turned directly to the bernardine sources and processed this
monastic heritage into his own theology of the cross, especially
in times of spiritual troubles. Even at so unexpected a place as
his late lectures on Genesis, the ageing Luther was reminded of
Staupitz's theological influence, especially concerning the meditation on the wounds of Christ.[19] With his specific passion piety,
i. e. devotion to the suffering Lord, Bernard had become the father
of subsequent devotional authors such as these augustinian friars
who concentrated their devotion on the Lord's passion.

---

kosten die allersuessisten parmherzikait ('you may enter through it to the soul
and through the soul to the godhead. There you shall taste and try the sweetest
mercy' (no. 9); see also no. 1 as quoted by Nicol, *Meditation bei Luther,* 134,
note 225. See Markwald, *A Mystic's Passion,* 95–128.

18 WA TR 1:245,9–12 (no. 526); LW 54:97. WA TR 2:112,9–11 (no.1490).
In 1532 Luther repeated that he had learned everything from Staupitz: WA
TR 1:80,16f (no. 173). Recent Reformation research pointed out that Luther's
theology of the cross is neither influenced by John Tauler, nor by the anonymous
'German Theology' (*Theologia Germanica*), nor in any direct way by the 'modern
devotion'; see Karl W. Eckermann, 'Luther's Kreuzestheologie: Zur Frage nach
ihrem Ursprung', *Catholica* 37 (1983) 306–317. I question, however, the author's
statement about Staupitz exerting no influence on Luther in this regard. Pesch,
Hinführung zu Luther, 50–60, 74, pointed out that Staupitz was mediating the
german mysticism to Luther; Pesch rightly spoke of a limited but definite influence
on Luther. He, however, did not take any particular bernardine influence into
consideration, in contrast to Reinhard Schwarz, who observed that Staupitz's
counseling was essentially shaped by Bernard's concept of Christ the suffering
Son of God, see R. Schwarz, *Luther,* 21. Unfortunately, Alister MacGrath, *The
Intellectual Origins of the European Reformation* (Oxford and New York: Basil
Blackwell, 1987) did not even hint at monastic theology or at Bernard as being
of influence on Luther. McGrath was preoccupied with refuting Oberman's
point of view in regard to the influence of 'Augustinianism' upon Luther. On
'affective theology' at the beginning of the sixteenth century, see Berndt Hamm,
Frömmigkeitstheologie am Anfang des 16. Jahrhunderts (Tübingen: Mohr, 1982)
330–33; Otto Gründler, 'Devotio Moderna'. *Christian Spirituality: High Middle
Ages and Reformation,* Jill Raitt, ed., 190f (on the imitation of Christ according
to Staupitz and Luther; however, I doubt whether Luther's theology marked such
clear a 'break with the spirituality of the monastic tradition which the *devotio
moderna* attempted to revive', as Gründler 191 assumed).

19 WA 43:461,1–14.

Plate 14: Saint Bernard's Meditation on the Man of Sorrows. Woodcut by Lucas Cranach the Elder, ca. 1515, in *Hortulus animae: Lustgertlin der Seelen* (Wittenberg: Georg Rhau, 1547/48). The National Gallery of Art, Washington, D.C.

S. Bernhards betrachtung.

Plate 15: Saint Bernard's Meditation on the Man of Sorrows. Woodcut, anonymous, mid-sixteenth century.

Two facts from the history of christian art seem to support these observations on the bernardine-colored piety in the reformed (i. e. observant) Order of the German Augustinians:

(1) At their (no longer extant) church at Nuremberg, these Augustinians possessed an altar painting which shows the *Amplexus Bernardi* on one of its wings. It was created by Michael Wolgemut in 1487 (Plate 13). By *Amplexus* we mean the embrace which Bernard, according to legend, is said to have received from the crucified Christ in a vision which another abbot witnessed. The Crucified whose feet are nailed to the cross, has lifted his hands from the beam and closes his arms around Bernard, who with his right hand holds Christ under his left armpit. His crozier is somehow balanced over his left shoulder. The heads of Christ and Bernard almost touch. Bernard appears to be ready to kiss Christ.[20] This motif may be taken as the artistic expression of Bernard's intimate, affective christ-centered and cross-centered spirituality, particularly as found in his *fasciculus myrrhae* (SC 43). This Nuremberg painting with its cistercian motif is extraordinary because it is found in a non-cistercian place.[21] It testifies to the observant Augustinians' predelection for Bernard in late fifteenth-century Germany.

(2) A woodcut by Lucas Cranach, the later 'lutheran' artist, who worked at the court of Frederick the Wise in Wittenberg, from about 1515. It shows Bernard adoring the Man of Sorrows. Christ is sitting on a bench, half naked, with the crown of thorns on his head, and the instruments of torture in his hands which he has crossed over his chest, making the mark of the nail visible on his hands. At Christ's feet is placed a heart with an arrow that has pierced it. At the right side, a figure with monastic tonsure

20 The painting is depicted in Herbert Paulus, *Die ikonographischen Besonderheiten in der spätmittelalterlichen Passions-Darstellung zwischen Tafelmalerei und zeitgenössischer geistlicher Literatur (Predigt, Andachtsbild und Gebet)* (Wurzburg: no publisher given, 1952) Plate XIII. The literary sources of this motif is *Vita Bern,* Book 7.10; Cawley 2:86; *see also* Herbert of Clairvaux, *Liber de miraculis* and the *Exordium magnum Cisterciense,* distinction 2c. 7.10; PL 185:419f.

21 On the history of this motif, see Franz Posset, 'The Crucified Embraces Saint Bernard: The Beginnings of the *Amplexus Bernardi*', CSQ 23 (1998) 289–314.

and habit prays with folded hands, making eye contact with the Man of Sorrows. An *abbatial* miter is shown below the praying hands. This woodcut was incorporated into the much later prayer-book *Hortulus animae: Lustgertlin der Seele* (Wittenberg: Georg Rhau [also spelled Rhaw, Raw], 1547/1548) with the german title, 'Saint Bernard's meditation' (Plate 14. *S. Bernhards Betrachtung*; *Betrachtung* may mean either 'meditation' or 'contemplation' or both). Art historians at times have posited that it is not Bernard, but Augustine, who is depicted here.[22] I opt for Bernard, having in mind the high esteem which Bernard enjoyed around 1500 in general and specifically with the observant Augustinians who in 1487 had the *amplexus* painting commissioned for their Nuremberg church and who made their presence felt at the University of Wittenberg, the city where Cranach had his shop. The artist quite possibly wanted to depict Bernard (and not Augustine) in this particular woodcut which is assumed to have been made originally around 1515, and in 1547/1548 re-used in the *Hortulus* edition produced at Wittenberg.

Could Luther have seen these depictions of Bernard? As for Cranach's woodcut, there is no reason to believe that his friend Luther was not aware of it. The *Amplexus Bernardi* was in the church of the Augustinian friary at Nuremberg, which Friar Luther visited on several occasions. In 1510–1511, while on his way to and from Rome on his Order's business, he stayed with his confrères there, as did any friars traveling from the north. In 1518, Luther again stopped at Nuremberg on his way to and from Augsburg after having been summoned to an interrogation by Cardinal Cajetan.

22 The Cranach woodcut shows Bernard according to the *New Catholic Encyclopedia* (1967) 2:335. Others claim that it shows Saint Augustine. For details, see Franz Posset, 'Saint Bernard of Clairvaux in the Devotion, Theology, and Art of the Sixteenth Century,' *Lutheran Quarterly* (1997) 345 with n. 23. Johannes Ficker has a reprint of the same woodcut in his article, 'Hortulus animae', *Buch und Bucheinband* (Leipzig 1923) 59–68, here 60, however, with the explicit title *S. Bernhards Betrachtung* [sic, styled in part after the capital 'B' in the last word] over the depiction which was used as an illustration for the prayerbook *Hortulus animae* (Wittenberg: Georg Rhaw, 1547/48). Ficker included at the end of his article (p. 68) another woodcut, styled in part after Albrecht Dürer's motif 'Christ resting' (*Christus in der Ruhe*) from his *Small Passion*, which appears to have been copied in books and Bibles of the Reformation time. This woodcut also carries the title *S. Bernhards betrachtung* [with a small 'b' in the last word]. See Pl. 14.

At that time the prior of the Nuremberg friary, Luther's good friend Wenceslas Linck, accompanied him from Nuremberg to Augsburg for that fateful encounter.[23] No explicit mention is made in the sources as to whether Luther noticed the painting on the Nuremberg altarpiece, or whether he made any comments about it. In the light of what was just said about the Nuremberg painting and Luther's presence at Nuremberg, we may corroborate this thesis, even though Luther never made explicit mention of the artistic motif or of the legend. Now let us turn to specific texts from Luther's *opus*.

Luther: 'Learn Christ and him crucified'

The religious environment of the observant Augustinians, in which Luther matured as a friar, included bernardine elements in word and image. It is not surprising that after praising Bernard's beautiful meditation in the Sermon on the Annunciation in his first exposition of the Psalms (1513–1515) as a young lector, Luther spoke of the abbot again when he began his exposition of Ps 83:4 (on birds' nests), the same verse Bernard had used in his interpretation of Christ's wounds. In his gloss, Luther referred to Bernard, quoting him as having said that the soul finds rest nowhere save in the wounds of Christ.[24] In his scholium he elaborated further: faith is to be equated with the nest. This faith-nest is built by meditation on the wounds of Christ, on his words and deeds, and on those of the saints. Then Luther referred to Bernard's *De fasciculo myrrhe* (SC 43).[25] Like the abbot of Clairvaux, the friar of Wittenberg quoted the same verse, 1 Cor 2:2, declaring that one understands nothing of the Scriptures if one does not understand Christ crucified.

---

23 For Luther's sojourn at Nuremberg in October 1518, see Martin Brecht, *Martin Luther*, trans. James L. Schaaf (Philadelphia: Fortress Press, 1985) 1:251. For the one in 1510/11, see internet 'Luther in Nuremberg'.

24 *Quia secundum Bernardum, Anima non habet requiem nisi in Vulneribus Christi*, WA 55-I:585 (=WA 3:640,40–43; gloss on Ps 83; *Dictata*, 1514); LW 11:36; see Erdai, *Auf dem Wege zu sich selbst*, 82; see Lohse, 'Luther und Bernhard von Clairvaux', 286.

25 *Sicut b. Bernardus de 'fasciculo myrrhe' disserit . . .* , WA 3:645,27–646,20; LW 11:140–41. There is no need to assume that Luther referred here to the pseudo-bernardine text *Vitis mystica*, as the index in WA 63:97 did in regard to this locus; *fasciculus myrrhe* is the medieval name for SC 43.

In the same vein Luther wrote to his confrère, George Spenlein, on 8 April 1516: 'Therefore, my sweet brother, learn Christ and him crucified.' In the same letter Luther mentioned his concept of the righteousness of God (*iustitia dei*) which is given us *gratis* in Christ.[26] Luther's utterances at the time (1513–1516) demonstrate quite impressively that for him the admonition to lead a true monastic life did not contradict the doctrine of justification which, by hindsight, he identified in 1545 as the core of his Reformation breakthrough.

In his theological theses 17 and 18 of the *Heidelberg Disputation* of 1518 (which was organized by Luther's superior, Johann von Staupitz, during a chapter meeting of the Augustinian Order) Luther's use of Bernard's doctrine of humility and grace is evident. Luther then declared in theses 20 and 21—parallel to Bernard's 'more refined and interior philosophy—that true theology and knowledge of God is found in the crucified Christ. In this context Luther spoke, just like Bernard, of 'God's backside' (Ex 33:23). In theses 19 and 20 he stated that the good theologian is someone who perceives what is visible of God, God's 'backside', by 'beholding the sufferings and the cross'.[27] From this perspective, Bernard was

26 See WA 4:153,27–29 (*Dictata*). WA Br 1:35,18–21 (April 8, 1516); see LW 48:12–13. James M. Kittelson, *Luther the Reformer* (Minneapolis: Augsburg Publishing House, 1986) 95, commented, in the context of referring to Luther's two letters of April 8 and 15, 1516, that 'Luther had turned late medieval theology and religious practice on its head'. In contrast, Manns, *Martin Luther: An Illustrated Biography*, 47f, pointed out that this correspondence shows 'impressively that for Luther the admonition to lead a true monastic life seamlessly connects with those approaches which he will identify as the core of his reformist breakthrough in the great retrospect of 1545'. Manns' view appears to be more appropriate than Kittelson's.

27 Theses 19 to 21, WA 1:361,32–362,22. On Bernard's impact on Luther in regard to the concept of Christ as 'hidden God', see Albrecht Peters, 'Verborgener Gott–Dreieiniger Gott: Beobachtungen und Überlegungen zum Gottesverständnis Martin Luthers'. *Martin Luther: 'Reformator und Vater im Glauben'. Referate aus der Vortragsreihe des Instituts für europäische Geschichte Mainz,* Peter Manns, ed. (Stuttgart: Franz Steiner Verlag Wiesbaden GMBH, 1985) 74–105. The bernardine matrix is neglected in two recent studies on this issue: Oddvar Johan Jensen, 'Deus absconditus und Deus revelatus im Lichte der Christologie Luthers'. *Die Kunst des Unterscheidens,* Joachim Heubach, ed. (Erlangen: Martin-Luther-Verlag, 1990) 59–71. Dennis Ngien, *The Suffering of God According to Martin Luther's 'Theologia Crucis'* (New York etc: Peter Lang, 1995) who referred to Bernard in general as being of influence on Luther, but not specifically in regard to the *Deus absconditus* issue in Luther's theology. For

indeed to be counted among the 'good theologians', the 'theologians of the cross'. Parallel expressions in Luther and Bernard are striking: both understood 'God's backside' to be the God-man's suffering on the cross; both connected the 'back of God' to the cross of Christ, Luther in thesis 20 and Bernard in SC 61.

In Luther research, the motif of the 'hidden God' (*Deus absconditus*) has sometimes been related to the thought-world of Nicholas of Cusa, in order to point out that Luther reshaped this thought 'already early', that is, in his *Heidelberg Disputation*.[28] This detour through Nicholas of Cusa—while possible—is not necessary once we realize that the matrix of the *Heidelberg Disputation* is the theology of the church fathers and in particular that of Bernard's SC 56 on 'the hidden God' and SC 61 on the 'clefts of the rock'. Both theologians drew on the same Scripture texts, namely, Is 45:15 (Vulgate), 'truly you are a hidden God',[29] and Ex 33:23,

our topic, see Walther von Loewenich, *Luther's Theology of the Cross,* trans. H. J. A. Bowman (1976); first published in German: Munich: Kaiser, 1929). Klaus Schwarzwäller, *Theologia crucis. Luthers Lehre von der Prädestination nach de servo arbitrio 1525* (Munich: Kaiser, 1970). Marc Lienhard, *Luther: Witness to Jesus Christ. Stages and Themes of the Reformer's Christology*, Edwin H. Robertson, trans. (Minneapolis: Augsburg Publishing House, 1982). Joseph E. Vercruysse, 'Luther's theology of the cross in the time of the Heidelberg Disputation', *Gregorianum* 57 (1976) 523–548; Vercruysse, 'Gesetz und Liebe. Die Struktur der 'Heidelberger Disputation' Luthers (1518)'. *Lutherjahrbuch* 48 (1981) 7–43. Critical of Vercruysse's view is James Arne Nestingen, 'Luther's Heidelberg Disputation: An Analysis of the Argument', *Word and World*, Supplement Series 1 (1992) 147–154. As to Luther's 25th thesis, one may see the program of the 'Wittenberg Augustinianism' at work which was directed against scholastic Aristotelianism; see Karl-Heinz zur Mühlen, 'Luther's Kritik am scholastischen Aristotelismus in der 25. These der Heidelberger Disputation von 1518', and his 'Die Heidelberger Disputation Martin Luthers vom 26. April 1518. Programm und Wirkung'. *Reformatorisches Profil: Studien zum Weg Martin Luthers und der Reformation*, Johannes Brosseder and Athina Lexutt, eds. (Göttingen: Vandenhoeck & Ruprecht, 1995) 40–65; 174–198. The anti-scholastic aspects were highlighted also by Ole Modalsli, 'Die Heidelberger Disputation im Lichte der evangelischen Neuentdeckung Luthers'. *Lutherjahrbuch* 47 (1980) 33–39. The anti-scholastic tendency in these lutheran theses fit nicely into the otherwise bernardine matrix as expressed in Luther's theses 17 to 21. See also Willigis Eckermann, 'Die Aristoteleskritik Luthers: ihre Bedeutung für seine Theologie', *Catholica* 32 (1978) 114–130; Eckermann, 'Luthers Kreuzestheologie. Zur Frage nach ihrem Ursprung', *Catholica* 37 (1983) 306–317. Bell in his *Divus Bernhardus* neglected the Heidelberg Disputation.

28 See Pesch, *Hinführung zu Luther*, 247f.

29 SC 56.2; SBOp 2:116,2; CF 31:89; on Luther and the biblical background of this passage, see Walther von Loewenich, *Martin Luther: Der Mann und das Werk* (Munich: List Verlag, 1982) 116f.

'so that you my see my back'.[30] Both the medieval monk and the sixteenth-century friar interpreted these verses christologically. What is exciting here is that Luther's contribution to the *Heidelberg Disputation* was permeated even in its details by Bernard's monastic theology, which was intrinsically non-scholastic, if not anti-scholastic, as the *Heidelberg Disputation* is notorious for being. This means that another major event in the career of the Reformer was influenced by 'Father Bernard'. Even those who cannot be convinced of Luther's direct dependence at this point must be struck by the general congeniality.

The bernardine imagery of 'nesting' in Christ's wounds like birds in a tree so impressed Luther that he evoked it again in a much later Table Talk. There he mentioned Bernard as his source: 'It is Bernard's saying: We must make for ourselves nests in Christ's wounds like birds in the holes of the trees'.[31] In his lectures on Rom 9:16 Luther admonished his listeners to meditate on the wounds of Christ in order to purge the eyes of the heart.[32] In his exposition on the Lord's Prayer, the reformer also recommended meditation on the wounds of Christ. There further bernardine thoughts surface, especially the metaphor of 'sucking' from the rock. Luther recommended that we 'suck from these wounds' the realization of our own sinfulness as the decisive aspect of our self-knowledge and the recognition of our need for penance.[33] This echoed Bernard's phrase, 'sucking honey' from the rock, which he used in his SC 61 (see note 7 above).

Bernard: 'I had no idea; I thought I was sound'

In his third Christmas sermon Bernard spoke not only of Christ's nativity, but also of Christ's passion and his affection for sinners. In the midst of the Christmas celebration he introduced a reminder of the cross. Onlookers weep 'from his passion' while Christ weeps 'from compassion' and, he continued:

30 SC 61. 6; SBOp 2:152,1–4; CF 31:145f; see Loewenich, *Martin Luther,* 116f.

31 *Bernhardi dictum* . . . , WA TR 5:395,1f (no. 5898).

32 WA 56:400,1–10; LW 25:389.

33 WA 9:145,31f (1518). Another section of his exposition shows Bernard's influence, namely WA 9:137,10–36.

Brethren, Christ's tears bring on in me at once shame and agony. There was I playing outside in the square, while in the secrecy of the royal bedroom a sentence of death was brought against me. His Only Begotten got to hear of it. He came out. He had put down his diadem. He was wearing sackcloth, and his head was spattered with ash. He was barefoot, and weeping and wailing, because his little slave-boy had been condemned to die. Quite suddenly, I see him coming out. I am struck dumb. New thing. I am told the reason why. I listen. What am I to do? Play on, make play of his tears? If I have taken leave of my senses, if I am not of sound mind, I will not follow him, will not weep with his weeping. This is the shame I felt. Agony and fear, how did they come about? Well, I have only to look at the remedy to get a picture of what danger I'm in. I had no idea. I thought I was sound. Then I found this: the virgin's son is sent for, Son of Highest God, and out goes the order he is to be killed, and this way my wounds are tended—with the precious balsam of his blood.[34]

Luther: 'Saint Bernard was so terrified by this'

Luther made reference to Bernard's affective christocentrism and Christ's tears in his commentary (1519) on his favorite pauline letter, at the point where he interpreted Gal 4:12: 'For thus, when our sins did not torment us, Christ, as Saint Bernard testifies, grieved and suffered for us, in order that by his grief on account of our sins he might the more strongly move us to mourn, just as he said to the women who were following him' (Lk 23:28).[35] The reference to the mourning women appears to be Luther's embellishment of the bernardine passage.

Luther also had in mind Bernard's words in Nat 3 when he wrote his own *Meditation on Christ's Passion* in 1519. He focused on the nails, the crown of thorns, and the sacred heart of Jesus: When one sees the nails penetrate his hands, one must believe that

34 SBOp 4:260f. I used the translation of Nat 3 by Peter Cramer, published in Pranger, *Bernard of Clairvaux and the Shape of Monastic Thought*, 240–44, here 242f; another version was provided in the same book on 264f (along with the latin text). Pranger 244–269 offered an interpretation of this sermon. Pranger, however, did not cover Luther's use of this passage.

35 *Sic enim et Christus, teste d. Bernardo*, WA 2:543,6–9; LW 27:300; see Bell, *Divus Bernhardus,* 264.

our evil thoughts are causing this. It is we who deserve those nails in hand and foot. Christ is 'the earnest mirror' which neither lies nor trifles: in him we recognize our sinfulness for which he suffered. Luther paraphrased Bernard's Christmas text, deleting Bernard's mention of the 'servant-boy', the 'diadem', and 'ash'. Bernard's phrase, 'There was I playing outside in the square, while in the secrecy of the royal bedroom a sentence of death was brought against me', was rendered in Luther's vernacular as 'I regarded myself secure, I was not aware of the eternal sentence that had been passed on me in heaven'. Bernard's original 'His Only Begotten got to hear of it. He came out', was paraphrased by Luther as 'I saw that God's only Son had compassion upon me and offered to bear this sentence for me'. Luther continued: 'What am I to do? Play on, make play of his tears? If I have taken leave of my senses, if I am not of sound mind, I will not follow him, will not weep with his weeping'. Luther paraphrased a substantial section here for his purposes, and in the process he again included a reference to the women of Lk 23:28:

> Saint Bernard was so terrified by this that he declared: 'I regarded myself secure, I was not aware of the eternal sentence that had been passed on me in heaven until I saw that God's only Son had compassion upon me and offered to bear this sentence for me. Alas, if the situation is that serious, I should not make light of it or feel secure. We read that Christ commanded the women not to weep for him but for themselves and their children.[36]

As Luther's meditation on Christ's passion was surely inspired by Bernard's Christmas sermon, so too were his Good Friday sermon of 1525 and his sermon for the fifth Sunday after Trinity in the Summer Postil.[37] In addition, one suspects his meditation

36 *eyn solchen erschrecken nam sanct Bernhard dar auss* . . . , (1519), WA 2:137,37–138,4; LW 42:9. In 1900 already, Köhler had worked on this locus and had to admit that he was unable to find the source in Bernard's works which Luther had in mind, see *Luther und die Kirchengeschichte*, 309. The index in WA 63:97 listed the reference as unidentified; Bell, *Divus Bernhardus*, 263–65, offered the solution by pointing to Bernard's Nat 3.4.

37 See WA 20:303,31–36 (1525); WA 22:87, 22–25 (Summer Postil); see WA 50:471,4; see Posset, 'Bernhard von Clairvauxs Sermone zur Weihnachts-, Fasten- und Osterzeit als Quellen Martin Luthers', *Lutherjahrbuch,* 98.

was also nurtured by Bernard's SC 61, in which he had preached on 'sucking from the rock' and on the sacred heart which is laid open through the clefts of his body. A mighty mystery (*magnum sacramentum*) of love, his heart is laid open; laid open are too the entrails (*viscera*) of the mercy of our God, in which the morning sun from on high has risen upon us. 'Surely, are not his *viscera* laid open through his wounds?'[38] These bernardine references to the sacred heart and divine *viscera* found their way into Luther's own meditation on the passion of Christ.[39] One should meditate on the heart of Christ and through it reach the heart of God. This surfaced again in a lutheran sermon of 1525. Speaking on Mk 14:34–49, the beginning of Christ's passion, Luther invited the frightened listeners to look into Jesus' sacred heart where they can discover his and the Father's love.[40]

Bernard: 'Because I shall remember the wounds of the Lord'

Yet one more phrase from Bernard's sermon 61 needs consideration here. It is part of the sermon passage which was introduced with the question: 'And really where is there safe sure rest for the weak except in the Saviour's wounds?' The phrase is: 'My conscience is disturbed, but not perturbed, because I shall remember the wounds of the Lord' (SC 61.3).

Luther: 'Because in my heart I shall remember the wounds of the Lord'

Luther repeated this phrase several times: 'I have sinned gravely, my conscience is disturbed but not perturbed, because in my heart I shall remember the wounds of the Lord'. He took the phrase as Augustine's, as he did in 1521 when he wrote on monastic vows, and again in 1536, when he wrote to Melanchthon,[41] and in 1544 when he wrote the preface to an anthology on 'consolation' by

38 SC 61.4; SBOp 2:150,29–151,3; CF 31:144.
39 See WA 2:140,27–141,7.
40 WA 17-I:353,23–25, and 354,1; see Nicol, *Meditation bei Luther,* 133–144.
41 Luther to Melanchthon: *Turbabor, sed non perturbabor, quia vulnerum Domini recordabor,* WA Br 12:193,91f.

George Spalatin, another humanist friend.[42] Even in an academic disputation on the divinity and humanity of Christ he held the same mistaken opinion.[43] Research has shown that this quotation cannot be localized in Augustine's works, but occurs only in Bernard's SC 61.[44] This demonstrates that Luther was more influenced by Bernard than even he was aware. Only once, in 1524, did Luther correctly attribute the phrase on 'perturbation' to Bernard, when he interpreted Habakkuk 3 with the help of Bernard's sentence on being mindful of God's mercy when one feels 'in trouble': 'Bernard treats this notion in an excellent way',[45] he commented.

Luther's great admiration for Bernard's passion piety can be detected throughout his career. In 1527, in his lectures on 1 John, he complimented the Cistercian by saying that he had not erred in his spirit since he knew Christ as his Saviour and felt him in his heart.[46] In 1532–33, when he preached on psalm 40, he remarked: 'I let you have the example of Saint Bernard and Saint Augustine. Wherever Saint Bernard preaches, whenever he is with himself in faith, he is a beautiful teacher. He ascribes everything to Christ, he praises and praises the man'.[47] 'The man' is the crucified Jesus, at the center of his religious attention. Several years later, in 1538, the ageing Luther was still fond of Bernard's christocentrism and 'theology of the cross' and noted: 'Whenever monks were saved, however, they were constrained to crawl to the cross of Christ again. This is what Saint Bernard did. I regard him as the most

---

42 *Et ipse quoque Augustinus . . . : 'Turbabor (inquit), sed non perturbabor, Vulnerum Domini recordabor'*, WA 54:114,20–23 (Luther's preface to George Spalatin's book *Magnifice consolatoria exempla et sententiae ex vitis et passionibus sanctorum collectae*). Spalatin in his book quotes the phrase under consideration here as Bernard's (fol. H2a); Luther keeps associating it with Augustine, even in this preface to a book where the phrase is marked as Bernard's.

43 See WA 39-II:99,3f (Disputation of February 28, 1540); WA TR 5:280,1f (no. 5623); see Posset, 'The Elder Luther on Bernard: Part I', 33f; Luther also mistook another quotation from Bernard as being augustinian, i. e. Pre, SBOp 3:292,24f.

44 See SC 61.3; SBOp 2:150,9–22; CF 31:142.

45 *Bernhardus egregie hunc locum tractat . . .* , WA 13:441,37–442,11 (on Habakkuk, 1524). On monastic vows (1521), WA 8:602,28–29; LW 44:292.

46 *Sic Bernardus spiritu non erravit, scivit Christum salvatorem et sensit corde*, WA 20:753,22–23.

47 WA 47:109,18–21, on Jn 3:19 (September 14, 1538); LW 22:388.

righteous of all the monks . . .'.[48] Still later, he made no secret of
his high regard for Bernard, when during one of his last battles he
wrote the following revealing words:

> To be sure, I did teach, and still teach, that sinners shall be stirred
> to repentance through the preaching or the contemplation of the
> passion of Christ, so that they might see the enormity of God's
> wrath over sin, and learn that there is no other remedy for this
> than the death of God's Son. This doctrine is not mine, but Saint
> Bernard's.[49]

Some further light may yet be shed from another perspective.
In 1530, in describing his personal seal, called the 'Luther Rose'
(see Plate 16) to his friend, Lazarus Spengler, the town clerk of the
imperial city of Nuremberg, the Reformer expressed this cross-
centered piety succinctly:

> It is a mark of my theology. . . . The first thing expressed in my
> seal is a cross, black, within the heart, to remind me that faith
> in Christ crucified saves us. 'For with the heart man believes
> toward righteousness' (Rom 10:10). . . . 'For the just shall live
> by faith' (Rom 1:17)—by faith in the crucified. But this heart is
> fixed upon the center of a white rose, to show that faith causes
> joy, consolation, and peace.[50]

In the preface to his 1535 commentary on Galatians, Luther
wrote: 'For in my heart there rules one article, namely, faith in
Christ; from it, through it and in it all my theological thoughts flow
and return day and night'.[51] In his subsequent exposition of Gal
3:6 he gave his theology of the cross an anti-*ratio*-nal twist when

---

48 WA 40-III:354,3f.

49 WA 50:471,1–5; LW 47:110 (Antinomians, 1539).

50 See WA Br 5:445,1–22 (no. 1628, Luther's letter to Lazarus Spengler
of July 8, 1530, from the Coburg castle); Luther's german letter contains one
quotation (Rom 1:17) in Latin. i. e. 'the righteous will live by faith, but by the
faith in the crucified [Lord]', see WA Br 13:155. See Wicks, 'Martin Luther:
The Heart Clinging to the Word', 79. Unfortunately, this collection of articles
in the *Spiritualities of the Heart* does not include Bernard as one of its greatest
representatives.

51 WA 40-I:33,7–9; see Posset, *Luther's Catholic Christology,* 15, with notes
1 and 2.

he declared that this faith (*fides*) kills reason (*ratio*): *fides occidit rationem.*[52] Luther decidedly by-passed the rationalistic theology of the scholastics (as he perceived it) and straightforwardly pressed back to the Fathers, *ad fontes*. He went back to such proven authorities of the Church as Bernard and Augustine, and beyond them to the 'naked text of the Bible'.

Plate 16: Luther's Seal (so-called 'Luther Rose'), described by Luther in 1530.

Excursus: Luther's further use of Bernard's Sermon 61 on the Song of Songs (SC 61)

As we have seen, Luther used Bernard's SC 61.3 for insights (a) on the clefts of the rock (*foramina petrae*) as a symbol of Christ's wounds, and (b) on the troubled conscience (*turbatur sed non perturbatur*). Altogether, Luther referred to this section of SC 61 about ten times, thinking he was relying on Augustine.[53] There

52 See Ebeling, *Lutherstudien,* 3:181–222. See Friedrich Beisser, 'Luthers Urteil über die 'Vernunft'. *Theologische Beiträge* 15 (1984) 150–162, where Luther's view of 'reason' is summarized.

53 WA 1:344,24; WA 2:148 (not listed in WA index); WA 3:640,40 (WA 3:645,31 is a reference to SC 43, and not to SC 61 as the index WA 63 has it); WA 8:602,28f; WA 9:145 (not listed in the WA index); WA 39-II:99,1; WA 46:515,8.30; WA 50:471 (not listed in the WA index); WA 54:114, 22. *Turbatur– perturbatur, inquit D. Augustinus,* WA 40-III: 660,35f.

is another section of this sermon, i. e. SC 61.8, which contains a
famous passage on suffering quoted by numerous contemporaries
of Bernard.[54] The later Ludolph of Saxony in his *Vita Christi* used it
in its exact bernardine wording, *nec deest dolor, sed contemnitur*[55]
('pain is not absent, it is scorned'). In SC 61.8 Bernard spoke of the
martyrs who find shelter in the bowels (heart) of Jesus. The martyr
does not feel his own wounds when he regards those of Christ. The
martyr's soul is in a safe place even while his body is tortured. The
soul finds safety with the 'Rock', and in the clefts of the rock (Sg
2:14) which represent Christ and his open wounds:

> While gazing on the Lord's wounds [the martyr] will indeed not
> feel his own. The martyr remains jubilant and triumphant though
> his whole body is mangled; even while the steel is gashing his
> sides he looks around with courage and elation at the holy blood
> pouring from his flesh. Where then is the soul of the martyr?
> In a safe place, of course; in the rock, of course; in the heart
> of Jesus, of course, in wounds open for it to enter. . . . Now
> that it dwells in the rock is it any wonder if it endures as rock
> does? . . . The feelings are not lost, they are leashed. And pain
> is not absent, it is scorned. From the rock therefore comes the
> courage of the martyr.[56]

Historical research has followed Erich Auerbach in holding
that this passage 'seems not to have left direct traces in Luther's
works'.[57] His observation is out-dated, however, because Luther
referred to and also quoted the phrase 'And pain is not absent, it
is scorned' in its original Latin. The first hint of Luther's use of
SC 61.8 is found in 1527, when he commented on 1 Jn 4:13. He
declared that the Holy Spirit works hiddenly in the heart. 'Affected
about Christ', the heart rejoices and is at peace in him. Through
remembrance of Christ (*per memoriam Christi*)[58] we feel him in

54 See Erich Auerbach, 'Gloria Passionis'. *Literary Language and Its Public
in Late Antiquity and in the Middle Ages* (New York: Pantheon Books, 1965) 70f.

55 See W. Baier, *Untersuchungen zu den Passionstraktaten in der Vita
Christi des Ludolf von Sachsen* (Salzburg 1977) 3:536, note 32, as referred to
by Bell, *Divus Bernhardus,* 334.

56 *Nec deest dolor, sed contemnitur*, SC 61.8; SBOp 2:153,15; CF 31:147.

57 Auerbach, 'Gloria Passionis', 70f.

58 WA 20:750,14.

the heart. This is not the spirit of the flesh or of the world at work here, but the Holy Spirit. When one feels joy over the works of Christ, then one has the Holy Spirit (see 1 Jn 4:13). If one rejoices in Christ, one rejoices in the Father, 'and this is meant by "that God is in us' ". 'Again, with confidence (*fiducia*) we flee to the Father and to Christ in any tribulations. If this sweetness (*ista dulcedo*) touches and affects my heart, it is from the Holy Spirit'.[59] At this point, Luther may have been mindful of Bernard's statement in SC 61.8 (*Nec deest dolor, sed contemnitur*) about the martyr who, although he experiences pain, 'scorns' it. Luther did not quote this particular phrase explicitly; he did mention the martyrs. They may have been disturbed and frightened, but not perturbed (as also in SC 61.3), as the martyr's spirit cleaves to Christ, so his spirit in Christ conquers the 'sadness of the flesh' and any malice through the 'sweetness of the Spirit'.[60] The flesh is terrified, but the spirit rejoices. Luther went so far as to identify human sweet affection with the Holy Spirit: 'This sweet and cheerful affection toward Christ is the Holy Spirit'.[61] This affection is not born 'of us' (*ex nobis*), but it is nevertheless 'in us' (*in nobis*).[62] The Spirit works sweetly in us, but does not come from our own capacity (*ex nobis*). In his johannine lectures of 1527, Luther did not use the exact bernardine wording, as he did seven years later when, in his *Sermon on Anger* According to Matthew 5, delivered in 1534 and published in 1536, we find the direct latin quotation of Bernard's phrase within the german sermon text: 'For we do not have, nor should we have, hearts of iron but of flesh, as Saint Bernard says: *Dolor est, sed contemnitur*; it is painful, but must be borne and overcome'.[63]

59 WA 20:750. Luther told his audience to look up Rom 8:15 and Gal 3:26, where this 'Spirit of liberty and confidence' is explained.

60 WA 20:750,26.

61 WA 20:750, see also 751.

62 WA 20:750; see Georg Eichholz, 'Der 1. Johannesbrief als Trostbrief und die Einheit der Schrift', *Evangelische Theologie* 5 (1938) 76.

63 . . . *Wie S. Bernhardus sagt: Dolor est, sed contemnitur (Eine predigt vom Zorn, auff das Evangelium Matth. V.*; printed version), WA 41:749,38f; this bernardine phrase is found already in Rörer's stenogram of that sermon: WA 37:383,37; cf. Bell, *Divus Bernhardus*, 334.

In Luther's *Church Postil* (model sermons), this phrase occurs in the third sermon for the Sixth Sunday after Trinity.[64] Because Luther referred to Bernard only in general terms ('as Saint Bernard says') no scholar identified the source until very recently, when Theo Bell[65] and I, independently of each other made the identification.

64 *One person should not be angry at another, an excellent sermon. An exhortation to patience and meekness, a second sermon by Dr. Martin Luther, Wittenberg, 1543*; printed by Joseph Klug, at Wittenberg; see *Sermons of Martin Luther,* ed. John Nicholas Lenker (Grand Rapids: Baker Book House, reprint of 1904 edition) 4:198.

65 See Bell, *Divus Bernhardus,* 334.

III. BERNARD REALLY LOVED CHRIST'S INCARNATION

1. *Longing for Christ's coming*

Bernard: 'The intense longing of those men of old . . . may be enkindled in me'

The Advent season is a time to remind the faithful that Israel waited for salvation. Bernard in his Second Sermon on the Canticle (SC 2), which is an Advent sermon, preached about longing for the coming of the Messiah:

> Even now I can scarcely restrain my tears, so filled with shame am I by the lukewarmness, the frigid unconcern of these miserable times. For which of us does the consumation of that event fill with as much joy as the mere promise of it inflamed the desires of the holy men of pre-christian times? Very soon now there will be great rejoicing as we celebrate the feast of Christ's birth. But how I wish it were inspired by his birth! All the more therefore do I pray that the intense longing of those men of old, their heartfelt expectation, may be enkindled in me. . . . [1]

Luther: 'Bernard says this: "When I look at the prophets . . ."'

Luther must have been moved by Bernard's passage from this sermon, for he recalled it in 1531 in words macaronically preserved in German and Latin by George Rörer: 'Bernard says this: "When I look at the prophets and their calling and clamor for Christ, I feel ashamed in my heart and am distressed because I see how ungrateful the present times are etc. while they are quite anxious because they did not see him"'.[2]

If we compare the latin wording of Bernard and Luther, we realize that Luther quoted not literally but liberally, yet without any change of meaning. Luther had internalized the bernardine insight to such a degree that it had become part of his own thought. He knew it 'by heart'. During the Advent and Christmas seasons the

---

1 SC 2.1; SBOp 1:8,20–9,6; CF 4:8. That we deal with an Advent sermon is derived from the introduction of SC 2: 'Very soon now there will be great rejoicing as we celebrate the feast of Christ's birth'. SBOp 1:8,25–9,1.

2 *Bernardus sic dicit . . .* (Rörer), WA 34-II:2–5; see lines 18f.

Plate 17: *Mary, the Christ Child, and Saint Bernard*. Enlarged detail of the illuminated page 88 of the *Antiphonale Cisterciense*, cistercian monastery of Altenberg, Germany, 1544. Universitätsbibliothek, Düsseldorf, Germany.

Plate 18: Bottom of illuminated page 88 (previous plate).

Plate 19: *Mary, the Christ Child, and Saint Bernard.* Illuminated page in *Manuale pietatis*, Saint Bernards-op-'t-Schelt, approx. 1524. Bibliotheek van de Faculteit der Godgeleerdheid, Catholic University of Louvain, Belgium.

elderly Luther appears to have been regularly inspired by Bernard's sermon: during Advent 1531,[3] at Christmas in 1537 and again in 1540, when the passage from Bernard's SC 2 came to his mind. Bernard spoke of the prophets' longing for the Messiah; Bernard contrasted this to his own shameful lukewarmness. The contrast impressed Luther deeply. In his Christmas sermon for 1537 he again referred to 'Bernard in a sermon' on the coming of the Lord.[4] Not only during the Advent and Christmas seasons did this bernardine phrase emerge in Luther's preaching; we find it also in a sermon of 12 September 1533, delivered at Schweinitz. There Luther identified his source very clearly: *Sic Bernardus in Canticis.*[5]

2. *Christ, the physician of souls*

Bernard: The heavenly physician is wise, but not rough

When Luther was reading Bernard's sermons, he must have come across the traditional image of Christ as the healer of afflicted souls. In his Third Sermon for Christmas Eve and in his Third Sermon for Christmas Day, Bernard spoke of Christ as 'the wise physician' who comes to the sick, the redeemer to slaves, the Way to wanderers, the Life to the dead.[6] Furthermore, in sermons SC 3 and SC 44 Bernard preached on the 'spiritual physician' and the Church as his 'inn' or hospital. In SC 3, he also spoke about the Word of God as 'medicine' and Christ as the 'heavenly physician'. Significantly, this sermon was also given during the Advent season.[7] 'The heavenly physician came with speed to her aid, because "his word runs swiftly". Perhaps you think the Word of God is not a medicine? Surely it is, a medicine strong and pungent, testing the mind and the heart'.[8] In SC 44, Bernard returned to this motif:

3 WA 34-II:453,18f (Advent 1531).

4 WA 45:348, 28–30 (Christmas 1537); WA 49:176,23 (Christmas 1540).

5 WA 37:142,7–10 (September 12, 1533); see Posset, 'The Elder Luther on Bernard: Part I', 46f.

6 V Nat; SBOp 4:211,14–16; Nat; SBOp 4:260:11.

7 *Caelestis medicus . . .* , SC 3.2; SBOp 1:15:9f; CF 4:17.

8 SC 3.2; SBOp 1:15,9–11; CF 4:17.

But let us consider the man who fell into the hands of brigands and was carried by the good Samaritan to that inn which is the Church. His wounds were healed not by oil alone but by wine and oil, to show that the spiritual physician must possess the wine of fervent zeal as well as the oil of gentleness, since he is called not only to console the timid but to correct the undisciplined. For if he sees that the wounded man, the sinner, rather than improving through the exhortations so gently addressed to him, rather disregards the kindness and becomes gradually more negligent, resting more securely in his sins, then, since the soothing oils have been tried in vain, the physician must use medicine with a more pungent efficacy. He must pour in the wine of repentence. . . . [9]

Luther: Christ as chief hospital administrator

Unless we allow mere coincidence of thoughts, Luther must have been familiar with these passages on Christ as the physician and the Church as his hospital, for they turn up in Luther's works. If Luther was not directly influenced by Bernard's sermons, then his independent congeniality with the cistercian's thought would be still striking. That he was influenced by the bernardine notion of Christ as the physician of souls, *medicus animarum,* can be verified by his explicit quotations of Bernard's Easter sermon on the leper Naaman (2 Kings 5). Luther referred to it in his first lecture on Psalm 42:7 to explain the name of the Jordan river as 'descent' (*descensus*). In this context Bernard had spoken of the Lord Jesus as the 'physician of souls' who dispensed seven purgatives before his passion and had been prefigured by Elisha, who as a sort of doctor told the leper Naaman to descend into the Jordan river seven times to be healed.[10]

The medical imagery in the tradition impressed Luther. I limit myself to two lutheran sources in which can be found traces of Bernard's interpretation of Christ as 'Doctor' and the Church as his hospital. One is a sermon of 1525, the other a passage in his 1527 course on 1 John. We must, however, be mindful that the concept of

9 SC 44.3; SBOp 2:45,27–46,10; CF 7:226f; see Posset, *Luther's Catholic Christology,* 201–204 with note 6.

10 Res 3, *De lepra Naaman*; SBOp 5:103,5; see WA 3:236,28 (on Ps 42:7).

Christ as Physician and Medicine had already been the conviction of Augustine who wrote in his *Christian Doctrine*: 'Thus the Wisdom of God, setting out to cure men, applied himself to cure them, being at once the Physician and the Medicine'.[11] Bernard employed this same imagery in his sermons. One could, of course, argue that Luther had found this medical language in Augustine and not in Bernard. In the light of the evidence that Luther was an enthusiastic reader of Bernard's sermons, however, we may assume that he was at least equally influenced by Bernard. In either case, we can safely say that Luther followed an augustinian/bernardine tradition based on Scripture.[12] For his local audience in 1525, Luther translated the church fathers' impressive presentation of *Christus medicus* into German, proclaiming Christ as 'master of the hospital' (*Spittalmeister* in his sixteenth-century german) and consequently declared the Church a *spital*, a hospital.[13]

Luther lectured on *Christus medicus* as well in his course on 1 Jn 2:1 and 2:12.[14] Man stands in need of a cure from sin, *curatio peccati*,[15] because his flesh is fatally afflicted[16] from fighting with sin. In this struggle, the best weapons and the real medications are faith, prayer, and meditation on the Word of God, because they drive the devil away. The power of Christ must be preached because it is the most valuable *medicina* against everything. Luther saw the Church as the hospital where patients are transferred from darkness to light, from sin to cure.[17] Clearly Luther used the concept of Christ the Physician of souls and the Church as his hospital in the same way Bernard had done in SC 44. Luther also

11 Book One.14, D. W. Robertson, Jr, trans. and ed. (Indianapolis: The Bobbs-Merrill Company, 1976) 15. *Medice meus intime, Confessiones* 10.3. See Schuck, *Das religiöse Erlebnis beim hl. Bernhard von Clairvaux,* 39–41.

12 Already in his first lectures Luther was influenced by this medical language; he understood justification as a healing process; see Adolf Hamel, *Der junge Luther und Augustin: Ihre Beziehungen in der Rechtfertigungslehre nach Luthers ersten Vorlesungen 1509–1518 untersucht* (reprint, Hildesheim, New York, 1980) 115ff.

13 . . . *ecclesia ist eyn spital,* WA 59:239–40 (on Mt 18:21ff, 1525).

14 WA 20:636,31 and 655,9–15.

15 See WA 20:655,14.

16 See WA 20:635,7; see WA 20:629,5; 759,19; 776,17f; 790,6–18.

17 See WA 20:655,13–15.

pointed to the good bedside manners of the 'spiritual physician' who can reveal an illness to the sick person without worsening the patient's condition; he uplifts the patient with the promise of cure. In Luther's version, the patient clings in good faith and hope to the physician's promise.[18] Bernard saw Christ as the wise, gentle, spiritual physician, but he also knew that many people take Christ as a 'rough physician' and that 'there are many who have perished in their flight from the physician, for, although they know Jesus, they do not recognize him as the Christ'.[19] Similarly, Luther was concerned with the right image of Christ whom he understood primarily as healer (*Heiland*), and not as legislator and angry Judge. Bernard's question of how the merciful God could also be the Judge could be Luther's question as well. And Bernard's response could have been Luther's answer: 'If he judges and condemns, it is because we in a certain sense compel him to, so that condemnation seems to come from his heart much more reluctantly than mercy'.[20]

3. *The three advents of Christ*

Bernard: The 'triple advent'

In his first Advent sermon, Bernard talked about the incarnation in connection with the spiritual advent of Christ as the 'physician of souls'. In Bernard's words: 'He comes from the heart of God the Father into the virgin's womb'. He comes because we are lying paralyzed on our beds and have not the power to reach the heights of God. 'So the most kind saviour and physician of souls came down from his lofty place, and tempered his brightness to the weakness of our eyes'.[21] Toward the end of that sermon he dealt with the spiritual coming of Christ which is a daily advent: 'Just as, in order to effect salvation in the midst of earth, he came once visibly in flesh, so also he comes daily, unseen and in the spirit, to save the souls of individuals. . . . Although the sick man cannot

18 See WA 20:655,13–15.
19 V Nat 6; SBOp 4:235,16–18.
20 Nat 4; SBOp 4:268,2.
21 SBOp 4:165,13; 167,5–13.

travel far to meet the great Physician, let him at least try to raise
his head when he draws near!' In this context he quoted Zech 2:10,
'The Word is near thee, in thy mouth and in thy heart'.[22] Bernard's
mystical concept of Christ's daily spiritual birth in the heart of the
believer is found again in one of his sermons for Christmas Eve:
just as Christ was born in Bethlehem and is sacrificed daily so long
as we proclaim his death, so he is also to be born daily in us.[23]

The first coming of Christ at his incarnation is the general advent to all people, *ad homines*. The *parousia*, the 'second coming',
is the advent on the Day of Judgment, which is his coming against
mankind, *contra homines*. The third advent is the spiritual birth in
the soul as a 'mystical' advent *in homines*. Bernard numbered these
three advents differently at times. What is here the 'second coming'
is sometimes called the 'third advent', and the spiritual advent in
the soul can be the 'second advent' by his count: Between the
incarnation in historical time and the *parousia* at the end of time,
then, the spiritual advent in the individual soul takes place as the
second (hidden) advent.[24]

Bernard also preached on the triple advent in his Fifth Advent
Sermon, where he repeated that the intermediate advent is the one
hidden and seen only by his chosen ones, in themselves, and so
their souls are saved.[25] In his Sixth Sermon he focused on the
guest's arrival, Christ's spiritual advent in the soul: 'You have a
noble guest, o flesh, a very noble guest; and your salvation depends
entirely on his. Give honor to so great a guest'.[26]

The presentation of the spiritual coming of Christ was not
restricted to Bernard's talk about 'advents'. He wrote about it
in other terms as well: 'Christ ascended once and for all above
heaven's height in corporeal fashion, but now he ascends every

22 SBOp 4:168,14–169,2. In Bernard's V Nat 4, we find Christ described as
the pious and wise physician, SBOp 4:221,12–13. In V Nat 6 he is the 'gentle
saviour' who nevertheless is powerful; he is not a 'rough physician', SBOp
4:235,9–15.
23 V Nat 6; SBOp 4:234–244. 'Physician' as a title for Christ is found also
in the SC 31.7 and SC 32.3.
24 S 3; SBOp 4:177,17–187,2 where Bernard included biblical references
to Jn 14:23, Prov 9:1 (?), Ps 88:15, and Ps 131:17.
25 SBOp 4:188,10–11.
26 SBOp 4:192,25–193,1.

day spiritually in the hearts of the elect'. And in another, rather short, sermon Bernard chose the terms 'utility', *de triplice utilitate*. Here he applied the triple advent to its usefulness for us: first, to illuminate our blindness; second, to remain with us to assist our infirmity; third, to protect us and fight for us in our fragility. All this occurs in the believing soul where Christ resides by faith.[27]

Luther: 'Saint Bernard spoke beautifully about these distinctions'

Bernard's concise concept of Christ's triple advent served Luther as the immediate matrix for his early interpretations of Ps 101:1 ('when will you come to me?'), Ps 102:2 ('do not turn your face away from me', *non advertas faciem tuam a me*), and Ps 118. In expounding Psalm 101:2, he declared that he understood the time of Christ's coming to mean any time—past, present, and future. He explicitly added that Bernard spoke beautifully (*pulchre*) about these distinctions.[28] Luther thought he had read about it in Bernard's Sermons on the Canticle, while it is more likely that he had encountered it in the Advent sermons. Luther, speaking in the words of Psalm 102:2, expressed the hope that Christ would not turn away his face from him. In this context, he spoke of Christ's triple 'face' because the psalm text on which he was reflecting used this image, 'face':

> Christ's face is triple. First, in his first advent when he was incarnated as Son of God who is the face of the Father. . . . Secondly, in the spiritual advent without which the first is good for nothing. And so one has to recognize his face through faith

27 SBOp 4:196,9–14. The 'ascending' terminology is found in Div 61.1; SBOp 6:293,14–16. In V Nat 6 Bernard repeated the idea that Christ is resident in the heart by faith, SBOp 4:242,10–13. The triple coming of Christ according to Bernard was further elaborated by Frischmuth, *Die paulinische Konzeption in der Frömmigkeit Bernhards von Clairvaux*, 46–87, and most recently by Stercal, *Il 'Medius Adventus'*; it found honorable mention also in McGinn, *The Growth of Mysticism,* 177, and in O'Brien, 'St. Bernard's Use of Sacred Scripture', 165.

28 *Intelligam, quocunque tempore venias. Et hunc distinctionem Bernardus in Canticis pulchre ponit,* WA 4:134,6f; LW 11:285. See Prenter, *Der barmherzige Richter,* 82–84. Prenter, unfortunately, did not mention Bernard as Luther's matrix in regard to the triple advent of Christ. See Posset, 'Bernard of Clairvaux as Luther's Source: Reading Bernard with Luther's "Spectacles" ', CTQ 54 (1990) 281–304, here 294f.

in which all good things are. . . . Thirdly, in the second and last
advent when his face will be fully visible.[29]

Luther did not refer to Bernard by name either here or at the
conclusion of his interpretation of Ps 118.[30] Yet the concept of
the triple advent of Christ is so distinctly bernardine that we must
assume Luther borrowed it from him. He used the sequence of the
three advents in the way Bernard had done. Bernard's concept of
the triple coming of Christ is also visible in Luther's Lectures on
Romans, to which we turn our attention now.

Luther: Christ's mystical coming to the Jews

'Christ's mystical advent to the Jews'! What an expression!
Luther did not specify what he meant by *mysticus* but in his
subsequent sentence he contrasted this 'mystical advent' to the
'corporal advent' of Christ. The 'corporal' or physical coming of
Christ in the flesh is the first coming, in fulfillment of prophecy:
'Usually, the authority of Isaiah is clearly fulfilled in the corporal
advent of Christ'. Using Bernard's sermons on the triple advent
as Luther's theological background, we may understand Luther's
teaching on the physical advent of Christ as the coming to the
people (*ad homines*), and see Luther's wording of 'the mystical
advent of Christ' as the third coming in which the advent 'to
the Jews' (*in Iudeos*) is included; Bernard spoke of it in terms
of Christ's coming 'to the people' (*in homines*), that is, into the
hearts of the people, Gentiles and Jews. Luther's concept of the
'mystical advent of Christ' is best interpreted within this bernardine
matrix. One may, therefore, conclude that Bernard helped Luther in
interpreting the Letter to the Romans, especially when Luther ran
into the difficulty with Rom 11:25, 'I do not want you to be ignorant
of this mystery. . . . Blindness has come upon part of Israel until

29 *Quia facies Christi est triplex . . .* , WA 4:147,10–20.

30 On Ps 118: *Vltimo Notandum, Quod quiquid in hoc psalmo et aliis quoque
dictum est de aduentu Christi in carnem, debet etiam intellegi moraliter de
adventu eius quottidiano per gratiam tam in incipientibus quam proficientibus,
quam Expositionem fere omnes elaborant hoc psalmo. Tertio, De futuro aduentu
per gloriam, Quia tunc Videbimus Verbum eius, eloquium, testimonium in sua
claritate, Et misericordiam, pacem et omnia habebimus,* WA 55-I:80,1–7. The
new critical edition (1993) does not provide any hint at Bernard at this point.

the full number of Gentiles enter in, and then all Israel will be saved', which as he himself admitted, appeared obscure to him.[31]

Luther: 'Spiritual birth'

Luther had an opportunity to process Bernard's concept of Christ's spiritual advent in the soul when he interpreted the johannine notion *nativitas ex deo* or *generatio dei*, i. e. man being born of God. Again, the mystical divine birth in the heart is also Augustine's theme, which was evidently further unfolded by Bernard.[32] Since Luther did not give any source reference at this point, it is useless to debate whether Luther picked up this concept from Augustine or from Bernard. He moved within the greater monastic tradition which was shaped by both.

When Luther arrived at 1 Jn 3:9, he spoke of *nativitas ex deo*, the birth from God which effects the cleasing of the soul.[33] On 1 Jn 4:7 ('begotten of God') he spoke of *nativitas spiritualis*, the spiritual birth which bears fruit in deeds of love.[34] And on 1 Jn 5:2 he lectured on *nativitas Dei*,[35] which is the equivalent of Bernard's 'spiritual advent' in the heart of the believer. On 1 Jn 5:4, on the need to be born of God, Luther proclaimed that this verse should be written 'in golden letters'.[36] Like Bernard, Luther also qualified the 'birth of God' as a happening in faith. To the Reformer, the *efficacia adventus* or the *energian adventus*, was important as it expresses the salvific purpose of Christ's incarnation.[37] Luther stressed the 'birth of God' as that 'faith in the preached Word' which is the spiritual advent of Christ as he is preached to us.[38] The tribute to the power of the Word of God as strong medicine for the soul was

31 WA 56:437f, especially 438,20f; see LW 25:430; see Posset, 'Bernard of Clairvaux as Luther's Source,' CTQ 54 (1990) 294–296 (on *Adventus Christi Mysticus in Iudeos*).

32 See Hugo Rahner, 'Die Gottesgeburt: Die Lehre der Kirchenväter von der Geburt Christi im Herzen der Gläubigen'. *Symbole der Kirche: Die Ekklesiologie der Väter* (Salzburg: Müller Verlag, 1964) 13–87, here 67.

33 WA 20:706,2–4.

34 WA 20:738,13f.

35 WA 20:766,11f.

36 WA 20:773,28–774,1.

37 See WA 20:726, 10–20 (on 1 Jn 4:2).

38 WA 20:778; 780,3f; see WA 20:772,20f.

prevalent in both Bernard and Luther, and Luther's theology of the Word of God may have been influenced by Bernard's emphasis on the Word of God as medicine. In this context Luther also talked of the 'coming' of Christ 'through blood and water' in interpreting 1 Jn 5:6,[39] referring to christian baptism.

4. *The three great miracles in connection with the Incarnation*

A further bernardine inspiration to Luther's preaching came when he reflected on the mystery of the incarnation. Bernard's admiration of the 'miracle' of the Virgin Mary's faith/humility in the mystery of the incarnation led him to preach on it extensively in his Third Sermon for Christmas Eve.

Bernard: 'Three works, three mixtures . . .'

Bernard's sermon focused on the mystery of the omnipotent divine majesty performing 'three works, three mixtures when assuming our flesh'. They are 'so wonderfully unique and uniquely wonderful' that they were never performed anywhere else again in the whole wide world. 'Indeed, conjunct to each other are God and man, mother and virgin, faith and the human heart'. The three conjunctions are: first, the incarnation; second, the mystery of the virgin becoming a mother; third, the coming together of faith and the human heart. This passage was integrated into the Christmas lesson of the *Legenda aurea*, whose author made clear that he had taken it from Bernard's *opus* by adding: 'As Bernard says'.[40] Whether Luther picked the bernardine thought from the secondary source, the *Legenda aurea,* or directly from the Third Sermon for Christmas Eve remains an open question.

Luther: 'Saint Bernard says that in this birth three great and remarkable signs occurred'

In his Christmas sermon of 1520, we find the Reformer making homiletic use of Bernard's marveling over the faith of the virgin.

39 WA 20:777,19.
40 SBOp 4:216,27–217,1; see *The Golden Legend*, Ryan 1:39.

His theme was Luke 2:14: the Saviour is born to persons of good will. One must feel this birth in one's heart, he said, and to do this the right way, one must do it in faith alone. At this point Luther introduced bernardine thoughts:

> Bernard says that in this birth three great and remarkable signs occurred. The first is that God and man became one by the unification of the divine and human nature. The second is that she who gave birth remained a virgin and nursed. The third is that in this event the human heart and faith in such matters could come together and became one. I tell you, the first sign is easy to believe, and [yet] moves only a few people. The second is easier yet to believe. The third is easiest of the three. Herein lies the real miracle, namely that the Virgin Mary believed that this will happen 'in her'. This is so great that we cannot marvel enough about it. . . . [41]

She became more his mother through her heart than through her flesh. If Christ's birth is to become of any use to us and move our hearts, Luther continued, we must follow Mary's example; the birth must occur in our hearts. Anyone who does not accept the Christ Child this way, loses this birth.

In Luther's sermons as they were collected by John Polliander between 1519 and 1521, Bernard's sermon on the three wonders surfaced again, not once, but twice. The first instance has it as follows:

> *Bernardos* [sic] reminds of the three miracles:
>   1. That God and man became one person.
>   2. That the virgin gives birth.
>   3. That the human heart and the word of the faith can come together and be united. This heart in which faith and the word is united must be reborn daily and renewed.[42]

41 *Sanctus Bernhardus sagt, das in dieser gepurt drey grosse und merck-liche wunderzeichen geschehen sindt . . .* , WA 7:188,18-189,14. On Luther's use of Bernard's sermons from Christmas to Easter, see Posset, 'Bernhard von Clairvauxs Sermone zur Weihnachts-, Fasten- und Osterzeit als Quellen Martin Luthers', *Lutherjahrbuch*, 93–116.
42 WA 9:498, 23–26.

The second locus within this particular collection occurs in Luther's sermon for Christmas 1520, the one already treated above, but here given in its latin version.[43] For the feast of the Annunciation in 1525, Luther again made use of Bernard's sermon on the threefold miracle, adding that such belief is possible only by the work of the Holy Spirit.[44] The idea emerged again in the Summer Postil for Pentecost Monday,[45] and yet again in his 1533 sermon for the feast of the Visitation (2 July).[46] Even as late as in his commentary on Genesis, Luther marveled at how 'Bernard really loved Christ's incarnation'. On Gen 28:14f, Luther again referred specifically to Bernard as an admirer of the faith of the Virgin Mary: 'Concerning the faith of the Virgin Mary when it had been announced to her by the angel that she would be the mother of Christ, Bernard says that the strength of the faith of the Virgin who could believe the words of the angel was no less a miracle than the incarnation of the Word itself.'[47]

This comment resembles what Luther said to Cardinal Cajetan, that Mary's exemplary faith was admired by '*Divus Bernhardus* and the universal Church'. On that occasion in Augsburg, Luther definitely had Bernard's Ann 1 in mind. Here, in his exposition of Gen 28:4–15, however, it is possible that he was referring to another sermon, Bernard's Second Christmas Sermon, which contains the following lines about Mary's faith:

> Happy is she, blessed among women, in whose chaste womb this bread was baked by the fire of the Holy Spirit which came down upon her. Happy, I repeat, is she who hid the leaven of her faith in these three measures. By faith she conceived, by faith she brought forth, as Elizabeth says: 'Blessed are you who has believed . . .'. And do not be surprised to hear me say that it was

43 *Unde Bernhardus dixit, Hic tria facta esse miracula . . .*, WA 9:517,14–28. The reference to Augustine follows, and again mention of Bernard, see 518,4–8.

44 WA 17-I:150,23–26 (March 25, 1525).

45 See WA 21:489,31.

46 WA 37:96,25–35 (July 2, 1533).

47 *Sic Bernardus de fide virginis Mariae*, WA 43:590,16–19; LW 5:234.

by means of her faith that the Word was united to flesh, since in fact he took his flesh from her flesh.[48]

5. *Not In-angel-ment, but In-human-ment*

Bernard: Lucifer and the Incarnation

Our cistercian preacher expressed his thoughts on the incarnation and Lucifer's envious reaction in several places: Adv 1, Miss 3, and SC 17.[49] We concentrate here on his Adv 1, in which he asks why the Son of God, and not the Father or the Holy Spirit, became man, and answered that it was certainly not without reason that the Son became man, adding the rhetorical question from Rom 11:34: 'Who knows the mind of the Lord?' Then he introduced his own speculation about what went on in heaven when the Holy Trinity decided on the incarnation of the Son. One of the chief angels, Lucifer, became jealous and wanted to usurp the *similitudo* of the Most High.[50] At that moment he was cast out of heaven. Bernard implied that Lucifer was annoyed at the decision that God should become human.

Luther: 'A good speculation'

Apparently, Bernard's homilies on Lucifer inspired the Reformer, for he integrated this particular thought into several of his own sermons: first, into one delivered in 1526; then into his Christmas sermons of 1533 and 1535;[51] and several times later on. This particular bernardine speculation was not picked up by the Reformer before the year 1526, i. e. almost a decade after the 1517 publication of his theses against the abuses of indulgences in 1517,

48 See Nat 2; SBOp 4:254,18–20. This reference is given in LW 5:234. See SBOp 4:13–21.

49 SC 17; SBOp 1:100,22–101,12. Miss 3; SBOp 4:44,6–23.

50 Adv 1; SBOp 4:162,8–25; see Posset, 'The Elder Luther on Bernard', 45. In SC 53.7f, Bernard wrote of Christ's leaping over the angels and archangels to descend from heaven to earth. The Son of God did not stop there to become so to speak in-angel-ated, but he went down further in order to take to himself the seed of Abraham, i. e. to be incarnated. B. McGinn pointed to this 'leaping' in his section on Bernard's teaching on redemption, see *The Growth of Mysticism*, 174.

51 See Posset, 'Bernard of Clairvaux as Luther's Source', 296–298.

and after he had broken with the monastic way of life. Here is what Luther preached in 1533:

> There were Fathers who gave some thought to this matter, and they said that the devil when living in heaven saw that God would become man, and this caused his downfall; that he assumed this nature, not the angelic one; thus there was envy and haughtiness. . . . [The Fathers] wanted to indicate the great joy and overwhelming goodness, that he took not the angelic but the adamitic semen and flesh and blood, and which is the one spoiled by the devil, by sin, death, and poison. How unhappy are those who do not know anything about this and who never experienced it. . . . It is preached to them first by angels, then by the apostles, preachers, that God has visited them and honored them so much that the human nature has become God and is placed so high that the angelic nature cannot reach it, and the human nature was made Lord over everything. Those, who do not sense this, have no consolation and joy from it.[52]

Two years later, on 25 December 1535, Luther gave the afternoon sermon on the Christmas gospel, focusing on Lk 2:10–13:

> Saint Bernard is a wonderful man, he believes that the devil in paradise has noticed that God will become man. . . . They do not mind at all and they are happy that God is not called an angelic God and that God does not become an angel, but a person, and they say: 'Be not afraid, we want to get together now.'[53]

On 1 September 1537, in his sermon about the johannine phrase *Et homo factus est*, the ageing Luther again took time to elaborate extensively on Lucifer and the incarnation. Deeply rooted in the Catholic tradition even at this late point in his career, Luther first praised the roman liturgical custom of genuflecting at the line of the Creed, *Ex Maria Virgine, et homo factus est* ('He was born of the Virgin Mary and became man'), a gesture which he interpreted as an expression of gratitude for the incarnation. Luther then observed

52 WA 37:235,10–22.

53 . . . *S. Bernardus est mirabile vir, putat diabolum in paradiso gemerckt, quod deus futurus homo . . .*, WA 41:486,13–28; see Posset, 'The Elder Luther on Bernard: Part I', 42–46.

that the church fathers were particularly joyful that God had not taken on the angelic nature, but had humiliated himself to take our flesh and blood and to be born as a human being:

> Saint Bernard especially in his meditation had many good thoughts about these words and wondered very much, and he said that he believed that the archdevil, Lucifer, fell over this idea and was pushed from heaven. . . . And furthermore, Saint Bernard said that the good angels enjoyed the idea and said: If it pleased our Lord, God and Creator, so well, it shall please us also; they stayed and recognized him as their God and Lord.[54]

This sermon exists also in part in a latin version with the same patterns on the incarnation and Lucifer's jealousy. This version includes Luther's compliment to Bernard that this 'is a good speculation'.[55] In the Reformer's commentary on Genesis, Bernard's thoughts on the incarnation and Lucifer reappear at least three times.[56] At one point, Luther distanced himself from the speculative character of Bernard's thought, but he did not discard it, nor did he compel anyone to believe in it. He declared them to be mere 'opinions'. He affirmed, however: 'This much is certain: the angels fell and the devil was transformed from an angel of light into an angel of darkness'.[57]

In his exposition of Gen 24:5–7, which deals with Abraham and includes the line, 'He will send his angel before you', he again brought up the story of the angels' fall and Bernard's 'poetic' interpretation of it:

> About the fall of the wicked angels there is a statement of Bernard, who as the poets do, invents the story that Satan fell from heaven because he saw that the Son of God was to become man and would take on this wretched mass of the human race, and that then the service and care of the human nature, which was far more wretched than they, would be entrusted to the

54 WA 46:625,1–10; see WA 46:625,20–626,17.

55 . . . S. Bernhardus habuit cogitationem. . . . Et est bona speculatio, WA 46:792; LW 22:103. Luther utilized Bernard's SC 2, SBOp 1:12,1f.

56 WA 42:18,6–21; LW 1:22f.

57 WA 42:18,30–35; LW 1:23.

angels. Therefore since, as Bernard says, he was irritated by the disgracefulness of the situation, he despised the Son of God and for this reason fell from heaven.[58]

Luther considered this thought excellent and pious.[59] He referred to it a third time when he provided his exposition of Gen 28:12–14 on Jacob's dream about the heavenly ladder. Having said that the passage gave reason to marvel at the mystery of the incarnation, i. e. that God had joined human nature to himself, Luther began a lengthy excursus on Bernard's speculation about the incarnation and Lucifer's fate:

> Ambrose and especially Bernard take great pleasure in this passage, which is exceedingly delightful. . . . And it is right and godly for them to do so. . . . *Bernard really loved Christ's incarnation.* So did Bonaventure. I praise these men very highly for the sake of that article on which they reflect so gladly and brilliantly, and which they practice in themselves with great joy and godliness. Bernard thinks and imagines piously enough that the devil fell because of that envy on account of which he begrudged men such great dignity, namely, that God would become man. For he thinks that when Satan was a good angel in the sight of God, he saw that one day the divinity would descend and take upon itself this wretched and mortal flesh and would not take upon itself the nature of angels. Moved by that indignity and envy, thinks Bernard, the devil raged against God, with the result that he was thrown out of heaven. These thoughts of Bernard are not unprofitable for they flow from admiration for the boundless love and mercy of God.[60]

This speculation on Lucifer was rooted so deeply in Luther's thought that he spoke of it even during his study of the Koran

---

58 *Extat Bernardi dictum de lapsu malorum Angelorum, qui fingit, sicut Poetae figmenta habent . . .*, WA 43:319,16–21; LW 4:256; see Posset, 'The Elder Luther on Bernard: Part II', 188–91.

59 *Satis pulchra et pia cogitatio est*, WA 43:319,22; LW 4:256.

60 WA 43:580,42–581,21. Note especially the line: *Bernardus valde dilexit incarnationem Christi*, 581,11; LW 5:220f. Luther apparently had Bernard's Adv 1 in mind, SBOp 4:162,20–24; see Posset, 'The Elder Luther on Bernard: Part II', 189. In the same breath of his praise for Bernard, Luther expressed his high esteem of Bonaventure, WA 43:581,11.

(in about the year 1542). Luther commented that this speculation is also part of the islamic teaching. He hinted at this phenomenon in continuing his excursus on Gen 28:12–14, where he compared Bernard's and Mohammed's teachings: 'This is almost in agreement with what Bernard imagined . . .'.[61] Luther added that the teaching about Lucifer stemmed from ancient interpreters who understood Is 14:13 as a reference to the action of the angel who would truly have become like God, if God had accepted the angel into the unity of his person. This would have amounted to 'in-angel-ment' instead of the 'in-human-ment', 'incarnation':

> The angel would have been adorned with the same glory if the Son of God had become 'inangelate', so to speak, and had taken up that most beautiful spirit. For then it would have been said: 'That Lucifer is true God, the Creator of heaven and earth'. This, says Bernard, is what the devil seems to have sought to achieve. But when he had been repulsed, he was inflamed with great hatred. . . . It is an ancient and inveterate hatred, conceived and rooted in heaven, so that it can never be eradicated. Accordingly, the ladder is the wonderful union of the divinity with our flesh. On it the angels ascend and descend, and they can never wonder at this enough.[62]

Although Bernard's ideas on Lucifer's reaction were highly speculative, the ageing expositor appraised them as profitable and found great inspiration in them.

6. Brother Christ

Bernard: 'After all he is my brother, and my own flesh'

On several occasions Bernard pointed out that at the incarnation Christ became our brother. In his famous *Aqueduct sermon* for the Feast of Mary's Birth he preached: 'Surely you are not afraid of approaching him? "He is your brother and your flesh" (Gen 38:27). . . . Him Mary has given you as your brother'.[63] In

61 WA 43:581,28–37; LW 5:222.
62 WA 43:582,4–17; LW 5:223.
63 Nat BVM 7; SBOp 5:279,14f.

his Sermons on the Canticle he mentioned this at two places: in SC 15.4, he declared: 'I share in his inheritance. I am a Christian, Christ's own brother. If I am what I say, I am the heir of God, co-heir with Christ'.[64] In SC 2, an Advent sermon, he meditated on Christ the Mediator:

> If the mediator is to be acceptable to both parties, equally dependable in the eyes of both, then let him who is God's Son become man, let him become the Son of Man, and fill me with assurance by this kiss of his mouth. When I come to recognize that he is truly mine, then I shall feel secure in welcoming the Son of God as mediator. Not even a shadow of mistrust can then exist, for after all he is my brother, and my own flesh. It is impossible that I should be spurned by him who is bone from my bones, and flesh from my flesh.[65]

Luther: 'He even calls us his brothers. Thus said Bernard'

Luther was fascinated by the idea that Christ is our brother. Of the three possible bernardine sermons Luther most likely read SC 2, as we know from other hints that he was familiar with it. His wording of 1535, too, came closest to SC 2: God will not be angry with us since Christ is our flesh and blood: 'He even calls us his brothers. Thus said Bernard the monk: Why should I despair? My flesh and blood is sitting up there. I hope that He does not become angry with me as he is of my flesh and bone. This is a good, heavenly, spiritual thought'.[66]

On later occasions Luther brought up the same idea in almost literal quotations: 'He [Bernard] says: God cannot be angry with me because he is my flesh and blood'.[67] And he exclaimed that there is 'no friendlier word on earth' than that Christ is 'bone from my bones and flesh from my flesh'.[68] If Luther did not consult Bernard's sermons directly in this regard, he may have found this bernardine

64 SC 15.4; SBOp 1:85, 9; CF 4:108.

65 SC 2.6; SBOp 1:12,1f; CF 4:12.

66 *Imo vocat nos fratres. Sic Bernardus* . . . , WA 41:97,1–98,1; LW 13:245.

67 German: *Gott . . . mir nicht gram ist, denn er ist mein fleisch und blut,* WA 46:627,4. Latin: *Dicit item: Deus non potest mecum irasci, quia est mea caro et sanguis* (September 1, 1537), WA 46:792; LW 22:103.

68 WA 45:304,1–3; 9–14 (1537).

idea in the *Legenda aurea*, in the reading for the Circumcision of the Lord: 'So says Bernard: "It is the name of our Saviour, of my brother, of my flesh and my blood" '.[69]

7. On Christ's circumcision

Bernard: 'He has the form of a sinner'
As if wanting to fill in the lines of the image of Christ our brother which he had painted in his previous sermons, Bernard plainly stated in his Third Sermon on the Circumcision (Circ 3) that Christ not only has the 'form of a man, but also 'the form of a sinner. . . . For what does circumcision mean', he asked, 'if not being an indication of superfluity and of sin'.[70]

Luther: Bernard gives the moral reason for the circumcision
When Luther preached on 1 January 1517, the Feast of the Circumcision of the Lord, he must have sought help from the sermons of Bernard, for he indicated that he followed the saint's explanation of the circumcision; that by being circumcised Christ wanted to take on the reputation of a sinner. Luther preached: 'Bernard gives the moral reason for Christ's circumcision, that indeed for us Christ wanted to take on the reputation of a sinner, which he was not'.[71]

By way of summary we may remark that not only implicitly, but also explicitly Luther taught bernardine concepts; among them

69 *The Golden Legend*, Ryan 1:73.
70 Circ 3; SBOp 4:283,19–284,1; see Circ 2; SBOp 4:280,13.
71 . . . *rationem Circumcisionis Christi moralem dat Berhardus, quod scilicet Christus pro nobis voluit reputari peccator quod non erat,* WA 1:120,7f. Interestingly, this particular bernardine thought had not found entry into the *Legenda aurea*. Luther's reflections on Christ being sin metaphorically were recently described by Gerhard Ebeling, ' "Christus . . . factus est peccatum metaphorice" ', *Tragende Tradition. Festschrift für Martin Seils zum 65. Geburtstag*, Annegret Freund, Udo Kern, Aleksander Radler, eds. (Frankfurt etc.: Peter Lang, 1992) 49–73; Wilfried Härle, ' "Christus factus est peccatum metaphorice": Zur Heilsbedeutung des Kreuzestodes Jesu Christi', *Neue Zeitschrift für Systematische Theologie und Religionsphilosophie* 36 (1994) 302–15. However, both theologians, Ebeling and Härle, did not point out that Luther made explicit reference to Bernard on this issue (i. e. in WA 1:120).

the triple coming of Christ, which is such a distinctively bernardine concept that no other source reference fit better than the Advent sermons. We also saw Luther dwelling on Bernard's teaching about the 'three great miracles' of the incarnation; on the in-human-ment rather than in-angel-ment; and on Christ who became our circumcised brother, but who is also the 'physician' of our souls. It is evident that Luther recognized that the mystery of the incarnation occupied a central place in Bernard's spirituality and in turn internalized it to a great extent. What is today generally acknowledged as a typical cistercian incarnation spirituality[72] was also the spirituality of Luther.

The hagiographer William of Saint Thierry had recognized Bernard's love of the incarnation and incorporated it into the story he told about Bernard' childhood vision of the nativity. William commented: 'To this day, Bernard seems to find deeper meaning, to have more material to speak of, when this mystery [of the incarnation] is his topic.'[73] William had also pointed out that Bernard preferred to give the moral sense in his interpretations of Scripture, by-passing 'more mysterious aspects'.[74] Bernard's preference is reflected in Luther's.

---

72 'Chez les Cisterciens, le mystère de l'Incarnation occupe la place centrale. . . . La figure du Christ au centre de la Règle . . .', Edmond Mikkers, article 'Robert de Molesmes. II. La Spiritualité Cistercienne', DSp (1988) 13:770.

73 *Vita Bern,* Book 1.2.4; PL 185:229; Cawley 1:9.

74 *Vita Bern,* Book 1.12.60; PL 185:259; Cawley 1:73.

1. *Bernard: Judge of the World and Gentle Saviour*

Bernard's affective Christocentrism found expression, as we said, in his *fasciculus myrrhae* (SC 43) which also contains the preacher's theology of the cross and the idea that Christ is both the 'Judge of the World' to be feared and the 'gentle and humble Lord' to be loved.[1] In his Sixth Sermon on the Canticle the abbot meditated on embracing the two feet of the Lord, one the foot of judgment, the other the foot of mercy, an allusion to Psalm 100:1. 'I have been instructed by the experience of my master [the psalmist], it is not judgment alone or mercy alone but both together that will be my song'.[2] In his Second Sermon on the Ascension Bernard described Christ sitting at the right hand of the Father, holding mercy in his right hand and judgment in his left.[3] As we saw earlier, for Bernard, Christ is the 'sweetest spouse' (SC 52.1)[4] and the crucified Saviour, 'sweet on the cross' (SC 61.6).[5]

2. *Luther: From 'Stern, Terrible Judge' to 'Sweetest Saviour'*

In absorbing these bernardine sermons, and in following the concept of Christ the 'sweet Saviour', held by his superior Staupitz,[6] which Staupitz may have drawn from Augustine,[7] Luther felt

1 SC 43.4; SBOp 2:43,16–18; CF 7:223.

2 SC 6.9, in the translation of Michael Casey, *Bernard of Clairvaux: Man, Monk, Mystic: Texts Selected and Translated* (Kalamazoo: CP, 1990)14; see CF 4:37.

3 Asc 2.5; SBOp 5:129,12–14; see Casey's translation 78.

4 SC 52.1; SBOp 2:90,12–13; see CF 31:48, where *dulcissimus sponsus* is rendered with 'completely tender bridegroom'.

5 SC 61.6; SBOp 2:152,1–14; CF 31:146.

6 Staupitz: *O sueser seligmacher / dulcis salvator* (no. 67; see no. 64), *Libellus de Exsecutione Aeternae Praedestinationis,* Johann von Staupitz, *Sämtliche Schriften*, 152–153. Staupitz's spirituality was centered around the saving Christ, not the judging Christ according to Adolar Zumkeller in his entry 'Staupitz', DSp 14 (1990) 1190: *Chez lui* (i. e. Staupitz) *ce n'est pas le Juge de l'univers, mais le Christ sauveur qui est le thème central.*

7 *Deus altissime et dulcissime,* (*Confessiones* 3.8.16) CSEL 33:58; *summa suavitas* (*Confessiones* 9.1.1) CSEL 33:197. *Factus est tibi suavis* (S 145), PL 38:792 and 794. See Posset, 'The Sweetness of God', 143–178.

secure in moving away from the 'stern judge' he had perceived as the dominant image. As he admitted: 'I did not believe in Christ but thought of him as nothing but a stern, terrible judge as he is depicted sitting on a rainbow'.[8] Luther probably had in mind a stone relief at the Wittenberg cemetery on which an artist depicted the stern Christ sitting on a rainbow with a sword in his mouth.[9] The Augustinians of the neighoring Grimma friary depicted the same image in their seal (Plate 19).[10] Under the influence of Bernard and Staupitz he eventually learned to understand the cross as the 'mercy seat'[11] and Christ as 'sweetest Saviour', *dulcissimus Salvator*, as Luther expressed himself to Staupitz in 1518.[12]

In 1519, Luther passed on the same advice which he had received to the readers of his *Meditation on Christ's Passion*, so that they would be warmed by it and receive 'strength and

8 *Denn ich gleubte nicht an Christum, sondern hielt jn nicht anders denn für einen strengen, schrecklichen Richter, wie man jn malet auff dem Regenbogen sitzend,* WA 45:482,15; see WA 38:147,30. See E. G. Schwiebert, *Luther and His Times* (St. Louis: Concordia Publishing House, 1950) 153. Reinhard Schwarz summarized the widespread medieval mentality concerning Christ as a merciless Judge which the young Luther had internalized, and from which he was liberated: Reinhard Schwarz, 'Die spätmittelalterliche Vorstellung vom richtenden Christus – ein Ausdruck religiöser Mentalität'. *Geschichte in Wissenschaft und Unterricht* 32 (1981) 526–553. Schwarz, 'Wurzeln evangelischen Verantwortungsbewusstseins'. *Kirchengemeinschaft – Anspruch und Wirklichkeit.* Festschrift für Georg Kretschmar zum 60. Geburtstag, Wolf-Dieter Hauschild, Carsten Nicolaisen, Dorothea Wendebourg, eds. (Stuttgart: Calwer Verlag, 1986) 149–164. Christoph Burger followed in Schwarz's tracks with his article on 'Die Erwartung des richtenden Christus als Motiv für katechetisches Wirken'. *Wissensorganisierende und wissensvermittelnde Literatur im Mittelalter. Perspektiven ihrer Erforschung. Kolloquium 5.-7. Dezember 1985,* Norbert Richard Wolf, ed. (Wiesbaden: Dr. Ludwig Reichert Verlag, 1987) 103–122. On the concept of the merciful Judge, see Prenter, *Der barmherzige Richter.* Otto Hermann Pesch also pointed to Luther's image of the merciful Judge: 'Im Angesicht des barmherzigen Richters. Lebenszeit, Tod und Jüngster Tag in der Theologie Martin Luthers', *Catholica* 42 (1988) 245–273.

9 On the location of the stone relief of Christ with sword and rainbow, see Loewenich, *Martin Luther,* 74.

10 *Urkundenbuch der Stadt Grimma und des Klosters Nimbschen,* ed. Ludwig Schmitt (Leipzig: Giesecke & Devrient, 1895) illus. 5 in Table I. I am grateful to Rudolf Markwald for pointing the seal out to me.

11 See Posset, *Luther's Catholic Christology,* 175–178, with note 101.

12 *Ita enim dulcescunt praecepta dei, quando non in libris tantum, sed in vulneribus dulcissimi Salvatoris legenda intellegimus* (Luther's letter to Staupitz of 30 May 1518); WA 1:525,21.

Plate 20: *Christ Enthroned on a Rainbow*; from each side of his face swords issue.
Green color seal of the former augustinian friary at Grimma, Saxony, used after
1426; circumscription: *S. Conventus fratrum heremitarum August. in Grimme.*

sweetness' when 'chewing' on it.[13] In his Christmas Sermon of
1520 he observed:

> It is true that it is impossible for one's heart to accept this Child
> and taste his sweetness, except if one has emptied oneself of all
> joy that is not of Christ. The heart must be left unmarried (*ledig*)
> and without consolation, and it must not seek help from any
> creature. The Child will not tolerate that one's heart is engaged
> with something else. . . . Christ will never become sweet to you
> unless you first become bitter to yourself.[14]

13 *Krafft und sussikeit*, WA 9:146,31–36.
14 *Nu ist es war, das es nicht kan moglich seyn, das sich das hertz dises
kindes also ahnnehme und schmeck seyn sussickeit. Er hab dann zuvor alle freud
auss geschut ausserhalb dem, das nicht Christus ist, das hertz muss ledig gelassen
stehen und trostlos sein, und muss kein hilff suchen bey keiner creatur, das kindt*

In 1527, ten years after the famous posting of the theses on indulgences, Luther remembered that he had carried this image of Christ as an exacting person (*exactor*) with him all the time:

> I had believed that Christ is like an *exactor* and, even more, I had become pale at the mention of Christ's name, as of Moses' and of Satan's, because I sensed that their laws were impossible [to keep]. So the heart was wounded by this prolonged craziness. So I truly tell you: You have to comprehend Christ not as an *exactor*, but as the Saviour, the liberal Giver.[15]

Still later in his life, in 1539, he stated: 'Saint Bernard is such a man who speaks and preaches sweetly'.[16] In encountering Christ one is 'drenched with divine sweetness and spirit', Luther wrote in his exposition on the *Magnificat*, and he stressed that the 'Blessed are those who trust in God' for they will 'experience God's work' in themselves and will thus arrive at the 'experiential sweetness' and 'through it at full understanding and insight'.[17] This sweetness was experienced in paradise before the fall when man lived a 'pleasant and sweet life'.[18]

In following Augustine, Bernard, and Staupitz, Luther remained with Christ, the 'sweetest Saviour'.[19] In encountering Christ Luther found 'the sweetest consolation'.[20] In a sermon of 1534, he identified from among the medieval authorities three by name, Augustine, Bernard, and Bonaventure, as those theologians

---

will nicht leyden, das sich das hertz etwas anders ahnnimpt. . . . Christus wirt dir nymmer suss werden, du seist dir dan vorhin selber bitter (Christmas Sermon 1520), WA 7:191,1–192,12. On Luther's spirituality of the heart, see Wicks, 'Martin Luther: The Heart Clinging to the Word', 79–96.

15 WA 20:770,22–25; see Posset, *Luther's Catholic Christology*, 235.

16 See WA 47:694,4–9. The one german notion *susse* was translated with *dulciter et suave* in the latin version of that sermon of March 24, 1539, WA 47:694,26.

17 WA 7:550,7–18.

18 WA 42:42,33; see WA 42:66,9 (Lectures on Gen). See Augustine, *Confessiones,* 3.1.1; CSEL 33:43–44; PL 32:683.

19 *Salvator suavissimus*, WA Br 4:299,15; see WA Br 4:294,7.

20 *Dulcissimam consolationem*, WA Br 1:35,29–32.

who speak to the heart which begins truly to understand the Scriptures, a heart that has the 'foretaste' of God.[21] Luther had learned, along with this patristic, monastic tradition, to see Christ sitting, not only on the judgment seat, but also on the mercy seat, the cross, and to experience personally the salvific sweetness of Christ.[22] This insight moved Luther to change the course of western christianity. At root he was simply retrieving for himself the monastic tradition of experiencing the sweetness of God on the mercy seat, and passing it on to eager Christians outside cloister walls.

The issue of Judgment Day was prevalent in medieval mentality and in Luther's works. When he found something consoling on this topic in the Bernard legend, he gladly made use of it, as we will now see.

3. Bernard: Christ's double right to heaven—for me

Bernard's spirituality had taken concentrated expression in his concept of Christ's double right to the kingdom of heaven: a person cannot possess the kingdom of heaven by personal merit but must receive it from Christ who shares it with sinners. As Brian P. McGuire points out, this summary of Bernard's faith in the redemptive merits of Christ's passion is the 'essence of christian theology'.[23]

Perhaps basing himself on a passage in SC 61.5, where Bernard spoke of merits which are credited to God's mercy, and said that Christ's righteousness suffices for both 'you [Christ] and me', the hagiographer articulated the insight in narrative form:

> There was a time when the man of God fell so seriously ill that he seemed about to breathe his last. He was rapt in ecstasy and saw

21 *Augustinus, Bernardus, Bonaventura praegustum vocant . . . , ut Petrus ait* (1 Pt 2:3), WA 37:474,22f (Sermon of 2 July 1534). See WA 46:524,20f (Christmas Sermon 1538).

22 See Posset, *Luther's Catholic Christology*, 175–178.

23 See McGuire, 'A Saint's Afterlife. Bernard in the Golden Legend and in Other Medieval Collections', *Bernard of Clairvaux. Rezeption und Wirkung im Mittelalter und in der Neuzeit*, Elm., ed., 194; *The Difficult Saint*, 163.

himself being presented before God's judgment seat, while Satan
stood opposite him and peppered him with malicious charges.
When Satan had exhausted his list and it was the man of God's
turn to speak for himself, fearless and unperturbed he said: 'I
admit I am unworthy, and unable by merits of my own to gain
entrance to the kingdom of heaven. On the other hand, my Lord
has won the kingdom by a twofold right, namely, by inheritance
from his Father and by the merits of his passion. The first he has
reserved for himself but the second he gives to me; and by that
gift I assert my right and shall not be confounded!' These words
threw the Enemy into confusion, the meeting was closed, and
the man of God came to himself.[24]

4. Luther: 'I Often Use the Example of Saint Bernard'—'Golden Words'

Luther deleted the introductory part of the story as found in the
medieval sources, which tells how Bernard 'being rapt in ecstasy,
saw himself before the judgment seat of God. . . .' Luther used
only the theological concept of Christ's double right to heaven. He
mentioned it for the first time in his first lecture (*Dictata*) on Psalm
15, where he explicitly spoke of the *duplex ius*:

> The Lord [Christ] has a double right with God: The first is
> inherited since he is the innocent one and the Son of God . . . ;
> and the second is [his] right by merit; and so he says: 'O Lord,
> my alloted portion and my cup' (Ps 15:5). But this [second right]
> is totally ours as we share with the Lord in this life the chalice
> and suffering of Christ. . . . [25]

24 I use my own translation of the original: *Caeterum duplici jure illud
obtinens Dominus meus, haereditate scilicet Patris, et merito passionis, altero
ipse contentus, alterum mihi donat ex cujus dono jure illud mihi vindicans, non
confundor. Vita Bern*, Book 1.12,57; PL 185:258; see Cawley 1:70. This passage
is also found in *Vita Secunda*, PL 185:491, and in the *Legenda aurea*, 533;
The Golden Legend, 471; Ryan 2:102f. See SC 61.5; SBOp 2:151; CF 31:144f.
Bernard's concept of the double right of Christ and his teaching about grace
and merits was recently dealt with briefly by Robert Thomas, 'Que pense saint
Bernard de ses mérites?' Coll 49 (1987) 201–217; see also Lane, 'Bernard of
Clairvaux: A Forerunner of John Calvin?' *Bernardus Magister*, 541.

25 *Et si bene Inspiciatur textus, Allegat hic Dominus duplex ius, quod
habet ad Deum. Primum Est hereditarium, quia innocens et filius Dei, merito*

This *locus* in Luther's works can easily escape attention because Bernard is not mentioned by name. Perhaps Luther was not at the time (1513) yet aware of the bernardine origin of the concept. This appears to be the case again in 1520, in Luther's treatise *The Freedom of a Christian*, where he also took up this bernardine thought without crediting his source:

> The birthright [in the Old Testament] was highly prized for it involved a twofold honor, that of priesthood and that of kingship. . . . Now just as Christ by his birthright obtained these two prerogatives, so he imparts them to and shares them with everyone who believes in him according to the law of the above-mentioned marriage, according to which the wife owns whatever belongs to the husband.[26]

In the early 1520s many decisive events occurred, which cannot be described here. Luther was excommunicated, banned, and taken into 'protective custody' at the Wartburg castle where, from 4 May 1521, he spent ten months incognito as 'knight George', busy with the translation of the New Testament into German. The theological faculties of Cologne, Louvain, and Paris rejected Luther's

---

habet omnia velut hereditarie; et secundum hoc dicit 'Dominus pars hereditatis mee' [sic], *quia ut supra, in hac vita Christus etiam non omnia habuit, que iure hereditatis ad eum pertinebant. Secundum est ius meriti, et sic dicit: 'Dominus pars calicis mei'. Sed hoc totum nostrum est, quia et nos participamus Dominum in hac vita in calice et passione Christi. Ideo sequitur tu es, qui restitues hereditatem meam mihi* . . . , WA 55-II,1:120,5ff (1513). See M. B. Pranger, 'Perdite Vixi: Bernard de Clairvaux et Luther devant l'echec existentiel', *Bijdragen: Tijdschrift voor Filosofie en Theologie* 53 (1992) 46–61; Pranger, *Bernard of Clairvaux and the Shape of Monastic Thought*, 24. Pranger featured the phrase from SC 20, 'I have been living miserably because I have been wasting my time' (*perdite vixi*), while my focus here is on Christ's double right to heaven, which is connected to the phrase of 'living miserably' ('unworthy') in the Bernard entry in *The Golden Legend*. It is noteworthy that Luther's teacher Staupitz did not give credit to Bernard either when he talked about the 'right to heaven'. See Franz Posset, 'St Bernard's Influence on Two Reformers 175–87. Only later did Luther make the explicit connection between the traditional concept of the 'double right to heaven' and Bernard.

26 WA 7:20–38;47–73. See Willibrord van Rijnsoever, 'Bernard en Luther over onze Vrijheid in Christus', Coll 23 (1961) 20f. By the way, in 1516/17 Staupitz again used the concept of the 'right to heaven', and again he did not indicate the bernardine origin of it; see Franz Posset, 'St Bernard's Influence on Two Reformers,' 175–187.

teachings in the spring of 1521. There was unrest at Wittenberg,
where in January 1522 the theology professor Karlstadt got married, as did several other friends of Luther. During some argument
over reforms Karlstadt even insulted Luther as a 'neo-papist'. A
third of the friars at Luther's Wittenberg friary left the cloister.[27]
During these events Luther was confined to the Wartburg Castle. He
had time to reflect on his religious vows when the bernardine line
quia perdite vixi ('I lived damnably [or: shamefully]'), originally
in Sermon 20 on the Canticle, came to his mind. He combined
that phrase directly with the statement (which, Luther pointed out,
Bernard made 'elsewhere', meaning in his defense in the vision of
the heavenly court) that Christ was ready to share his 'double right
to the kingdom of heaven', the part Christ has earned for the sinners
by his salvific suffering and death for humankind. Luther stressed
that on his sickbed Saint Bernard 'put total trust in Christ' alone,
despairing over his own works. Bernard at that point said nothing
about monastic poverty, obedience, chastity; he even called his a
'lost life': 'And elsewhere: "By a double right does Christ possesss
the kingdom; by the first because he is the Son, by the second
because he has suffered. And since he did not need the second
merit, he gave it to me and all who believe." '[28] At the Wartburg,
for the first time, Luther apparently made the connection between
Bernard and the concept of the 'double right to heaven' which he
had previously used without mentioning Bernard by name.

Luther returned to his friary on 6 March 1522 to encounter the
mess which had been created at Wittenberg during his absence. He
resumed his preaching duties. On 13 March 1524, he delivered
a homily on Gen 31:40–43 about Jacob and Laban, which for
some reason gave him yet another opportunity of making use of
the bernardine line on the wasted life in combination with the
'double right' to the kingdom of God.[29] Two years later, in 1527,
Luther published a sermon in which he made readers aware of the
two different bernardine sources which he so often combined in

27 See Heinrich Bornkamm, *Luther in Mid-Career 1521–1530*, E. Theodore
Bachmann, trans. (Philadelphia: Fortress Press, 1983) 1–68.

28 WA 8:601,18–24. SC 20; SBOp 1:14,14–19; see WA 8: 528f; see Bell,
Divus Bernhardus, 199, 208.

29 WA 14:425,6.

one train of thought. Already in *On Monastic Vows* Luther had
indicated that he worked from two different sources. Here he did
so again. First, Luther quoted the phrase *quia perdite vixi* (SC 20),
and then he repeated that 'elsewhere' (*alibi*) Bernard was talking
about Christ and his double right to heaven.[30] The 'elsewhere', the
locus where he may have read Bernard's story, could well have
been *The Golden Legend*. This admittedly apocryphal utterance
had an impact on Luther, who quoted it throughout his life.[31]
His theological genius spotted this simultaneously simple and
complex concept, and once he had internalized it he very often
quoted it. When Erasmus took up his pen against Luther on the
issue of free will in September 1524, Luther in his counter-attack
used the one bernardine thought, the line from SC 20. Bernard's
learned contribution on this subject, *On Grace and Free Choice*,
he apparently neglected.

In 1527, when Luther gave his course on the First Epistle of
John, he referred again to Bernard's self-deprecation and Christ's
double right to the kingdom of heaven. Luther felt compelled to
speak out against those fathers of the Church, such as Gregory
and Bernard, who had established monasteries. Nevertheless, he
continued with an eulogy of the cistercian abbot and his declaration
about his wasted life: ' . . . There is no better phrase in all of
Bernard, another one is in the sermon about the Annunciation'.
Apparently bernardine self-deprecation and the passage in the First
Annunciation Sermon (which was treated above) were of equal
significance to Luther. When the Reformer preached on the Feast
of John the Baptist in 1529, he again referred to the familiar line
about the lost life and declared that the saint was 'an excellent
man' who was strict about his religious Order. When ill, however,
he had admitted his lost cause. At this point in the sermon text, the
latin and the german version are given: *Perdite vixi", habs übel
zugebracht.* Saint Bernard had realized, Luther elaborated, that
his life had become a 'hull' (*hulssen*) without substance. Luther
carried on with this thought, declaring that this was so 'with all the
teachings' which are based on human wisdom and do not have the

30 WA 24: 550,6–8 (latin); line 22 (german); see WA 24: 551,1–3.
31 See Posset, 'St Bernard's Influence on Two Reformers', 182–187.

Spirit or any power. In a sermon of November 1531, Luther again
spoke of Bernard's self-deprecation; and yet again in 1533, when
he realized that Jean Gerson had also made use of this bernardine
phrase. Gerson, however, did not combine the 'lost life' phrase
with the concept of the double right to heaven in the way Luther
usually did, and to pursue Gerson as Luther's source in this regard
therefore seems pointless.[32]

In 1537 Luther had the honor of speaking to an assembly of
Reformation theologians at Schmalkald. His sermon contained a
lengthy passage with Bernard's concept of Christ's double right in
combination with the phrase from SC 20:

> In such horrible error and darkness, our dear Lord nevertheless
> has miraculously preserved many people in the right faith, yes
> to some of them he revealed it on their deathbed, as one reads
> about Saint Bernard who with his writings has given much cause
> to the effect that one has elevated the virgin Mary so highly
> in Christendom, and that one ascribed to her what otherwise
> is Christ's alone. The same Bernard had high regards of the
> monastic life; he was so chaste, pure, disciplined and moderate,
> and he so strongly mortified his body with extra fasting that as it
> is written finally his breath stank so badly that one could not stay
> close to him. If ever there was a righteous monk, it was he. But
> then, when he was about to die, he did not only forget about his
> good works and holy life, since he saw very well that he would
> be unable to subsist with them before God, but raised his voice:
> 'I have lived an evil life; but I find consolation in this: my Lord
> Christ possesses the kingdom of heaven through a double right,
> first as a natural heir and Son of God, which therefore I do not
> claim. The other right he has through his own merit of innocent
> suffering and death; this right I claim because he did not die for
> himself but for me and for all sinners.' Yes, dear Bernard, if you
> had died in your cowl without this confidence in the Lord Christ,

32 WA 18:644, 8f; LW 33:77; see WA 20:624,3 (lecture notes); see LW
30:230; WA 48:319,25 (scholium). Furthermore: WA 20:672,11–12; WA 20:746,
13–18; WA 29:427,17–20; WA 34-II:441,10–14 (November 26, 1531); *wie es
auch Gerson an zeucht,* WA 38:154,10 (1533); see Gerson, *Oeuvres complètes,*
P. Glorieux, ed. (Paris etc: 1962) 5:393; see Bell, *Divus Bernhardus,* 131f, who
at this point featured only Bernard's phrase *perdite vixi,* but not his concept of
the 'double right to heaven' which normally for Luther was connected with it.

you would have gone straight to hell. But God through the Holy Spirit taught you at that hour to say that Christ has died for you and by his death has earned heaven for you.[33]

This, the central passage of the sermon, demonstrates how important Bernard's model was to Luther and the Reformers. Luther was fully aware of his redundancy in repeating this bernardine idea. In 1538 he declared: 'I often use the example of Saint Bernard'.[34] It remained one of his favorite references in his entire Bernard repertoire. On one occasion the Wittenberg preacher combined this favorite reference with another unidentifiable legendary source. When he delivered his sermon on the Third Sunday of Advent (on Mt 24, between 1537 and 1540) he said:

> And now I must tell you a story which I read about Saint Bernard. But I do not know whether it is true . . . But it is a fine story and doubtlessly written by a fine man, namely that when Bernard was about to die, somebody received the revelation that at the same hour many thousands of people also died, but from among all of them only Bernard and one common layman entered heaven and were saved . . . [35]

Time and again, Luther utilized the bernardine concept of the sinners' right to heaven earned by Christ. We find it in his lecture on Gal 4:31 of 1531;[36] in a table talk of 1531,[37] and again in 1532 in his published german sermons on the Sermon on the Mount.[38] In 1533, in his response to Duke George he brought up it up,[39] and again in

33 WA 45:45,23–46,8 (on Mt 4:11, February 18, 1537).

34 *Wie ich den offt das Exempel von S. Bernhardo pflege zu gebrauchen. Der hielt auch darfur, das der Bapst Gott were.* . . . *Erblich und keufflich durch sein blut vergissen,* WA 47:585,19–20.

35 See WA 47:598,23–34; see WA 46:79,15–20; 86,34–39 (on Jn); WA 22:228,7–20 (Cruciger's Summer Postil).

36 WA 40-I:687,6f; LW 26:5; see WA 45:265,8.

37 WA TR 1:45,26f (no. 118, 1531).

38 WA WA 32:534,20–38; LW 21:283.

39 *Kleine Antwort auf Herzog Georgen nächstes Buch,* WA 38:154,7–36. In LW 12:335 with note 11, the editor claimed that Luther quoted Bernard's phrase, 'I have lived shamefully', also in his lecture on Ps 51:3; however, the critical edition, WA 40-II:341 (1532/1538), does not show any reference at all to Bernard, nor does WA include any phrase which would sound similar to the one in question.

1537.[40] We find it in the german printed version of his exposition of the first two chapters of John's Gospel, emphasizing that Christ did it *für mich*, 'for me'.[41] On 18 November 1537, Luther concluded his sermon with the same reference macaronically preserved in Latin-German.[42]

5. Luther: 'These are golden words'

Luther called Bernard's phrase from SC 20 and the concept of the double right 'golden words'. Religious tradition refers to a text written 'with golden letters' to signify a precious word or phrase. In the medieval tradition of text interpretation some words were written with 'bad' and some with 'golden' letters.[43] The mystical vision of a medieval nun of Kirchberg was described as a theophany, with the biblical text [*Qui vult venire post me, abneget semetipsum*] written in gold.[44] Bernardino of Siena, at the end of a moving sermon, lit two candles and showed the audience a board bearing the name 'Jesus' in golden letters on an azure ground, surrounded by the sun's rays.[45] The lore surrounding Bernard includes a legend according to which certain messages were inscribed in gold.[46]

Into this medieval tradition we may place Luther's statements about certain texts which he wanted to see written with 'golden letters' (*guldene wort*). Among such texts in Luther's view one

40 WA 46:580,24–32; LW 22:52. LW gives the impression that the entire text, as quoted here, was a direct citation from Bernard's SC 20, while actually only the part *quia perdite vixi* is found in that sermon.

41 WA 46:784,1–16; see Posset, 'St Bernard's Influence on Two Reformers', 185, where the original was quoted in full in note 40, and where further utilizations of the story were given.

42 See WA 45:265,7–13.

43 As Friedrich Ohly pointed out in his 'Vom geistigen Sinn des Wortes im Mittelalter', *Zeitschrift für deutsches Altertum und deutsche Literatur* 89 (1958–59) 6f.

44 F. W. E. Roth, 'Das mystische Leben der Nonnen von Kirchberg bei Sulz', *Alemannia: Zeitschrift für Sprache, Kunst und Altertum* 21 (1893) 131.

45 See J. Huizinga, *The Waning of the Middle Ages* (Garden City: Doubleday, 1954) 200.

46 See *Vita Bern*, Book 7.5; Cawley 2:82.

was the Bernard legend which mentions the double right to heaven (*zweierlei recht*) and Bernard's self-judgment about his wasted life. Luther interpreted this as departure from reliance on monastic life and the substitution of reliance on Christ alone. Luther explained on John 3 (1538–1540): 'He [Bernard] fell away from the monks' order, cowl and rules and unto Christ . . . Therefore Bernard was saved. These are golden words which one must very well keep in our Christendom, because they alone make a person a Christian'.[47]

To my knowledge this is the only non-biblical text Luther ever considered worthy of being written with 'golden letters'. The importance of this bernardine text can be best appreciated if one compares it with the Scripture verses Luther wanted to see written in gold:

(1) Rom 8:15: the cry 'Abba' is such a 'noble and comforting text, worthy of being written in letters of gold'.[48]

(2) 1 Jn 5:4: being 'born of God' is a 'text to be written with golden letters'.[49]

(3) On Jn 3:16–21, 'God so loved the world that he gave his only Son', Luther exclaimed: 'This is one of the most glorious Gospel lessons to be found in the entire New Testament, so that it is worthy to be written, if that were possible, with golden letters upon the heart. And every Christian should know at least this [one] text by heart and recite it daily to his heart.'[50]

(4) The Gospel (in general) 'is to be written with golden letters upon the heart'.[51]

(5) Psalm 118 (119) is the 'Golden Psalm'.[52]

It may be hard to believe, but it is nevertheless true, that Luther ascribed equal value to Bernard's saying. Apparently this legend, with its highly theological, christocentric content at least in the way Luther viewed it, to his mind qualified as gospel truth. The

47 WA 47:85,12–26.
48 WA 22:136,21f (Eighth Sunday after Trinity, Summer Postil).
49 WA 20: 773,28–774,4.
50 WA 52:326,3–5 (on Jn 3, House Postil, 1544).
51 WA 21:479,26 (1544).
52 Luther's text of 1522; see Hagen, *Luther's Approach to Scripture*, 118.

cistercian father with his christocentric focus—as Luther perceived it—had a lasting impact on the career of the Reformer. Bernard's authentic words from his sermons and the legendary words spoken from his sick-bed were of equal value to Luther because they expressed insights which he found laudable and worthy of being handed on. Our modern sensibilities would probably take a more critical attitude towards quotations from hear-say and legends, but Luther liked what was handed down to him and readily passed it on to his audience.

However, Luther probably did not correctly interpret Bernard's phrase 'I wasted my life'. Most likely Bernard meant, not that his monastic way of life had been a waste, but that, because of many worldly distractions, he had not been able to lead a fuller contemplative life, as a real monk should do. Bernard deplored his life style because it was not spent in contemplation leading toward the union with God. Luther, for his reform-minded, pastoral, and homiletic purposes, always productively misunderstood Bernard's phrase and therefore drew down upon himself the wrath of a scholar of the caliber of Heinrich Denifle at the beginning of the twentieth century.[53]

Besides that, Luther was not consistent in his use of bernardine thoughts on the Last Judgment and Christ as Judge. While in his thirtieth sermon on Jn 3 and 4 of 1538 he had praised Bernard's words on the double right to heaven as 'golden', he accused Bernard in his thirty-second sermon of that same 1538 series of having 'erred horribly' in presenting Christ as the angry Judge and 'hangman' (*Hencker*) and the Virgin in contrast as 'always friendly' and as 'pure sweetness and love'. In that sermon Luther seems to have forgotten that earlier in his career he had relied on Bernard's concept of the salvific self-accusation. He now spoke of it without giving Bernard credit for the insight, and instead referred

53 Heinrich Denifle, *Luther and Lutherdom: From Original Sources*. Translated from the Second Revised Edition of the German [1904] by Raymund Volz (Torch Press, 1917) 1:43–61. Denifle charged Luther with having distorted Bernard's saying about the monastic vows, and pointed out with some right that the passage simply proves to be the humble confession of a contrite heart. If Denifle actually thought that Luther deliberately 'distorted' Bernard, one would have to question him on this, see Bell, *Divus Bernhardus*, 209f, 221–226.

for some reason to Rom 1 in interpreting Jn 3:17, 'God did not send the Son into the world to condemn the world, but that the world might be saved through him'.[54]

54 See WA 47:85,25 (thirtieth sermon, 1538). WA 47:99,24–100,6 (thirty-second sermon, 1538): . . . *Solch Gerichte ist schon durch Gesetz Mosi, unser Gewissen und hertz angezeiget, wie Rom 1. gesaget wird, das unser eigen gewissen uns anklage und verdamme, und also keines Richters mehr von nothen sei. . . . Ich hielt Christum fur einen Richter. Irreten also greuliche. S. Bernhard, der sonst ein from man gewesen ist, saget auch also: Sihe im gantzen Euangelio, wie greulich offt Christus schieltt, strafft und verdammet die Phariseer und geschwinde mit ihnen fehret, dargegen die Jungkfrau Maria imerdar freundlich und sanfftmuttig ist und hatt nie kein hard wortt geredet, und dohehr dan die gedancken geschopfft: Christus schielt, strafft, aber bej Maria, do ist eittel sussigkeit und liebe . . . Christus war allein der Hencker, die Heiligen aber waren unsere Mitteler.*

Plate 21: *Bernard's Vision of Mary and the Christ Child*, combined with Bernard's fight with a demon. Enlarged detail of an illustration in an *Antiphonale Cisterciense*, originally from the cistercian monastery of Altenberg, 1547. Universitätsbibliothek. Düsseldorf, Germany. The illuminated page marks the Feast Day of Saint Bernard of Clairvaux, August 20. The initial 'P' in the upper left-hand corner of the page is filled out with the image of Saint Bernard with opened book and staff, clothed in a white habit. Bernard is positioned between the heavenly and the sub-terrestrial realms. A demon at his feet grabs the end of his staff; he looks up to the Virgin Mary with the Christ Child. She has her right breast exposed. The strawberries to the left of the letter 'P' are a symbol of Mary and her sweetness.

Plate 22: Further enlargement of the *letter 'P'* (previous plate). One may perhaps decipher the letters in Bernard's book to mean *Monstra te esse matrem* ('Show yourself to be a mother')

Bernard's cross centered spirituality and his love of the mystery of the incarnation naturally lead us to his marian piety. To his mind, honoring the Son does not detract from honor to his mother or vice versa. In this section, we will deal not with Bernard's and Luther's mariology, but primarily with the issue of intercession, taken for granted by Bernard, strongly debated by Luther. In treating this issue, we are forced to take a closer look at the iconography of Bernard and Mary, because Luther referred to it, and to distinguish among the motifs of *Maria lactans, Lactatio Bernardi*, and the *Intercessio* (*Tribunal of Mercy*) all of which show Mary with a bare breast (to say nothing of the mixture of motifs seen in Plate 20). First we deal briefly with bernardine and other cistercian texts, before we investigate Luther's opinions in this regard.

1. *Bernard and the Cistercians*

In his Second Sermon on the Canticle (SC 2) Bernard welcomes as mediator the Son of God who became our brother in the incarnation. In his famous Aqueduct Sermon for the Feast of Mary's Birth, Bernard reflects expressly on the relationship between Christ and Mary, the 'sweetness of her milk' and her intercession. Bernard assures readers that the Son will listen to his Mother, and the Father will listen to his Son; it is, nevertheless, by grace alone that we are saved, because Jesus is our mediator. Bernard kept intact the theological priority of Christ and belief in salvation by his grace alone:

> You have enjoyed the sweetness of the milk: perhaps if we labor the subject a little more we shall succeed in extracting therefrom the fat of the butter. . . . He [the Father] gave you Jesus as your Mediator. What shall not such a Son be able to obtain for you from such a Father? Doubtless he shall be heard. . . . Surely you are not afraid of approaching him also? He is your brother and your flesh . . . Him Mary has given you for your brother. But perhaps you stand in awe of the divine majesty of Jesus? For although he has become human he has not ceased to be God.

Perhaps you desire to have an advocate even with him? If so, have recourse to Mary. I do not deem it doubtful that she likewise shall be heard for her reverence. Assuredly the Son will listen to the Mother and the Father will listen to the Son. My little children, behold the sinners' ladder, behold the main source of my confidence, the principal reason for my hope. What? Can the Son refuse respect to his own mother or be refused respect by his Father?. . . . Dearest brethren, Mary shall always find grace with God, and grace alone is what we have need of. . . . For it is by grace alone that we shall be saved.[1]

This intercession motif is repeated in his Second Advent Sermon:

Through you, O blessed Lady, we have access to the Son, for you are the one who has found grace, the one who has given birth to life, the one who is the mother of salvation. . . . You are our Lady, our mediatrix, our advocate. Reconcile us with and recommend us to your Son. Be our representative with him.[2]

In his First Sermon on the Octave of the Assumption, Bernard wrote that although the glorified Christ may appear an austere and distant judge, he is merciful:

The human Christ Jesus is the faithful and efficacious mediator between God and human beings (1 Tim 2:5), but people are afraid of the divine majesty in him. . . . Not only is his mercy chanted, but also his judgment (Ps 100:1). The fact is that though he learned compassion through what he suffered (Heb 5:8) so that he might become merciful, nevertheless he retains his judicial

1 Nat BVM 4; SBOp 5:278,23–279,27; see Norbert Mussbacher, 'Die Marienverehrung der Cistercienser'. *Die Cistercienser. Geschichte, Geist, Kunst.* Ambrosius Schneider, ed. (Cologne: Wienand, 1986) 151–77; Michael Casey, 'Bernard of Clairvaux and the Assumption'. *Word and Spirit* 12 (1990) 21–42, here 26; Emmanuele Iablczynski, 'Maria nella gloria. Assunzione e mediazione di grazia in san Bernardo'. *Respice Stellam. Maria in san Bernardo e nella tradizione cistercense.* Atti del Convegno Internazionale (Roma, Marianum 21–24 ottobre 1991), Ignazio M. Calabuig, ed. (Rome: Edizioni 'Marianum', 1993) 143–177.
2 Adv 2.5; SBOp 4:174,10–22. The passage Adv 2.5 was used as a prayer text in the *Liber precum* (appr. 1425) from the lower Rhine valley, see Ochsenbein, 'Bernhard von Clairvaux in spätmittelalterlichen Gebetsbüchern'. *Bernhard von Clairvaux*, Elm, ed., 221.

power. Remember that our God is a consuming fire (Heb 12:29). A sinner may well fear to approach. . . . [3]

Bernard tried to counteract a contemporary perception of a judgmental Christ, and with Michael Casey we may state that Bernard preached for 'pastoral purposes'[4] here: If you are afraid to approach Christ, feel free to approach his mother. If you are afraid of him as the judge, take his mother as your advocate. If you are afraid of the king, go to the queen of heaven:

> Our queen has gone ahead of us. She has gone ahead of us and is gloriously welcomed so that we, her serving men, may faithfully follow the Lady, crying out, 'Draw us and we will run in the fragrance of your ointments' (Sg 1:3). Our advocate has gone in advance of our pilgrimage. Because she is the mother of the Judge and the mother of mercy, she will be able to negotiate successfully in the business of petitioning our salvation.[5]

Clearly these marian titles are derivatives of Bernard's christology. Christ means mercy; his mother is the 'mother of mercy'. Christ means salvation; Mary is the 'mother of salvation'. Christ means all graces; she is 'mother of all graces'.

For our purposes here, we have to look not only at the genuine bernardine texts, but also at a pseudo-bernardine but cistercian text about Christ and Mary, a text which may have been in Luther's mind when he began to distance himself from belief in the intercession of Mary and the saints. The text is found in the book on the praises of Mary by Bernard's contemporary, the cistercian abbot Ernald of Bonneval (= Arnold of Chartres, †1156). Writing about the 'exchange' (*commercium*) between heaven and earth at the incarnation of the Son of God, Ernald connected it to the idea of intercession:

> In the exchange of this blessedness are united human and divine matters, earthly and heavenly matters. A person has safe access

3 O Asspt 1; SBOp 5:262f; see Bell, *Divus Bernhardus*, 316–318.

4 Casey, 'Bernard of Clairvaux and the Assumption', 26.

5 Asspt 1.1; SBOp 5:229,12–16; see Jean Leclercq, ' "Marie Reine" dans les sermons de Saint Bernard'. *Recueil d'Études sur Saint Bernard et ses Écrits* (Rome: Editioni di Storia e Letteratura, 1992) 5:125–36.

to God where the Son is mediator of his cause before the Father, and the mother before the Son. Christ with exposed side shows the Father his side and wounds; Mary [shows] Christ her bosom and breasts.[6]

This passage connects the patristic and liturgical notion *commercium* with that of Christ as the 'Merchant'[7] who brings the great gift of salvation and thus redeems sinners with his own blood. This christological image serves Ernald as the basis on which to establish the concept of Mary's intercession; humans gain access to God by having recourse first to Mary. Mary reminds Christ of her motherhood by displaying her breast, while Christ points to his side wound as a reminder to God the Father that he suffered and died for the salvation of the sinners, and that the Father should therefore mitigate his judgment of the sinners.

This cistercian spirituality, expressed here in Ernald's words, found its way into Jacobus de Voragine's *Golden Legend*. There

---

6 PL 189:1726–34, here 1726. The oldest german version of Ernald's text appeared between 1270 and 1290 in the book *Geistlicher Herzen Baungart*, where we find the embellishment that Mary showed 'her heart and breast' to her son; see Ochsenbein, 'Bernhard von Clairvaux in spätmittelalterlichen Gebetsbüchern'. *Bernhard von Clairvaux*, Elm, ed., 222 (with additional examples of the use of this sermon text in the vernacular around 1300); see *Speculum humanae salvationis*, Jules Lutz and Paul Perdrizet, eds. (Mühlhausen/Leipzig, 1907) 293–298; see Leopold Kretzenbacher, 'Schutz- und Bittgebärden der Gottesmutter: Zu Vorbedingungen, Auftreten und Nachleben mittelalterlicher Fürbitte-Gesten zwischen Hochkunst, Legende und Volksglauben'. *Bayerische Akademie der Wissenschaften. Philosophisch-Historische Klasse, Sitzungsberichte Heft 3* (1981) 1–112, here 67. Susan Marti and Daniela Mondini, ' "Ich manen dich der brüsten min, das du dem sünder wellest milte sin!" Marienbrüste und Marienmilch im Heilsgeschehen', Jezler, *Himmel Hölle Fegefeuer*, 80. The text referred to at the beginning of this note was attributed to Bernard by the artist, who provided the caption for the painting of 1503 for the cloister at Rüti, Switzerland; see Jezler, *Himmel Hölle Fegefeuer*, 198, illus. 21. On the iconographic motif 'breast', see Hans Biedermann, *Dictionary of Symbolism: Cultural Icons and the Meaning Behind Them,* trans. James Hulber (New York: Meridian, 1994) 49; G. Brandmann, entry 'Brust, Brüste', *Lexikon der christlichen Ikonographie* (Rome, Freiburg, Basel, Vienna: Herder, 1973) 1:336f; Diane Apostolos-Cappadona, *Dictionary of Christian Art* (New York: Continuum, 1994) 66f. Margret Miles, 'The Virgin's One Bare Breast: Female Nudity and Religious Meaning in Tuscan Early Renaissance Culture'. *The Female Body in Western Culture, Contemporary Perspectives,* Susan Rubin Suleiman, ed. (Cambridge, Mass.: Harvard University Press, 1986) 193–208.

7 Augustine: 'The Son of God came as a merchant, bringing a great gift, but only finding birth and death . . .', as quoted in James A. Mohler, *A Speechless Child is the Word of God* (New Rochelle, NY: New City Press, 1992) 43.

Christ and Mary appear as intercessors in the lesson for the Feast of the Ascension. The legend mistakenly attributes to Bernard (not Ernald) the belief that Mary shows her breast to her Son, who in turn shows his wounds to the heavenly Father. As Jacobus introduced this concept, he included this quotation from Pseudo-Bernard (Ernald):

> Christ ascended in order to be our advocate with the Father. We can be secure indeed when we realize that we have such an advocate to plead our cause; 1 John 2:1: 'We have an advocate with the Father, Jesus Christ the just; and he is the propitiation for our sins'. About this security Bernard says: 'O man, you have sure access to God, when the mother stands before the Son and the Son stands before the Father, the mother shows her Son her bosom and her breasts, the Son shows his Father his side and his wounds. Surely then, where there are so many marks of love, there can be no refusal.[8]

Thus Bernard was improperly credited with the image of the intercessory Mary baring one of her breasts. Yet it remains impressive that this lesson in *The Golden Legend* was introduced with the clear understanding that, after the Ascension, our 'advocate' is Christ.

Cistercian spirituality may have influenced—directly or indirectly through *The Golden Legend*—texts from the end of the thirteenth or early fourteenth century in which marian intercession is conspicuous. Editions of *The Mirror of Human Salvation* (*Speculum humanae salvationis*), a manual for preachers widely used in the late Middle Ages, contain the oldest illustrations of this. Manuscripts exist in the original Latin and in translations into Czech, Dutch, English, French, and German. The *Speculum* contains the following lines: 'Christ showed the Father his wounds

---

8 *Legenda Aurea*, 326; *The Golden Legend,* 293; Ryan 1:297f; see Posset, 'The Elder Luther on Bernard: Part I', 48–50. In this article I stated in a too abbreviated way that the motif of Mary exposing her breast was found first in *The Golden Legend.* This observation needs to be qualified to the effect that it was widely *popularized* first by *The Golden Legend.* Bernard in his Ep 322 spoke in general terms of a mother (not Mary) baring her breast, as he quoted Jerome; see Pennington, *Bernard of Clairvaux,* 30; see Jerome's Letter 14 (PL 22:348f; *The Letters of St. Jerome,* trans. Charles Christopher Mierow [New York: Newman Press, 1963] 60).

[which he suffered] for us. And Mary showed the Son her bosom and breasts.' In the text immediately accompanying the illustrations, Christ says to the Father: 'Take note of the wounds; Father, do what my mother asks.'[9]

Besides the *Maria lactans* and *Lactatio Bernardi* motifs which involve the *infant* Jesus, Christian art also depicts Mary with one bare breast in conjunction with her *adult* Son. When she is shown with the adult Christ, she is presented as interceding for sinners, or in negotiation directly with the heavenly Father, as happens in some early sixteenth-century depictions. This composition, called the *Tribunal of Mercy* or *Intercessio* by Mary and Christ before the Father, places Mother and Son visibly before a sometimes angry-looking God the Father, the heavenly Judge. This depiction enhanced the mariological concept of the Virgin as the motherly 'advocate' of sinners in the heavenly court. This type of marian devotion was also expressed in hymnic form in the famous *Salve Regina* of the eleventh century, which salutes Mary as the 'mother of mercy, life, sweetness, and hope', and invokes her as 'our advocate'.

This spirituality found expression in a painting in the style of Konrad Witz from *c.* 1450,[10] and again in woodcuts, one of which was used for a 1495 german translation of Jean Gerson's book

9 *Speculum*, ed. Lutz and Perdrizet, 80f; see Erwin Panofsky, ' "Imago Pietatis". Ein Beitrag zur Typengeschichte des "Schmerzensmanns" und der "Maria Mediatrix" '. *Festschrift für Max J. Friedländer zum 60. Geburtstage* (Leipzig: Verlag von E. A. Seemann, 1927) 261–308, here 281 with illus. 27 (fourteenth century) and illus. 30 (1418). Adrian Wilson and Joyce Lancaster Wilson, *A Medieval Mirror: Speculum humanae salvationis 1324–1500* (Berkeley, Los Angeles, London: The University of California Press, 1984); Wolfgang Augustyn, 'Passio Christi est meditanda tibi. Zwei Bildzeugnisse spätmittelalterlicher Passionsbetrachtung'. *Die Passion Christi in Literatur und Kunst des Spätmittelalters,* Walter Haug and Burghart Wachinger, eds. (Tübingen: Max Niemeyer Verlag, 1993) 235.

10 See Gertrud Schiller, *Iconography of Christian Art. Vol. 2: The Passion of Jesus Christ,* Janet Seligman, trans. (Greenwich, Connecticut: New York Graphic Society Ltd., 1972) illus. 798; see Caroline Walker Bynum, *Fragmentation and Redemption: Essays on Gender and the Human Body in Medieval Religion* (New York: Zone Books, 1991) 113, illus. 3.13; in contrast to Bynum, who interprets this painting as 'double intercession', I tend to take it as a sequential intercession from Mary through the Son to the Father. Later artists who took up this composition added banderoles with texts which clearly indicate that Mary asks the Son who in turn asks the Father. The so-called 'double intercession' would by definition require the concept of both as co-equal intercessors.

of sermons, which Luther may have known.[11] Another is found
in a single-leaf print of 1500 in which the banderoles connected
to each figure can be deciphered and translated as follows: Mary
says to Christ: 'Child, because of these breasts have mercy on
sinners'. Christ says to the Judge: 'Father, see my wounds, and
grant what she who gave birth to me asks for'. The Father says
to the Son: 'O Child, we cannot deny anything to you and your
mother'.[12] Clearly the sequential chain of intercession is preserved
here, as is also the case in a triptych made for Antonius Tsgrooten
of Tongerloo in 1507 by Goswyn van der Weyden[13] (a depiction
with which Luther very likely was not familiar): Bernard, holding
his staff, is placed behind the Virgin and so incapable of being
fed from Mary's breast; thus, it is not a *lactatio Bernardi*, as in

11 See Hans Düfel, *Luther's Stellung zur Marienverehrung* (Göttingen:
Vandenhoeck & Ruprecht, 1968) illus. 2 (Gerson's sermons), where the space
for Mary's line is provided, but nothing is written into it.

12 The single-leaf woodcut of 1500 is reproduced in Jezler, *Himmel Hölle
Fegefeuer*, 201, no. 23.

13 See Bynum, *Fragmentation and Redemption,* 115, ill. 3.14; 106. In her
concentration on the parallelism of Mary's milk and Christ's blood, Bynum sees a
parallel where there is actually an intercessory sequence in the traditional sense of
the cistercian spirituality. Bynum also read into this motif 'an association of two
sacrifices: Christ's bleeding and dying for us on the cross, Mary's suffering for
her baby and therefore for all sinners'. Bynum would like us to believe that there
is a parallel not merely between 'two sacrifices' but also 'between two feedings'.
Her interpretation of this motif is questionable because she worked here with the
mistaken concept of a 'double intercession', whereas there is actually a sequence
of intercessions from Mary to Christ to the Father; she also worked with the
untenable thesis of a marian sacrifice which supposedly is depicted there. I see
only Christ's bloody sacrifice depicted here. Mary's bare breast is meant here
as a symbol not of sacrifice, but of motherly care. The primary intent of Mary's
gesture is to remind her Son of the mother who cared for him as a baby. Thus,
Bynum's interpretation of the c. 1450 picture in the style of Konrad Witz (her
ill. 3.13) and the 1507 picture of Goswyn van der Weyden (her ill. 3.14) does
not do justice to these two pictures in classifying them as 'double intercessions',
along with the 1508 painting by Holbein, which indeed is a 'double intercession'.
Even in Holbein's 'double intercession', there is no trace of Mary's sacrifice, but
only a hint that the Son of God sucked on her breast, as Mary's banderole clearly
says in her address to the Father: ' . . . and see my breast the Son has sucked'. I
also doubt whether it is helpful and legitimate to interpret paintings of 1450 and
1507 in the light of a later painting, i. e. Holbein's 'double intercession' of 1508.
I prefer to interpret the last as a daring departure from the older concept of the
hierarchical spirituality which began the intercession process with Mary through
the Son to the heavenly Father. As to the phenomenon of vernacular inscriptions,
we observe them also, for example, in the earlier fresco in Graz (1485), and in
the 1506 painting of the Lower Rhine Master.

a true *lactatio Bernardi* drops or a stream of milk issuing from
Mary's breast on Bernard's lips or face are required. Bernard is
inserted into the scene because at the time he was associated with
the promotion of the cult of Mary and credited as the 'inventor' of
the path of intercession. This path begins with Mary, who reminds
her adult Son (placed in the center) that it was she who nurtured
him. Clearly the primary purpose of Mary's gesticulation with her
breast is as a reminder of her motherly care; in this context the
breast is meant only secondarily a symbol of lactation. The viewer
of the triptych is led from Bernard (on the far right) to Mary, and
from her to Christ who is depicted in his suffering for sinners.
All the instruments of the crucifixion and the 'way of the cross'
are assembled in the background around Christ as the Lord who
points with his right hand to the wound in his side, and with his head
slightly turned towards his Father. Christ is expected to carry the
sinner's plea for mercy to the Judge who is shown on the left wing
of the triptych. While it is correct to say (with Bynum) that Mary's
display of her bare breast is not 'a symbol of pity' alone, it would be
incorrect to deny that here the artist wanted to depict the classical
intercession sequence (which Bynum appears to neglect). Artists
on other occasions detailed this scene still further by including
banderoles to indicate that Mary speaks to the Son, and the Son
in turn speaks to the Father on behalf of the sinner. Mary's bare
breast is shown primarily in support of her advocacy, and not so
much as a general 'symbol of food'.

For our purposes, let us concentrate on an early sixteenth-
century version of this motif by Hans Holbein the Elder, as there is a
good chance that Luther actually saw it (Plate 23). Holbein painted
at Augsburg where, I suspect, the motif of double intercession
(as distinguished from the sequential intercession) had its origin.
By double intercession, we mean positioning Christ and Mary
on an equal level. Holbein painted Mary in the ordinary dress of
any Augsburg citizen's wife, similar to the women below her for
whom she intercedes. She is showing her bare right breast to both
Father and Son. Being the *advocata*, however, she speaks to the
Father alone, who is shown slightly elevated in heaven. Holbein
audaciously shows Mary in a standing position and on the same

Plate 23: *Double Intercession before the Heavenly Father* (Votive picture for
Ulrich Schwarz), painting by Hans Holbein the Elder, 1508. Städtische Kunst-
sammlungen Augsburg, Germany.

level as Christ. She remains in her traditional position on the left
hand of the Father while Christ is on his right. The Father holds
a half sheathed sword, either in the act of drawing the sword or,
having been pacified already by Christ and Mary, of placing it
back after he had drawn it in his holy anger. The lower half of the
painting shows the donor and his relatives. The female relatives
are clustered under Mary's cloak, in the traditional pose of the
'Madonna with the protective cloak' (Mantle Madonna; Mother of
Mercy), a symbol of her protection. The men are grouped below
Christ, but not under a mantle. These human figures do not have
eye contact with either Mary or Christ. The inscriptions above
the heads of Father, Son, and Mary are no longer in Latin, but in
Early New High German. The inscriptions represent the heavenly
conversations between Mary and God the Father, as distinct from
the conversation between Son and Father on the other side. Since all
their words are in rhyme (which is lost in the english translation below), they allowed easy memorization by common people. A self-
confident and commanding Mary addresses the Father directly:
'Lord, sheathe the sword you plucked; behold the breast the Son
has sucked'. At the same level as Mary, Christ also speaks to the
Father, simultaneously pointing with the fingers of his right hand
to the wound in his side, and in doing so manifesting the wound
on his hand. The intention is to manifest primarily the symbols
of Christ's bloody suffering, and not so much his side wound as
a parallel to Mary's breast (as Bynum has it). Christ says to the
Father: 'Father, see my red wounds. Help the people in their need,
through my bitter death'. The Father responds: 'I will show mercy
on all those who depart from there [the earth] with true contrition'.
Gone is the traditional concept of a staircase that leads sinner(s)
first to Mary, who intercedes with the Son, who then convinces the
Father. Mary has attained the same powerful status as Christ. By
the early sixteenth century Mary had *direct* access to the Father.
She is now an intercessor in her own right, next to and equal to
Christ. Holbein and others obviously painted what they perceived
as people's convictions. This folk piety, considerably removed
from Bernard's own, genuine spirituality, became intolerable to
the reform-minded theologians such as Luther.

2. *Luther: Christ is the breasts and the lap*

The Reformers rejected any marian devotion which assigned divine power to the Mother of God as *advocata*. Depictions of Mary's daring gesture suggested that her adult Son was compelled by his mother to champion whatever she asks, and that she by-passes Christ altogether in directly addressing the Father. To the Reformers Christ may have appeared belittled. It is not surprising therefore, that this marian spirituality and the corresponding artistic depictions of Mary began to wane with the introduction and spread of a deliberately Christ-centered humanistic piety under Erasmus' leadership and the subsequent lutheran, and later calvinist, Reformation.

Several preliminary observations regarding Luther and his criticism of marian piety and the concept of marian intercession need to be made:

(1) As a young friar Luther was interested in religious art. When he was in Rome in 1510–11 on business for his Order, he visited the painting of the Madonna attributed to the Evangelist Luke, located in the Augustinians' church, S. Maria del Popole, next to the monastery where he stayed.[14]

(2) Luther may be influenced by Erasmus' efforts to reform popular piety, including the humanist's criticism of devotion to Mary's milk, as these are expressed in Erasmus' notorious *Colloquia*.[15]

(3) One of Luther's best known reformation axioms, 'whatever promotes Christ', simultaneously means a reduction in marian devotion: Mighty Mary, queen of heaven, becomes the meek maiden and mother. Even so, Luther had no problem concluding his explanation of the *Magnificat* in 1521 with the line, 'May Christ grant us this through the intercession and for the sake of his dear Mother Mary. Amen'.

(4) Luther assumed that Bernard had started the custom of showing Mary addressing Christ with her breast bare. His mistake

---

14 *Ego vidi quasdam imagines, quas Lucae etc*, WA 47:817,3–4; see WA 31–I:226.

15 On Erasmus' criticism in his Colloquy of Ogygius and Menedemus, see Patrick Arabeyre, 'La lactation de saint Bernard (Chatillon-sur-Seine): données et problèmes'. *Vies et légendes de saint Bernard de Clairvaux: Creation, diffusion, reeception (XIIe–XXe Siècles)* (Cîteaux: Commentarii Cistercienses, 1993) 173.

is excusable, as most of his contemporaries attributed it to Bernard, as we see, for example, in a picture of 1503 at Rüti, Switzerland; in the caption we find Bernard's name associated with the phrase about the hierarchical access to the Father via Mary and her Son.

(5) Luther seemes unaware that Bernard himself actually spoke of mystically drinking from Christ's breasts, not Mary's.

(6) Relatively late in his career, about eight years after going public with his reform efforts and three years after the iconoclastic riots at Wittenberg, Luther in November 1525 began to object to depictions of Mary's breast. At first, Luther did not mention Bernard by name in this context: 'People like to depict Him with Mary showing Him her breasts; this is preaching the devil and not Christ who alone is the one who gives; he does not take'.[16]

Luther wanted to preach on Christ alone. Any pictures that showed Mary on the same or almost the same level as Christ ran counter to his christocentric theological intention, and so he found them objectionable. Luther may have seen Holbein's 1508 oil painting during his sojourn at Augsburg in 1518, when he was interrogated by Cardinal Cajetan. The painting then hung in the church of Saint Ulrich and Saint Afra. Luther was critical of exaggerated marian advocacy, because he understood it to be in rivalry with Christ's, especially if she was shown having access to the Father directly without going through the Mediator.

In 1523, Luther wrote to the mayor of Regensburg that until the 'beautiful Mary' (the nickname of a marian shrine at Regensburg) does not turn ugly, the gospel cannot become beautiful.[17] Here, as again in 1527, when he lectured on the First Letter of John, Luther's perception of the assumed rivalry between Christ/gospel and Mary is visible. According the Vulgate terminology of 1 Jn 2:1, Christ is the *advocatus* of sinners. We need not send his mother to him, for he himself 'is the breasts and the lap', Luther declared. Christ himself is the immaculate, the paraclete, the mediator, the consoler.

16 WA 17-I:472,11–12 (sermon of November 19, 1525), reprinted in German in his *Summer Postil* of 1526, WA 10-I, 2:434,13–17; see Bell, *Divus Bernhardus*, 314.

17 *Das Euangeli nicht kan schon werden, die schone Maria werde denn hesßlich,* WA Br 3 (no. 652), as quoted by Bernd Moeller, 'Probleme des kirchlichen Lebens in Deutschland vor der Reformation'. *Die Reformation und das Mittelalter,* 93.

Luther strongly favored this johannine Christ and so he turned away from Mary the *advocata*. Not surprisingly then, in 1528 Luther commented, in writing on Jn 2:1–11, that in the past people 'have made the mother a mediatrix, and Christ a serious, strict judge, as paintings display how Mary shows her breasts to her child as she intercedes for us before Christ'.[18] Not until 1531, however, did Luther mention his beloved Bernard in this connection. From 1531 on, Luther was (mistakenly) convinced that the motif of Mary exposing her breast was based directly on 'Bernard's books'. And in this he also mixed another rejection, that of the ancient *deësis* concept, which by definition consists of Mary and John the Baptist (not the Evangelist) as intercessors before Christ (not the Father). When a John figure appears along with Mary in scenes of the Last Judgment, it is always John the Baptist and never John the Evangelist:

> As it is a shameful and blasphemous image or painting of the Last Judgment when one painted the Son falling down in front of the Father showing him his wounds; and Saint John [the Baptist] and Mary asking Christ for us on the Last Day; and that the mother shows her breasts to the Son who sucked on them. This is taken from Saint Bernard's books, and it is not spoken nor painted nor done well by Saint Bernard, and one should put away these depictions.[19]

18 *Qui ubera et schos* (Rörer's macaronic notes), WA 20:636,8; see Posset, *Luther's Catholic Christology*, 124. The 1528 text is found in WA 21:65,29–34. See also Luther's polemic against the image of Christ as Judge, WA 45:86,1 (1537), and his repeated objection to the portrayal of Christ as Judge, and Mary with her breast exposed: *Christus pictus ut Iudex, et Maria ubera. Ut erat pictum, ita cor affectum*, WA 37:420,30–32.

19 I use my own translation of the original which reads as follows: *wie dan dis auch ein schendtlich und lesterlich bildt oder gemelde ist von dem Jungsten tage, do man gemahlet hat, wie der Son fur dem vater niderfellet undt zeiget ihm seine wunden, undt S. Ioannes undt Maria bitten Christum fur uns am Jungsten gerichte, undt die mutter weiset dem Sohn ihre bruste, die ehr gesogen hat, Welches aus S. Bernhards buchern genommen ist undt ist nicht wohl geredet, gemahlet oder gemacht gewesen von S. Bernhardt, unndt man solte noch solche gemelde wegthuen*, WA 33:83,25–42 (1531); see LW 23:57; Bell, *Divus Bernhardus*, 315, note 150, is critical of the translation in LW. In his comments on the Sg (1530–1531) Luther again connected Bernard to the treatment of the breast theme, WA 31-II:597,10–12. On *deësis*, see *Dictionary of Christian Art*, 101; Christopher Walter, 'Two Notes on the Deesis', *Revue des Études byzantines* 26 (1968) 311–36; Franz Posset, 'Martin Luther on *Deësis*. His Rejection of the Artistic Representation of "Jesus, John, and Mary"', *Renaissance and Reformation* (1997) 57–76.

We do not know exactly what artistic depiction(s) Luther had in mind. Several images may have converged in his mind. He was wrong in tracing the motif of Mary exposing her breast to a bernardine text, yet he may be excused if he had in mind the *Libellus* of Ernald which circulated under Bernard's name; there is no proof, however, that Luther read Ernald. He may simply have followed Gabriel Biel, whom he had read earlier, in thinking that this was a bernardine motif.[20]

When Luther spoke of 'shameful and blasphemous' pictures of intercessors before the Judge on the Last Day, he may have had in mind the *deësis* composition at Erfurt's main church, where he was ordained to the priesthood: There Mary and John the Baptist flank the Trinity (Plate 24). Or it may have been a *Speculum* woodcut which he criticized.[21]

Plate 24: *Deësis*. Stone sculpture at the *Dom* of Erfurt, Germany. Fourteenth century.

20 Gabriel Biel, *De fest. Mariae 18*, as referred to by Bell, *Divus Bernhardus*, 315, note 151.

21 See Friedländer and Rosenberg, illus. 100. Wilson, *A Medieval Mirror*, 198. The *Speculum* woodcut shows Christ enthroned, with a sword to the right of

At about the time Luther first mentioned Bernard in connection with marian depictions, November 1531, one of his many Table Talks (no. 118) was recorded. In it Luther criticized the church fathers Jerome, Gregory, Augustine, Bernard and others for unspecified 'errors'. He immediately added, however, that they had not remained in their errors, especially not Bernard and Augustine, even though Bernard had written many things about Mary in a 'most impious' way in the sermons on 'The angel was sent' [*Missus est Angelus*, Lk 1:26] and in other places:

> [Bernard] nevertheless at the end of his life said: 'I wasted my life; Lord Jesus, you have the double right . . .'. The same is true of Augustine who at the end of his life prayed the seven psalms etc. While they were living, they did not pursue the proper doctrine, yet at the end of their lives they became [true] confessors.[22]

At about the same time, in 1532, the Reformer spoke rather favorably in another Table Talk about a depiction of the Virgin and Christ Child. While talking at table he apparently pointed to a painting on the wall of his dining room which showed Mary with the Child in her arms.[23] The painter is not identified. Luther

---

his mouth (a motif Luther mentioned in another context), lilies to his left, below him on the left is Mary with her hands folded, and on the right John the Baptist also with folded hands. The picture does not, however, fit Luther's wording, 'the mother shows her breasts to the Son who sucked on them'. Nor does it fit the Erfurt *deësis*, because Mary's breast is not shown there. These representations do not precisely match Luther's objection. Furthermore, the depictions show Christ enthroned, and thus do not correspond well with Luther's text, which says that Christ is 'falling down in front of the Father'. The Son on his knees is an element not of the *deësis*, but of the *Tribunal of Mercy* composition such as is found in Holbein's painting of 1508.

22 See WA TR 1:45,21–29 (no. 118, 1531); see WA TR 1:219,6f (no. 494, 1533). Luther's use of the singular ('sermon') in both these table talks for Bernard's *Homelium super Missus est in laudibus virginis matris* means that he had taken these four texts as one 'disputation'; see my remarks in this regard in the Introduction. The Table Talk no. 118 was used as the major source for establishing an argument that Luther was critical of Bernard (along with the later text in his *House Postil* of 1544). See Georg Söll, 'Maria in der Geschichte von Theologie und Frömmigkeit', *Handbuch der Marienkunde,* Wolfgang Beinert and Heinrich Petri, eds. (Regensburg: Friedrich Pustet, 1984) 92–231, here 169.

23 On the painting in Luther's dining room, see WA TR 2:207,22–24 (no. 1755, 1532); see Josef Lieball, *Martin Luthers Madonnenbild. Eine ikonographi-*

apparently approved of pictures of Mary and the Child that supported his theology of the incarnation by showing Mary as a mother and humble virgin. In general, Luther avoided two extremes: the traditional folk veneration of images which came close to idolatry; and radical iconoclasm on the other side. To Luther, pictures had value only insofar as they assisted in preaching and promoting Christ. In his Sermon for the Second Sunday of Advent in 1533 (on Lk 21), Luther stressed the priority of Christ, and complained again about Bernard and marian piety, disregarding the centrality Bernard gave to Christ:

> Christ as Redeemer was not talked about; instead he was painted like a judge with rod and sword, i. e. being angry, as he wanted to punish the world; then they painted John [the Baptist] and Mary; to them we ran. And Bernard says that the Mother shows her breasts to the Son. These are signs of what we believed: Christ is supposed to come as the Judge. But no, the text says, that he comes as the Saviour and that he wants to give what he is asked for: 'Thy Kingdom come'. He comes as a Judge to the impious whom he punishes as enemies of the pious.[24]

In this particular Advent sermon Luther contrasted Bernard and the Bible, mistakenly claiming that Bernard presented Christ more as

sche und mariologische Studie mit 53 Abbildungen (Stein am Rhein: Christiana Verlag, 1981) 14f; see Rosemarie Bergmann, 'A "tröstlich pictura": Luther's Attitude in the Question of Images', *Renaissance and Reformation* 5 (1981) 15–25, here 20; see Eric W. Gritsch, 'The Views of Luther and Lutheranism on the Veneration of Mary'. H. George Anderson, J. Francis Stafford, and Joseph A. Burgess, eds. *The One Mediator, the Saints, and Mary*: Lutheran and Catholics in Dialogue VIII (Minneapolis: Augsburg, 1992) 240. Luther was not opposed to crucifixes and simple pictures of Mary, see WA 18:80,6–14. Holy cards were also acceptable to him as *Merckbilde*, WA 28:677,37 (1529).

24 WA 37:207,34–208,5 (sermon on 7 December 1533). See Bell, *Divus Bernhardus*, 315; however, one may question Bell's opinion that Luther meant the Apostle John and Mary under the cross. Luther most likely meant John the Baptist as he and Mary appear as intercessors in the traditional *deësis* composition, a grouping which shows Christ in majesty with Mary and the Baptist flanking him; see entry 'deësis', *Dictionary of Christian Art*, 101. One of the editions of Johannes von Paltz, *Himlische Funtgrub* (Cologne: Hermann Bungart, 1512) has the *deësis* as an illustration at the end of the book; see print description in Johannes von Paltz, *Werke 3: Opuscula,* Christoph Burger et al., eds. (*Spätmittelalter und Reformation Texte und Untersuchungen*, ed. Heiko A. Oberman) vol. 4:183 (Berlin and New York: Walter de Gruyter, 1989).

Judge than as Redeemer, as someone who needs to be reminded of
his incarnation by his mother, while the biblical message, 'the text',
proclaims Christ as the sole Saviour. Here again Luther reflects the
late medieval emphasis on Christ coming in Judgment,[25] which is
usually found in art as a *deësis* composition, and which he saw
as a distortion of the biblical message. In Luther's reformation
teaching, Christ is the merciful God. The late medieval image
of God as an angry Judge had become so intolerable that some
form of mitigation and motherly intervention was called for. If it
is true that late medieval spirituality was dominated by fear of the
Last Judgment, then people had two choices: either go to Mary as
the *advocata* and ask her to try to pacify the Judge (as medieval
spirituality tended to do) or deemphasize the angry-Judge image
and emphasize the merciful nature of the divine judge (as the
Reformers saw him).

In the sermon of 5 June 1535, Luther again polemicized against
certain pictures, this time without mentioning Bernard by name:
'We were afraid of the man; [we] called upon Our Dear Lady
and reminded her of her breasts which she gave to Christ; she
was supposed to ask her Son that he may have mercy on us
because of her intercession'.[26] In 1537 Luther again criticized
marian intercession, calling it 'dangerous', all the while assuming
that it was Bernard's idea: '[Here is] Bernard's dangerous word:
"The Son shows his wounds to the Father, and the mother her
breasts to the Son"'.[27] In his late lecture on Gen 3:13, Luther spoke
again about sequential intercession, repeating that 'the Mother
Mary shows her breasts to the Son, the Son his wounds to his
Father', and that by her intercession people thought to obtain
salvation.[28] At about the same time (1537/38) Luther also repeated
his criticism of certain artistic works. Which depiction(s) Luther
had in mind can be debated: 'And someone has painted Saint
Bernard in this way, that he adores the Virgin, who shows her
breasts to her Son, Christ, who [had] sucked on them. Oh, how did

25 See R. Schwarz, 'Die spätmittelalterliche Vorstellung vom richtenden
Christus', 149–164.

26 WA 41:198,6–9 (sermon on 5 June 1535); printed version: WA 41:198,
33–35.

27 WA 49:713,46.

28 WA 42:134,29–32 (1535–1545).

we give kisses to Mary; but I do not like Mary's breasts or her milk, because she did not redeem me nor did she make me blessed'.[29] Luther's description suggests popular pictures which show Bernard kneeling in front of the Virgin Mother and her baby, perhaps with a stream of milk flowing from her breast onto Bernard's mouth or face. This can be seen, for example, in the frontispiece of the 1520 edition of Bernard's works[30] (Plate 25). However, Luther may not have had this in mind at all, since in the immediate context

29 WA 46:663,32–36 (on Jn 1); see Posset, 'The Elder Luther on Bernard: Part I', 48–50. In that essay and also in my book *Luther's Catholic Christology*, 122f, I should have differentiated more between the two motifs: (1) Mary exposing her breast as a gesture with which she emphasizes her role in the life of Christ and being the motherly advocate for the sinner before God on the one side; and (2) the *Lactatio Bernardi* in the strict sense, on the other side. Bell, *Divus Bernhardus*, 321, also associated this text with the *Lactatio Bernardi*. We both overlooked that the text refers to the image of Mary showing her breast to Christ (not to Bernard!). Such a connection to the *Lactatio Bernardi* motif appears questionable to me now, if by *Lactatio Bernardi* we mean depictions which show a stream or drops of Mary's milk issuing from her nipple to Bernard's mouth or face, as it is the case with numerous pictures of this motif; see Rafael M. Durán, *Iconografía Espanola de San Bernardo* (Poblet: Monasterio, 1953; [revised edition, Poblet 1990]) ills. IV (1290), XXXI (1460), XXXIV (fifteenth century), XXXV (second half of the fifteenth century), XXXVI (end of fifteenth century), LII (about 1550), LIX (sixteenth century) and others; Paffrath, *Bernhard von Clairvaux* (1984), ills. 92, 193, and 279. Bell, *Divus Bernhardus,* 321, note 181, was unnecessarily critical of Jean Wirth, 'Le dogme et image: Luther et l'iconographie', *Revue de l'art* 52 (1981) 11, who (like Düfel) saw primarily the motif of the stairway to salvation at work here. If Luther actually had the *Lactatio Bernardi* in mind, he would have had to say that the Virgin directs her breast to Bernard. But Luther spoke of Mary 'who directs her breasts to *her Son*'. On 'Bernard and Mary's Milk', see McGuire, *The Difficult Saint,* 189–225.

30 See Riccardo Cataldi, ed., *Melliflui Doctoris Opera: Le edizioni delle opere di san Bernardi di Clairvaux dei sec. XV–XVIII della Biblioteca Statale des Monumento Nazionale di Casamari e di altre Biblioteche cistercensi* (Casamari: Ministero per i beni culturali e ambientali biblioteca statale de monumento nazionale di Casamari, 1992) 32f. This frontispiece would qualify for what Luther had in mind except that Luther spoke of Mary showing her breast to Christ, while the picture clearly has Mary, with a royal crown, pointing her breast towards Bernard's forehead, and the Christ Child looking at him as drops of milk fly past him toward Bernard. Bernard's banderole reads: *Monstra te esse matrem.* The woodcut of 1495, as shown in *Sermones Bernardi in Duytssche,* at Zwolle, by Peter van Os, 1495 (Plate 3), also bears this legend. A glass window, (called *Lactatio Bernardi* in the wider sense) today in the National Museum in Madrid, shows Bernard before bare breasted Mary as the Christ Child turns to Bernard; but no stream of milk is visible; see Paffrath, *Bernhard von Clairvaux* (1984),190, ill. 55a. Bell, *Divus Bernardus,* 321, mentioned a manuscript of about 1470 in the Rijksmuseum in Utrecht with the motif under discussion here. For a recent survey, see Jean-Claude Schmitt, 'Saint Bernard et son image'. Colloque de Lyon-Cîteaux-Dijon. *Bernard de Clairvaux: Histoire, Mentalités, Spiritualité* (Paris: Cerf, 1992) 639–657, especially 651.

Plate 25: *Lactatio Bernardi*. Frontispiece of the 1520 edition of Bernard's works
*Melliflui deuotique doctoris sancti Bernardi abbatis Clareuallensis Cisterciensis
ordinis opus preclarum*. Queen Mary exposes one of her breasts and squirts three
drops of her milk toward Bernard's face while the Christ Child looks on. Bernard
asks 'Show yourself a mother' (*Monstra te esse matrem*), a direct quotation from
the fourth stanza of the ninth century hymn *Ave Maria stella*. Three monks witness
the event. The caption reads: 'Come to me, all of you' (*Uenite ad me omnes* [Mt
11:28]).

he was criticizing marian intercession, which is definitely not the theme of the frontispiece. Nor is it very likely that he had a picture of Mary feeding her baby in mind, because Luther never objected to the *Maria lactans* motif.

Another possible image would be a picture of Mary holding the Christ Child, but feeding Bernard, the *Lactatio Bernardi*. The 1520 frontispiece can be interpreted in this way. If Luther had this mystical lactation in mind, however, he would have said that Mary gave her milk to Bernard. Instead he explicitly said that Mary displayed her breasts 'to her Son, Christ'. Because of this specific reference and because of the immediate context that speaks of intercession, I think that Luther meant primarily the illustrations showing the intercession of Mary with her breast exposed to her *adult* Son before the heavenly Judge, that is the *Tribunal of Mercy* motif. Luther's further criticism, that it was not Mary who redeemed us, but Christ, points to the issue of salvation and mercy at the Last Judgment, and not to the mystery of the incarnation or mystical lactation.

Luther likely had in mind pictures of Mary with the adult Christ or he may have meant a depiction in the well-known *Schedel Chronicle* or the woodcut in the 1495 German edition of Gerson's sermons. In the last one sees a human figure kneeling and praying directly below Mary. This figure could be any sinner or it could be Bernard. If it is Bernard, then this illustration would match Luther's words that someone has depicted 'Saint Bernard in this way, that he adores the Virgin, who gives her breasts to her Son, Christ, who sucked on them'. We know that Luther was fond of Gerson's works, and so it is likely that he knew this german edition of Gerson's sermons, and had come across this particular woodcut while reading them.[31]

One of the best matches with Luther's words of 1537/38 is a painting by Monte di Giovanni, *Intercessione di Cristo e della Vergine con san Bernardo* dating to the end of the fifteenth century,

---

31 I tend to agree with Düfel, *Luther's Stellung zur Marienverehrung,* who correlated the woodcut in Gerson's book with Luther's saying of 1537/38. As to Luther being fond of Gerson, one may point to Luther's table talk: 'God began to shine with Gerson' (*Durch den Gersonen hat Gott angefangen zu leuchten*), WA TR 5:327 (no. 5711).

it hangs today in the Museum of Fine Arts in Montreal. On the lower level Bernard, in a kneeling position, points with his right index finger to Mary, on the next higher level on the right side; she shows her breast to her adult Son opposite her, on the same level. Christ with his right hand points to his wound while looking up to the Father in heaven on the uppermost level of the picture.[32] It is, however, very unlikely that Luther could have seen this italian painting. But perhaps pictures like it were in existence in Luther's area before being destroyed by sixteenth-century iconoclasts.

In 1531 Luther had disapproved of Last Judgment scenes with Mary and John. Several years later, in 1538, Luther explicitly spoke of 'John the Baptist' and Mary in once more criticizing medieval spirituality: 'They make out of Christ nothing but a strict, angry Judge of whom one has to be afraid, as he wants to throw us into hell; in this way one has painted him as sitting in judgment, on the rainbow, with his mother Mary and John the Baptist on each side as intercessors against his terrible anger'.[33] His criticism is clearly aimed at the *deësis* without using this *terminus technicus*.

In a text from 1537/1540, Luther again objected to Mary's intercession and advocacy. This time he combined his criticism with a rejection of Mary as the Mantle Madonna (*Schutzmantelmadonna*; *Mater misericordiae*) under whose wide cloak even emperors and kings find protection from an angry Christ. Such devious devotional avoidance 'against her Son' he called an 'abomination'.[34] Luther objected to it in another text from the same period, this time referring to a legend about Saint Francis presented by the 'preaching friars'. The Reformer called trust in Mary's mantle a heresy; in his opinion the rival preaching friars (Dominicans and Franciscans) were wrong to put their trust in it. Luther did not connect the

32 *Bernardo Cistercense. Atti del XXVI Convegno storico internazional. Todi, 8–11 ottoble 1989* (Spoleto: Centro Italiano di studi sull'alto medieoevo, 1990), Figure 14.

33 *Wie man jn gemalet hat auff dem Regenbogen zu gericht sitzend und seine Mutter Maria und Johannes den Teuffer zu beiden seiten als furbitter gegen seinem schrecklichen zorn*, WA 46: 8,32–36 (on John 16).

34 See WA 47:257,9–15 (on Mt 18–24); Luther did not mention Bernard here.

Cistercians with this image.[35] It is doubtful whether the augustinian Luther was familiar with typical cistercian art, and probably did not associate the Mantle Madonna with the cistercian traditions.

In Luther's *Haus Postille* of 1544, in the Sermon for the Second Sunday of Advent, we again find his familiar objection to Bernard and the concept attributed to him. 'As the dear Father Bernard thought about the mother Mary, that when she was showing her breasts to her Son, he would be unable to deny anything to her. This surely is an indication that one believed Christ to be coming as a judge'.[36] Clearly, Luther believed Mary's intercessory role was derived from the misguided image of the Son of God as an angry Judge. To him Christ is not merely the Judge, but also and primarily the *Heiland*, the Saviour of sinners.

In his very last sermon before his death, delivered on 17 January 1546, on the second Sunday after Epiphany, the Reformer spoke out once more against an exaggerated marian devotion derived from a distorted image of God and of Christ as Judge. Luther called Bernard an exaggerator who overdid it, 'doing too much to

35 See WA 47:275,34–276,26, where Bernard is mentioned by name as promoter of Mary *mediatrix*, but he is not directly connected to the motif of the Mantle Madonna. Luther associated Bernard with the motif of Mary showing her breast. He accused the *Prediger Munche* (276,23; the 'Order of Preachers' i. e. the Dominicans), of having presented Mary with her mantle as a protection against God's three arrows of pestilence. Luther also accused the *Francisci Bruder* (276,28; the Franciscan Friars) of spreading the dream of Saint Francis according to which Mary opened up her cloak to reveal that no Franciscans were under it. She consoled him, however, that his brethren were already in the state of perfection and therefore did not need her protection. Luther may have confused Francis with Bernard here; the mantle motif emerged earlier in the cistercian legends, as in the last chapter of Book VII of Caesarius of Heisterbach, *The Dialogue of Miracles* (trans. H. von E. Scott and C. C. Swinton Bland; London: George Routledge & Sons, Ltd. Broadway House, Carter Lane, 1929) 546. On the history of the motif of marian protection, see Paul Perdrizet, *La Vierge de miséricorde* (Paris: A. Fontemoing, 1908); Vera Sussman, 'Maria mit dem Schutzmantel'. *Marburger Jahrbuch für Kunstwissenschaft* 5 (1929) 285–352; N. H. Baynes, 'The Finding of the Virgin's Robe'. *Byzantine Studies and Other Essays* (London 1955) 240–247; Christa Belting-Ihm, *'Sub matris tutela'. Untersuchungen zur Vorgeschichte der Schutzmantelmadonna* (Heidelberg: Carl Winter Verlag, 1976); numerous illustrations of the motif are found in Paolo Dal Poggetto, ed., *Piero e Urbino, Piero e le Corti rinascimentali* (Marsilio Edizione, 1992) 401–416; Francesca Rita Alimonti, 'La *Mater misericordiae* nella tradizione cistercense'. *Respice Stellam*, Calabuig, ed., 203–221.

36 WA 52: 22, 2–5 (Advent Sermon in his *Haus Postille*, 1544).

him' [Christ]. He was convinced that Bernard presented Christ as a son who gave too much honor to his mother, and portraying Mary as a compelling, dominating woman who displayed her womanly power by showing her breasts. Here is the entire passage of the printed version of that sermon:

> When we thus preach about the faith, we should worship nobody else but God alone who is the Father of our Lord Jesus Christ as we say in the creed: I believe in God the Father, the Almighty, and in Jesus Christ. . . . 'You will find him in a manger' (Lk 2:12); he alone shall be sufficient. But reasoning leads to the opposite: Should one worship Christ alone? Should one not also honor the holy mother of Christ? She is the woman who crushed the serpent's head; hear us, O Mary, since your Son honors you so much that he cannot deny you anything [you ask for]. Here, Bernard in [his interpretation of] the gospel *Missus est Angelus* etc. has done too much to him [german *jhm* = Christ]. [While] God has commanded [us] to honor father and mother, I want to call upon Mary; she will ask the Son for me, and he will ask the Father who will listen to the Son. [From this kind of thinking] we have this picture of the irate God and how Christ shows his wounds to the Father, and Mary [shows her] breasts to Christ.[37]

Luther disapprovingly referred to the homily *In laude virginis Mariae* in a Table Talk in 1533,[38] but he can only mean Bernard's *Homelium Super Missus est in laudibus virginis matris* (Miss) known also as four sermons on *Missus est Angelus*. Luther always

---

37 WA 51:128,19–34 (print); 128,1–15 (Rörer's notes). See Bell, *Divus Bernhardus*, 316 (and 342f, note 2). Bell is mistaken in wanting to amend the text of the critical edition (WA), where he thought he had discovered a mistake (*Rörers Fehler [jhm statt jhr]*): Bell inexplicably preferred to read *jhr* (Mary) in place of the *lectio difficilior jhm*, as WA has it. Luther meant to refer to Christ (and not to Mary) by using the Early New High German pronoun *jhm*. Luther wanted to say that Bernard 'did too much' to Christ (*jhm*); in Luther's view Christ was not presented correctly by Bernard when he showed a Christ who allowed so much honor to be given to his Mother that the Son would be unable to deny her anything she asked. Bernard also 'did too much' damage to Christ (*jhm*) when he made Christ look like the dreadful Judge and Mary the sweet mother and advocate (as Luther mistakenly perceived Bernard doing).

38 WA TR 1:219,6f (no. 494). See Bell, *Divus Bernhardus,* 342. Luther's over-critical attitude toward Bernard's *homelium Super Missus* may have originated from his reading of Erasmus' annotations of the New Testament; see Bell, *Divus Bernhardus*, 344, n. 12.

disliked this *homelium* as much as he appreciated Bernard's First Sermon on the Annunciation (Ann 1).

Some odd curiosities deserve to be mentioned yet. The title page of Luther's own sermon on the Holy Cross (for the Feast of the Exultation of the Cross, 14 September), edited in 1522 by the progressive (i.e. friendly to Luther) publisher Melchior Ramminger in Augsburg, shows the Virgin Mary and her gesture of intercession, exposing one breast. Here, however, Mary served as the symbol of the Gospel in contrast to Moses, the symbol of the Law. Both Mary and Moses serve as background to the crucifix which dominates the page.[39] Apparently this ostentatious marian gesture was so deeply ingrained in the artist that he used it here, even though he was a rather reform-minded person.

Within the traditional Catholic world of the second half of the sixteenth century, reformation criticism of artistic representations caused some reaction. Toward the end of the Council of Trent, on 3 December 1563, the council fathers decreed that 'the images of Christ, of the Virgin Mother of God, and of the other Saints, are to be retained'. Having decreed this, the Church wanted to make sure that the right kind of religious paintings and statues were allowed and that no provocation was given to further protestant criticism. Churches were to be entirely free from secular elements, particularly traces of ancient paganism. While in the Middle Ages the Church appears to have allowed great freedom, with Jean Gerson at the beginning of the fifteenth century, protests were heard against naked figures in ecclesiastical decorations. The Council of Trent legislated that 'all lasciviousness must be avoided; so figures shall not be painted or adorned with a beauty inciting to lust'.[40]

39 The woodcut was created by Hans Burgkmair (†1531, at Augsburg), who was the leader of Augsburg's renaissance art. See *Martin Luther und die Reformation in Deutschland: Ausstellung, Germanisches Nationalmuseum, 1983* 369, no. 492.

40 See Anthony Blunt, *Artistic Theory in Italy 1450–1600* (Oxford: Clarendon Press, 1959) 101–136; see Marti and Mondini in *Himmel Hölle Fegefeuer*, ed. Jezler, 84. The Council thus may have taken the reformation criticism into consideration which Ulrich Zwingli, too, had expressed in 1525 concerning Mary being depicted with her bare breast: *Ja, die ewig, rein, unversert magt und müter Jesu Christi, die müss ire brüst harfürzogen haben,* as quoted in Robert W. Scribner, 'Vom Sakralbild zur sinnliche [sic] Schau. Sinnliche Wahrnehmung und das Visuelle bei der Objektivierung des Frauenkörpers in Deutschland im

Nude bodies, like those shown in the sistine frescos, were discreetly covered with loin cloths. Perhaps as part of these developments, Mary's bare breast came under review. We know that one catholic author pleaded in 1570 for the depiction of Mary's bare breast by arguing that the motif went back to the recognized authority of Saint Bernard of Clairvaux.[41] It may be as a result of these developments that the Cistercians at Wettingen, Switzerland, by 1590 commissioned a glass window portraying an intercession scene with a fully dressed Mary who points to the breast under her dress rather than exposing it. The words put into her mouth still express the traditional intercessory petition before her Son: 'Son, because of my breast have mercy on this sinner'. The Crucified, having his left hand still nailed to the wood, points with his right to the wound in his side and says to the heavenly Father: 'Father, listen to the prayers of my mother through the wounds which I have suffered'. The Father's gracious response is: 'Son, whoever asks for something in the name of your mother will not be damned eternally'. The entire sequence is written on the glass window in the Swiss-German dialect.[42]

Luther wanted to change the image of Christ from that of a merciless Judge to the merciful Saviour. His reformation christo-centrism required that Mary's role and the display of her breast in token of her advocacy had to come to an end. A new phase in the veneration of Mary set in: Mary as the meek maiden and the model of obedient faith, to which the renaissance 'Madonna of Humility' was the likely forerunner.[43] Luther provided the bib-

---

16. Jahrhundert'. *Gepeinigt, begehrt, vergessen: Symbolik und Sozialbezug des Körpers im späten Mittelalter und in der frühen Neuzeit*, Klaus Schreiner and Norbert Schnitzler, eds. (Munich: Wilhelm Fink Verlag, 1992) 309–336, here 309.

41 See Johannes Molanus, *De picturis et imaginibus sacris liber unus*, as referred to by Marti and Mondini in *Himmel Hölle Fegefeuer*, 85.

42 See Jezler, *Himmel Hölle Fegefeuer*, 85, illus. 54.

43 See Peter Meinhold, 'Die Marienverehrung im Verständnis der Reformatoren des 16. Jahrhunderts', *Saeculum* 32 (1981) 43–58. Meinhold preferred to think of the Reformers as 'renewers' of the veneration of Mary from a biblical basis. On Luther and the renaissance concept of the 'Mary of humility', see Heinz-Meinolf Stamm, 'Die "Humilitas' Mariens als Ansatzpunkt der Marientheologie und Marienverehrung bei Martin Luther'. *De cultu Mariano Saeculo XVI* (Rome, 1985) 3:161–76.

lical/theological rationale for this image of Mary, and she was consequently perceived as the model of passivity and humility. Luther had little use for images of Mary as mighty mother and queen of heaven because he feared that this image came too close to idolatry. He featured biblical images of Mary as mother and thus preferred scenes of the Annunciation and Christmas, with Mary and the Christ Child. Mary was made into an 'inner-worldly mother', as the painters Cranach[44] and Holbein sometimes depicted her. Once the reformed image of Christ was accepted, there was no more need for a 'mother of mercy' to placate the angry godhead. Luther thought that since Bernard's day Christ had been perceived as the strict, condemning judge, while Mary had become the friendly virgin, full of sweetness and love.[45] This assumed medieval split between justice and mercy should not, however, be blamed on Bernard, who tried to keep both together. Luther's criticism may apply less to Bernard than to other witnesses of medieval spirituality and art.[46] Yet Luther was quite correct in his general evaluation when he recognized the increase in marian devotion after Bernard's (twelfth) century, and the increase of prayers for her merciful intercession at the heavenly court.

In this Luther was no longer willing to follow his beloved Bernard, whom he otherwise readily accepted as his mentor in spiritual and theological matters. Because Luther, like other late medieval authors, did not differentiate between authentic bernardine and pseudo-bernardine sources, he criticized Bernard for statements he never made. Luther's objections were directed against

44 Scribner, 'Vom Sakralbild', 316. See WA 7:569–75; see Reinhard Schwarz, ' "Die zarte Mutter Christi': Was uns Luther über Maria lehrt', *Zeitwende: Die Neue Furche* 57 (1986) 204–216, here 214. Certain marian feasts such as the Feasts of Mary's conception on 8 December, her birth on 8 September, and her assumption into heaven on 15 August, were no longer celebrated at Wittenberg after 1524.

45 *S. Bernhard, der sonst ein from man gewesen ist, saget auch also* . . . WA 47:99,39–100,16 (on John 3:17); see last note of previous section.

46 'Mary gives us the milk of devotion and mercy . . . for in her nothing remains severe, nothing austere', Jacob de Voragine, *Mariale* (Venice 1497) 33 as referred to by Pierroberto Scaramella, *Le Madonne del Purgatorio. Iconografia e religione in Campania tra rinascimento e controriforma* (Genova: Marietti, 1991) 53f. For a recent overview of marian devotion, see Mary E. Hines, art. 'Mary', *New Dictionary of Catholic Spirituality*, Michael Downey, ed. (Collegeville: The Liturgical Press, 1993) 637.

a late medieval marian spirituality which was probably shaped by cistercian authors. Luther's chief concern with preserving the centrality of Christ meant that no saint, not even Mary, could be allowed to dislodge him from this center. Teachings of Bernard and others were valuable to Luther only if they led to Christ:

> You may not go only to Saint Bernard or Ambrose, but together with them also to Christ, and [you should] check whether their teachings rhyme with his. If this would not be the case, and if they thus invent and teach something from their own devotion beyond that which Christ had taught, they will have to be responsible for this, and I will not make it an article of faith.[47]

Since we are not certain that Luther was familiar with Bernard's collection of letters, we cannot know for sure whether he read Bernard's letter to the canons of Lyons (Ep 174), with its critical attitude toward the feast of Mary's immaculate conception. Had Luther known Bernard's opinion, however, one may rest assured that he would have quoted it approvingly:

> The royal virgin does not need false honor; she had been accumulated with true titles of honor, with headbands of dignity. Sanely give honor to the integrity of the flesh, the holiness of life; admire the fecundity in the virgin, venerate the divine offspring. Praise the one who does not know concupiscence in conceiving nor pain in giving birth.'[48]

So persuasive (and evidently so joined with Erasmus' critical influence in this regard[49]) was Luther's christocentric view that a church in Erfurt in 1525 turned the marian antiphon *Salve regina*, with its invocation to Mary as *advocata nostra*, into a christocentric song.[50]

---

47 WA 46:769,2–9.

48 SBOp 7:388,18–21; see Casey, 'Bernard of Clairvaux and the Assumption' 28 with the discussion of the bernardine ambiguity of Mary being exempt or purified from original sin.

49 See L. Halkin, 'La mariologie d'Erasme', ARG 68 (1977) 32–55.

50 See F. Falk, 'Die Gegner der Antiphon Salve regina im Reformationszeitalter', *Der Katholik* 83 (1903) 350–354; Hans-Ulrich Delius, 'Luther und das "Salve regina"', *Forschungen und Fortschritte* 38 (1964) 249–251.

By way of a summary, we may say that cistercian and lutheran spiritualities are centered not only on Christ's incarnation, but also on his passion, cross, and resurrection and on his role as Judge at the Last Judgment. From Bernard, Luther learned to concentrate on Jesus, the crucified Lord. His cross is the 'mercy seat' which has priority over the 'judgment seat'; the Lord shares his double right to heaven with the sinners for whom he earned it on the cross. Bernard's sermons on the passion and on the 'sweet spouse' of the soul helped Luther, relieving him of the burden of a lop-sided image of the stern Christ in judgment. Luther's 'theology of the cross' was his version of Bernard's *fasciculus myrrhae* (SC 43), to which the Reformer repeatedly referred, as he did in his own commentary on Sg 1:13 (the subject of SC 43): 'Bernard [said] many things here about the memory of the suffering of the Lord'.[51] This monastic theology had great influence on the spirituality of Luther and of subsequent Christianity. Luther's central concern for the sinner's salvation was intimately tied to traditional catholic christology.[52]

When one reviews Luther's deep appreciation of Bernard's sermons on the advent, incarnation, and passion of Christ, and of the bernardine concepts of contrition, humility, self-knowledge, God-knowledge, self-judgment, grace, faith, and Christ's double right to heaven—which taken all together we call his affective christocentrism—one can better understand why the reformer ranked Bernard 'higher than any monk or priest on earth' and could state unequivocally that 'Bernard is above all the teachers in the Church'.[53]

In regard to Mary, however, Luther did not want to learn from Bernard, who appears to have provided ampler room for her than Luther was willing to grant. The reformer perceived

51 *Bernhardus multa hic de memoria passionis Christi*, WA 31-II:628,26 (Rörer). There is no need to suggest that Luther meant the pseudo-bernardine work which has a similar title (*Vitis mystica seu tractatus de passione Domini*), as the index in WA 63:97 opines.

52 George Yule, 'Luther's Understanding of Justification by Grace Alone in Terms of Catholic Christology', 87–112; David P. Scaer, 'Sanctification in Lutheran Theology', CTQ 49 (1985) 165–182.

53 See Posset, 'Divus Bernhardus'. *Bernardus Magister*, 530–531.

the elevated place she had come to hold over the centuries as inappropriate competition to Christ's unique salvific role. Luther had early distanced himself from any Mary-centered spirituality[54] as deriving from a mentality which appeared to impede his pastoral principle of doing everything to promote Christ (*was Christum treibet*). 'The Thousand Faces of the Virgin Mary'[55] which patristic and medieval theologies had produced, Luther, true to his Christ-focus, reduced in number and left his followers only with those that are biblically grounded.

Luther was not anti-Mary. His objection was to the marian intercession concept, whether in theology or in the artistic form of *deësis* or the *Tribunal of Mercy*. He was no less against John the Baptist's intermediary role. When the Baptist was depicted as a pointer to Christ, Luther was all for it. It was a depiction which agreed with his theological hermeneutical principle *was Christum treibet*:

> [John 1:29] is a bright and clear text with strong words which are confirmed by the beautiful, glorious painting which shows Saint John with the lamb, as he [John the Baptist] points with his fingers toward the lamb. I like those pictures, and especially when one painted the easter lamb as a standard-bearer; and [I also like pictures] of Christ crucified.[56]

For his depiction of the Baptist with his index finger pointing toward Christ, Luther may have had in mind the altar painting in the church at Neustadt on the Orla river which Cranach had painted in 1511 and which Luther had seen when he preached there in 1524.[57] As Luther said, he favored Christ-centered and cross-centered pictures. The older Cranach gave artistic expression to exactly this theological concern when he and his son painted the

54 See WA 60:188,25–28 (approx. 1516).

55 See George H. Tavard, *The Thousand Faces of the Virgin Mary* (Collegeville: The Liturgical Press, 1996).

56 ... *das man S. joan mit dem Lemlin gemalt hat, wie er mit den fingern aff das Lamb weise, und ich hab solch gemelde gerne gesehen.* ... (Sermon for All Saints Day 1537), WA 46:683,35–684,1.

57 See Christoph Markschies, ' "Hie ist das recht Osterlamm". Christuslamm und Lammsymbolik bei Martin Luther und Lucas Cranach', ZKG 102 (1991) 209–230, here 222f.

center section of the altarpiece in the town church of Saints Peter and Paul in Weimar in 1555. In it we see John the Baptist under the cross of Christ, next to a self-portrait of the older Cranach himself and a portrait of Luther. The Reformer points in the open Bible to three verses on the first page: (1) 'The blood of Jesus his Son cleanses us from all sin', 1 Jn 1:7. (2) 'So let us confidently approach the throne of grace to receive mercy', Heb 4:16; and on the other page (3) 'Just as Moses lifted up the serpent in the desert, so must the Son of Man be lifted up, that all who believe may have eternal life in him', Jn 3:14–15. Luther's finger rests on verse Heb 4:16, the promise of God's mercy.[58]

Luther constantly focused on the grace of God in Christ. The elder Luther also recognized Saint Bernard's Christocentrism and his appropriate view of the relationship between Christ and Mary when—alluding to John 1:16—he said in a sermon of 1537: 'Saint Bernard writes that all the saints, yes even the dear Holy Mary, Mother of God, have received from the fullness that is in Christ Jesus.'[59]

---

58 See Manns, *Martin Luther: An Illustrated Biography*, 9, ill. no. 36.

59 *S. Bernhardus schreibet, das alle Heiligen, Ja auch die Heilige, werde Mutter Gottes, Maria, von der Fulle, so in Christo Jhesu ist, genommen habe*, WA 45:319, 22–25 (sermon of 22 November 1537). Luther may have had in mind Bernard's second sermon *In Praise of the Virgin Mother* (Miss 2.7; SBOp 4:25, 20–22). See Posset, 'The Elder Luther on Bernard: Part I: Martin Luther's Permanent Indebtedness to Bernard,' *ABR* 42 (1991) 33; Bell, *Divus Bernhardus*, 322.

5

Evangelization Alone

$\mathfrak{I}$N CHAPTER FIVE, we shall study the priority of pastoral care in Bernard's teaching and Luther's perception of it. We deal first, with Bernard's diagnosis of the state of the Church and then proceed in section two to investigate his advice to Pope Eugene III, his disciple, in the *Five Books on Consideration,* examining in both cases the use Luther made of it for his purposes. In the third section, we will highlight the johannine concept of 'feeding my sheep' in terms of evangelization according to Bernard and Luther.

I. 'A FOUL CORRUPTION PERMEATES
THE WHOLE BODY OF THE CHURCH'

In the context of their biblical exposition, both Bernard and Luther expressed their concern for the spiritual welfare of the Catholic Church, which they considered always under attack by the devil. To discover and demonstrate the impact Bernard had on Luther in this regard, we shall look at Bernard's interpretation of Ps 90:5–6 (Vulgate) and Luther's reaction to it.

1. *Bernard's diagnosis*

The great abbot of Clairvaux dedicated seventeen sermons to an exposition of the sixteen verses of Ps 90, which in Latin begins with the words *Qui Habitat*, 'He who dwells in the shelter of the Most High'. The first four sermons deal with the initial four verses of the psalm; the fifth treats the first half of verse 5; the sixth refers to the verses 5b and 6: 'You shall not fear the terror of the night nor the arrow that flies by day, nor the pestilence that prowls in darkness nor the devastating plague at noon'. Bernard treated these verses not only in these special lenten sermons, but also in sermon 33 on the Song of Songs. We will concentrate on SC 33, because other indications in Luther's works make it clear that he had read Bernard's SCs, whereas there is not clear evidence that he had read the *Qui Habitat* sermons.[1]

In the second part of SC 33, Bernard spoke of Ps 90. He understood it as a text about the 'mystical noontide' and the four temptations to be avoided. He arrived at this topic because Sg 1:7 speaks of 'the rest' which is given to the flock at midday. The bride's question about the place where the groom pastured his flock at noon, Bernard took as a hint at the clear light of the day. He understood the groom's companions as people devoid of the truth that gives true stability. They are people who never attain knowledge of the truth although they are always learning; they are identified as philosophers and heretics. Because of them, and also because of the deceits of invisible powers and spirits who lie in ambush, 'fitting their arrows to the string to shoot in the dark at the upright in heart' (Ps 10:3), one must yearn for the noonday. Only in the clear light of the day can one detect the devil's tricks and recognize Satan masquerading as an angel of light. One cannot

1 SBOp 4:383–492. See QH 6; SBOp 4:404–11. QH 7 interprets verse 7. SC 33 is found in SBOp 1:241,24–242,22. See Marie-Noel Bouchard, 'Une lecture monastique du psaume 90: les sermons de saint Bernard sur le psaume *Qui habitat*', Coll 49 (1987) 156–72. The conjecture that Luther most likely referred to SC 33 (and not to QH 6) may be corroborated by the fact that Luther referred to the 'bitterness' of the Church (speaking with Isaiah) which is the catch-word found only in Bernard's SC 33; it is missing in QH. My conjecture may be supported further by the observation that references to Bernard's SC 33 belong to the medieval augustinian tradition as represented by Conrad von Zenn, according to Zschoch, *Klosterreform und monastische Spiritualität im 15. Jahrhundert*, 197. See Posset, 'Bernhard von Clairvauxs Sermone zur Weihnachts-, Fasten- und Osterzeit als Quellen Martin Luthers', *Lutherjahrbuch* 61, pp. 103–106; Bell, 'Bernhard von Clairvaux als Quelle Martin Luthers' (1995), 7–10, is not convincing in insisting that Luther was familiar with QH.

defend oneself against the attack of the noonday devil except by the midday light.

Bernard believed that Satan was styled the noonday devil because some wicked spirits can become as bright as midday light. If this kind of devil sets out to tempt someone, there is no chance of escape, unless the Sun from heaven shines in his heart with noonday brightness. The abbot cited examples from the monastic life to illustrate the devil's work: 'How often, for example does [the devil] not persuade a monk to anticipate the hour of rising, and mock him as he sleeps in choir while his brothers pray?' The preacher went on to explain the four kinds of temptations described by the psalmist in the verses five and six: 'His truth will surround you with a shield: you will not fear the pestilence that stalks in the darkness, nor invasion, nor the noonday devil'.

Nocturnal fear is understood as the monk's fearfulness at the beginning of his conversion, the fear of all the adversities of life. Beginners on the way to God must watch and pray against this first temptation or they will be overtaken by faintheartedness as suddenly as by a storm. When this first temptation is conquered, the second immediately appears. Here one must take up arms against the arrow that flies by day, the inane glory of men who find cause for compliments 'in the praiseworthy life we lead'. This is because fame is said to fly by day while it springs from works done in the night. When this second temptation has been blown away, one is confronted with a still stronger one. This is the temptation the Lord experienced when the devil asked him to pitch himself from the temple for the sake of vanity and all the kingdoms of the world (Mt 4:8). If one does not follow the Lord in refusing what is offered, one will become a victim of the ' "pestilence that stalks in darkness" which is hypocrisy'. This evil has its source in ambition, its dwelling place in darkness; it conceals what it really is and pretends to be what it is not. It may retain the appearance of piety as a mask to hide behind. The last temptation is the 'noonday devil' who lays ambushes for the perfect who have survived all the previous snares—pleasures, applause, and honors. The apostles experienced the noonday devil in the boat when they saw the Lord walking over the sea, and mistook him for a ghost.

After identifying these four temptations in the course of his exposition on Psalm 90, the abbot proceeded to apply them to the Church, describing the course of church history from its origins to his own times. He took this interpretation to be the fulfillment of Isaiah's prophecy, rendered in the Vulgate as *ecce in pace amaritudo mea amarissima* ('see how in peace my bitterness is most bitter' [Is 38:17]). Astoundingly, Bernard explicitly applied these criticisms to the concept of the Church as the 'Body of Christ' in the following words: 'If you are not worn out by the length of this sermon, I shall try to apply these four temptations in due order to the Church as the Body of Christ (Col 1:24). I shall try to be as brief as possible'. He equated the fate of the early Church with the bitter affliction of 'the terror of the night'. To him it was surely night when anyone who killed the saints thought he was doing a service to God, an allusion to Jn 16:2. Centuries later, the enemy changed his tactics from 'the terror of the night' to the 'arrow that flies by day'. Bernard considered the Church's members wounded by the arrows of ambition and the praises of men. 'The times in which we live are, by the mercy of God, free from these two evils, but are obviously contaminated by 'the pestilence that stalks in darkness'. He continued with some acerbic observations on the sad condition of the Body of Christ:

> Today a foul corruption permeates the whole body of the Church, all the more incurable the more widespread it becomes, all the more dangerous the more it penetrates inwardly. For if a heretic were to rebel in public, he would be cast out to wither; if an enemy were to attack her violently, she could perhaps hide from him. But as things stand, whom will she cast out, or from whom will she hide herself? Everyone is a friend, everyone an enemy; everyone is indispensible, everyone is an adversary; everyone is a member of the household, and none is peace-making (*nulli pacifici*); all are neighbors to each other, but all seek their own. Called to be ministers of Christ, they are servants of Antichrist.[2]

At the end of his sermon he again evoked the figure of the Antichrist:

---

2 SC 33.15; SBOp 1:243,27–244,9; CF 7:157f; see Glenn W. Olsen, 'Recovering the Homeland', *Word and Spirit* 12 (1990) 109.

He pretends that he is not only the day but the very noon, who 'exalts himself above every so-called god or object of worship' (2 Thes 2:4), 'whom the Lord Jesus will slay with the breath of his mouth' (2 Thes 2:8), whom he will destroy with the light of his coming, because he is the true and eternal noonday, the Bridegroom and advocate of the Church; he is God above all, blessed for ever. Amen.[3]

Between those two hints at the Antichrist, Bernard inserted a passage from Is 38:17 on the bitterness in peace as being most bitter. After he had castigated the false ministers of Antichrist, he continued with his penetrating diagnosis:

Promoted to honors over the possessions of the Lord, they do not honor the Lord. Hence that bogus splendor that you see every day. . . . Hence the gold embossments on their bridles . . . spurs that carry more costly adornment than their altars. Hence . . . the carousing and drunkenness. . . . Hence the painted casks, hence custom purses. Such is the goal they aim at when they seek a prelacy in the Church, to be deans or archdeans, bishops or archbishops. Nor do they come to this by way of merit, but by a transaction that works in darkness (Ps 90:6). Long ago the following prophecy was made, and now we see its fulfillment. 'See how in peace my bitterness is most bitter' (Is 38:17). It was bitter at first in the slaughter of the martyrs, more bitter in later times in the struggle with heretics, but most bitter now in the moral of the members of the household. She cannot drive them away nor flee from them, so strong have they grown, so multiplied beyond counting. This plague of the Church is intestinal and incurable, which is why during peace her bitterness is most bitter.[4]

Bernard's criticism of the deeply rooted and *insanabilis plaga* of the Church sounds more devastating than many of Luther's attacks on the papal Church. Bernard spoke harshly because for

---

3 SC 33.16; SBOp 1:245,5–9; see CF 7:158f.

4 . . . *Intestina et insanabilis est plaga Ecclesiae, et ideo in pace amaritudo eius amarissima*, SC 33.16; SBOp 1:244,19–24; CF 7:158. The modern translation of the prophetic text, based on the Hebrew original and not on the Vulgate, differs considerably: 'Thus is my bitterness transformed into peace' (*The New American Bible*).

the Church's welfare his concern was undergirded by his affective christocentrism and his love for the Church as the Body of Christ and for her true ministers.

2. *Luther's use of Bernard's diagnosis*

Luther found his own convictions about the bitter incurability of the Church anticipated in this bernardine sermon. In his First Psalm Lectures *(Dictata)*, on Ps 68, he quoted the passage from Bernard's sermon practically word for word, particularly the phrase, 'It was bitter at first in the slaughter of the martyrs, more bitter in later times in the struggle with heretics'.[5] Bernard's critical words provided fertilizer (if not the hotbed) for Luther's efforts at reforming of the head and the body of the Church. As we shall see below, Luther found further support in Bernard's *De consideratione*. Immersed in the bernardine thought world, Luther, too, experienced the contemporary Church as 'most bitter'.

If one compares Luther's citations with Bernard's entire sermon, one observes that at this early point in his career Luther did not even refer to the severest bernardine criticisms; there is no hint at the servants of the Antichrist mentioned by Bernard. Luther did not quote Bernard's phrases about the inveterate, 'intestinal', and incurable illness of the Church. In short words, Luther, not yet the outspoken reformer, was less pointed in his criticism than was the saint of Clairvaux. But Luther was on his way towards Reformation, confident that he was spiritually accompanied and mentored by Bernard. At the time of Luther's First Lectures on the Psalms, between 1513 and 1515, the beauty of the Church in her 'spiritual men' and the bitterness of the Church in her corrupt members passed in review before the friar's eyes, still through his bernardine glasses. It took several years and many

5 *Ut Bernardus ait: que fuit amara sub tyrannis, amarior sub hereticis, amarissima sub pacificis et securis*, WA 3:417,7–9 (scholium on Ps 68; WA gives an incorrect source reference (no. 13); the correct one is SC 33.16; LW 10:352. The second text in which Luther referred to this passage is found in WA 3:420,14–16; LW 10:356; see Bell, *Divus Bernhardus,* 48–50; see Lohse, *Luthers Theologie,* 78.

spiritual struggles before Luther turned Bernard's holy rage against abuses in the 'incurable' twelfth-century Church into his own anger against the Church of the Pope as the Church of the Antichrist, the Church enslaved in 'babylonian captivity'. Yet there can be little doubt that Luther's critical attitude toward the Church of the renaissance popes developed within the same monastic tradition which had produced Bernard's scathing diagnosis in his interpretation of Ps 90:5f in SC 33.[6] Luther found his bernardine evaluation corroborated by the contemporary humanist and carmelite poet Ioannes Baptista Mantuanus, whom the young Luther adored, as is demonstrated elsewhere.[7]

Luther's use of Bernard's SC 33 to comment on the grave illness of the Church did not go unnoticed in 1521, when Luther was confronted by the authorities at the famous Diet of Worms. Luther had included Bernard's thoughts in his published commentary on the Psalms, a work which grew out of his *Operationes in psalmos*, his second lectures on the psalter between 1519 and 1521. At Worms, a substantial number of Luther's publications were put on the table for scrutiny; one of them was listed as 'the exposition of the first thirteen Psalms'.[8] In them one member of the Diet found Luther's reference to Bernard's interpretation of the 'noonday devil'. This member, Dr Jerome Vehus, chancellor of Baden, examined Luther and used exactly this Bernard reference to warn Luther against the very demon Luther had himself mentioned. He admonished Luther to take the unity of the Church into consideration and not to tear apart the seamless garment of the Lord by his teachings and opinions. Even if councils had erred, Vehus continued, no one should despise their power and authority.

6 See Schwarz, 'Luther's Inalienable Inheritance of Monastic Theology', note 17.
7 On the impact of the carmelite poet Mantuanus on Luther, see Morimichi Watanabe, 'Martin Luther's Relations with Italian Humanists: With Special Reference to Ioannes Baptista Mantuanus'. *Lutherjahrbuch* 54 (1987) 23–47; Franz Posset, ' "Heaven is on Sale". The Influence of the Italian Humanist and Carmelite Baptist Mantuanus on Martin Luther', *Carmelus* 36 (1989) 134–144.
8 Among the books at hand at the diet of Worms was the *Expositio in tredecim psalmos primos,* WA 7:840,32. The reference to Bernard is found in the context of the interpretation of Ps 5: *ut Bernhardus psal. 90 [:6] vocat, per 'daemonium meridianum'*, AWA 2:240,15–17. According to Bell, *Divus Bernhardus*, 112f, Luther referred to QH 6, while I remain with SC 33.

We are all humans and may err; that, however, is no reason to scorn authority. Much good had come from conciliar decisions. And even if all these historical reminders could not move Luther, his own conscience should move him not to be so stubborn. At this point, chancellor Vehus quoted Bernard's sermon 'with many words' (*mit vil worten*) on the noonday devil and told Luther that brotherly love demanded that he (Luther) should give in, mindful of the many dangers he would give rise to if he refused to concede. The alternative would be that the Emperor would step in. If that occurred, then all the good things Luther had written would be thrown out with the bad. Luther's 'good' books were mentioned explicitly: *On the Triple Righteousness, On Christian Liberty*, and *On Good Works*.[9] This acknowledgment achieved no change in Luther's position, and he completely ignored Vehus' reference to Bernard.

Also in the year 1521 the *Passional Christi und Antichristi* was published at Wittenberg.[10] This polemical volume contained thirteen antithetical pairs of woodcuts by Cranach which were meant to contrast the life of Christ with the lives of renaissance popes. We may wonder to what degree the editors of this vicious publication felt encouraged by Bernard's diagnosis of the state of the Church and his criticism of the popes, to which Luther alluded.

In 1538, more than twenty years after his *Dictata* and after many conflicts with the concrete Church and Empire of his day, the ageing Reformer still remembered Bernard's application to the bitterness of the Church of Hezekiah's hymn of thanksgiving.[11] This late use of the passage is a reminder that Bernard's SC 33 served not only the young developing critic, but also the mature accomplished Reformer. In an undated Table Talk Luther is recorded as having referred to this same passage: 'Saint Bernard used to say, said D. M. Luther, "See how in peace my bitterness is most bitter" [Is 38:17], that is, in peace [time] my sadness is greatest. The Church is never more troubled than when she has peace and quiet.'[12]

9 WA 7:844,15–845,34; Bell, *Divus Bernhardus*, 170.

10 A description of the *Passional* of 1521 is found in Koepplin and Falk, *Lukas Cranach*, 330.

11 WA 50:262 (1538); see LW 34:215, where the editors failed to indicate Luther's source, Bernard's SC 33.

12 *St. Bernhardus hat pflegen zu sagen . . .* , WA TR 6:222,4–7 (no. 6835).

Luther was not the only reformer to be influenced by this particular bernardine thought. Martin Bucer, the reformer of later days, quoted the same extensive passage from SC 33 in his tract on the 'Kingdom of God', written in 1550:

> Saint Bernard complained of these and similar things nearly five hundred years ago. But these evils of the Church have greatly increased and accumulated in the meantime. Truly, therefore, the churches of Christ in Europe never were in worse condition than after the Roman Antichrist established over so many Christian peoples the tyranny in which he maintains himself today with the support of so many great monarchs and nations.[13]

Luther and later protestant leaders readily accepted the church-critical passages they found in Bernard's application of Ps 90:5–6 to the incurable malaise of the Church. The difference between them and Bernard lay not so much in the sharpness of their devastating accusations as in the fact that their diagnosis of the 'incurable plague' no longer remained on the rhetorical level, but led to violent reactions as the sixteenth-century reformers turned their backs to the stricken patient.

Luther only slowly followed Bernard in his severest criticism. As a young professor he had been a rather tame disciple of the medieval castigator. In his earliest interpretation of Ps 90:5f, Luther explicitly referred to the four temptations which Bernard had distinguished and concluded: 'And thus somehow it agrees with Bernard'.[14] More than fifteen years later, the Reformer took a more critical posture toward Bernard's scriptural interpretation, and suggested his own allegorical (!) interpretation of Ps 90:5f. Although Luther accepted the four temptations, he applied them not primarily to the monastic-spiritual way of life, but in opposition to the 'establishment' of Empire and Papacy. He turned what had grown on monastic ground against the 'world'. Luther spoke of the fear of the night as threats, hatred, envy, and harm (still similar to Bernard). At the second temptation, Luther deviated from the

---

13 See *De Regno Christi*, in *Melanchthon and Bucer,* Wilhelm Pauck, ed. (Philadelphia: The Westminster Press, 1969) 211.
    14 WA 4:74,21–30; LW 11:223.

bernardine pattern and spoke of the arrows that fly by day as open slander, contradiction, reviling, backbiting, cursing, and condemnation, such as that found in the papal bulls and imperial edicts of his day. To Luther the third evil, the pestilence in the darkness, meant attacks and plots. The fourth, the pestilence that lays waste at noon, was open persecution, burning, and hanging. Luther saw all four as attacks against the Word of God, which he believed was on his side. Luther was quite aware of the subtle differences between his and Bernard's interpretations of this psalm: 'I know, of course, that Bernard has a different interpretation, which is all right; though in my opinion, it savors all too strongly of monkishness'.[15] Apparently, after his emancipation from the monastic life, Luther moved away from the specifically monastic applications which Bernard provided, and focused more broadly on the 'four plagues or mischief which the just man must suffer for God's sake'. Luther generalized by applying the text not only to monks but to the 'just man' who suffers for God's sake anywhere. Despite their differences, both interpreters shared the effort of trying to read the biblical text in a life-related, 'existential' way, of applying the message in their contemporary Church, although they did not draw the same practical conclusions. Bernard applied the text within his monastic life experience; Luther saw in it a prophecy of the persecution of his followers and himself through imperial edicts and papal bulls. One may call Bernard's exposition internalizing and Luther's externalizing.[16] The basic pattern of interpreting the psalm verse in an 'existential' way remained the same.

On yet another occasion Luther distanced himself from what he observed in Bernard's preaching on Ps 90. Luther summarized his objections to the effect that Scripture verses and psalms are not to be applied personally in the way Bernard did. He 'distorted' the text, for instance, by connecting the flying arrow of Ps 90:5, by a moral and monastic interpretation to vainglory. According to Luther, Scripture must instead be related to the remission of sins and

---

15 ... *Weis aber wol, das Sanct Bernhard einen andern hat, den ich lasse gut sein, wie wol er allzu viel mich dunckt muenchentzen ...* , WA 38:13,22–14,13 (*Defense on the Translation of the Psalms* [1531]); LW 35-I:217.

16 See LW 35-I:217.

to the Church.[17] Apparently, the Reformer disregarded Bernard's acerbic criticism of the bitterness and incurability in the Church; otherwise he could not have criticized the saint while demanding that Scripture relate 'to the Church', something Bernard had done.

Luther's departure from Bernard's specific interpretation does not, however, invalidate our thesis: his fundamental indebtedness to the spiritual master of whose influence he was keenly aware. In fact, his precise reference to Bernard's specific interpretation of a certain psalm verse in SC 33 indicates Luther's close familiarity with the abbot's scriptural exegesis and with his subsequent evaluation of the miserable condition of the Church. Besides SC 33, Luther found further encouragement from Bernard's *On Consideration* to which we now turn our attention.

17 WA TR 1:355,23–26 (no. 740); see Bell, *Divus Bernhardus*, 351.

Secuntur quinqz libri de consideratione domini Bernhardi
Abbatis Clareuallensis ad Eugenium papam.

Incipit liber primus.

Obit animus dictare aliquid quod
te papa beatissime Eugeni vel edi
ficet vel delectet vel consoletur. Sz
nescio quomodo vult/ et non vult exire
leta quidem seo lenta oratio du cer
tatim illi contraria imperare conten-
dunt. maiestas atqz amor. Nempe
vrget iste inhibet illa. Sz interuenit
dignatio tua. quia hoc ipsum non p
cipis/ seo petis. cum precipere magis
te deceat. Maiestate igitur tam dignanter decente. et quid deceat
mi pudor? Quid enim si kathedra ascendisti. Nec si ambules sup
pennas ventorum. subduceris affectui. amor dnm nescit. agnoscit
filium. et in insulis per se satis subiectus est. obsequit sponte. gra
tia obtemperat. libere veretur. Non sic aliqui non sic seo aut ti
more ao ista compelluntur. aut cupiditate. Dij sunt qui in facie
benedicunt. mala autem in cordibus eorum. Blandiuntur cocam
in necessitate desidunt. At cautus nunqz exoit. Ego et verum
fatear. matris libratus sum officio/ seo non podatus affectu. olim
mihi muisceratus es. non tam facile erueris. Ascende in celos. de
scende in abyssos/ non recedes a me. sequar te quocunqz ieris amaui
pauperem. amabo et pauperum et diuitum patrem. Non enim si
bene noui te. quia pater pauperum factus. ideo non paup spiritu
es. In te hanc mutationem factam esse confido/ non se te. nec pu
ou statui tuo successisse promotionez seo accessisse. Monebo pinde
te. non vt magister. seo vt mater. plane vt amans. Amens magis videar. seo ei qui non amat. qui non sentit vim amoris. Dn
ergo iam incipiaz: Libet occupationibus tuis/ quia in his maxie
condoleo tibi. Condoleo dixeram/ si tamen doles et tu. Alioquin
doleo magis dixisse debueram/ quia non est condolere vbi nemo q
doleat. Itaqz si doles. condoleo. si non doles. tamen et maxime
sciens. a salute longius abfistere membrum qd obstupuit. et egru
se se non sentientem. periculosius laborare. absit autez vt de te io

1. *Bernard's advice to a pope*

As the subtitle of Bernard's treatise *On Consideration* (Csi) indicates, the five books were written as advice to a pope, concrete admonition to the contemporary pope Eugene III (1145–53), a fellow cistercian monk, who was elected pope in 1145. From 1149 to about 1152/53, i. e. shortly before his death, Bernard wrote these five books for his disciple on the papal throne. He included criticisms of papal administration and outlined the timeless, pastoral duties of a pope. The work became not only an instrument for an examination of conscience for popes and other rulers during the Middle Ages, but also a tool for those who, like Erasmus and Luther, became critical of the higher clergy and the papacy in Rome. Like all the works of Bernard, Csi is permeated by biblical theology.[1]

By 'consideration' Bernard meant searching for the truth. Books One and Two emphasize the necessity of meditation in a pope's spirituality. The first part is an inquiry about the demands of the papal office, the dangers of being overburdened, and the limitlessness of the burden. The pope was told to take time out for 'consideration' of things unknown to him, including his own self.

On the 'hard heart'

When Bernard wrote about the danger of being overburdened, he warned of ending up with a hardened heart, like Pharaoh in

---

1 See Appendices in *Five Books on Consideration: Advice to a Pope,* John D. Anderson and Elizabeth T. Kennan, trans. (Kalamazoo: CP, 1976) CF 37:185–188. See Karl Bihlmeyer and Hermann Tüchle, *Church History,* Victor E. Mills and Francis J. Miller, trans. (Westminster, Md: The Newman Press, 1963) 2:170; see Jaroslav Pelikan, *The Christian Tradition: A History of the Development of Doctrine. The Growth of Medieval Theology [600–1300]* (Chicago and London: The University of Chicago Press, 1978) 3:300; see 4:71; Posset, 'Recommendations by Martin Luther of St Bernard's *On Consideration',* 25–36; Posset, 'Bernard of Clairvaux as Luther's Source: Reading Bernard with Luther's 'Spectacles,' CTQ 54 (1990) 281–304, here 288f. On the coming into existence of Bernard's *On Consideration,* see the new german edition: *Bernhard von Clairvaux: Sämtliche Werke,* ed. Gerhard Winkler (Innsbruck: Tyrolia, 1990) 612–620. On Erasmus: Winkler, 'Die Bernhardrezeption bei Erasmus von Rotterdam'. *Bernhard von Clairvaux,* Elm. ed., 264–66. Bell, *Divus Bernhardus,* 138–150.

Ex 7:13. Bernard reflected on the meaning of a 'hard heart' (a
description Luther picked up) by asking:

> Now what is a hard heart? One that is not torn by compunction
> nor softened by piety, or moved by entreaty. It does not yield
> to threats; it becomes obdurate with beatings. It is ungrate-
> ful for kindness, treacherous in its advice, harsh in judgment,
> unashamed of disgrace, fearless in danger, inhuman toward hu-
> manity, brazen toward divinity, unmindful of the past, neglectful
> of the present, improvident toward the future.[2]

Discontent with the papal business

Bernard expressed his discontent with the vileness (*indignitas*)
associated with the papal office, and deplored that its chief business
had become litigation[3] rather than the edification of the Church:

> What is more servile and more unworthy, especially for the
> Supreme Pontiff, than every day, or rather every hour, to sweat
> over such affairs [finances etc]. . . . Tell me this, when are we to
> pray or to teach the people? When are we to build up the Church
> or meditate on the law? (Ps 1:2) Oh yes, every day laws resound
> through the palace, but these are the laws of Justinian, not of
> the Lord.[4]

In Book Two he dealt with the 'three-fold consideration of
self'. If one does not know oneself, one is like a building without
a foundation. The pope was reminded that the apostle Peter's
successor did not inherit silver and gold: 'For the apostle could
not give you what he did not have. What he had he gave: respon-
sibility for the churches, as I have said'.[5] To Bernard it was clear
that 'dominion is forbidden to apostles'.[6] The abbot admonished
further: 'You are the one shepherd not only of all the sheep, but of
all the shepherds',[7] referring to Jn 10:16. The pope was told that he

2 SBOp 3:396,11–14; CF 37:28.
3 SBOp 3:397,4–6; CF 37:29.
4 SBOp 3:399,2–4; CF 37:31f.
5 SBOp 3:418,3; CF 37:58.
6 SBOp 3:418,7f; CF 37:58f.
7 SBOp 3:423,15f; CF 37:65.

should consider whether he was proficient in virtue, how he ought
to act in various situations, how he could avoid idleness, frivolity,
partiality, and easy credulity. He should always stay on the royal,
middle road:

> Stand firm in yourself. Do not fall lower, do not rise higher.
> Do not proceed to greater length; do not stretch out to greater
> width. Hold to the middle if you do not want to lose the mean.
> The middle ground is safe. The middle is the seat of the mean,
> and the mean is virtue. Every dwelling place beyond the mean
> is counted an exile by a wise man.[8]

'You instruct me to feed dragons and scorpions, not sheep'
Apparently, Bernard anticipated objections, which he formulated, again in metaphor, in Book Four: 'You instruct me to feed
dragons and scorpions, not sheep'.[9] Since the pope found himself
in a dangerous position, Bernard offered advice about the kind of
men he ought to choose as his colleagues and assistants, and how
he should preside over his *familia*, his household. Good helpers
would not despoil but repair the churches. They would not empty
pockets but renew spirits and correct faults. They would not rush to
enrich themselves or their friends 'from the dowry of the widow'.[10]
He reminded Eugene of 1 Tim 3:5, 'If anyone does not know
how to rule his own house, how will he care for the Church of
God?' In this section, the abbot admitted that he was quite weary
of the roman curia[11] and suggested hiring for the papal household
a general manager who would be invested with full authority, so
that the pope would not be lost 'in this labyrinth'.[12] At this point,
Bernard's sarcasm showed through: 'A strange situation! Bishops
have at hand more than enough people to whom they can entrust
souls, but they find no one to whom they can commit their paltry
possessions: obviously they have made the best evaluation of the

---

8 SBOp 3:426,24f; CF 37:72.

9 SBOp 3:454,4f; CF 37:117.

10 SBOp 3:455,12–59,2; CF 37:120–125; see Posset, 'The Elder Luther on
Bernard: Part II', 188.

11 SBOp 3:461,14; CF 37:130.

12 SBOp 3:463,15; see 462,20–23; CF 37:133.

situation—they have great concern for the least matters, little or
no concern for the greatest.'[13]

A little later he continued: 'Many things you may not know,
several things you may pretend not to know, quite a few you
forget'.[14] The pope should, however, know the character and the
pursuits of each person in his household. And, 'In the palace
show yourself pope; at home show yourself the father of your
household'.[15] In Bernard's epilogue to Book Four he wanted the
pope to see that the Holy Roman Church of which he is the head,
is the mother of the churches, and not the mistress (*domina*). He
reminded him that he was not the lord of bishops, but one of them,
the brother of those who love God and the companion of those who
fear him. He ought to be a friend of the Bridegroom (Christ), an
attendant of the Bride (Church), the shepherd of the people.

'What is God?'

The first four books of Csi discuss many things pertaining to
earthly action, the last book deals with the consideration of things
which are above: the unity of soul and body, the angels, God in
unity and trinity. Luther was especially impressed with the section
on God, which deserves to be quoted in full:

> What is God? He is not less the punishment of the perverse
> than the glory of the humble; for he is, so to speak, the spiritual
> [rational] principle of equity, unalterable and uncompromising,
> indeed, pervading everywhere, and every evil that comes in
> contact with this principle must necessarily be confounded. And
> why should everything inflated or distorted not dash against such
> a principle and be shattered? Woe to anything which might be
> struck by a righteousness which knows not how to yield since
> it is also fortitude. What is so contrary and adverse to an evil
> will than always to strive, always to clash, but in vain? Woe to

13 SBOp 3:463,25–28; CF 37:133f.

14 The translation is mine. The latin original reads: *Multa nescias, plura
dissimules, nonulla obliviscaris,* SBOp 3:464,14f; CF 37:134 has this translation:
'Remain unaware of many things, neglect even more, and forget about some'.

15 *In palatio papam, domi te patremfamilias exhibe*, SBOp 3:465,7; CF
37:136.

rebellious wills who reap only punishment for their opposition. What is so punishing as always to will what will never be and always to oppose what will always be. What is so condemned as a will given over to this compulsion to desire and aversion, so it no longer experiences either except perversely and, therefore, wretchedly. Never will it obtain what it wishes, and what it does not wish it will nonetheless endure forever. It is completely just that he who is never attracted to what is right should never attain what pleases him. Who arranges this? The righteous Lord our God, who deals perversely with the perverse (Ps 91:16; 17:27). Never do right and wrong agree, for they are adverse to one another even though they do not harm one another. . . . God is also the punishment of the base man, for he is light. And what is as hateful to obscene, profligate minds? Truly, 'everyone who does evil hates the light' (Jn 3:20).

This is the worm which does not die (Mk 9:43): the memory of things past (Ws 11:3). Once it is inserted, or rather is born in a person through sin, it clings there stubbornly, never after to be removed. It does not stop gnawing at the conscience; and, feeding on this truly inexhaustible food, it perpetuates its life. I shudder at this gnawing worm and such a living death. I shudder to fall into the hands of this living death, this dying life.

Such is the second death (Rv 20:14) which never annihilates but always kills. . . . Therefore, a wrong you have done and remember for eternity must of necessity torment you for eternity. . . . Thus it is, Eugene. No being can be opposed to God and in harmony with itself; whoever is accused by God is likewise accused by himself . . . Do you see that nothing is lacking for the confusion of base men when they will be brought forth to become a spectacle to God, the angels, and to men themselves (1Cor 4:9)? O how badly all the evil have been disposed, indeed they are set in opposition to this torment of unyielding justice, and exposed to the light of naked truth. Is this not to be buffeted perpetually and perpetually confounded? The prophet says, 'Destroy them with a double destruction, O Lord, our God' (Jer 17:18).[16]

16 SBOp 3:467,6ff; CF 37:170–173; on soul and body, see 483,20–484,33; CF 37:164–166; on 'What Is God', see 487,8–488,19; CF 37:173–179.

2. Luther: 'I am following the example of Saint Bernard in his book'

There is no question that reformers through the ages read Bernard's book. The bohemian reformer John Hus quoted it in his book on the Church and at least twice in his treatise on simony (1413). During the Great Schism, especially at the Council of Basel (1431), copies of Bernard's book were sold and read. Numerous editions have been preserved in the Vatican Library. The humanist pope Nicholas V (†1453) esteemed Bernard's work so highly that he had a magnificent copy of it made for himself. *De consideratione* was available in print as early as 1473.[17] Erasmus of Rotterdam, the prince of the humanists, used it in support of his criticism of the roman court and his accusation in a letter in 1521 that Rome was lacking in evangelical spirit.[18] It is thus not surprising that Bernard's book exercised an influence on Luther, who referred to it at least ten times, for the first time in his lectures on Rom in 1515/1516.

'Bernard says: "That heart is called hardened" '

The developing Reformer made use of Bernard's notion of the 'hardened heart' in his interpretation of Rom 2: 'Bernard says: "That heart is called hardened which is not softened by piety, which does not yield to threats and is hardened even further when whips are used," as in the case of the Jews'. The slant against the Jews is not found in Bernard's Csi. Luther added it as his own explication. In his scholium he made a precise reference to Book One: *Vnde b. Bernardus 1. de Consyderatione* [sic]: 'A heart is called hardened because it cannot be softened by well-doing, frightened by threats,

17 See Appendices in *Five Books on Consideration*, 213. On John Hus' *On Simony*, see *Advocates of Reform: From Wyclif to Erasmus*, Matthew Spinka, ed. (Philadelphia: The Westminster Press, 1953) 221 and 232; see Köhler, *Luther und die Kirchengeschichte,* 311–312.

18 *Vel diuus Bernardus in libris quibus titulum fecit De consideratione: quanquam non defuerunt et ex recentioribus celebrati nominis autores qui publicam instaurationem ecclesiasticae disciplinae flagitarent* (Erasmus' Letter to Jodocus Jonas, May 10, 1521) Allen edition, 4:487 (no. 1202).

corrected by punishment, or moved by promises'.[19] Apparently Luther had memorized Bernard's definition of a 'hardened heart', and so was able to weave it into this exposition and to use it again later on, for the last time in his *Commentary on Genesis*[20] toward the end of his life.

'With right, therefore, Blessed Bernard says: "A strange situation!" '

In Luther's interpretation of Rom 4:7, Bernard's work emerged again, but only indirectly. Luther did not refer to him by name when he spoke of the concept of the royal, middle road which had to be held.[21] By the time Luther arrived at his exegesis of Rom 13:1, however, he had a full, direct quotation ready from Bernard's book, the passage quoted above on the bishops' neglect of pastoral care. Luther interpreted Rom 13:1, 'Let everyone obey the authorities that are over him, for there is no authority except from God, and all authority that exists is established by God' with the help of Csi 4, 'With right, therefore, Blessed Bernard in a ridiculing way says in Book Four of his *De consideratione*: 'A strange situation! . . .'.[22] This passage seems to be one of the major ones which Luther cited literally from the abbot's manual, and it is perhaps noteworthy that this sarcastic passage came to Luther's mind as he dealt with the issue of authority in Rom 13. It appears, however, that while Luther used this text in his scholium, he did not quote it in his lectures. We must remember that Luther was not yet the fully developed Reformer. He still moved along the track of Bernard's criticism of the hierarchy. And, as if wanting to draw

19 WA 56:19,26–27; LW 25:17; WA 56:192,28–30; LW 25:176; see *Bernhardus: 'Durum cor dicitur . . .', WA 57-I:23,5; Et Bernhardus 1. de consideratione: 'Cor durum dicitur . . .', WA 57-I:143,5. Bernard's original reads as follows: Quid ergo cor durum? Ipsum est quod nec compunctione scinditur, nec pietate mollitur, nec movetur precibus: minis non cedit, flagellis duratur. Ingratum ad beneficia est . . . , SBOp 3:396,11–14; see Bell, Divus Bernhardus, 85.* Luther used this definition also in WA 27:253,14; WA 39-I:400,21 and 401,26.

20 WA 43:36,2f; LW 3:225.

21 WA 56:283,7–12; LW 25:270.

22 *Recte itaque B. Bern[ardus] li 4 [de] consyd[eratione] irridet dicens: 'Mira res!', WA 56:480,12–16; LW 25:472–73; see Bell, Divus Bernhardus, 87; Lohse, Luthers Theologie, 95.*

back from the path of criticism, Luther concluded his excursus on the abuses in the Church by saying: 'But this is enough. Let us return to the Apostle'.[23]

An older Luther, during his lectures on Gen 21:25, quoted a sentence from the same Csi 4 concerning 'government': 'Therefore Bernard writes admirably to Pope Eugenius: "Of necessity you have no knowledge of many things, and of necessity you pretend not to know many things you do know." Ignorance is an error of the will with which we tolerate that which we do not want.'[24] Here, Luther may be remembering Bernard's advice that a pope should beware petitioners and flatterers; when people approach him, he should pretend not to know many things which he does know. At another time Luther remembered Bernard's advice that one should know the character and the pursuits of each person in one's household, and that in the palace the pope should show himself pope, while at home he should be the father of his household.[25] When, during his late lectures on Genesis, the expositor arrived at Gen 25:1–4, he may again have recalled Bernard's *De consideratione* (Csi 4.12) about people who get rich from the 'dowry of a widow', for he lectured that there are men of base motives who marry old ladies for the sake of their wealth or honor. Luther laconically commented without quoting Bernard verbatim: 'May God give them the cup of suffering, as Bernard says'.[26]

'About this matter, Saint Bernard speaks beautifully and extensively'

During the decisive years of the early Reformation, Luther gave lectures not only on Paul's *Letter to the Romans* but also on the *Letter to the Hebrews* (1517–1518). There one finds traces of

23 *Sed hec satis. Reuertendum ad Apostolum*, WA 56:480,17; LW 25:473; see Schmidt-Lauber, *Luthers Vorlesung über den Römerbrief 1515/16*, 128.

24 *Praeclare igitur Bernhardus ad Eugenium Papam scribit. Multa cogeris ignorare, et multa cognita dissimulare . . .*, WA 43:194,15–17 (on Gen 21:25). Luther paraphrased Bernard's text of Csi 4.20 (see note 14); see Posset, 'The Elder Luther on Bernard: Part II', 187 with note 25; see Bell, *Divus Bernhardus*, 333.

25 See WA 20:98, 3f, but without mention of Bernard's name.

26 See WA 43:354,39–42; see Posset, 'The Elder Luther on Bernard: Part II', 188 with note 27. Bell, *Divus Bernhardus*, 334, did not discuss Csi 4.12 as a possible source for Luther.

Bernard's *De consideratione* once again. When Luther treated Heb 4:12, 'Indeed, God's word is living and effective, sharper than any two-edged sword', a passage from Bernard's 'Fifth Book' came to his mind:

> The unbelievers will be tortured with endless, eternal, and incurable cutting. About this matter, Saint Bernard speaks beautifully and extensively in the Fifth Book of his *On Consideration*. From this the punishment follows as 'the dissolution of the mind and the soul, of joints and marrow', the incision, the trouble, and the confusion of all internal and external forces.[27]

Luther seems here to refer to the section on the question 'What is God?', where Bernard answered that God is 'no less the punishment of the perverse than the glory of the humble'. This Luther took as a graphic illustration of the verse being expounded. Never before had Luther referred to this particular section, and never again did he return to it.

'All popes should know it by heart'
In addition to using the book as background reading for his lectures on Romans and Hebrews, the friar also relied on Csi in the explications to his Ninety-Five Theses on Indulgences of 30 May 1518. In his forty-eighth thesis he explicitly referred to the very apt words of Bernard to pope Eugene: Christians are to be taught that in granting indulgences the pope needs and thus desires their devout prayer more than their money. The Reformer commented that the pope's heart must be nourished by prayer and that Bernard had written about this in a very attractive way in *On Consideration*.[28] Luther hit the nail on the head by juxtaposing money and prayer. Bernard had done the same. Clearly, as Luther pondered the extinction of abuses in the Church, Bernard's efforts at influencing the papacy were in his mind and motivated him to action. When Luther addressed the pope in his Open Letter of

27 *De qua re Beatus Bernhardus libro 5. de consideratione pulchre et late,* WA 57-III:162,9–12; LW 29:165; see Bell, *Divus Bernhardus,* 106.
28 *Sed de hac re omnium pulcherrime B. Bernhardus ad Eugenium Papam de Consideratione* (1518), WA 1:601,28f; LW 31:204f; see Bell, *Divus Bernhardus,* 138.

1520, he thought it helpful to make the pope once more aware of Bernard's book. Luther knew that his own address to the pope might be interpreted as impudent (*unvorschampt*). Nevertheless he recommended that 'all the popes should know it by heart',[29] and implied that they should also take it to heart and act accordingly. There is a german as well as a latin version of this Open Letter. The german expression Luther used is *ausswendig künden*, which means: able to recite fully from memory what has been learned by heart, without glancing at the text. To know something *auswendig* implies turning outward what had been internalized by previous memorization. Thus, this adverb suggests that the popes should at all times have Bernard's words impressed on their minds and ready to be articulated and applied. The verb Luther chose, *künden*, is related etymologically to the german verb, *können*, to be able to do or to know something. In modern German, *künden* means 'to proclaim'.[30] Luther expected the popes to be able to proclaim by heart or express from the heart the deeply internalized message of Bernard's book.

The Augustinian affirmed that he attacked not the person of the pope, but the ungodly corruption and teachings which surrounded the papacy. Evoking some of the images Bernard had employed, Luther opened his letter to the pope with the following words: 'Living among the monsters of this age with whom I am now for the third year waging war, I am compelled occasionally to look up to you, Leo, most blessed Father.'[31] The 'war' going on for the third year was the controversy over indulgences. The friar felt truly sorry for the pope, whom he envisaged, in biblical images, sitting

29 *Ich byn villeycht unvorschampt. . . . Aber ich folge hyrynn S. Bernard ynn seynem buch zu Bapst Eugenium, wilchs billich solten alle Bepst außwendig künden*, WA 7:10,30; LW 35:342; WA 7:48,22 has the latin version with the identical meaning: *omni pontifici memoriter noscendo*. Decot pointed out that Luther's criticism of the popes must be seen in the context of Bernard's criticism, see 'Ansatzpunkte und Gründe von Luther's Papstkritik', *Theologie der Gegenwart* 26 (1984) 75–85. See Bell, *Divus Bernhardus*, 140.

30 See *Der Grosse Duden: Etymologie, Herkunftswörterbuch der deutschen Sprache* (Mannheim, Vienna, Zurich: Dudenverlag, 1963), s. v. 'kund' and 'wenden'; see Posset, 'Recommendations by Martin Luther of St Bernard's *On Consideration*', 32; see Bell, *Divus Bernhardus*, 140.

31 *Epistola Lutheriana ad Leonem X. summum pontificem, Tractatus de libertate christiana* (1520), WA 7:42,6–10; LW 31:334.

like a lamb among wolves—Mt 10:16—like Daniel in the lions' den—Dan 6:16—or like Ezekiel among scorpions—Ez 2:6.

Luther stated in his Open Letter how very upset he was with the way Dr Eck had drawn him into the *Leipzig Disputation* in 1519, and he warned the Holy Father of flatterers like Eck. In religious humility (and perhaps humanist understatement) Luther continued: 'So I come, most blessed father, and, prostrate before you, pray that if possible you will intervene and stop those flatterers who are the enemies of peace while they pretend to keep peace'. Luther declared that he was not about to acknowledge any 'fixed rules for the interpretation of the Word of God, since the Word of God, which teaches freedom in all other matters, must not be bound', a reference to 2 Tim 2:9. Luther told the pope that 'they err who exalt you above a council and the Church Universal. They err who ascribe to you alone the right of interpreting Scripture'. A few sentences later Luther cited the example of Bernard:

> Perhaps I am presumptuous in trying to instruct so exalted a personage from whom we all should learn and from whom the thrones of judges receive their decisions, as those pestilential fellows of yours boast. But I am following the example of Saint Bernard in his book, *On Consideration*, to Pope Eugenius, a book every pope should know from memory. I follow him, not because I am eager to instruct you, but out of pure and loyal concern which compels us to be interested in all the affairs of our neighbors.[32]

There is no doubt that the Reformer consciously imitated[33] Bernard in addressing a pope, for in this Open Letter he referred directly to Bernard's book more than once:

> O most unhappy Leo, you are sitting on a most dangerous throne. I am telling you the truth because I wish you well. If Bernard

---

32 WA 7:48,19–31.

33 See Thomas W. Best, 'Ulrich von Hutten and Luther's Open Letter to Leo X'. *The Martin Luther Quincentennial*, Gerhard Dunnhaupt, ed. (Detroit: Wayne State University Press, 1985) 66: 'Luther overtly mimics Saint Bernard'; 'copying Saint Bernard' (69). On the relationship between Luther and the papacy, see Scott H. Hendrix, *Luther and the Papacy: Stages in a Reformation Conflict* (Philadelphia: Fortress Press, 1981).

felt sorry for pope Eugenius at a time when the Roman See, although even then very corrupt, but still having been ruled with better prospects of improvement, why should not also we complain who for three hundred years have had so great an increase of corruption and wickedness? Is it not true that under the vast expanse of heaven there is nothing more corrupt, more pestilential, more offensive than the Roman Curia?[34]

If Bernard could address a pope, so could Luther. Bernard had written to one of his own cistercian monks now on the papal throne; the fairly young friar of Wittenberg was in a far less authoritative position in his saxon friary at the outskirts of civilization, at a recently (1502) founded academy with no tradition. Furthermore, Bernard's work was probably welcomed by the cistercian pope, while Luther's was bothersome. Both the white monk of Clairvaux and the black friar of Wittenberg aimed at reform of the Church. But several hundred years separated them, and by the time Luther entered the scene the situation had worsened. As the text above indicates, Luther distinguished the person of the pope from his office and its appurtenances. He deplored the fact that Leo had to occupy so dangerous a see and be surrounded by corruption and power-hungry cardinals. Perhaps Luther had in mind here the conspiracy of April 1517, when a twenty-seven year-old cardinal had tried to poison the pope. This stirred great concern all over Europe and especially in Germany.[35]

Without doubt Luther's criticism of the papacy was inspired by Bernard's handbook for Eugene III. There Luther found a pastoral concept of the papal office much to his liking. He simply applied Bernard's ideal to his own contemporary situation. He kept Bernard's pastoral efforts constantly in mind, as we have seen here in works from 1515 to 1520, the high tide of Luther's reformation

---

34 WA 7:45,2–6 (Latin version). German version: *O du aller unseligst Leo . . . . Szo S. Bernhard seynenn bapst Eugenium klagt, da der Romische stuel, wie wol er schon auch zu der selben tzeyt auffs ergist ware, doch noch ynn guter hoffnung des besserniss regiert, Wie viel mehr sollen wyr dich klagen, die weyl ynn dissen drey hundert jarenn die bossheyt und das vorterben sso unwidderstatlich hatt tzu ubir hand genummen!* WA 7:6,18–25; LW 31:337, see 342; see Bell, *Divus Bernhardus,* 139.

35 *Encyclopedia of the Papacy,* s. v. 'Leo X' (New York and London, 1958).

activities. It was during these critical years that Luther returned to the 'sources', to the Church Fathers and to Bernard and his book *On Consideration* with its biblical concept of the petrine office, a concept which Bernard and Luther shared. This was advice given, we may conclude with M. Basil Pennington, not only to a pope, but 'to us all'.[36]

36 M. Basil Pennington, 'Advice to a Pope And to Us All', *Word and Spirit* 12 (1990) 118–147.

The eminent Luther scholar Gerhard Ebeling has studied the history of the word 'pastoral care' (in German: *Seelsorge*) with special attention to Luther's use of it.[1] Unfortunately, Ebeling by-passed Bernard in his review of the history of this notion and did not realize the close relationship between Luther's and Bernard's evangelical concept of pastoral care. Bernard understood the duty of caring for the sheep in terms of the 'feeding' of Jn 21:15–17, where Christ repeats himself three times during the 'job interview' with Peter. Luther followed closely in Bernard's footsteps. He, too, aimed at retrieving the meaning of 'feeding' the flock, which the johannine Christ has in mind for Peter.

Here we will look at five bernardine texts concerning this 'feeding': a letter, a treatise, two sermons, and one *sententia*. We begin with the examination of the concept in the treatise *De consideratione*, which appears to have been a decisive influence on Luther, and we end with a chart of Luther's use of Bernard's concept.

1. *Bernard on the triple feeding of the flock*

'To preach the gospel is to feed'

In Csi 3, Bernard reminded Eugene III that Christ is the head of the Church, her Lord; the pope is only his steward. Christ claims possession of the earth for himself by right of creation, by merit of redemption, and by gift from the Father. The pope should leave possession and rule to Him. 'You take care of it. This is your portion; beyond it do not stretch your hand'.[2] The pope was to correct heretics, to convert gentiles, and to check the ambitious. These are his specific pastoral duties. In Book Four, Bernard described the pope's immediate companions in powerful

---

1 See Ebeling, 'Luthers Gebrauch der Wortfamilie "Seelsorge" '. *Luther-jahrbuch* 61 (1994) 7–44. A brief introduction to Bernard's pastoral care by means of his letter writing is found in Gerhard B. Winkler, 'Bernhard von Clairvaux: Der Brief als Mittel der Seelsorge', *Theologisch-Praktische Quartalschrift* 141 (1993) 368–372.

2 *Ultra ne extendes manum tuam*, SBOp 3:432,3–4.

images: 'I know where you dwell; unbelievers and subversive men are with you. They are wolves, not sheep; but still you are the shepherd'.[3] The pope was told to provide a pastoral example. Again, the simple model of Saint Peter was evoked. He never went in procession adorned with jewels or silks, covered with gold, carried on a white horse, attended by a knight or surrounded by clamoring servants:

> But without these trappings, he believed it was enough to be able to fulfill the Lord's command, 'If you love me, feed my sheep' (Jn 21:15). In this finery, you are the successor not of Peter, but of Constantine. . . . You are the heir of the Shepherd and even if you are arrayed in purple and gold, there is no reason for you to abhor your pastoral responsibilities: there is no reason for you to be ashamed of the Gospel. . . . To preach the Gospel is to feed. Do the work of an evangelist and you have fulfilled the office of shepherd.[4]

Bernard wanted to guide the pope back to the original task of shepherding the people and away from ruling them like an emperor. Bernard's reform program for the petrine office in the Church centered primarily on the duty of 'evangelization', and the pope was summoned to be 'an evangelist'. Apparently, in Bernard's (as in Luther's) thinking, this title was not reserved to the authors of the four gospels.

'Feed your sheep by word, by example, and with the fruit of holy prayer'
    In his Ep 201 Bernard wrote to Abbot Baldwin of Rieti that pastoral care must consist of three things: (1) preaching, (2) exemplary living, (3) praying:

---

3 SBOp 3:453,10f.
4 SBOp 3:453,10–454,3; CF 37:117; see Bell, *Divus Bernhardus*, 85–87; Bell revised his position in his 'Bernhard von Clairvaux als Quelle Martin Luthers', 12, based on my investigations: 'Der Aufsatz Possets hat mich einsehen lassen, daß meine Schlußfolgerung hier nicht ganz richtig war'. Bell referred to my contribution in *Lutherjahrbuch* 1994. I register with some satisfaction the fact that Theo Bell conceded that my contribution gave him some new insight. On the significance of Bernard's Csi in the history of the Church and on Luther's reliance upon it, see Appendices in CF 37:187–189; Bell, *Divus Bernhardus*, 138–150.

Remember to 'give to your voice the voice of power'. That is to say, see that your deeds accord with your words, or rather your words with your deeds, by being careful to practice before you preach. It is a beautiful and sound order of things that you should bear first yourself the burden you are to place upon others, and so learn from your own experience how to temper all things for other people. . . . The example given is indeed 'a living and effectual word', easily making what is said persuasive, by showing that what is ordered can be done. Therefore on these two commands of word and example, understand that the whole of your duty and the security of your conscience depends. But if you are wise, you will add a third, and that is devotion to prayer, so as to fulfil that threefold repetition of the command in the gospel of Saint John to feed the sheep. You will find that you can only fulfil the demands of the threefold sacrament if you feed your sheep by word, by example, and with the fruit of holy prayer. Therefore, these three remain: word, example, prayer, but the greatest of these is prayer.[5]

'Feed my flock with the prayer of the spirit, with the exhortation of the word, with the exhibition of the example'

In one of Bernard's Easter sermons we encounter this threefold pastoral concept again, as he interprets in an allegorical way how the three women approach Jesus' burial place and then turn to Peter with their spices: (1) 'praying'; (2) 'exhortation', by which is meant 'preaching'; and (3) 'exhibiting' a good example in one's daily life. To preaching is assigned the mouth; to giving good examples the hands; to praying the mind:

What did the holy women do? . . . 'They bought spices, that they might come and anoint Jesus' (Mk 16:1). . . . So let these three women, the mind, the tongue, and the hands, buy their spices. For I think that from them Peter accepts the triple mandate as the feeding of the flock of the Lord: Feed my flock, he said, with your mind, feed it with your mouth, feed it with your work: Feed it with the prayer of the spirit, with the exhortation of the word, with the exhibition of the example.[6]

5 *Manent itaque tria haec: verbum, exemplum, oratio*, SBOp 8:61,3f.
    6 SBOp 5:96,21–24. In my article 'Recommendations by Martin Luther of St Bernard's *On Consideration*', 30f, I only discussed Csi and Ep 201 to Abbot

'The sheep must all be pastured on the Scriptures'

In SC 76, one of his late sermons, Bernard dwelt on the meaning of the 'watchmen' of Sg 3:2–3 and in doing so he once again incorporated the three basic elements of his pastoral concept:

Who are these watchmen? Surely those of whom the Saviour said in the Gospel, 'Blessed are they whom the Lord finds watching when he comes'. . . . (1) [They] pray a lot for their people. . . . They watch and pray . . . Remember how the Lord in his wisdom entrusted the sheep to the first shepherd—I mean Saint Peter— and urged him with such persistence to tend it lovingly. . . . It was not pointlessly that Our Lord, in handing over the sheep, said three times, 'Peter, do you love me?' It was, I think, as though Jesus had said: Unless your conscience bears witness that you love me and love me so strongly and completely—more than you love your possessions, your family, and even yourself— that this threefold command of mine is fulfilled, you must not, on any account, take this charge upon you. . . . Therefore, give heed, you who have been chosen for this ministry. . . . (2) The sheep must all be pastured on the Scriptures, which are the Lord's legacy. . . . Good and faithful shepherds never cease to feed their flock (3) with good and choice examples—from their own lives rather than from other people's. . . . It is sheer temerity for anyone to undertake this task unless he has the necessary knowledge and lives an exemplary life.[7]

'Feed by . . . living, teaching, praying'

In his *Sententia* (third series, 41) Bernard summarized his message: 'On the triple interrogation and response of the Lord to Peter: The Lord to Peter: Love, love, love. Feed, feed, feed by [your way of] living, teaching, praying'.[8]

Badwin as possible sources for Luther. In my contribution to the *Lutherjahrbuch* 1994, I argued (hopefully more convincingly) that Luther may have relied on Bernard's Second Easter Sermon (Res 2.3).

7 The numbers have been added for purposes of clarity. (Referring to Jn 21:17) *Petre, amas me . . . Et haec tria ad Domini trinam sciscitationem forte non in congrue pertinere dicentur . . . pastus ovium communiter quidem in pascuis Scripturarum . . . bonis. . . . exemplies . . . orant pro populo*, SC 76.7–10; SBOp 2:258,16- 261,14; CF 40:115–119. Bell did not take SC 76 as a source into any consideration at all.

8 *Series Tertia*, 41, SBOp 6-II:89,6.

These five texts present Bernard's view of the johannine Christ's command to Peter to feed the flock. Bernard's concept of pastoral care centered on (1) pasturing the flock on the Scriptures, (2) living an exemplary life, and (3) praying for the flock. This threefold concept was taken up by Luther at various times throughout his career.

2. *Luther's explicit and tacit use of Bernard's concept*

Before taking a closer look at Luther's use of the bernardine concept of pastoral ministry, we need to realize, first of all, that Luther's early reform efforts were purely theological in nature.[9] His starting point was not so much anticlericalism[10] or issues of church organization or offices, as the Word of God. As late as 1518, Luther delivered a sermon on the dignity of the priesthood, reminding his audience that God gave us priests so that He can more easily facilitate our salvation.[11] Only later did the role of the preacher and the role of the congregation become major, yet derivative issues, in the reform movement. The Reformer's great concern was always the preaching of the pure gospel of grace, and he focused on the duty of preaching as a pastoral function separate from celebrating the liturgy. Luther's responsibilities at the Wittenberg friary were not those of a choir monk or a Mass priest, but of a preacher and a college teacher. In the process of studying and teaching the Bible, friar Luther began to realize the fundamental significance of baptism as the theological ground for the 'common priesthood' of all Christians. Gradually, the separation of clergy and laity became unacceptable to him because he could not find it in the New Testament. This insight was not yet present to him in 1516, however, when he worked on his *Lectures on Romans* and utilized Bernard's concept of ministry for the first time.

9 'The Reformation starts in the lecture hall' (*Die Reformation beginnt im Hörsaal*), Pesch, *Hinführung zu Luther*, 48–70.

10 Recently, the issue of anticlericalism in the Reformation time was discussed, including its medieval matrix, see Peter A. Dykema and Heiko A. Oberman, eds., *Anticlericalism in Late Medieval and Early Modern Europe* (Leiden, New York, Köln: Brill, 1993).

11 See *De sacerdotium dignitate Sermo,* WA 4:655–659.

Luther's explicit use in his *Lectures on Romans*

As Luther prepared glosses on Rom 15:5, he reflected on the pastoral work of the Apostle Paul. As he did so, Bernard's thoughts on this subject came to his mind, specifically those on ministry (*officium*) and its three dimensions: (1) working (i. e. living by good example), (2) teaching/ preaching, and (3) praying:

> The Apostle [here] prays for those whom he instructs, for that is the obligation of a good teacher. He must not only water, but also ask God to give the increase. First he must work; then he must teach, lastly also he must pray for them. Saint Bernard, in his writing to Eugene, explains the threefold 'Feeding', which our Lord inculcated in Saint Peter.[12]

Luther was well aware of Bernard's three-fold concept of pastoral ministry. When he spoke of the 'three-fold feeding', he used the latin adjective *trinum,* which means 'three at a time' or 'three together', thus referring to the bernardine interpretation of Christ's thrice repeated command in the Gospel of John. The command itself, according to Bernard in *On Consideration*, essentially means to proclaim the gospel. There was no particular reason why Bernard should enter Luther's mind at this point, except that he valued him as a great preacher of the biblical message. Bernard's concept must have been so impressive to Luther that at this moment he called on Bernard to help him in interpreting Paul's letter. Not so clear is which bernardine text Luther had in mind when he referred to *B. Bernardus ad Eugenium*. The three components under discussion are not found in Bernard's *On Consideration* to Eugene III. If the Wittenberg lecturer had this treatise in mind, he was mistaken. Since Luther definitely worked with the triple feeding concept, he must have encountered it in some other bernardine source(s) which explicitly speak(s) of the three elements as part of the one 'feeding'.

---

12 *Sic enim B. Bernardus ad Eugenium Exponit trinum illud 'pasce' ad Petrum a Domino dictum,* WA 56:137,26–27; LW 25:120. *Orat Apostolus pro incremento illorum, quos docuit, et hoc ipsum est boni doctoris officium: facere primum, docere deinceps, tandem orare pro eis, ut exponit Beatus Bernardus ad Eugenium trinum illud 'Pasce' ad Petrum dictum Ioann. ultimo,* WA 57-I:117,19–22.

There are several ways of interpreting Luther's line, 'as Blessed Bernard expounds to Eugene'. He spoke of 'expounding' and cited a text to a certain person. Since Luther never mentioned any 'letters' of Bernard, one can argue that he is unlikely to have taken it from the letter to Baldwin (Ep 201). The 1470 printed edition of the collection of letters may or may not have been available to Luther, while we know for certain that *De consideratione*, 'to Eugene', in the 1477 edition, was available to him at the Erfurt Library (Plate 25).

Therefore, the *Sententia* and the two sermons remain to be examined as Luther's possible sources. One must remember that Luther was first and foremost a preacher, and therefore mainly interested in Bernard's sermons. With the *Sententia* there is the difficulty that Luther never spoke of any of Bernard's *Sententiae* anywhere else. Arguing that the sequence exemplary life, teaching, praying is identical in Bernard's *Sententia* and in Luther's interpretation of Rom 15[13] is not convincing, as the sequence here appears accidental. Luther elsewhere used other sequences. One may point out, further, that for Bernard as for Luther the top priority was not ethics ('life', as the *Sententia* terms it in one place), but preaching and teaching. Bernard defined 'feeding' as 'evangelizing' and Luther focused on the good preacher/teacher in expounding Paul's text. Therefore, listing 'life' in the first place is not significant. If there is any priority at all, it is given to preaching, both by Bernard and by Luther. The better choices for Luther's potential sources remain the two sermons.

SC 76 is not to be precluded. Luther was fond of most of Bernard's SC, to which he referred at times explicitly. Yet he does not refer directly to SC 76 anywhere in his works and one cannot be absolutely sure that he had read this particular sermon. We are more certain about the bernardine Easter sermons, as Luther indicated already in his *Dictata* that he had read Bernard's Third Easter Sermon.[14] One may safely assume then that he had also read the

---

13 Theo Bell in his 'Bernhard von Clairvaux als Quelle Martin Luthers', 12, opted for the *Sententia* as Luther's source. Bell's position would be more convincing, if it could be demonstrated that Luther actually quoted directly from *Sententiae* also elsewhere, which appears not to be the case.

14 WA 3:236,27f.

preceding, second, sermon, which contains a passage on the three-fold pastoral ministry. And since this Second Easter Sermon is more concise than SC 76, it might have been easier to recapitulate; thus it may likely constitute Luther's source for the *trinum* concept of pastoral care. Since Luther's reading of the Easter sermons had taken place during his first course on the Psalms, the *Dictata*, it may very well be that he did not remember it distinctly. Perhaps the various bernardine sources ran together in Luther's mind, and the most famous of them, *On Consideration*, dominated. Luther's verb, *exponit*, points more to an exegetical sermon than to anything else, as in monastic sermons the scriptural texts were 'expounded'.

Luther's tacit use of Bernard's concept

In 1519, when Luther entered into disputation with his opponent, Dr Eck, he defended his position on the nature of the clerical office in the Church in terms of 'feeding' the flock. In his view this meant (1) 'to teach the Word of God', (2) 'to pray for the sheep', (3) 'to be a good example'.[15] Luther no longer mentioned Bernard by name, as he had in 1516, yet Bernard's threefold concept was clearly in his mind. During the decisive years of the Reformation, Luther kept Bernard's reform efforts in mind and felt supported by his monastic theology. In his explications of the Ninety-Five Theses, written in May 1518 and later sent to Pope Leo X, he made explicit reference to Bernard's *On Consideration* (in the context of thesis 48). The pope's heart 'must be nourished by prayer', Luther insisted: 'Saint Bernard has written about this matter in a very attractive way to Pope Eugene in his work *On Consideration*'.[16]

Early in 1521 Luther was summoned before the international imperial congress, the so-called Diet of Worms. On his way to Worms, on 7 April 1521, Luther stopped at Erfurt. He was by now so famous that the entire university, led by the rector, welcomed him at the city gate. In the overcrowded augustinian church at Erfurt Luther preached on the meaning of 'feeding the sheep' according to Jn 21, declaring that it meant proclaiming the Word of God,[17]

15 WA 1:601,28f; LW 31:204f.
16 WA 7:10, 30; LW 35:342; WA 7:42,6–10; LW 31:334.
17 See WA 7:811,17–20.

exactly as Bernard had conceptualized. At about the same time, Luther was working on his second investigation into the psalms (*Operationes in Psalmos*). In the preface to this work, he once again wrote: ' "Feed my sheep", that is, give [them] what they feed on; they feed on the Word of God alone, not on opinions or human traditions'.[18]

At that time Luther began to add to his biblical-bernardine focus the radical questioning of the concept of an external priesthood, arguing, especially after 1521, from his heightened christocentric point of view, that the New Testament does not know any external priesthood at all. Christ is the only priest and pastor, Luther pointed out in a number of sermons for the traditional Good Shepherd Sunday (the second Sunday after Easter).[19] 'Ordination' now began to mean for him a call and commitment to a specific ministry in the Church, in essence the proclamation of the gospel, and no longer to a man's priestly 'consecration' by anointing.

In 1522, in talking about Mk 7, he again used the three-fold pastoral concept of preaching, exemplary living, and praying for others:

The preachers and apostles lead the common folks to God. This happens now in a threefold way: by preaching, good [exemplary] living, and praying for others. With the Word and preaching they lead the people to God; their exemplary life serves the purpose to enforce all the more the [preached] word and its power.[20]

When, in 1523, Luther expounded 1 Peter, he again integrated the threefold bernardine concept into his deliberations: 'This is the right priesthood: it consists of three parts . . . , spiritual sacrifice, praying for the community, and preaching'.[21] Toward the end of his

18 AWA 2:11,19f.

19 Three sermons on the Good Shepherd are collected conveniently in John Nicholas Lenker, ed., *Sermons of Martin Luther* (Grand Rapids: Baker Book House, n. d.) 3:17–71.

20 WA 10-III:311,4–12; see Posset, 'Bernhard vom Clairvauxs Sermone zur Weihnachts-, Fasten- und Osterzeit als Quellen Martin Luthers', 111. Bell differs.

21 WA 12:309,24–26.

life, in 1545, Luther once again made use of the threefold concept as part of his polemics against the papacy. Luther stressed the familiar three aspects of Bernard's concept, which he saw lacking in the Roman Church: preaching the gospel, praise and thanksgiving to God without end, praying for all the world and living a disciplined (*zuchtig*) life by which one gives a good example.[22]

This overview of Luther's use of Bernard's pastoral concept has covered several decades, from 1516 to 1545, and it demonstrates that the idea was always in the Reformer's mind. Early on, Luther made it clear that he followed Bernard in this regard. Unfortunately, the connection to Bernard has not always been given due consideration in past and present ecumenical deliberations on pastoral ministry. This connection needs to be emphasized again today.[23] As Luther learned from Bernard, so should we. It does

22 WA 54:280,4–11.

23 There is a need to clarify Luther's doctrine of the pastoral ministry, as the large number of recent studies in this regard demonstrates. None of them take Bernard's concept as Luther's matrix into consideration. From among the recent literature on this subject (after 1980), see especially the following: David Bagchi, '*Eyn Mercklich Underscheyd*: Catholic Reactions to Luther's Doctrine of the Priesthood of All Believers, 1520–25'. *The Ministry: Clerical and Lay*, W. J. Sheils and Diana Wood, eds. (Oxford: Basil Blackwell, 1989) 155–65; Hans-Martin Barth, 'Allgemeines Priestertum der Gläubigen nach Martin Luther', *Una Sancta* 43 (1988) 331–342; Barth, *Einander Priester sein. Allgemeines Priestertum in ökumenischer Perspektive* (Göttingen: Vandenhoeck & Ruprecht, 1990); Remigius Bäumer, 'Luthers Ansichten über das Priestertum'. *Luther und die Folgen für die Geistesgeschichte. Festschrift für Theobald Beer,* Remigius Bäumer and Alma von Stockhausen, eds. (Weilheim-Bierbronnen: Gustav-Siewerth-Akademie, 1992) 9–30; Mark Ellingsen, 'Luther's Concept of the Ministry: Creative Tension', *Word and World* 1 (1981) 338–346; Charles J. Evanson, 'The Office and Order of the Holy Ministry: Luther and Lutheran'. *And Every Tongue Confess. Essays in Honor of Norman Nagel on the Occasion of His Sixty-fifth Birthday*, Gerald S. Krispin and Jon D. Vieker, eds. (Dearborn, MI: The Nagel Festschrift Committee, 1990) 153–178; Ramon Arnau García, *El ministro legado de Cristo, según Lutero* (Valencia, 1983), and the review of it by Jared Wicks, *Theological Studies* 46 (1985) 366–368; Christine Globig, *Frauenordination im Kontext lutherischer Ekklesiologie. Ein Beitrag zum ökumenischen Gespräch* (Göttingen: Vandenhoeck & Ruprecht, 1994); Robert J. Goeser, 'Word of God, Church, and Ministry', *Dialog* 29 (1990) 195–206; Irwin J. Habeck, 'Luther's Attitude Toward the Public Ministry'. *Luther Lives: Essays in Commemoration of the 500th Anniversary of Martin Luther's Birth* (Milwaukee: Northwestern Publishing House, 1983) 33–43; Gert Haendler, *Luther on Ministerial Office and Congregational Function,* Ruth C. Gritsch, trans., Eric W. Gritsch, ed. (Philadelphia: Fortress Press, 1981); Kurt K. Hendel, 'The Doctrine of the Ministry: The Reformation Heritage', *Currents in Theology and Mission* 17

not matter which approach we use, whether we study Bernard's insights first as representative of Catholic thought and then realize, with Luther, their ecumenical significance; or whether we study Luther first and then realize the compatibility of the sixteenth-century Reformer's ideas with the medieval monk's concept; or, whether, with Bernard and with Luther, we meditate on their common biblical ground, the text of Jn 21:15–17. Whichever approach we choose, we will arrive at the same bernardine and lutheran conclusion: 'Feeding means evangelizing'. What is (ecumenically) exciting is the fact that a Catholic saint provides the basis for a concept of the care of souls (*Seelsorge*) which all Christians can share and build on. If only all Christians in defining pastoral ministry would take Bernard as seriously as did Luther!

The following chart shows the loci where the pastoral concept is mentioned in Bernard (chart two), and and where in Luther's works it is taken up (chart one). The original sequences in the sources (preaching – exemplary living – praying) are indicated by the numbers in parentheses:

(1990) 23–33; Eugene R. Klug, 'Luther on the Ministry', CTQ 47 (1983) 293–304; Robert Kolb, 'Ministry in Martin Luther and the Lutheran Confessions'. *Called and Ordained: Lutheran Perspectives on the Office of Ministry,* Todd Nichol and Marc Kolden, eds. (Minneapolis: Augsburg Fortress Press, 1990) 49–66; *The Condemnations of the Reformation Era. Do They Still Divide?* Karl Lehmann and Wolfhart Pannenberg, eds., Margaret Kohl, trans. (Minneapolis: Fortress Press, 1989,147–159 (Chapter 4 on Ministry); in critical response to *The Condemnations,* the Faculty of Theology at the University of Göttingen, Germany, came out with its expert opinion *Outmoded Condemnations? Antitheses between the Council of Trent and the Reformation on Justification, the Sacrament, and the Ministry—Then and Now,* Oliver K. Olson and Franz Posset, trans. (Fort Wayne, Indiana: Luther Academy, 1992) 99–106 (on 'The Office of the Ministry'); Carter Lindberg, 'The ministry and vocation of the baptized', *Lutheran Quarterly* 6 (1992) 385–401; Heinz Schütte, 'Ist Luther's Sakramentsverständnis kirchentrennend?' *Martin Luther im Spiegel heutiger Wissenschaft,* Knut Schäferdiek, ed. (Bonn: Bouvier Verlag Herbert Grundmann, 1985) 185–199. The Journal of catholic and evangelical Theology *Pro Ecclesia* dedicated the entire vol. 2 (1993) 261–295 to 'A Symposium on Ministry'. The first edition of the electronic journal *Semper Reformanda: A Journal for Lutheran Reformation* 1 (1997) has three articles on ministry, by Ruben Josefson, Lowell C. Green, and David P. Scaer (internet).

Luther in 1545 WA 54: 280,4–11	(1) preaching *predige*	(3) live a good example *zuchtig leben zum guten Exempel*	(2) pray for all the world *bete für alle welt*
Luther in 1523 WA 12:309	(3) preaching *predige*	(1) spiritual sacrifice *geystlich opffere*	(2) praying *beten*
Luther in 1522 WA 10-III:311,4–10	(1) preaching *predigen*	(2) exemplary living *guttem leben*	(3) praying for *fürbitten*
Luther in 1519 WA 2:635,16–18	(1) teach God's Word *verbum dei docere*	(3) lead with good example *exemplo bono praeesse*	(2) pray for the sheep *orare pro ovibus*
Luther in 1516 WA 56:137,25–27 WA 57-I:117,19ff	(2) teaching *doceat*	(1) laboring *faciat*	(3) pray for *oret pro*

Chart 1

Bernard's Sent 3:41 SBOp 6-II:89,6f	(2) teaching *doctrina*	(1) living *vita*	(3) prayer *oratio*
Bernard's Ep 201 SBOp 8:61,3f	(1) word *verbum*	(2) example *exemplum*	(3) prayer *oratio*
Bernard's Second Easter Sermon SBOp 5: 96,21–24	(2) exhort by word *verbi exhortatione ore lingua*	(3) exhibition of example *exempli exhibitione opere manus*	(1) praying of the mind *animi oratione mente mens*
Bernard's SC 76 SBOp 2:258,16– 261,14	(2) pastures of the Bible *in pascuis Scripturarum*	(3) good and choice examples *bonis . . . exemplis*	(1) pray for the people *orant pro populo*
Bernard's Csi SBOp 3:454,1	Feeding means evangelizing *Evangelizare, pascere est.*		

Chart 2

Conclusion

BEFORE DRAWING THIS investigation to its conclusions, I need to point out that I have not elaborated on the trinitarian theology of Bernard and Luther or mentioned that both men moved without question within the orthodox christian theological tradition.[1]

The subject of our investigation has been whether there is a theological congeniality between the two diverse personalities of the Cistercian abbot, Saint Bernard of Clairvaux, and the Augustinian friar and later Reformer, Martin Luther. In terms of their theology and spirituality, the answer is emphatically affirmative. Bernard, the extraordinary *doctor mellifluus*, was given by Luther the honorific title 'father'; *Pater Bernhardus* he preferred 'over all the others, for he had the best knowledge of *religio*, as his writings show'. In Luther's view, 'Father Bernard' was an outstanding witness to the gospel truth. 'The Last of the Church Fathers' had a great influence on the inner development of the sixteenth century Reformer, who wanted to by-pass the scholastics and return to the sources (*ad fontes*), to the Church Fathers and, with them, ultimately to the Bible. He did this in terms of the biblical and monastic humanism (*Klosterhumanismus*) of his time and territory.

---

1 On Bernard, see Michael Stickelbroeck, *Mysterium Venerandum: Der trinitarische Gedanke im Werk des Bernhard von Clairvaux* (Münster: Aschendorff, 1994); Anne Morris, 'The Trinity in Bernard's Sermons on the Song of Songs', CSQ 30 (1995) 35–57; on Luther, see for example Lohse, *Luthers Theologie*, 223–235.

Luther became well versed in Bernard's spirituality and regarded
him 'as the most righteous of all the monks'.

In following Luther's recommendation that Bernard 'should be
studied diligently', I have tried to explore Luther's repertoire of the
works of Bernard, all of which were available in the new medium
of that time, the printed text. Luther's high esteem for Bernard was
part of the wider reception of this medieval master in the fifteenth
and sixteenth centuries. Bernard enjoyed an enormous popularity
in the late Middle Ages, and his influence may be compared to that
of Augustine.[2] Luther did not, however, make use of the entire
bernardine *corpus*. He either did not know it in its entirety or
simply ignored great parts of it, mostly the treatises (*The Steps of
Humility and Pride, On Loving God, On the Conduct and Duties
of Bishops, In Praise of the New Knighthood, On Grace and Free
Choice, Apology to William of Saint Thierry, On Conversion to
Clerics,* and the *Life of Malachy*).[3] *On Grace and Free Choice*,
I have demonstrated, Luther probably did not read, despite the
fact that an adage he used in the vernacular appears to have come
straight out of this treatise. Luther's source reference was to an
obscure (unidentifiable, pseudo-bernardine?) sermon on the gospel
text about Mary Magdalene. Luther appears to have shared in the
reception of Bernard as model preacher, which the renaissance
humanists promoted, and he therefore showed no interest in his
treatises, with the exception of *On Consideration*.

Luther owed much of his erudition to contemporary 'monastic
humanism' and to the revival of a monastic theology of which
Bernard was one of the most articulate representatives. Luther's
own 'orational', *sacra pagina* approach to Scripture studies by way
of *oratio, meditatio, tentatio* is unthinkable outside the matrix of
the monastic tradition. Further traces of monastic theology found
in Luther's spiritual and theological concepts have been presented

2 See Constable, 'Twelfth-Century Spirituality and the Late Middle Ages',
Medieval and Renaissance Studies 5 (1971) 31; see Posset, 'Saint Bernard in
Devotion, Theology, and Art of the Sixteenth Century', *Lutheran Quarterly* 11
(1997) 308–352.

3 Franz Posset, 'Bernaed of Clairvaux as Luther's Source: Reading Bernard
with Luther's "Spectacles" ', CTQ 54 (1990) 281–304.

in Chapter One. The german Reformation grew primarily, not out of criticism of the deformation and abuses within the renaissance Church, but out of Luther's pastoral and spiritual concerns and his theological studies, which included the Church Fathers up to Bernard, and, of course, the Bible. In this he belonged within sixteenth-century biblical humanism. From this came the theological axioms which made him famous: Scripture alone, grace alone, faith alone, Christ alone. These axioms should not be claimed as Luther's inventions, however, as has sometimes been insinuated in post-reformation and post-tridentine histories of the Church. They are grounded largely in the bernardine (and augustinian) monastic legacy which Luther retrieved and which he processed in his own way, at times polemically in defending himself, and mainly against such friars of the rival Order of Preachers (Dominicans) as John Tetzel op, Sylvester Mazzolini op, called Prierias, Marcus von Weida op, or Cardinal Cajetan op, and their specific spirituality, scholasticism, and last but not least their overwhelming influence in Rome.[4]

The friar, then ex-friar, of Wittenberg sharpened his monastic theological and contemporary humanistic emphasis on the Scriptures, an emphasis he inherited from his own augustinian Order, and he radicalized it in his own hermeneutical principle of 'Scripture alone'. Luther learned from Bernard how to internalize the Scriptures. Even though one does not find the expression 'Scripture alone' in the bernardine *opera*, Bernard certainly employed and applied this axiom in his writings, for his texts are permeated by biblical language. In his sermons on the Song of Songs alone,

---

4 The list of Luther's opponents from the Order of Saint Dominic could easily be expanded by names such as John Faber from Augsburg, John Mensing, a preacher at Magdeburg and Dessau, Jacob Hochstraten, the head of the inquisition in Cologne, and Conrad Köllin, a member of the theological faculty in Cologne whose members Luther denounced as asses, dogs, and swine. See Nikolaus Paulus, *Die deutschen Dominikaner im Kampfe gegen Luther, 1518–1563* (Freiburg 1903); Hartmann Grisar, *Martin Luther: His Life and Work* (Westminster: The Newman Press, 1953) 367f. Luther's opponent, Hieronymus Dungersheim, was a friend of the Leipzig Dominicans. More recently, the pamphlet war between the Franciscans and Luther and his followers was investigated by Geoffrey Dipple, *Antifraternalism and Anticlericalism in the German Reformation* (Aldershot, England: Scolar Press, 1996).

5526 biblical quotations can be identified.[5] This surely constitutes a scriptural principle characteristic of monastic theology. Bernard's and Luther's fundamental congeniality is grounded in their love of Scripture studies. We have learned of Luther's opinion that nobody could teach the Word of God better than monks like Bernard. Bernard had advised people to read the Bible in a 'cautious and simple way'. Luther practised this type of reading and also the interpretation of the Bible in simplicity, as he had learned in the friary. Monastic 'rumination' of the Word of God had taught Luther to 'taste' and to experience the 'sweetness' of that Word. Convinced that those who have a soul like Bernard's will understand the Bible, Luther demanded that all Christians read and ponder the Bible not as ancient literature but as the Word of God which, in his words, 'wants to be grasped with a quiet mind and be meditated on'. None but a 'quiet, meditating mind'[6] can grasp the meaning of the Word of God. Thus monastic meditation was transferred from the cloister and recommended to Christians in the world. Luther may be set within the broad late medieval practice of carrying theological and sometimes monastic concepts to lay people. This transfer was known by the carthusian maxim *de cella in seculum*, 'from the [monastic] cell to the world [at large]'.[7]

Luther wanted Scripture to be read not only with a 'quiet meditating mind', but also 'with closed eyes', so that nothing— whether pagan, aristotelian, or scholastic or any other human imagining or fabrication—nothing but the Word of God alone could influence his thinking. This 'orational' approach to the Bible, which Luther shared with the monastic tradition, was enriched by the 'monastic humanism' (biblical humanism) of Luther's time

5 See Denis Farkasfalvy, 'St Bernard's Interpretation of the Psalms in his Sermons *Super Cantica*', *Erudition at God's Service: Studies in Medieval Cistercian History*, XI, John R. Sommerfeldt, ed. CS 98 (Kalamazoo: CP, 1987)109.

6 . . . *mit stillem geyst gefasset und betrachtet,* WA 10-I:728,9–22. See on this Bernhard Lohse, 'Entstehungsgeschichte und hermeneutische Prinzipien der Lutherbibel', *Evangelium in der Geschichte. Studien zu Luther und der Reformation*, 182 and 198; see Posset, 'Bible Reading "With Closed Eyes"', 293–306.

7 See Michael G. Sargent, ed., *De cella in seculum: Religious and Secular Life and Devotion in Late Medieval England* (Cambridge: D. S. Bewer,1988).

with its 'sacred philology' and its emphasis on returning to the original biblical languages in order better to understand the Word of God. From this monastic-humanistic perspective, the typical modern Roman Catholic picture of Luther as a 'subjectivist' in interpreting the Sacred Scriptures no longer makes sense and should, therefore, be abandoned.

In Chapter Two, we pointed out how Bernard's concept of 'grace alone' (Ann 1) was ingrained in Luther's thinking early in, and throughout, his career. Luther's longest literal quotation from Bernard's works came from Ann 1, which dealt with the priority of grace. Already in his first exposition of Psalm 31 Luther very likely referred to the decisive passage in that sermon, and shortly afterwards, during his famous 1515/1516 lectures on Paul's *Letter to the Romans*, he quoted explicitly from Ann 1 for the first time, and then very extensively. At that same time he recognized in Bernard the same spirit, *plenus eodem spiritu,* as in Saint Paul. These observations lead one to give credibility to Melanchthon's remark about the young Luther that, already during his stay at the Erfurt friary (1505–1508 and 1509–1511), he had heard a senior friar talk about the message of Bernard's Ann 1.[8] Furthermore, this same sermon was used by Luther not only in his lectures, but also in his defense against Cardinal Cajetan op, who as the great Thomist of his time was Luther's roman curial counterpart at the Diet of Augsburg in 1518. There we observe the clash of two schools of thought: monastic theology and scholastic theology.

Bearing these central theological concepts in mind, I proposed that we view Luther as *Bernardus redivivus*.[9] A Catholic fellow scholar has called this 'questionable'.[10] I do not insist on it here.

8 See *Praefatio Melanthonis in 'Tomum secundum omnium operum Reverendi Domini Martini Lutheri, Doctoris Theologiae'* (Wittenberg 1546), *Corpus Reformatorum* 6:158f; see Posset, *'Bernardus Redivivus'*, especially note 52; see Posset, 'Divus Bernhardus', *Bernardus Magister,* 520; see Theo Bell, *Bernhardus Dixit* (1989), 27- 74; *Divus Bernhardus* (1993), 27–82.

9 *'Bernardus Redivivus'*, CSQ 22 (1987) 239–249.

10 See Theo Bell, 'Pater Bernardus. Luthers visie op Bernhardus van Clairvaux', *Luther-Bulletin* 1 (1992) 41; Bell, 'Bernhard von Clairvaux als Quelle Martin Luthers', 13–15; Ann 1 is 'doubtlessly, one of the most important, if not the most important Bernard quotation in Luther', 14.

But one must insist that Luther embodied many of Bernard's theological concerns and certainly his concept of pastoral care as evangelization.

We discussed in Chapter Three how Luther early took up Bernard's teaching on humility as the 'virtue of Christ', his differentiation between humility and humiliation, and his thoughts about the interdependence of the knowledge of self and the knowledge of God without which one is led into despair. The two men shared the belief that Christ dwells in the believer's heart by faith. Although the doctrine of forensic justification had often been identified as the chief and distinct axiom of reformation teaching on salvation, we noticed that Bernard occasionally sounds like sixteenth-century reformers in this regard. Yet, Luther in his spirituality and theology did not accentuate the doctrine of forensic justification in the way in which it was promoted in the 1530s, especially by Luther's friend, Melanchthon.[11]

In Chapter Four, we focused first on Bernard's affective christocentrism and his theology of the cross. Then we saw how the Cistercian's theology of the incarnation influenced Luther to such a degree that at one point he exclaimed in admiration that 'Bernard really loved the Incarnation'. Luther learned important insights from Bernard's sermons on longing for the coming of Christ as the physician of souls, on Christ's 'three advents', and on the 'three miracles' connected to Christ's incarnation (in-*human*-ment, not in-*angel*-ment). Luther also took up Bernard's peculiar speculation about Lucifer, and his emphasis on Christ as our circumcised brother who for us was made in the 'form of sin'.

Bernard, fascinated by 1 Cor 2:2, had no other philosophy than to know Christ and him crucified. Luther was quite familiar with this bernardine thought and its context in SC 43 (*fasciculus myrrhae*), which also includes the distinctive concept of self-judgment which leads to happiness and obviates the need for condemnation by a Judge. Under Bernard's influence, Luther was able to balance his initially distorted image of Christ as nothing but the stern Judge with his acceptance of the bernardine concept of Christ as the 'most sweet Saviour' on the mercy seat, the cross.

11 See Strehle, *The Catholic Roots of the Protestant Gospel*, 66.

In the tradition of Luther's religious Order and in obedience to his superior, Johann von Staupitz, Luther followed a wise recommendation that he meditate on the wounds of Christ and on his Sacred Heart. By this practice, Bernard's *fasciculus myrrhae* became the matrix for Luther's theology of the cross. For both Bernard and Luther, the 'hidden God' is the crucified Christ. Late in his career, Luther came in retrospect to the conclusion that his own emphasis on the contemplation of Christ's salvific passion was identical with Bernard's teaching, and in 1539 he declared that this doctrine was not his, but Bernard's, and ultimately the apostle Paul's. No doubt Luther's interest in pauline theology matched Bernard's. The Reformer's simple comment was that Bernard 'ascribed everything to Christ' and that he 'crawled to the cross' as to his salvation. Bernard's talk of 'Christ's double right to the kingdom of heaven', one by divine sonship, the other by meritorious suffering on the cross, turns out to have been a constant image in Luther's teaching up to his death. By calling this legendary saying 'golden', Luther made a bernardine saying comparable to key verses in Scripture.

In Chapter Five, we investigated the medieval monk's diagnosis of the state of the Church and his impulses for reform, which forcefully resurfaced in Luther's teaching. Bernard's Csi was valued so highly by the Reformer that he wanted all popes to learn it by heart. Luther quoted from or referred to passages in every one of the five books originally addressed to Pope Eugene III. In his pastoral concept of the petrine office, Luther simply picked up Bernard's idea that it is essentially, 'evangelization' and applied it to the pastoral ministry of ecclesiastical ministers in general. On this specific ecclesiological and pastoral issue, too, one may view Luther as *Bernardus redivivus*. Bernard and Luther perceived the Church as a 'hospital' filled with patients stricken by a 'foul corruption' which Luther felt at least as intensely as had Bernard. In trying to cure her, the cistercian abbot from France had more 'success' and became a great saint of the Church, while the augustinian friar from Saxony was excommunicated and became 'the Reformer' outside the Church of Rome.

Having said this, one must realize that Luther was not at all interested in Bernard as a politician, nor even as an ecclesiastical politician. He was impressed primarily by the preacher, specifically the preacher of the incarnation and of the *Kreuz*, the cross, but not of the *Kreuzzug*, the crusade. The Reformer shared his selective interest in Bernard the preacher with Erasmus and with the great medieval theologian, Bonaventure, who quoted Bernard more than four hundred times and also classified Bernard primarily as a preacher, a person well versed in Bible studies and, because of this, considered him a very eloquent speaker.[12] In following this medieval classification, Luther, as a preacher and *Seelsorger* (provider of pastoral care, 'pastor'), viewed and used Bernard as a pastoral, homiletic, spiritual, and theological authority. In doing so, he evaluated him in an 'evangelical' way, measuring him with the yardstick of the Bible. In this regard then, Bernard's 'mystical' sermons were a *chose négligeable* to Luther. He favored the abbot's 'affective christocentrism' which mirrored his intense love for the Word of God found in Scripture.

We may suspect that Luther entered religious life for all the wrong reasons, if he initially wanted to 'earn' his salvation by his own efforts at becoming a perfect religious, as some contemporary popular opinions have insinuated. Authentic monastic spirituality and his own biblical-humanistic theological studies under the leadership of Staupitz soon taught him something else: that Christ alone, grace alone, faith alone, and evangelization alone are essential. From faith in Christ, good works flow naturally. No one can perform good works without grace, Luther learned from Bernard. On the basis of his studies Luther must have realized that his initial motivation for the religious life was no longer tenable. Once his pre-monastic outlook on life brought him into the cloister he had been straightened out behind augustinian walls and, as a friar, began to apply these (new to him) monastic insights (especially about grace and faith) to the popular practices

12 Bonaventure: . . . *beatus Bernardus parum sciebat, sed quia in Scriptura multum studuit, ideo locutus est elegantissime*, as quoted by Jacques Verger, 'Saint Bernard et les scolastiques'. *Vies et légendes*, 210. See also Heiko A. Oberman, 'Luther and Mysticism'. *The Reformation in Medieval Perspective*, ed. Steven Ozment (Chicago: Quadrangle Books, 1971) 226f. On Luther the preacher, see John T. Pless, 'Martin Luther: Preacher of the Cross', CTQ 51 (1987) 83–101. Luther's 2300 sermons as published in WA, reveal his primary calling and vocation. Luther claimed to have equaled the preaching activity of both Augustine and Ambrose.

and devotions of his day. Some of these—such as indulgence trafficking—he and his augustinian confrères consequently sought to purify and reform. Luther soon began to proclaim to the wider audience outside monastic walls the ideas he had learned from a Bible–based, humanistic, and monastic, mainly bernardine and augustinian theology, which he gradually internalized and which is known today as his Reformation theology. From our perspective, Luther's Reformation theology appears to be fundamentally monastic, and the so-called Reformation breakthrough emerges as a monastic process in which Bernard, (along with Augustine, the patron of both his Order and the University of Wittenberg), plays the role of Luther's great mentor.

When we look at Luther's theological career throughout his life in detail, an unbroken chain of references to Bernard's works becomes visible.[13] Unfortunately, no notes [as such exist in his books of Augustine, Anselm, and Lombard] are extant from Luther's personal reading in Bernard's works. The *demonstrable* chain of Bernard references begins in 1509–10, in his notes on Peter Lombard's *Sentences*, where the friar's first use of a Bernard quotation was probably meant as a critical comment on Peter Lombard. The chain of references continues with Luther's entry on the inside cover of the *Opuscula Anselmi,* which he consulted probably in preparation for his First Lectures on the Psalms in 1513. From this time through the critical years of the effervescent Reformation, direct and indirect references to Bernard can be retrieved. As a friar and as an ex-friar, Luther treated Bernard as his mentor, guide, and helper in interpreting the Scriptures, whether in an academic or a pastoral setting, in polemical writings, in confrontations, in talks at table, in letters, or in preaching the Good News to ordinary people. Bernard's spiritual insights were always vividly present in Luther's mind.

13 It should be noted that Theo Bell's investigation in *Divus Bernhardus* largely followed Luther's biography in demonstrating the younger Reformer's references to Bernard: Chapter 1: 1505–1515; Chapter 2: 1515–1521; Chapter 3: The controversies in 1521; Chapter 4: The Reformation writings; Chapter 5: Bernard in Luther's sermons up to 1520; Chapter 6: Bernard in Luther's writings after 1521; Chapter 7: Who was Bernard to Luther? Concentrating on Bernard as topic of table talks.

When one traces only Luther's most direct references to Bernard's works step by step throughout his career, a clear picture of Luther's repertoire of Bernard's theological insights emerges. By the time he gave his first course on the psalms, Luther was familiar with proverbial sayings gleaned from some of Bernard's letters and sermons, probably by someone other than Luther. He read the Sermons on the Song of Songs and the sermons for the liturgical year, particularly those for Advent, Christmas, and Easter. Especially impressive is the long quotation which Luther copied out from Bernard's first sermon for Epiphany. The most important of all his Bernard quotations, however, turns out to have come from the first sermon for the feast of the Annunciation. Furthermore, prior to or during his lectures on Romans (1515/1516), the young professor had certainly read *On Consideration*. Beginning with these lectures, and continuing into his second course on the psalms in 1519, he occasionally repeated some previously used Bernard references, but he also integrated new quotations, especially the passage from Bernard's fifth Lenten sermon about prayer which Luther liked very much. Other passages quoted before 1519 come from Sermon 61 on the Song of Songs (SC 61), on the clefts of the rocks as symbols of the wounds of Christ.

Along with many others, such as the fourteenth-century Dominican, Johannes Tauler, Luther thought at times that he was quoting Augustine, when he cited a phrase from Bernard; he mistakenly ascribed to Augustine a line actually taken from Bernard's SC 61 on gaining consolation from meditation on the wounds of the Lord. If one integrates these allegedly augustinian, but in fact bernardine, quotations into Luther's theological sources, one realizes that Bernard's impact on Luther was even greater than the Reformer himself realized.

During the period between his second lectures on the psalms in 1519 and the year 1525, when his political protector, Frederick the Wise, died and he married a former cistercian nun, he continued to refer to Bernard's works, quoting for the first time from Bernard's Sermons on the Song of Songs 2, 34, 37, and 38. After 1525, references to familiar phrases from the cistercian father's works were repeated and some new ones were added; speculation about Lucifer turned up after 1526, and references to Sermons 51 and 65 surfaced as late as in his commentary on Genesis (and only there). Thus, one may assert that Luther found recurrent help by consulting Bernard's works, and did not simply indirectly soak up some 'late medieval' concepts of piety which more or less happened to have been shaped by Bernard and were still floating around. In the decisive period of his life Luther enjoyed the steady company of bernardine works, which therefore constitute the spiritual and theological 'context' in which he moved. Contemporary Luther research needs to take this influence into serious consideration, if the real Luther is to be uncovered.

There are many of Bernard references in Luther's works in mid-career and beyond, and one may rightly conclude that he remained a life-long admirer of Bernard. Luther found in this medieval spiritual director a genuine father and teacher of the christian faith. Luther's christocentric interest felicitously meshed with Bernard's. Luther was seeking 'whatever promotes Christ' (*was Christum treibet*), and Bernard, being such a promoter, was of inestimable aid to him. In 1535 Luther said in his *Preface to the Commentary on Galatians*: 'In my heart there rules one article, namely, faith in Christ; from it, through it and in it all my theological deliberations flow and return day and night'.

The side-effect of this affective christocentrism was the diminution of devotions to the Virgin Mary. Probably under humanistic influence, Luther became very critical of folk piety with its trust in Mary's intercession on behalf of sinners. Ecumenical dialogues today and in the future need to concentrate on the sometimes murky marian folk piety of past and present more than on academic mariology. Further studies are needed to determine whether Bernard will be a teacher for all Christians on the veneration of the Virgin Mary, and whether Catholics can learn from Luther's view of Mary. What becomes clear here is that Luther learned from Bernard not a marian spirituality, but a Christ-centered spirituality of the heart.

In looking at Luther's Bernard citations, one must note that there are several works which Luther apparently never quoted at all. It is, of course, impossible to tell whether Luther neglected these writings because they did not appeal to him, because they were not useful to his task of preaching, or because they simply were not available to him. The number of neglected treatises is unusually high in view of the great esteem Luther had for Bernard. But if one takes into account that Luther by profession and passion was a preacher, then his selective interest in Bernard's sermons appears natural. As a gifted preacher, who has been dubbed the 'German Cicero', Luther valued the sermons over the treatises or 'disputations', of the Cistercian Cicero. From this perspective, Luther's lack of interest in Bernard the polemicist, treatise writer, and mystic is perhaps easier to understand. As a critical evaluator of contemporary monasticism, he appears to have taken Bernard's interpretation of monastic rules into account. He did not at all share the concept of monastic profession as a 'second baptism', yet he did not associate this idea with Bernard, who wrote about it in *On Precept and Dispensation*. One must, therefore, wonder whether Luther ever studied it.[14]

Luther's selective reading of the sermons of the *doctor mellifluus* may have been wider than is demonstrable by research today. That he read Bernard cannot, however, be disputed. It is evident from our comparisons of their texts and may also be deduced from Luther's own words: 'I hold Saint Bernard higher than any monk or priest on earth. I have not heard or *read* anything like him' (1525); 'it is a joy to *read* him'.[15] Luther did not read bernardine texts as historical literature; he 'came to know and study Bernard in view of his existential and theological questions'.[16]

Not only genuine bernardine texts, but also devotional texts ascribed to Bernard were known to Luther, as is the case with the prayer called the *Eight Verses of Bernard*. Early in his career as a Scripture professor Luther 'demythologized' this prayer, probably following Erasmus, by uncovering it as a pastiche of various psalm verses. Luther's familiarity with this and other pious products of the tradition, and his numerous, at times critical, references to Bernard's life story demonstrate once more his vast knowledge

---

14 Bell, 'Luther's Reception of Bernard' 252, wrote: 'Luther, indeed, knew the work'. The question remains: Really, and to what degree?

15 *das ein lust ist, quando quis legit* (1539); WA 47:694,5f; *Jch hab seines gleichen nicht gehort und gelesen*, WA 16:400,20f; see Posset, 'Bernhard von Clairvauxs Sermone', 93–116.

16 See Lohse, 'Luther und Bernhard von Clairvaux', 284.

of the Cistercian's spirituality, life, and work.[17] While ideas from Bernard's many letters left their impression on Luther, one may question whether Luther actually read them, and then ask for what purpose a busy preacher and teacher like Luther should have read them.

More significant than determining what exactly he read or did not read is the concentration Luther learned from Bernard on the essentials of the christian faith. From him he learned that Christ is 'for me' my personal saviour. By gradually 'demystifying' Bernard by neglecting his predominantly mystical sermons, and by focusing on the reformation-sounding passages in Bernard's works, Luther made Bernard a hero to his own and the younger generation of protestant Reformers. Luther laid the foundation for the reception of Bernard in later Lutheranism.[18]

Anyone who has followed the train of this investigation may have got the impression that I would like to explain the phenomenon 'Luther' in only one, mono-causal way, as if Luther were under the exclusive spell of Bernard. The careful reader will see that the contrary is true: I have tried to present Luther in his extreme complexity, a man influenced by many sources and formed by factors within the contemporary milieu of augustinian monastic and biblical humanism in which he came of age. He was also strongly influenced by the rivalry between his own reformed Augustinian Order and the Dominican Order.

The further objection could be raised that the connection between the spiritualities of the reformed augustinian friars on the one side and of the benedictine/cistercian monks on the other side has been more assumed here than demonstrated. This observation is correct. My goal has not been to demonstrate the relationship between two religious Orders as traditions. Even so, it is known that augustinian libraries such as those at Erfurt and Wittenberg

17 Posset, 'Bernard of Clairvaux as Luther's Source', CTQ (1990) 281–304; Posset, 'The Elder Luther on Bernard; Part I', 23–52; 'Part II: Last Exegetical Work', 179–201.

18 See Ernst Koch, 'Die Bernhard-Rezeption im Luthertum des 16. und 17. Jahrhunderts', *Bernhard von Clairvaux: Rezeption und Wirkung*, Elm, ed., 333–352; Posset, 'Saint Bernard in Devotion, Theology, and Art of the Sixteenth Century'.

included bernardine works. Furthermore, it is an historical fact that Johann von Staupitz, Luther's esteemed superior and the leading officer of the reformed Order of Saint Augustine in Germany, became a benedictine abbot at Salzburg, Austria, later in his life, in 1522. The benedictine monk and humanist Veit Bild (1481–1529) of Augsburg found Luther's *Resolutiones* on the indulgence issue 'excellent', and the cistercian abbot Valentine of Lehnin carried to Luther a letter from a bishop who pronounced his *Resolutiones* 'good catholic' teaching; this same abbot informed him that he himself thoroughly condemned the new indulgence preaching of the Dominicans.[19] In short, some familiarity and congeniality between the two religious Orders may be assumed. We also know of several cisterican monks who were friends of Luther and other Reformers: Antonius Corvinus (1501–1553), from the abbey of Loccum, Germany; Albert R. Hardenberg (1510–1574) from the monastery of Aduard (Adwert, Holland); and Michael Meurer (= *a Muris Galliculus*, who died in 1537) a monk of the cisterican abbey of Celle, near Dresden. It appears that their benedictine/cistercian formation opened them up to Luther's concerns.[20] Several religious Orders in German speaking lands, especially the Augustinian and Benedictine/Cistercian but also others, shared in what is known as 'monastic humanism' (*Klosterhumanismus*). Because of its influence, Europe experienced not only an 'Augustinréveil'[21] and enthusiasm for Jerome,[22] but also a return to Bernard's monastic

19 See Heinrich Boehmer, *Martin Luther: Road to Reformation,* trans. John W. Doberstein and Theodore G. Tappert (New York: Meridian, 1957) 199 (on Valentine of Lehrin); on Veit Bild: Junghans, *Der junge Luther und die Humanisten,* 293.

20 See Robert Stupperich, *Reformatorenlexikon* (Gütersloh: Gütersloher Verlagshaus Gerd Mohn, 1984), 62, 95, 145.

21 Heiko A. Oberman, ' "Tuus sum, salvum me fac". Augustinréveil zwischen Renaissance und Reformation'. *Scientia Augustiniana. Studien über Augustinus, den Augustinismus und den Augustinerorden.* Festschrift Adolar Zumkeller OSA zum 60. Geburtstag, eds. Cornelius Petrus Mayer and Willigis Eckermann (Würzburg: Cassiacum, 1975) 349–394.

22 See Eugene F. Rice Jr., *Saint Jerome in the Renaissance* (Baltimore and London: The Johns Hopkins University Press, 1985). See Berndt Hamm, 'Hieronymus-Begeisterung und Augustinismus vor der Reformation. Beobachtungen zur Beziehung zwischen Humanismus und Frömmigkeitstheologie (am Beispiel Nürnbergs)'. *Augustine, the Harvest, and Theology (1300–1650),* Hagen, ed., 127–235.

Conclusion   393

theology. Thus, this investigation may be considered a contribution to the history of Bernard's impact on subsequent thought (*Wirkungsgeschichte*), even though the full story of his influence on later centuries has yet to be written. Historians of theology have not known quite what to make of him. He remains a figure known to many but read by only a few modern theologians[23]—in contrast to the medieval theologians and protestant Reformers who knew the value of Bernard's works and eagerly studied them.

Finally, we may ask whether the observations made here on Bernard's impact on Luther are useful for a better understanding not only of Luther, but also of Bernard. I think they are. Reading Bernard through Luther's eyes highlights timeless aspects of the faith in Bernard's works, and thus sheds new light also on him. Whether all the essential elements of Bernard's theology were correctly viewed by the Reformer is a question which I leave to those who know Bernard better than Luther.

By tracing the far-reaching congeniality of these two giants in the history of christian spirituality, we have pursued a timely ecumenical purpose: introducing Catholic readers to Luther *via* Bernard, and familiarizing Protestants with Bernard via Luther. A second ecumenical concern I have is to let the 'protesting' Catholics—by which I mean Reformed (originally French and Swiss), Lutheran (originally German), and Anglican (originally English) Catholics—see how deeply the german Reformer was rooted in the catholic monastic, non-scholastic, theological tradition, at a time before ecclesiastical disintegration took place through the confessionalization of western christianity in the sixteenth century.

In the spirit of ecumenical Church history and theology, I have tried to elucidate the significance of the *doctor mellifluus* for the german preacher, professor, and Reformer, Martin Luther, and to sketch the Bernard image he gained over the years. Perhaps the benedictine/ cistercian tradition is predestined—because of its specific bernardine spirituality and its affinity with Reformation

---

23 See Constable, 'The Popularity of Twelfth-Century Spiritual Writers in the Late Middles Ages', 13. See Brian Stock, 'Experience, Praxis, Work, and Planning in Bernard of Clairvaux', 222.

concerns—to become the agent of further *redintegratio* between
the two now separated streams of western Christianity, Catholicism
and Protestantism. There is no doubt that 'Bernard can be a meeting ground for catholic-protestant dialogue'.[24] In the future, the
two streams may again flow together to form one gospel-centred
Catholic Church by reappropriating these two giants of western
spirituality, Bernard and Luther. That there is, indeed, a real chance
for such *rapprochement* is attested to by the late Jean Leclercq,
who observed some thirty years ago that 'Catholic tradition, and
an entire stream of Lutheran tradition as well, has always been
sensitive to the profoundly religious element in anything [Saint
Bernard] says about God, about man, and the manner in which
God and man are united in Christ and Christians'.[25] I am not
convinced by the opinion of a Lutheran contributor to a recent
intra-lutheran 'dispute' that the 'Catholic Middle Ages' are fundamentally different from 'the Reformation'.[26] In contrast, I would
point out with Bernd Moeller that Luther's reliance on Scripture
alone, grace alone, faith alone, and Christ alone referred back to
axioms in the Middle Ages which were always valid and that no
one argued against them in any direct way, although some did say
'yes, but'.[27] It seems to me that the historical Luther was very much
grounded in the best of medieval catholic monastic theology, in its
bernardine coloring, and that we need to examine further whether
Luther's *theology* can be understood as a real catholic possibility,
a legitimate version of 'evangelical catholicity'.

We must come to a conclusion, however, and end with Bernard's words to Eugene III:

> God must still be sought who has not yet sufficiently been
> found and who cannot be sought too much; but he is perhaps

24 See A. N. S. Lane, 'Bernard of Clairvaux: A Forerunner of John Calvin?'
Bernardus Magister, 544; Lane, *Calvin and Bernard of Clairvaux* (Princeton:
Princeton Theological Seminary, 1996).

25 Jean Leclercq, 'Bernard and the Christian Experience', *Worship* 41 (1967)
222.

26 See Berndt Hamm, 'Einheit und Vielfalt der Reformation–oder: was die
Reformation zur Reformation machte'. *Reformationstheorien*, 127.

27 See Bernd Moeller, 'Die Rezeption Luthers in der frühen Reformation'.
Reformationstheorien, 25f.

more worthily sought and more easily found by prayer than by discussion. Therefore, let this be the end of the book but not the end of the search.[28]

---

28 *Proinde is sit finis libri, sed non finis quaerendi,* Csi; SBOp 3:493,25; CF 37:179.

Selected Bibliography

I. PRIMARY SOURCES

A. The Works of Bernard of Clairvaux

Opera Sancti Bernardi. 8 vols. Jean Leclercq, Henri Rochais, Charles H. Talbot, eds. Rome: Editiones Cistercienses, 1957–1977.

Oeuvres complètes, introductions, traductions, notes et index. Sources chrétiennes. Paris: Editions du Cerf, 1990–1996.

Sämtliche Werke lateinisch/deutsch. 9 vols. Gerhard B. Winkler, ed. Innsbruck: Tyrolia-Verlag, 1990–1998.

Letter 77 to Master Hugh of Saint Victor. Hugh Feiss, trans. *Bernardus Magister.* John R. Sommerfeldt, ed. (see below) 360–77.

Selected Works. G. R. Evans, trans., Jean Leclercq, intro., Ewert H. Cousins, preface. New York, Mahwah: Paulist Press, 1987.

St. Bernard's Sermons on the Blessed Virgin Mary. A priest of Mount Melleray, trans. Chulmleigh Devon: Augustine Publishing Company, 1984 (reprint).

The Letters of St. Bernard of Clairvaux. Bruno Scott James, trans. London: Burns Oates, 1953. Rpt. Stroud Kalamazoo, 1998.

The Works of Bernard of Clairvaux. Cistercian Fathers Series. Kalamazoo: Cistercian Publications, 1970-:
– *Apology to Abbot William.* Michael Casey, trans., CF 1. 1970, 1985.

– *Five Books on Consideration: Advice to a Pope*. John D. Anderson and Elizabeth T. Kennan, trans. CF 37. 1976.

– *In Praise of the New Knighthood*. Conrad Greenia, trans. CF 19. 1977.

– *Magnificat: Homilies in Praise of the Blessed Virgin Mary*. Marie-Bernard Saïd and Grace Perigo, trans. CF 18. 1979.

– Monastic Obligations and Abbatial Authority: St. Bernard's Book on *Precept and Dispensation*. Conrad Greenia, trans. CF 1. 1970.

– *On Grace and Free Choice*. Daniel O'Donovan, trans. CF 19a. 1988.

– *On Loving God*. Robert Walton, trans. CF 13. 1974.

– *On the Song of Songs I*. Kilian Walsh, trans. CF 4. 1981.

– *On the Song of Songs II*. Kilian Walsh, trans. CF 7. 1988.

– *On the Song of Songs III*. Kilian Walsh and Irene M. Edmonds, trans. CF 31. 1979.

– *On the Song of Songs IV*. Irene M. Edmonds, trans. CF 40. 1980.

– *Sermons for the Summer Season: Liturgical Sermons from Rogationtide and Pentecost*. Beverly Mayne Kienzle and James Jarzembowski, trans. CF 53. 1991.

– *Sermons on Conversion: On Conversion, a Sermon to Clerics and Lenten Sermons on the Psalm 'He Who Dwells'*. Marie-Bernard Saïd, trans. CF 25. 1981.

– *The Steps of Humility and Pride*. M. Ambrose Conway, trans. 1974.

B. The Works of Martin Luther

D. Martin Luthers Werke. Kritische Gesamtausgabe. Weimar: Hermann Böhlaus Nachfolger; Graz: Akademische Druck u. Verlagsanstalt, 1883-.

Luther's Works. Jaroslav Pelikan and Helmut T. Lehmann, eds. St. Louis: Concordia Publishing House; Philadelphia: Fortress Press, 1955–1987.

Sermons of Martin Luther. John Nicholas Lenker, ed. Grand Rapids: Baker Book House, n. d. 8 volumes.

C. Others

Bernard of Clairvaux. Early Biographies. 2 vols. Martinus Cawley, trans. Lafayette, OR: Guadalupe Translations, 1990.

Concilium Tridentinum. Societas Goerresiana, ed. Freiburg: Herder, 1950–1967. Vols. 5 and 12.

Corpus Reformatorum. Carolus Gottlieb Bretschneider and H. E. Bindseil, eds. Halis Saxonum: C. A. Schwetschke, 1834–1860. Vol. 6.

Jacobus a Voragine. *Legenda aurea Vulgo Historia Lombardica Dicta.* Th. Graesse, ed. Osnabrück: Otto Zeller Verlag, 1965 (reprint).

———. *The Golden Legend of Jacobus de Voragine.* Granger Ryan and Helmut Ripperger, trans. New York, London, Toronto: Longmans, Green and Co., 1948 (reprint).

———. *The Golden Legend: Readings on the Saints,* 2 vols. William Granger Ryan, trans. Princeton: Princeton University Press, 1993.

Patrologiae cursus completus, series Latina. J.-P. Migne, ed. 221 volumes. Paris: 1844–1864.

The Book of Concord: The Confessions of the Evangelical Lutheran Church. Theodore G. Tappert, trans. and ed. Philadelphia: Fortress Press, 1981, fourteenth printing.

II. SECONDARY LITERATURE

Altermatt, Alberich. 'Christus pro nobis: Die Christologie Bernhards von Clairvaux in den Sermones per annum.' AC 33 (1977) 3–176.

Althaus, Paul. *The Theology of Martin Luther.* R. C. Schultz, trans. Philadelphia: Fortress Press, 1966.

Anderson, H. George and James R. Crumley, Jr, eds. *Promoting Unity. Themes in Lutheran-Catholic Dialogue.* Minneapolis: Fortress Press, 1989. Anderson, H. George, J. Francis Stafford, and Joseph A. Burgess, eds. *The One Mediator, the Saints, and Mary:* Lutheran and Catholics in Dialogue VIII. Minneapolis: Augsburg, 1992.

Apostolos-Cappadona, Diane. *Dictionary of Christian Art*. New York: Continuum, 1994.

Arabeyre, Patrick, Jacques Berlioz, and Philippe Poirrier, eds. *Vie et Légendes de saint Bernard de Clairvaux. Création, diffusion, réception (XIIe-XXe Siècles)*. Actes des Rencontres de Dijon, 7–8 juin 1991. Cîteaux: Commentarii Cistercienses, 1993.

Asendorf, Ulrich. *Die Theologie Martin Luthers nach seinen Predigten*. Göttingen: Vandenhoeck & Ruprecht, 1988.

Atkinson, James. *Martin Luther, Prophet to the Church Catholic*. Grand Rapids: Eerdmans, 1983.

Bach, Hedwig. 'Bernhard von Clairvaux und Martin Luther'. *Erbe und Auftrag* 46 (1970) 347–351, 453–459; 47 (1971) 36–43, 121–125, 193–196.

Balge, Richard D. 'Martin Luther, Augustinian'. *Luther Lives. Essays in Commemoration of the 500th Anniversary of Martin Luther's Birth*, Edward C. Fredrich, Siegbert W. Becker, David P. Kruske, eds. Milwaukee: Northwestern Publishing House, 1983. 7–20.

Bamberger, John Eudes. 'The Influence of St Bernard'. CSQ 25 (1990) 101–114.

Bauer, Dieter R. and Gotthard Fuchs, eds. *Bernhard von Clairvaux und der Beginn der Moderne*. Innsbruck and Vienna: Tyrolia, 1996.

Bayer, Oswald. 'Oratio, Meditatio, Tentatio: Eine Besinnung auf Luthers Theologieverständnis.' *Lutherjahrbuch* 55 (1988) 7–59.

Bell, Theo. 'Bernard of Clairvaux in Luther-Legend and Tower Experience'. *Bijdragen: Tijdschrift voor filosofie en theologie* 53 (1992) 62–72.

———. 'Bernhard von Clairvaux als Quelle Martin Luthers'. *Bijdragen: Tijdschrift voor filosofie en theologie* 56 (1995) 2–18.

———. *Bernhardus Dixit. Bernardus van Clairvaux in Martin Luthers werken*. Delft: Eburon, 1989. Revised german edition: *Divus Bernhardus: Bernhard von Clairvaux in Martin Luthers Schriften*. Mainz: Verlag Philipp von Zabern, 1993.

———. 'Der Mensch als Esel Christi: Jesu Einzug in Jerusalem

nach Mt 21 als Bildrede bei Bernhard von Clairvaux, Wenzes-
laus Linck und Martin Luther'. *Luther* 65 (1994) 9–21.

———. 'Luther's Reception of Bernard of Clairvaux'. CTQ 59
(1995) 245–277.

———. 'Pater Bernardus. Bernard de Clairvaux vu par Martin
Luther'. *Cîteaux* 41 (1990) 233–255.

———. 'Pater Bernhardus. Luther's visie op Bernardus van Clairvaux'. *Luther-Bulletin: Tijdschrift voor interconfessioneel
Lutheronderzoek* 1 (1992) 20–44.

———. 'Sermon von der Geburt Christi: Bernard van Clairvaux
en Johann Tauler in Luther's Kerstpreek van 1520'. *Bijdragen:
Tijdschrift voor filosofie en theologie* 39 (1978) 289–309.

———. 'Testimonium Spiritus Sancti—An Example of Bernard-
Reception in Luther's Theology'. *Bijdragen: Tijdschrift voor
filosofie en theologie* 53 (1992) 62–72.

Beer, Theobald. *Der fröhliche Wechsel und Streit. Grundzüge der
Theologie Martin Luthers*. Einsiedeln: Johannes-Verlag, 1980,
second revised edition.

Belting, Hans. *Das Bild und sein Publikum im Mittelalter: Form
und Funktion früher Bildtafeln der Passion*. Berlin: Mann, 1981.

Bennet, Renée H. 'The Song of Wisdom in Bernard's *Sermones
Super Cantica Canticorum*.' CSQ 30 (1995) 147–178.

Benzig, Josef, and Claus, Helmut. *Lutherbibliographie: Ein Ver-
zeichnis der gedruckten Schriften Martin Luthers bis zu seinem
Tod*. Vol. 2 (1522–1546). Baden-Baden: Verlag Valentin Koerner, 1994.

Bergmann, Rosemarie. 'A "tröstlich pictura": Luther's Attitude in
the Question of Images', *Renaissance and Reformation* 5 (1981)
15–25.

Berlioz, J. "La lactation de saint Bernard dans un exemplum du "Ci
Nous Dit" (Début du XIVe siècle)', *Cîteaux* 39 (1988) 270–284.

Benz, Ernst. 'Luther und Bernhard von Clairvaux.' *Eckart* 23
(1953/54) 60–64.

Bernhards, M. 'Zur Verbreitung der Bernhardflorilegien'. *Studien
und Mitteilungen zur Geschichte des Benediktinerordens und
seiner Zweige* 64 (1952) 234–241.

Bernardo Cistercense. Atti del XXVI Convegno storico interna-

zionale. Todi, 8–11 ottobre 1989. Spoleto: Centro italiano di studi sull'alto medioevo, 1990.

Blaumeiser, Hubertus. *Martin Luthers Kreuzestheologie. Schlüssel zu seiner Deutung von Mensch und Wirklichkeit. Eine Untersuchung anhand der Operationes in Psalmos (1519–1521).* Paderborn: Bonifatius Verlag, 1995.

Bouchard, Marie-Noel. 'Une lecture monastique du Psaume 90: les sermons de saint Bernard sur le Psaume *Qui habitat'.* Coll 49 (1987) 156–172.

Bougerol. Jacques Guy. 'Saint Bonaventure et Saint Bernard'. *Antonianum* 46 (1971) 3–79.

———. 'L'influence de saint Bernard sur la pensée franciscaine'. Coll 52 (1990) 284–298.

Bredero, Adriaan H. *Bernard of Clairvaux: between cult and history.* Grand Rapids: W. B. Eerdmans, 1996.

———. 'St. Bernard and the Historians'. *Saint Bernard of Clairvaux: Studies Commemorating the Eighth Centenary of his Canonization.* M. Basil Pennington, ed. Kalamazoo: Cisterican Publications, 1977.

Brooks, Peter Newman. 'A Lily Ungilded? Martin Luther, the Virgin and the Saints.' *Journal of Religious History* 13 (1984) 136–149.

Bungert, Hans, ed., *Martin Luther: Eine Spiritualität und ihre Folgen.* Vortragsreihe der Universität Regensburg zum Lutherjahr 1983. Regensburg: Mittelbayerische Verlagsanstalt, 1983.

Butler, Cuthbert. *Western Mysticism: The Teaching of SS. Augustine, Gregory and Bernard on Contemplation and the Contemplative Life.* New York: Harper & Row, 1966.

Calabuig, Ignazio M., ed. *Respice Stellam. Maria in San Bernardo e nella tradizione cistercense.* Atti del Convegno Internazionale. Roma, Marianum 21–24 ottobre 1991. Rome: Edizioni 'Marianum', 1993.

Casey, Michael. *Athirst for God. Spiritual Desire in Bernard of Clairvaux's Sermons on the Song of Songs.* CS 77. Kalamazoo: Cistercian Publications, 1988.

———. 'Bernard of Clairvaux: Forty Years of Scholarship'. *St Bernard of Clairvaux: The Man.* John S. Martin, ed. Parksville: University of Melbourne Press, 1992. 31–45.

————. *Bernard of Clairvaux: Man, Monk, Mystic: Texts Selected and Translated*. Kalamazoo: CP, 1990.

————. ' "Emotionally Hollow, Esthetically Meaningless and Spiritually Empty": An Inquiry into Theological Discourse'. *Colloquium* 14 (1981) 54–61.

————. 'Herbert of Clairvaux's "Book of Wonderful Happenings" '. CSQ 25 (1990) 37–64.

————. *Sacred Reading: The Ancient Art of Lectio Divina*. Liguori: Triumph Books, 1996.

————. *The Advent Sermons of Bernard of Clairvaux*. Australian Benedictine Studies Series 1. Belgrave, 1979.

————. *The Undivided Heart: The Western Monastic Approach to Contemplation*. Petersham: St. Bede's Publications, 1994.

————. *Toward God: The Ancient Wisdom of Western Prayer*. Liguori: Triumph Books, 1996.

Cavallera, Ferdinand. 'Bernard (Apocryphes attribué à saint)'. DSp 1:1499–1500. Paris: Gabriel Beauchesne et ses Fils, 1937.

Celletti, M. C. 'Bernardo di Chiaravalle. Iconografia'. *Bibliotheca Sanctorum*. Rome: Instituto Giovanni XXIII nella Pontificia Università Lateranense, 1963. 3:37–41.

Chrétien, J.-L. 'L'humilité chez saint Bernard'. *Communio* 10 (1985) 113–127.

Colloque de Lyon-Cîteaux-Dijon (1990). *Bernard de Clairvaux: Histoire, Mentalités, Spiritualité*. Sources Chrétiennes 380. Paris: Éditions du Cerf, 1992.

Constable, Giles. *Culture and Spirituality in Medieval Europe*. Brookfield, Vt: Variorum, 1996.

————. 'The Popularity of Twelfth-Century Spiritual Writers in the Late Middle Ages'. *Renaissance Studies in Honor of Hans Baron*. Anthony Molho and John A. Tedeschi, eds. DeKalb: Northern Illinois University Press, 1971, 5–28.

Dal Prà, Laura, ed. *Bernardo di Ciaravalle nell' arte italiana dal XIV al XVIII secolo*. Catalogo. Milan 1990.

————. *Iconografia di san Bernardo di Clairvaux in Italia*. II.1. La Vita. Rome: Editiones Cistercienses, 1991.

Damerau, Rudolf. *Die Demut in der Theologie Luthers*. Giessen: Wilhelm Schmitz Verlag, 1967.

Davy, Marie-Madeleine. *Bernard de Clairvaux*. Paris: Éditions du Félin, 1990.

Decot, Rolf. 'Ansatzpunkte und Gründe von Luthers Papstkritik'. *Theologie der Gegenwart* 26 (1984) 75–85.

Delfgaauw, Pacificus. 'An Approach to Saint Bernard's Sermons on the Song of Songs'. Coll 23 (1961) 148–161.

Diers, Michaela. *Bernhard von Clairvaux: Elitäre Frömmigkeit und begnadetes Wirken*. Münster: Aschendorff, 1991.

Dumont, Charles. 'Saint Bernard: A Mystic According to the Rule of Saint Benedict'. Richard Summers, trans. CSQ 16 (1981) 154–167.

————. 'La spiritualité de saint Bernard'. *Nouvelle Revue Théologique* 112 (1990) 502–515.

Dunnhaupt, Gerhard, ed. *The Martin Luther Quincentennial*. Detroit: Wayne State University Press, 1985.

Eastman, P. W. H. 'The Christology in Bernard's "De Diligendo Deo" '. CSQ 23 (1988) 119–127.

Ebeling, Gerhard. *Evangelische Evangelienauslegung. Eine Untersuchung zu Luthers Hermeneutik*. Darmstadt: Wissenschaftliche Buchgesellschaft, 1962 (first printing, 1942).

————. *Lutherstudien* 1–3. Tübingen: J. C. B. Mohr (Paul Siebeck), 1977–1985.

————. 'The Beginnings of Luther's Hermeneutics'. *Lutheran Quarterly* 7 (1993) 129–158; 315–338; 451–468.

————. *The Study of Theology*. Duane A. Priebe, trans. Philadelphia: Fortress Press, 1978.

Eckermann, Willigis. 'Die Aristoteleskritik Luthers: Ihre Bedeutung für seine Theologie'. *Catholica* 32 (1978) 114–130.

Eis, Gerhard. 'Fasciculus myrrhae'. *Leuvensche Bijdragen* 49 (1960) 90–96.

Elder, E. Rozanne, ed., *The Joy of Learning and the Love of God: Studies in Honor of Jean Leclercq*. CS 160. Kalamazoo: Cistercian Publications, 1995.

Elm, Kaspar, ed. *Bernhard von Clairvaux. Rezeption und Wirkung im Mittelalter und in der Neuzeit*. Wiesbaden: Harrassowitz Verlag, 1994.

————, and P. Joerißen, H. J. Roth, eds., *Die Zisterzienser: Ordensleben zwischen Ideal und Wirklichkeit. Eine Ausstellung des Landschaftsverbands Rheinland, Rheinisches Museumsamt, Brauweiler. Aachen, Krönungssaal des Rathauses, 3. Juli–28. September 1980.* Bonn: Rheinland-Verlag in Kommission bei Rudolf Habelt Verlag GmbH, 1980.

Elze, Martin. 'Das Verständnis der Passion Jesu im ausgehenden Mittelalter und bei Luther'. *Geist und Geschichte der Reformation: Festgabe Hanns Rückert zum 65. Geburtstag dargebracht von Freunden, Kollegen und Schülern.* Berlin: Walter de Gruyter & Co., 1966. 127–151.

———. 'Züge spätmittelalterlicher Frömmigkeit in Luthers Theologie'. *Zeitschrift für Theologie und Kirche* 62 (1965) 381–402.

Erdai, Klára. *Auf dem Wege zu sich selbst: Die Meditation im 16. Jahrhundert: Eine funktionsanalytische Gattungsbeschreibung.* Wiesbaden: Otto Harrassowitz Verlag, 1990.

Evans, G. R. ' "Lectio, disputatio, predicatio": St. Bernard the Exegete'. *Studia monastica* 24 (1982) 127–145.

———. 'The Classical Education of Bernard of Clairvaux'. *Cîteaux* 33 (1982) 121–134.

———. *The Language and Logic of the Bible: The Earlier Middle Ages.* Cambridge etc: Cambridge University Press, 1984.

———. *The Language and Logic of the Bible: The Road to Reformation.* Cambridge etc: Cambridge University Press, 1985.

———. *The Mind of St Bernard of Clairvaux.* Oxford: Clarendon Press, 1983.

Farkasfalvy, Denis. 'St Bernard's Interpretation of the Psalms in His Sermons *Super Cantica*'. *Erudition at God's Service.* John R. Sommerfeldt, ed. CS 98. Kalamazoo: CP, 1987. 109–116.

———. 'The Role of the Bible in St. Bernard's Spirituality'. AC 25 (1969) 3–13.

———. 'Use and Interpretation of St. John's Prologue in the Writings of St. Bernard.' AC 35 (1979) 205–226.

Fassetta, Raffaele. 'Le mariage spirituel dans les sermons de saint Bernard sur le Cantique'. Coll 48 (1986) 155–180, 251–265.

Feiss, Hugh. 'St Bernard's Theology of Baptism and the Monastic Life'. CSQ 25 (1990) 79–91.

Ficker, Johannes. "Hortulus animae'. *Buch und Bucheinband.* Leipzig 1923. 59–68.

Fijan, D. W. 'Bernard van Clairvaux en zijn Invloed op de Reformatie'. *Studio Studiosorum*. C. T. Boerke and C. M. Désirée de Vries-Hofland, eds. Apeldoorn: Kerkhistorisch Werkgezelschap, 1991. 9–24.

Forde, Gerhard O. *Justification by Faith—A Matter of Death and Life*. Philadelphia: Fortress Press, 1983.

Frahling, Bernhard. 'Formen der Kreuzesfrömmigkeit in der Geschichte und was sie uns zu sagen haben'. *Theologie und Glaube* 86 (1996) 534–551.

Frischmuth, Gertrud. *Die paulinische Konzeption in der Frömmigkeit Bernhards von Clairvaux*. Gütersloh: Bertelsmann, 1933.

Geurs, H. *Te bevrijden vrijheid. Een dogmenhistorische beschouwing over het vrijheidsbegrip bij Augustinus, Bernard van Clairvaux en Luther.* Assen Amsterdam: Van Gorcum, 1976.

Gilson, Étienne. *History of Christian Philosophy in the Middle Ages*. New York: Random House, 1955.

———. *The Mystical Theology of Saint Bernard*. A. H. C. Downes, trans. New York: Sheed and Ward, 1940. Reprint: Kalamazoo: Cistercian Publications, 1990.

Gleumes, Heinrich. 'Gerhard Groot und die Windesheimer als Verehrer des hl. Bernhard von Clairvaux'. *Geist und Leben: Zeitschrift für Aszese und Mystik* 10 (1935) 90–112.

———. 'Der geistige Einfluss des heiligen Bernhard von Clairvaux auf Thomas von Kempen'. *Geist und Leben: Zeitschrift für Aszese und Mystik* 13 (1938) 109–120.

Gnädiger, Louise, 'Der minnende Bernhardus: Seine Reflexe in den Predigten des Johannes Tauler'. *Cîteaux* 31 (1980) 387–409.

Goodrich, W. E. 'The Reliability of the Vita Prima S. Bernardi. The Image of Bernard in Book I of the Vita Prima and his own Letters: A Comparison'. AC (1987) 153–180.

Grane, Leif, Alfred Schindler and Markus Wriedt, eds. *Auctoritas Patrum. Contributions on the Reception of the Church Fathers in the 15th and 16th Century*. Mainz: Verlag Philipp von Zabern, 1993.

Grill, Severin. 'Bernhard von Clairvaux als Exeget'. *Festschrift zum 800-Jahrgedächtnis des Todes Bernhards von Clairvaux*. Vienna and Munich: Verlag Herold, 1953. 9–21.

Grislis, Egil. 'Piety, Faith, and Spirituality in the Quest of the

Historical Luther'. *Consensus: A Canadian Lutheran Journal of Theology* 19 (1993) 29–51.

—. 'The Spirituality of Martin Luther', *Word & World* 14 (1994) 453–459.

Grossmann, Maria. *Humanism in Wittenberg 1485–1517.* Nieuwkoop: B. de Graaf, 1975.

Hagen, Kenneth. *Luther's Approach to Scripture as seen in his 'Commentaries' on Galatians 1519–1538.* Tübingen: J. C. B. Mohr (Paul Siebeck), 1993.

—and Franz Posset. *Annotated Bibliography of Luther Studies.* Sixteenth Century Bibliography 24. Saint Louis: Center for Reformation Research, 1985.

—, Franz Posset, Terry Thomas. *Annotated Bibliography of Luther Studies 1984–1989.* Sixteenth Century Bibliography 29. Saint Louis: Center for Reformation Research, 1991.

Hägglund, Bengt. *The Background of Luther's Doctrine of Justification in Late Medieval Theology.* Philadelphia: Fortress Press, 1971.

Hamm, Berndt. *Frömmigkeitstheologie am Anfang des 16. Jahrhunderts.* Tübingen: J. C. B. Mohr (Paul Siebeck), 1982.

—. 'Was ist reformatorische Rechtfertigungslehre?' *Zeitschrift für Theologie und Kirche* 83 (1986) 1–38.

—. 'Von der Gottesliebe des Mittelalters zum Glauben Luthers.' *Lutherjahrbuch* 65 (1998) 19–44.

Haug, Walter and Burghart Wachinger, eds. *Die Passion Christi in Literatur und Kunst des Spätmittelalters.* Tübingen: Max Niemeyer Verlag, 1993.

Hausherr, Irénée. *Penthos: The Doctrine of Compunction in the Christian East.* Anselm Hufstader, trans. Kalamazoo: Cistercian Studies, 1982.

Heller, Dagmar. *Schriftauslegung und geistliche Erfahrung bei Bernhard von Clairvaux.* Würzburg, 1990.

Hendrix, Guido, ed. *Bernardina en Cisterciensia in de Universiteitsbibliotheek. Leesboek-kataloog.* Gent: Rijksuniversiteit, 1990.

—. *Conspectus Bibliographicus Sancti Bernardi Ultimi Patrum 1989–1993.* Deuxième Édition Augmenté. Louvain: Peeters, 1995.

Herz, Martin. Article 'Commercium'. LThK. Freiburg: Herder, 1962, second edition. 3:22.

———. *Sacrum Commercium: Eine begriffsgeschichtliche Studie zur Theologie der römischen Liturgiesprache.* Munich: Kommissionsverlag Karl Zink, 1958.

Hiss, Wilhelm. *Die Anthropologie Bernhards von Clairvaux.* Berlin: Walter de Gruyter, 1964.

Hoffman, Bengt. 'Lutheran Spirituality'. *Spiritual Traditions for the Contemporary Church,* Robin Maas and Gabriel O'Donnell, eds. Nashville: Abingdon Press, 1990. 145–161.

Hümpfner, P. Tiburtius. *Ikonographia S. Bernardi Abbatis Claravallensis.* Augsburg, Cologne, Vienna: Dr. Benno Filser Verlag, 1927.

———. *Ikonographie des hl. Bernhard von Clairvaux.* Augsburg, Cologne, Vienna: Dr. Benno Filser Verlag, 1927.

Jezler, Peter, ed. *Himmel Hölle Fegefeuer: Das Jenseits im Mittelalter.* Zurich: Verlag Neue Zürcher Zeitung, 1994.

Junghans, Helmar. *Der junge Luther und die Humanisten.* Weimar: Hermann Böhlaus Nachfolger, 1984; Göttingen: Vandenhoeck & Ruprecht, 1985.

———. ed. *Leben und Werk Martin Luthers von 1526 bis 1546. Festgabe zu seinem 500. Geburtstag.* Berlin: Evangelische Verlagsanstalt; Göttingen: Vandenhoeck & Ruprecht, 1983.

Kallas, Endel. 'The Spirituality of Luther: A Reappraisal of his Contribution'. *Spirituality Today* 34 (1983) 292–302.

Kantzenbach, Friedrich W. 'Christusgemeinschaft und Rechtfertigung: Luther's Gedanke vom fröhlichen Wechsel'. *Luther* 35 (1964) 34–45.

Kardong, Terrence. *The Benedictines.* Wilmington, Delaware: Michael Glazier, 1988.

Kasper, Clemens, and Schreiner, Klaus, eds. *Zisterziensische Spiritualität. Theologische Grundlagen, funktionale Voraussetzungen und bildhafte Ausprägungen im Mittelalter.* Studien und Mitteilungen zur Geschichte des Benediktinerordens und seiner Zweige, vol. 34 Ergänzungsband. St. Ottilien: EOS Verlag Erzabtei St. Ottilien, 1994.

Kaufman, Peter Iver. 'Luther's "Scholastic Phase" Revisited:

Grace, Works and Merit in the Earliest Extant Sermons'. *Church History* 51 (1982) 80–89.

Kelly, Robert A. *'Oratio, Meditatio, Tentatio Faciunt Theologum*: Luther's Piety and the Formation of Theologians'. *Consensus: A Canadian Lutheran Journal of Theology* 19 (1993) 9–27.

Kennan, Elizabeth T. 'The "De Consideratione" of St. Bernard of Clairvaux and the Papacy in Mid-Twelfth Century: A Review of Scholarship'. *Traditio* 23 (1967) 73–115.

Kilga, Klemens. 'Der Kirchenbegriff des hl. Bernhard von Clairvaux'. *Cistercienser Chronik* 54 (1947) 46–64; 149–179; 235–253. 55 (1948) 39–56; 86–114; 156–186.

Kleinig, John W. 'The Kindred Heart: Luther on Meditation'. *Lutheran Theological Journal* 20 (1986) 142–154.

Kleineidam, Erich. 'Ursprung und Gegenstand der Theologie bei Bernhard von Clairvaux und Martin Luther'. *Dienst der Vermittlung. Festschrift zum 25-jährigen Bestehen des philosophisch-theologischen Studiums im Priesterseminar Erfurt.* Wilhelm Ernst, K. Feiereis, and Fritz Hoffmann, eds. Leipzig: St. Benno Verlag, 1977. 221–247.

Knotzinger, Kurt. 'Hoheslied und bräutliche Christusliebe bei Bernhard von Clairvaux'. *Jahrbuch für mystische Theologie* 7 (1961) 7–88.

Köhler, Walther. *Luther und die Kirchengeschichte nach seinen Schriften, zunächst bis 1521.* Hildesheim, Zurich, New York: Georg Olms Verlag, 1984 (reprint; first printing: Erlangen 1900).

Köpf, Ulrich. 'Das Blut Christi in Frömmigkeit und Theologie des Protestantismus'. *900 Jahre Heilig-Blut-Verehrung in Weingarten 1094–1994.* Festschrift zum Heilig-Blut-Jubiläum am 12. März 1994, Norbert Kruse and Hans Ulrich Rudolf, eds. Sigmaringen: Jan Thorbecke Verlag, 1994. 399–413.

———. 'Die Rolle der Erfahrung im religiösen Leben nach dem Heiligen Bernhard.' AC 46 (1990) 307–319.

———. 'Ein Modell religiöser Erfahrung in der monastischen Theologie: Bernhard von Clairvaux'. *Religiöse Erfahrung. Historische Modelle in christlicher Tradition.* Walter Haug and Dietmar Mieth, eds. Munich: Wilhelm Fink Verlag, 1992.

———. 'Monastische Theologie im 15. Jahrhundert'. *Rottenburger Jahrbuch für Kirchengeschichte* 11 (1992) 117–135.

————. *Religiöse Erfahrung in der Theologie Bernhards von Clairvaux*. Tübingen: J. C. B. Mohr (Paul Siebeck), 1980.

————. 'Wesen und Funktion religiöser Erfahrung. Überlegungen im Anschluss and Bernhard von Clairvaux'. *Neue Zeitschrift für Systematische Theologie und Religionsphilosophie* 22 (1980) 150- 165.

Kusukawa, Sachiko. *A Wittenberg Library Catalogue of 1536*. Binghamton, N.Y.: Medieval & Renaissance Texts & Studies, 1995.

Lanczkowski, J. 'Der Einfluss der Hohe-Lied-Predigten Bernhards auf die drei Helftaer Mystikerinnen'. *Erbe und Auftrag* 66 (1990) 17- 28.

Lane, A. N. S. *Calvin and Bernard of Clairvaux*. Princeton: Princeton Theological Seminary, 1996.

————. 'Calvin's Sources of St. Bernard.' ARG 67 (1976) 253–283.

Leclercq, Jean. 'Bemerkungen zu den Predigten des hl. Bernard für die Fastenzeit'. *Cistercienser Chronik* 97 (1990) 1–9.

————. *Bernard of Clairvaux and the Cisterican Spirit*. Claire Lavoie, trans. Kalamazoo: Cistercian Publications, 1976.

————. *Bernard de Clairvaux*. Paris: Desclée, 1989; german trans.: *Bernhard von Clairvaux: Ein Mann prägt seine Zeit*. Munich: Verlag Neue Stadt, 1990; spanish trans.: *Bernardo de Claraval*. Valencia: Edicep, 1991.

————. ' "Curiositas" and the Return to God in St Bernard of Clairvaux', CSQ 25 (1990) 92–100.

————. 'Die Verbreitung der bernhardinischen Schriften im deutschen Sprachraum'. *Bernhard von Clairvaux: Mönch und Mystiker*. Internationaler Bernhardkongress Mainz 1953. Joseph Lortz, ed. Wiesbaden: Franz Steiner Verlag, 1955. 176–191.

————. 'Essais sur l'ésthetique de saint Bernard'. *Studi medievali* 9 (1968) 688–728.

————. 'Études sur Saint Bernard et le texte de ses écrits'. AC 9 (1953).

————. 'Introduction.' *Bernard of Clairvaux. Selected Works*. New York, Mahwah: Paulist Press, 1987. 13–57.

————. 'Monastic and Scholastic Theology in the Reformers of the Fourteenth to Sixteenth Century'. *From Cloister to Class-*

room: Monastic and Scholastic Approaches to Truth. E. Rozanne Elder, ed. CS 90. Kalamazoo: Cistercian Publications, 1986.

———. 'Naming the Theologies of the Early Twelfth Century'. *Medieval Studies* 53 (1991) 327–336.

———. *Recueil d'Études sur Saint Bernard et ses Écrits.* 5 volumes. Rome: Editioni di Storia e Letteratura, 1962–1992.

———. 'Saint Bernard écrivain d'après les sermons sur le psaume Qui Habitat'. *Revue benedictine* 77 (1967) 364–374.

———. 'Saint Bernard et l'Écriture Sainte'. *Saint Bernard mystique.* Bruges and Paris: Desclée de Brouwer, 1948. 483–489.

———. 'St. Bernard and the Christian Experience'. *Worship* 41 (1967) 222.

———. *The Love of Learning and the Desire for God: A Study of Monastic Culture.* Catharine Misrahi, trans. New York: Fordham University Press, 1960.

———. Francois Vandenbroucke, Louis Bouyer. *The Spirituality of the Middle Ages.* New York: The Seabury Press, 1968.

Loewenich, Walther von. *Martin Luther: The Man and His Work.* Lawrence W. Denef, trans. Minneapolis: Augsburg Publishing House, 1986.

———. *Luther's Theology of the Cross.* H. J. A. Bowman, trans. Minneapolis: Augsburg Publishing House, 1976.

Lohse, Bernhard, ed. *Der Durchbruch der reformatorischen Erkenntnis bei Luther. Neuere Untersuchungen.* Stuttgart: Franz Steiner Verlag Wiesbaden GMBH, 1988.

———. *Evangelium in der Geschichte. Studien zu Luther und der Reformation.* Zum 60. Geburtstag des Autors herausgegeben von Leif Grane, Bernd Moeller und Otto Hermann Pesch. Göttingen: Vandenhoeck & Ruprecht, 1988.

———. 'Luther and the Protestant Tradition'. *Encounters With Luther* 3 (1980–84). Eric W. Gritsch, ed. Gettysburg: GAM Printing, 1986. 201–214.

———. *Luthers Theologie in ihrer historischen Entwicklung und in ihrem systematischen Zusammenhang.* Göttingen: Vandenhoeck & Ruprecht, 1995.

———. *Martin Luther: An Introduction to His Life and Work.* Philadelphia: Fortress Press, 1986.

———. *Martin Luther. Eine Einführung in sein Leben und sein*

Werk. Dritte, vollständig überarbeitete Auflage. Munich: Beck, 1997.

Lossky, Victor. 'Études sur la terminologie de S. Bernard.' *Archivum Latinitatis Medii Aevi* 17 (1943). 79–96.

MacCandless. 'Meditation in Saint Bernard.' *Coll* 26 (1964) 277–293.

Machilek, Franz. 'Klosterhumanismus in Nürnberg um 1500'. *Mitteilungen des Vereins für Geschichte der Stadt Nürnberg* 64 (1977) 10–45.

Mannermaa, Tuomo. 'Das Verhältnis von Glaube und Liebe in der Theologie Luthers.' Mikka Ruokanen, ed. *Luther in Finnland. Der Einfluss der Theologie Martin Luthers in Finnland und finnische Beiträge zur Lutherforschung.* Helsinki: Luther-Agricola- Gesellschaft, 1986 (second printing). 99–110.

Malatesta, Edward, ed. *Jesus in Christian Devotion and Contemplation.* St. Meinrad: Abbey Press, 1974.

Manns, Peter. 'Fides absoluta—Fides incarnata: Zur Rechtfertigungslehre Luthers im Grossen Galaterkommentar.' *Reformata Reformanda, Festgabe für Hubert Jedin.* Erwin Iserloh and Konrad Repgen, eds. Münster: Aschendorff, 1965. 1: 247–264.

————and Meyer, Harding, eds. *Luther's Ecumenical Significance. An Interconfessional Consultation.* Philadelphia: Fortress Press, 1984.

————. *Martin Luther: An Illustrated Biography.* New York: Crossroad, 1983.

————, ed. *Martin Luther: Reformator und Vater im Glauben. Referate aus der Vortragsreihe des Instituts für europäische Geschichte, Mainz.* Stuttgart: Franz Steiner Verlag Wiesbaden, 1985.

————. *Vater im Glauben: Studien zur Theologie Martin Luthers. Festgabe zum 65. Geburtstag am 10. März 1988.* Rolf Decot, ed. Stuttgart: Steiner Verlag Wiesbaden, 1988.

————. 'Zum Gespräch zwischen M. Luther und der katholischen Theologie. Begegnung zwischen patristisch-monastischer und reformatorischer Theologie an der Scholastik vorbei.' *Thesaurus Lutheri: Auf der Suche nach neuen Paradigmen der Luther-Forschung. Referate des Luther-Symposiums in Finnland 11.–12. November 1986.* Tuomo Mannermaa, Anja Ghiselli and Simo Peura, eds. Helsinki: Luther-Agricola-Gesellschaft, 1987. 63–154.

Mantovani, Giovanni Battista. 'San Bernardo nella cultura e nell'arte del XII secolo'. *Rivista Cistercense* 8 (1991) 155–165.

Margerie, Bertrand de. 'The Heart of Christ: Revelation of the Heart of the Father According to Martin Luther'. *Faith and Reason* 17 (1991) 109–114.

Matsuura, Jun. 'Restbestände aus der Bibliothek des Erfurter Augustinerklosters zu Luthers Zeit und bisher unbekannte eigenhändige Notizen Luthers'. *Lutheriana: Zum 500. Geburtstag Martin Luthers von den Mitarbeitern der Weimarer Ausgabe.* Cologne: Böhlau, 1984.

Maurer, Wilhelm. 'Cisterciensische Reform und reformatorischer Glaube'. *Cistercienser Chronik* 84 (1977) 1–13.

Maynard, Theodore. 'St. Bernard of Clairvaux, Doctor and Mystic.' ABR 4 (1953) 230–249.

Metzger, Günther. *Gelebter Glaube: Die Formierung reformatorischen Denkens in Luthers erster Psalmenvorlesung, dargestellt am Begriff des Affekts.* Göttingen: Vandenhoeck & Ruprecht, 1964.

McGinn, Bernard. St. Bernard and Meister Eckhart'. *Cîteaux* 31 (1980) 273–286.

————. *The Growth of Mysticism.* Vol. II of *The Presence of God: A History of Western Christian Mysticism.* New York: Crossroad, 1994.

McGuire, Brian Patrick. *The Difficult Saint: Bernard of Clairvaux and his Tradition.* CS 126. Kalamazoo: CP, 1991.

Mikkers, Edmond. Article 'Robert de Molesmes II. La Spiritualité Cistercienne.' *Dictionnaire de Spiritualité.* Paris: Gabriel Beauchesne et ses Fils, 1988. 13:738–814.

Miquel, Pierre. *Le vocabulaire latin de l'expérience spirituelle dans la tradition monastique et canoniale de 1050 à 1250.* Paris: Beauchesne, 1989.

Moeller, Bernd. *Die Reformation und das Mittelalter: Kirchenhistorische Aufsätze.* Johannes Schilling, ed. Göttingen: Vandenhoeck & Ruprecht, 1991.

Morris, Anne. 'The Trinity in Bernard's Sermons on the Song of Songs'. CSQ 30 (1995) 35–57.

Mousnier, Roland. 'S. Bernard and Luther'. ABR 14 (1963) 448–462.

Mussbacher, Norbert. 'Die Marienverehrung der Cistercienser'. *Die Cistercienser. Geschichte, Geist, Kunst.* Ambrosius Schneider, ed. Cologne: Wienand, 1986. 151–177.

Nicol, Martin. *Meditation bei Luther.* Göttingen: Vandenhoeck & Ruprecht, 1984.

Oberman, Heiko A. *Luther. Man Between God and the Devil.* Eilee Walliser-Schwarzbart, trans. New Haven and London: Yale University Press, 1989.

Ohly, Friedrich. 'Süsse Nägel der Passion. Ein Beitrag zur theologischen Semantik'. Günther Heintz and Peter Schmitter, eds. *Collectanea Philologica. Festschrift für Helmut Gipper zum 65. Geburtstag.* Baden-Baden: Verlag Valentin Koerner, 1985. 403–616.

Ozment, Steven E., ed. *The Reformation in Medieval Perspective.* Chicago: Quadrangle Books, 1971.

Paffrath, Arno. *Bernhard von Clairvaux: Leben und Wirken, dargestellt in den Bilderzyklen von Altenberg bis Zwettl.* Cologne: Du Mont, 1984.

———. *Bernhard von Clairvaux: Band 2. Die Darstellung des Heiligen in der bildenden Kunst.* Bergisch Gladbach: Heider: 1990.

Paulsell, William O. 'The Use of Bernard of Clairvaux in Reformation Preaching'. *Erudition at God's Service.* John R. Sommerfeldt, ed. CS 98. Kalamazoo: CP, 1987. 327–338.

———. 'Bernard of Clairvaux as a Spiritual Director'. CSQ 23 (1988) 223–231.

Paulus, Herbert. *Die ikonographischen Besonderheiten in der spätmittelalterlichen Passions-Darstellung zwischen Tafelmalerei und zeitgenössischer geistlicher Literatur (Predigt, Andachtsbild und Gebet).* Würzburg: no publisher given, 1952.

Pelikan, Jaroslav. *The Christian Tradition: A History of the Development of Doctrine.* Chicago and London: The University of Chicago Press, 1971–1978.

———. *Jesus Through the Centuries: His Place in the History of Culture.* New Haven and London: Yale University Press, 1985.

———. *Mary Through the Centuries: Her Place in the History of Culture*. New Haven and London: Yale University Press, 1996.

Pennington, M. Basil. *The Last of the Fathers: The Cistercian Fathers of the Twelfth Century: A Collection of Essays*. Still River: St. Bede's Publications, 1983.

———and Yael Katzir. *Bernard of Clairvaux: A Saint's Life in Word and Image*. Huntington: Our Sunday Visitor, 1994.

Pérès, Jacques-Noël. 'Où il est question de source et de rivière: saint Bernard et Martin Luther à propos du rapport de l'Église à l'Écriture'. Coll 52 (1990) 299–306.

Pesch, Otto Hermann. 'Luther and the Catholic Tradition.' Eric W. Gritsch., ed. *Encounters With Luther* 3 (1980–84). Gettysburg: GAM Priniting, 1986. 179–197.

Pless, John T. 'Martin Luther: Preacher of the Cross'. CTQ 51 (1987) 83–101.

Posset, Franz. 'Bernard of Clairvaux as Luther's Source: Reading Bernard with Luther's "Spectacles" '. CTQ 54 (1990) 281–304.

———. *Bernardus Redivivus*: The *Wirkungsgeschichte* of a Medieval Sermon in the Reformation of the Sixteenth Century'. CSQ 22 (1987) 239–249.

———. 'Bernhard von Clairvauxs Sermone zur Weihnachts-, Fasten- und Osterzeit als Quellen Martin Luthers'. *Lutherjahrbuch* (1994) 93–116.

———. 'Bible Reading "With Closed Eyes" in the Monastic Tradition: An Overlooked Aspect of Martin Luther's Hermeneutics'. ABR 38 (1987) 293–306.

———. '*Christi Dulcedo:* The 'Sweetness of Christ' in Western Christian Spirituality'. CSQ 30 (1995) 245–265.

———. 'The Crucified Embraces Saint Bernard: The Beginnings of the *Amplexus Bernardi*'. CSQ 33 (1998) 289–314.

———. ' "Heaven is on Sale". The Influence of the Italian Humanist and Carmelite Baptist Mantuanus on Martin Luther'. *Carmelus* 36 (1989) 134–144.

———. *Luther's Catholic Christology According to his Johannine Lectures of 1527*. Milwaukee: Northwestern Publishing House, 1988.

———. 'Martin Luther on *Deësis*. His Rejection of the Artistic

Representation of "Jesus, John and Mary"'. *Renaissance and Reformation* 21 (1997) 57–76.

———. 'Monastic Influence on Martin Luther'. *Monastic Studies* 18 (Montreal: The Benedictine Priory, 1988) 136–163.

———. 'Preaching the Passion of Christ on the Eve of the Reformation'. CTQ 59 (1995) 279–300.

———. 'Recommendation by Martin Luther of St Bernard's *On Consideration*'. CSQ 25 (1990) 25–36.

———. 'Saint Bernard of Clairvaux in Devotion, Theology, and Art of the Sixteenth Century'. Festschrift Oliver Olson. *Lutheran Quarterly* 11 (1997) 308–352.

———. 'St. Bernard's Influence on Two Reformers: John von Staupitz and Martin Luther'. CSQ 25 (1990) 175–187.

———. 'The Elder Luther on Bernard: Part I: Martin Luther's Permanent Indebtedness to Bernard: Commemorating the 900th Birthday of Bernard of Clairvaux'. ABR 42 (1991) 22–52; 'Part II: Last Exegetical Work'. ABR 42 (1991) 179–201.

———. 'Sensing God with the "Palate of the Heart" According to Augustine and Other Spiritual Authors'. ABR 49 (1998) 356–386.

———. 'The Sweetness of God'. ABR 44 (1993) 143–178.

Pranger, M. B. *Bernard of Clairvaux and the Shape of Monastic Thought—Broken Dreams*. Leiden and New York: E. J. Brill, 1994.

———. 'Perdite Vixi: Bernard de Clairvaux et Luther devant l'échec existentiel'. *Bijdragen: Tijdschrift voor filosofie en theologie* 53 (1992) 46–61.

Prenter, Regin. *Der barmherzige Richter: Iustitia dei passiva in Luthers Dictata super Psalterium 1513–1515*. Kopenhagen: Universitetsforlaget Aarhus, 1961.

Pressouyre, Léon, and Terryl N. Kinder, eds. *Saint Bernard & le monde cistercien*. Paris: Caisse Nationale des Monuments Historiques et des Sites/Sand, 1990.

Raitt, Jill. 'Calvin's Use of Bernard of Clairvaux.' ARG 72 (1981) 98–121.

———, ed. *Christian Spirituality: High Middle Ages and Reformation*. New York: Crossroad, 1987.

Rasmussen, Tarald. *Inimici Ecclesiae. Das ekklesiologische Feind-*

bild in Luthers Dictata super psalterium (1513–1515) im Horizont der theologischen Tradition. Leiden: Brill, 1989.

Reinke, Darrell R. 'The Monastic Style in Luther's *De libertate christiana'. Studies in Medieval Culture.* John R. Sommerfeldt and Thomas H. Seiler, eds. Kalamazoo: The Medieval Institute, Western Michigan University, 1977.

Ries, Joseph. *Das geistliche Leben in seinen Entwicklungsstufen nach der Lehre des Hl. Bernard.* Freiburg: Herder, 1906.

Rochais, Henri and Figuet, Jean, 'Le jeu biblique de Bernard.' Coll 47 (1985) 119–128.

Ruhbach, Gerhard and Kurt Schmidt-Clausen, eds. *Kloster Amelungsborn 1135–1985.* Hannover: Missionshandlung Hermannsburg, 1985.

Ruhbach, Gerhard and Josef Sudbrack, eds. *Grosse Mystiker: Leben und Wirken.* Munich: Verlag C. H. Beck, 1984.

Ruh, Kurt. 'Zur Theologie des mittelalterlichen Passionstraktats.' *Theologische Zeitschrift* 6 (1950) 16–26.

Ruppert, Fidelis. 'Meditatio—Ruminatio: Zu einem Grundbegriff christlicher Meditation.' *Erbe und Auftrag* 53 (1977) 83–93.

Sabbe, M., M. Lamberigts, and F. Gistelinck, eds., *Bernardus en de Cisterciënzerfamilie in België 1090–1990.* Louvain: Bibliotheek van de Faculteit der Godgeleerdheid, 1990.

Sabbe, Maurits, and Gistellinck, Frans, eds. *Early Sixteenth Century Printed Books, 1501–1540 in the Library of the Leuven Faculty of Theology.* Louvain: Bibliotheek Godgeleerdheid, Uitgeverij Peeters, 1994.

Sabersky-Bascho, Dorette. *Studien zur Paronomasie bei Bernhard von Clairvaux.* Freiburg/Schweiz: Universitätsverlag, 1979.

Said, Sr. Marie-Bernard. 'The Doctrine of Grace in St Bernard.' CSQ 16 (1981) 15–29.

Scribner, Bob. 'Luther's Anti-Roman Polemics and Popular Belief'. *Lutherjahrbuch* 57 (1990) 93–113.

Scheel, Otto. *Martin Luther: Vom Katholizismus zur Reformation.* Two volumes. Tübingen: Mohr, 1930, fourth printing.

Schmidt-Lauber, Gabriele. *Luthers Vorlesung über den Römerbrief 1515/16: Ein Vergleich zwischen Luthers Manuskript und den studentischen Nachschriften.* Cologne, Weimar, Vienna: Böhlau Verlag, 1994.

Schreiber, Wilhelm Ludwig. *Handbuch der Holz- und Metallschnitte des XV. Jahrhunderts.* Leipzig: Hiersemann, 1926–1930.

Schuck, Johannes. *Das religiöse Erlebnis beim hl. Bernhard von Clairvaux. Ein Beitrag zur Geschichte der christlichen Gotteserfahrung.* Würzburg: C. J. Becker, 1922.

Schwager, Raymund. *Der wunderbare Tausch. Zur Geschichte und Deutung der Erlösungslehre.* Munich: Kösel Verlag, 1986.

Schwarz, Reinhard. 'Gott ist Mensch: Zur Lehre von der Person Christi bei den Ockhamisten und bei Luther'. *Zeitschrift für Theologie und Kirche* 63 (1966) 289–351.

———. *Luther.* Die Kirche in ihrer Geschichte. Ein Handbuch, begründet von Kurt Dietrich Schmidt und Ernst Wolf, herausgegeben von Bernd Moeller, vol 3, I. Göttingen: Vandenhoeck & Ruprecht, 1986.

———. 'Luther's Inalienable Inheritance of Monastic Theology'. Franz Posset, trans. ABR 39 (1988) 430–450.

———. 'Mystischer Glaube—die Brautmystik Martin Luthers'. *Zeitwende: Die Neue Furche* 52 (1981) 193–205.

Siegmund, Johannes Jürgen. 'Bernhard von Clairvaux und Martin Luther—Ein erfahrungstheologischer Vergleich'. *Cistercienser Chronik* 98 (1991) 92–114.

Sint Bernardus van Clairvaux. Gedenkboek Door Monniken van de Noord- en Zuidnederlandse Cistercienser Abdijen Samengesteld bij het Achtste Eeuwfeest van Sint Bernardus' Dood 20 Augustus 1153–1953. Rotterdam: N. V. Uitgeverij de Forel, 1953.

Sommerfeldt, John R., ed. *Bernardus Magister. Papers Presented at the Nonacentenary Celebration of the Birth of Saint Bernard of Clairvaux Kalamazoo, Michigan. Sponsored by the Institute of Cistercian Studies, Western Michigan University, 10–13 May 1990.* CS 135. Kalamazoo: CP, 1993.

———. *The Spiritual Teachings of Bernard of Clairvaux. An Intellectual History of the Early Cistercian Order.* CS 125. Kalamazoo: CP, 1991.

Southern, R. W. *The Making of the Middle Ages.* New Haven and London: Yale University Press, 1976, 23rd printing.

Spitz, Lewis W. *The Protestant Reformation*. Englewood Cliffs: Prentice-Hall, Inc., 1966.

Stange, Carl. *Bernhard von Clairvaux: Studien der Luther-Akademie*. Berlin: Verlag Alfred Toepelmann, 1954.

Steinmetz, David C. 'Luther and the Late Medieval Augustinians: Another Look.' *Concordia Theological Monthly* 44 (1973) 245–259.

———. *Luther in Context*. Bloomington: Indiana University Press, 1986.

Stepsis, Robert P. 'Fulfillment of Self and Union with God in the Writings of Bernard of Clairvaux'. ABR 24 (1973) 348–364.

Stercal, Claudio. *Il "Medius adventus": Saggio di lettura degli scritti di Bernardo di Clairvaux*. Rome: Editiones Cistercienses, 1992.

Stickelbroeck, Michael. *Mysterium Venerandum: Der trinitarische Gedanke im Werk des Bernhard von Clairvaux*. Münster: Aschendorff, 1994.

Stiegman, Emero J. Jr. 'The Literary Genre of Bernard of Clairvaux's Sermones Super Cantica Canticorum, Simplicity and Ordinariness'. John R. Sommerfeldt, ed. *Studies in Medieval Cistercian History* 4. Kalamazoo: CP, 1980. 68–93.

Stock, Brian. 'Experience, Praxis, Work, and Planning in Bernard of Clairvaux: Observations on the *Sermones in Cantica*'. *The Cultural Context of Medieval Learning: Proceedings of the First International Colloquium on Philosophy, Science, and Theology in the Middle Ages—September 1973*. John Emery Murdoch and Edith Dudley Sylla, eds. Dortrecht-Holland and Boston: D. Reidel Publishing Company, 1975. 219–268.

Stoeckle, Bernhard. 'Amor carnis—abusus amoris: Das Verständnis von der Kupiszens bei Bernhard von Clairvaux und Alred von Rieval.' *Analecta Monastica* 7, *Studia Anselmiana* 54. Rome: Herder, 1965. 147–174.

Studi su S. Bernardo di Chiaravalle nello ottavo centenario della canonizzazione. Convegno Internationale Certosa Di Firenze (6–9 Novembre 1974). Rome: Editiones Cistercienses. 1975.

Storm, Heinrich G. J. *Die Begründung der Erkenntnis nach Bernhard von Clairvaux*. Frankfurt am Main, Bern, Las Vegas: Peter Lang, 1977.

Strehle, Stephen. *The Catholic Roots of the Protestant Gospel: Encounter Between the Middle Ages and the Reformation.* Leiden and New York: E. J. Brill, 1995.

Strohl, Henri. *Luther Jusqu'en 1520.* Paris: Presses Universitaires de France, 1962; second revised edition.

Stupperich, Robert. 'Luthers itio spiritualis'. ZKG 107 (1996) 19–28.

Swietek, Francis R. and John R. Sommerfeldt. *Studiosorum Speculum: Studies in Honor of Louis J. Lekai, O.Cist,* eds. CS 141. Kalamazoo: CP, 1993.

Tavard, George H. *The Thousand Faces of the Virgin Mary.* Collegeville: The Liturgical Press, 1996.

Thomas, Robert. 'Que pense saint Bernard de ses mérites?' Coll 49 (1987) 201–217.

———. 'Saint Bernard and the Psalms'. *Liturgy O. C. S. O.* 29 (1995) 63–72.

Vacandard, Elphege. *Vie de St. Bernard.* Paris: V. Lecoffre, 1927, fifth edition.

Vallée, Gerard. 'Luther and Monastic Theology: Notes on *Anfechtung* and *Compunctio*'. ARG 75 (1984) 290–297.

Van den Bosch, Amatus. 'Christ and the Christian Faith'. *Cîteaux* 12 (1961) 105–19; 193–210.

———. 'The Christology of St. Bernard: A Review of Recent Work.' *Cîteaux* 8 (1957) 245–251.

———. 'Dieu devenu aimable d'après S. Bernard'. Coll 23 (1961) 42–57.

———. 'Dieu devenu connaissable dans le Christ d'après S. Bernard'. Coll 22 (1960) 11–20; 341–355.

———. 'Dieu rendu accessible dans le Christ d'après S. Bernard'. Coll 21 (1959) 135–205.

———. 'Le mystère de l'Incarnation chez S. Bernard.' *Cîteaux* 10 (1959) 85–92; 165–177; 245–267.

———. 'Presupposes à la Christologie chez S. Bernard.' *Cîteaux* 9 (1958) 5–17; 85–105.

Van Rijnsoever, Willibrord. 'Bernard en Luther over onze vrijheid in Christus.' Coll 23 (1961) 16–41.

Vercruysse, Jos E. 'Eine rechte Weise in der Theologia zu studirn. Oratio–Meditatio–Tentatio. Luthers Vorrede von 1539'. *Denk-*

ender Glaube in Geschichte und Gegenwart. Festschrift aus Anlaß der Gründung der Universität Erfurt vor 600 Jahren und aus Anlaß des 40jährigen Bestehens des Philosophisch-Theologischen Studiums Erfurt. Wilhelm Ernst and Konrad Feiereis, eds. Leipzig: Benno Verlag, 1992. 297–307.

―――. 'Gesetz und Liebe. Die Struktur der "Heidelberger Disputation" Luthers (1518)'. *Lutherjahrbuch* 48 (1981) 7–43.

―――. 'Luther in der römisch-katholischen Theologie und Kirche'. *Lutherjahrbuch* 63 (1996) 103–128.

―――. 'Luther's Theology of the Cross in the Time of the Heidelberg Disputation'. *Gregorianum* 57 (1976) 523–548.

―――. 'The Catholic View of Luther Five Hundred Years After His Birth'. *Pro Mundi Vitae. Europe, North American Dossier* 21 (1983) 2- 22.

Vetter, Ewald M. 'Iconografía del "Varon de Dolores". Su significado y origen'. *Archivo español de Arte* 36 (1963) 197–231.

Vogelsang, Erich. *Die Anfänge von Luthers Christologie nach der ersten Psalmenvorlesung insbesondere in ihren exegetischen und systematischen Zusammenhängen mit Augustin und der Scholastik dargestellt.* Berlin and Leipzig: Verlag von Walter de Gruyter & Co., 1929.

Volz, Carl. 'Martin Luther's Attitude Toward Bernard of Clairvaux'. *Studies in Medieval Cistercian History, Presented to Jeremiah F. O'Sullivan.* Spencer: Cistercian Publications, 1971. 186–204.

Von Martin, Alfred, ed. *Luther in ökumenischer Sicht. Von evangelischen und katholischen Mitarbeitern.* Stuttgart: Fr. Frommanns Verlag (H. Kurtz), 1929.

Wagner, Wilhelm. 'Die Kirche als Corpus Christi mysticum beim jungen Luther.' *Zeitschrift für katholische Theologie* 61 (1937) 29- 98.

Ward, Sr. Benedicta, ed. *The Influence of Saint Bernard: Anglican Essays with an Introduction by Jean Leclercq.* Oxford: SLG Press, 1976.

Wenzel, Horst. *Hören und Sehen. Schrift und Bild. Kultur und Gedächtnis im Mittelalter.* Munich: Verlag C. H. Beck, 1995.

Werner, Ernst. 'Reformation und Tradition—Bernhard von Clairvaux in den Schriften Martin Luthers'. *Martin Luther*

Kolloquium: Sitzungsberichte der Akademie der Wissenschaften der DDR, Gesellschaftswissenschaften 11G/1983. Berlin: Akademie-Verlag, 1983. 28–33.

―――. 'Reformatorischer Konservatismus? Bernhard von Clairvaux als Autorität bei Jan Hus und Martin Luther'. *Jahrbuch für Geschichte des Feudalismus* 7 (1983) 185–214.

Wicks, Jared. *Luther's Reform. Studies on Conversion and the Church*. Mainz: Verlag Philipp von Zabern, 1992.

―――. *Man Yearning for Grace: Luther's Early Spiritual Teaching*. Washington: Corpus, 1968.

―――. 'Martin Luther: The Heart Clinging to the Word'. *Spiritualities of the Heart. Approaches to Personal Wholeness in Christian Tradition*. Annice Callahan, ed. New York/Mahwah: Paulist Press 1990. 79–96. Reprinted in *Luther's Reform* 43–58.

Wilmart, Andre. *Le 'Jubilus' dit de Saint Bernard*. Rome: Edizioni di 'Storia E Letteratura,' 1944.

Winkler, Gerhard B. 'Bernhard von Clairvaux: Der Brief als Mittel der Seelsorge.' *Theologisch-Praktische Quartalschrift* 141 (1993) 368- 372.

Wolter, Hans. 'Meditation bei Bernhard von Clairvaux.' *Geist und Leben* 29 (1956) 206–218.

Word and Spirit: A Monastic Review 12 (1990): *St. Bernard of Clairvaux (1090–1153)*.

Yule, George, ed. *Luther: Theologian for Catholics and Protestants*. Edinburgh: T. & T. Clark, 1986, second printing.

―――. 'The Spirituality of Luther and Calvin', *Christian Spiritual Theology*, Noel J. Ryan, ed. (Melbourne: Dove, 1976) 205–210.

Zschoch, Hellmut. *Klosterreform und monastische Spiritualität im 15. Jahrhundert: Conrad Zenn OESA (+1460) und sein Liber de vita monastica*. Tübingen: J. C. B. Mohr [Paul Siebeck] 1988.

Zumkeller, Adolar. 'Das Ungenügen der menschlichen Werke bei den deutschen Predigern des Spätmittelalters.' *Zeitschrift für Katholische Theologie* 81 (1959) 265–305.

Zur Mühlen, Karl-Heinz. *Reformatorisches Profil: Studien zum Weg Martin Luthers und der Reformation,* Johannes Brosseder and Athina Lexutt, eds. Göttingen: Vandenhoeck & Ruprecht, 1995.

Index of Persons

Biblical names, Bernard of Clairvaux, and Martin Luther are not included, nor is information in footnotes.

CISTERCIAN TEXTS

Bernard of Clairvaux

- Apologia to Abbot William
- Five Books on Consideration: Advice to a Pope
- Homilies in Praise of the Blessed Virgin Mary
- Letters of Bernard of Clairvaux / by B.S. James
- Life and Death of Saint Malachy the Irishman
- Love without Measure: Extracts from the Writings of St Bernard / by Paul Dimier
- On Grace and Free Choice
- On Loving God / Analysis by Emero Stiegman
- Parables and Sentences
- Sermons for the Summer Season
- Sermons on Conversion
- Sermons on the Song of Songs I–IV
- The Steps of Humility and Pride

William of Saint Thierry

- The Enigma of Faith
- Exposition on the Epistle to the Romans
- Exposition on the Song of Songs
- The Golden Epistle
- The Mirror of Faith
- The Nature and Dignity of Love
- On Contemplating God: Prayer & Meditations

Aelred of Rievaulx

- Dialogue on the Soul
- Liturgical Sermons, I
- The Mirror of Charity
- Spiritual Friendship
- Treatises I: On Jesus at the Age of Twelve, Rule for a Recluse, The Pastoral Prayer
- Walter Daniel: The Life of Aelred of Rievaulx

John of Ford

- Sermons on the Final Verses of the Songs of Songs I–VII

Gilbert of Hoyland

- Sermons on the Songs of Songs I–III
- Treatises, Sermons and Epistles

Other Early Cistercian Writers

- Adam of Perseigne, Letters of
- Alan of Lille: The Art of Preaching
- Amadeus of Lausanne: Homilies in Praise of Blessed Mary
- Baldwin of Ford: Spiritual Tractates I–II
- Geoffrey of Auxerre: On the Apocalypse
- Gertrud the Great: Spiritual Exercises
- Gertrud the Great: The Herald of God's Loving-Kindness (Books 1, 2)
- Gertrud the Great: The Herald of God's Loving-Kindness (Book 3)
- Guerric of Igny: Liturgical Sermons Vol. I & 2
- Helinand of Froidmont: Verses on Death
- Idung of Prüfening: Cistercians and Cluniacs: The Case for Cîteaux
- Isaac of Stella: Sermons on the Christian Year, I–[II]
- The Life of Beatrice of Nazareth
- Serlo of Wilton & Serlo of Savigny: Seven Unpublished Works
- Stephen of Lexington: Letters from Ireland
- Stephen of Sawley: Treatises

MONASTIC TEXTS

Eastern Monastic Tradition

- Besa: The Life of Shenoute
- Cyril of Scythopolis: Lives of the Monks of Palestine
- Dorotheos of Gaza: Discourses and Sayings
- Evagrius Ponticus: Praktikos and Chapters on Prayer
- Handmaids of the Lord: Lives of Holy Women in Late Antiquity & the Early Middle Ages / by Joan Petersen
- Harlots of the Desert / by Benedicta Ward
- John Moschos: The Spiritual Meadow
- Lives of the Desert Fathers
- Lives of Simeon Stylites / by Robert Doran
- The Luminous Eye / by Sebastian Brock
- Mena of Nikiou: Isaac of Alexandra & St Macrobius
- Pachomian Koinonia I–III (Armand Veilleux)
- Paphnutius: Histories/Monks of Upper Egypt
- The Sayings of the Desert Fathers / by Benedicta Ward
- Spiritual Direction in the Early Christian East / by Irénée Hausherr
- The Spiritually Beneficial Tales of Paul, Bishop of Monembasia / by John Wortley
- Symeon the New Theologian: The Theological and Practical Treatises & The Three Theological Discourses / by Paul McGuckin
- Theodoret of Cyrrhus: A History of the Monks of Syria
- The Syriac Fathers on Prayer and the Spiritual Life / by Sebastian Brock

CISTERCIAN PUBLICATIONS

TITLES LISTING

Western Monastic Tradition

- Anselm of Canterbury: Letters I–III
  / by Walter Fröhlich
- Bede: Commentary…Acts of the Apostles
- Bede: Commentary…Seven Catholic Epistles
- Bede: Homilies on the Gospels I–II
- Bede: Excerpts from the Works of St Augustine
  on the Letters of the Blessed Apostle Paul
- The Celtic Monk / by U. Ó Maidín
- Life of the Jura Fathers
- Maxims of Stephen of Muret
- Peter of Celle: Selected Works
- Letters of Rancé I–II
- Rule of the Master
- Rule of Saint Augustine

Christian Spirituality

- The Cloud of Witnesses: The Development
  of Christian Doctrine / by David N. Bell
- The Call of Wild Geese / by Matthew Kelty
- The Cistercian Way / by André Louf
- The Contemplative Path
- Drinking From the Hidden Fountain
  / by Thomas Spidlík
- Eros and Allegory: Medieval Exegesis of the
  Song of Songs / by Denys Turner
- Fathers Talking / by Aelred Squire
- Friendship and Community / by Brian McGuire
- Gregory the Great: Forty Gospel Homilies
- High King of Heaven / by Benedicta Word
- The Hermitage Within / by a Monk
- Life of St Mary Magdalene and of Her Sister
  St Martha / by David Mycoff
- Many Mansions / by David N. Bell
- Mercy in Weakness / by André Louf
- The Name of Jesus / by Irénée Hausherr
- No Moment Too Small / by Norvene Vest
- Penthos: The Doctrine of Compunction in the
  Christian East / by Irénée Hausherr
- Praying the Word / by Enzo Bianchi
- Rancé and the Trappist Legacy
  / by A. J. Krailsheimer
- Russian Mystics / by Sergius Bolshakoff
- Sermons in a Monastery / by Matthew Kelty
- Silent Herald of Unity: The Life of
  Maria Gabrielle Sagheddu / by Martha Driscoll
- The Spirituality of the Christian East
  / by Thomas Spidlík
- The Spirituality of the Medieval West
  / by André Vauchez
- Tuning In To Grace / by André Louf
- Wholly Animals: A Book of Beastly Tales
  / by David N. Bell

MONASTIC STUDIES

- Community and Abbot in the Rule of
  St Benedict I–II / by Adalbert de Vogüé
- The Finances of the Cistercian Order in the
  Fourteenth Century / by Peter King
- Fountains Abbey and Its Benefactors
  / by Joan Wardrop
- The Hermit Monks of Grandmont
  / by Carole A. Hutchison
- In the Unity of the Holy Spirit / by Sighard Kleiner
- The Joy of Learning & the Love of God: Essays
  in Honor of Jean Leclercq
- Monastic Odyssey / by Marie Kervingant
- Monastic Practices / by Charles Cummings
- The Occupation of Celtic Sites in Ireland
  / by Geraldine Carville
- Reading St Benedict / by Adalbert de Vogüé
- Rule of St Benedict: A Doctrinal and Spiritual
  Commentary / by Adalbert de Vogüé
- The Rule of St Benedict / by Br. Pinocchio
- St Hugh of Lincoln / by David H. Farmer
- The Venerable Bede / by Benedicta Ward
- Western Monasticism / by Peter King
- What Nuns Read / by David N. Bell
- With Greater Liberty: A Short History of
  Christian Monasticism & Religious Orders
  / by Karl Frank

CISTERCIAN STUDIES

- Aelred of Rievaulx: A Study / by Aelred Squire
- Athirst for God: Spiritual Desire in Bernard of
  Clairvaux's Sermons on the Song of Songs
  / by Michael Casey
- Beatrice of Nazareth in Her Context
  / by Roger De Ganck
- Bernard of Clairvaux: Man, Monk, Mystic
  / by Michael Casey [tapes and readings]
- Bernardus Magister...Nonacentenary
- Catalogue of Manuscripts in the Obrecht
  Collection of the Institute of Cistercian
  Studies / by Anna Kirkwood
- Christ the Way: The Christology of Guerric of
  Igny / by John Morson
- The Cistercians in Denmark / by Brian McGuire
- The Cistercians in Scandinavia / by James France
- A Difficult Saint / by Brian McGuire
- A Gathering of Friends: Learning & Spirituality
  in John of Ford / by Costello and Holdsworth
- Image and Likeness: Augustinian Spirituality
  of William of St Thierry / by David Bell

- Index of Authors & Works in Cistercian Libraries in Great Britain 1 / by David Bell
- Index of Cistercian Authors and Works in Medieval Library Catalogues in Great Britian / by David Bell
- The Mystical Theology of St Bernard / by Étienne Gilson
- The New Monastery: Texts & Studies on the Earliest Cistercians
- Nicolas Cotheret's Annals of Cîteaux / by Louis J. Lekai
- Pater Bernhardus: Martin Luther and Saint Bernard / by Franz Posset
- Pathway of Peace / by Charles Dumont
- A Second Look at Saint Bernard / by Jean Leclercq
- The Spiritual Teachings of St Bernard of Clairvaux / by John R. Sommerfeldt
- Studies in Medieval Cistercian History
- Studiosorum Speculum / by Louis J. Lekai
- Three Founders of Cîteaux / by Jean-Baptiste Van Damme
- Towards Unification with God (Beatrice of Nazareth in Her Context, 2)
- William, Abbot of St Thierry
- Women and St Bernard of Clairvaux / by Jean Leclercq

MEDIEVAL RELIGIOUS WOMEN

edited by Lillian Thomas Shank and John A. Nichols:
- Distant Echoes
- Hidden Springs: Cistercian Monastic Women (2 volumes)
- Peace Weavers

CARTHUSIAN TRADITION

- The Call of Silent Love / by A Carthusian
- The Freedom of Obedience / by A Carthusian
- From Advent to Pentecost
- Guigo II: The Ladder of Monks & Twelve Meditations / by Colledge & Walsh
- Halfway to Heaven / by R.B. Lockhart
- Interior Prayer / by A Carthusian
- Meditations of Guigo II / by A. Gordon Mursall
- The Prayer of Love and Silence / by A Carthusian
- Poor, Therefore Rich / by A Carthusian
- They Speak by Silences / by A Carthusian
- The Way of Silent Love (A Carthusian Miscellany)
- Where Silence is Praise / by A Carthusian
- The Wound of Love (A Carthusian Miscellany)

CISTERCIAN ART, ARCHITECTURE & MUSIC

- Cistercian Abbeys of Britain
- Cistercians in Medieval Art / by James France
- Studies in Medieval Art and Architecture / edited by Meredith Parsons Lillich (Volumes II–V are now available)
- Stones Laid Before the Lord / by Anselme Dimier
- Treasures Old and New: Nine Centuries of Cistercian Music (compact disc and cassette)

THOMAS MERTON

- The Climate of Monastic Prayer / by T. Merton
- Legacy of Thomas Merton / by P. Hart
- Message of Thomas Merton / by P. Hart
- Monastic Journey of Thomas Merton / by P. Hart
- Thomas Merton/Monk / by P. Hart
- Thomas Merton on St Bernard
- Toward an Integrated Humanity / edited by M. Basil Pennington

CISTERCIAN LITURGICAL DOCUMENTS SERIES

- Cistercian Liturgical Documents Series / edited by Chrysogonus Waddell, ocso
- Hymn Collection of the…Paraclete
- *Institutiones nostrae:* The Paraclete Statutes
- Molesme Summer-Season Breviary (4 volumes)
- Old French Ordinary & Breviary of the Abbey of the Paraclete (2 volumes)
- Twelfth-century Cistercian Hymnal (2 volumes)
- The Twelfth-century Cistercian Psalter
- Two Early Cistercian *Libelli Missarum*

STUDIA PATRISTICA

- Studia Patristica XVIII, Volumes 1, 2 and 3

CISTERCIAN PUBLICATIONS

HOW TO CONTACT US

Editorial Queries

Editorial queries & advance book information should be directed to the Editorial Offices:

- Cistercian Publications
  WMU Station
  1201 Oliver Street
  Kalamazoo, Michigan 49008

- Telephone   616 387 8920
- Fax   616 387 8390
- e-mail   mcdougall@wmich.edu

Cistercian Publications is a non-profit corporat-ion. Its publishing program is restricted to mo-nastic texts in translation and books on the monastic tradition.

A complete catalogue of texts in translation and studies on early, medieval, and modern monas-ticism is available, free of charge, from any of the addresses above.

How to Order in the United States

Customers may order these books through booksellers, from the editorial office, or directly from the warehouse:

- Cistercian Publications
  Saint Joseph's Abbey
  167 North Spencer Road
  Spencer, Massachusetts   01562-1233

- Telephone 508 885 8730
- Fax   508 885 4687
- e-mail   cistpub@spencerabbey.org
- Web Site   www.spencerabbey.org/cistpub

How to Order from Canada

- Novalis
  49 Front Street East, Second Floor
  Toronto, Ontario M5E 1B3

- Telephone 416 363 3303
                     1 800 387 7164
- Fax   416 363 9409

How to Order from Europe

- Cistercian Publications
  97 Loughborough Road
  Thringstone, Coalville, Leicester LE67 8LQ

- Fax   44 1530 45 02 10
- e-mail   MsbcistP@aol.com